'An Iron Pillar'

The Life and Times of
William Romaine

The Rev'd Mr. William Romaine, A.M.

'An Iron Pillar'

The Life and Times of William Romaine

Tim Shenton

EP — **EVANGELICAL PRESS**

EVANGELICAL PRESS
Faverdale North Industrial Estate, Darlington, DL3 OPH,
England

Evangelical Press USA
P. O. Box 825, Webster, New York 14580, USA

e-mail: sales@evangelicalpress.org

web: www.evangelicalpress.org

First published 2004

British Library Cataloguing in Pulication Data available

ISBN 0 85234 562 3

Unless otherwise indicated, Scripture quotations in this
publication are from the King James and the New King
James versions of the Bible.

Portrait of William Romaine by Francis Cotes (1758),
reproduced by courtesy of The National Portrait Gallery,
London.

Printed and bound in Great Britian by Creative Print & Design
Wales, Ebbw Vale

Contents

Acknowledgements

I would like to record the debt I owe to the following: S. J. Taylor of the Evangelical Library, London, for his prompt and efficient service; the staff at the British Library, London, for their courtesy and helpfulness; William Hodges of the Bodleian Library, Oxford; Peter Nockles of John Rylands University, Manchester; Martin Beckett of the State Library of New South Wales, Sydney; Anette Hagan of Edinburgh University Library; Eileen Dickson of New College Library, Edinburgh; Anne Marie Menta of the Beinecke Rare Book and Manuscript Library, New Haven; Robert Oliver, for his readiness to help; Faith Cook, for writing the foreword; Steve Brady, for allowing me the use of Moorlands College Library; the staff at Winton Library; my father Townley, for his exhilarating company on my 'research travels' and for proof reading the MS; and my wife, for her constant support and encouragement.

Tim Shenton

Foreword

A man who can write 'Christ is all light and life and love and joy, an infinite and everlasting fullness of all blessing. I would lead you to him in the direct road, which is to lead you out of self entirely. Christ is the way...' is certainly a man worth reading about. We may know much about the great men of the eighteenth-century Evangelical Revival, about John and Charles Wesley and about George Whitefield; names such as Daniel Rowland, Howell Harris and William Grimshaw may have a familiar ring. But who was William Romaine, and how did his life and ministry fit into the amazing jigsaw of God's mighty acts in that era? We are much indebted to Tim Shenton for this comprehensive and detailed account of Romaine's life and influence. Following his well-received biography of *Christmas Evans, the life and times of the one-eyed preacher of Wales*, Mr Shenton has turned his attention to an earlier period of church history, first with the life of Samuel Walker of Truro and now with William Romaine.

A successful biographer must be in sympathy with his subject, and the style and emphasis of this book bears ample testimony to the fact that the writer understands his man and has entered fully into his thoughts and character. The task of writing such a biography is immense with letters to be analysed, contemporary views to be sifted and references to be culled from a wide range of sources, each to be woven into the narrative. I can well imagine that William Romaine has, metaphorically speaking, been a guest in Tim and Pauline Shenton's home for many months if not years in order to achieve a biography of this nature. Nor is he an easy man to live with – few truly great men are. Tim Shenton does not shield us from Romaine's faults, some quite glaring at times, but he understands them, and shows us that Romaine, often brusque and quick-tempered, was always quick to apologize when he knew he had been in the wrong, and that he would grieve deeply over his shortcomings.

As you read this book, you will find that you have more than a biography of one man. Here is a microcosm of the times – mini biographies within a biography – as Tim Shenton leads us aside from his main subject and introduces us to Romaine's contemporaries, and includes many sub-themes and pen portraits.

If ever we needed 'Pillars of Iron' in the church, it is in our own day, when compromise and worldliness are sapping its spiritual power and eroding its influence. May this new biography encourage many, both young preachers and all Christians alike, to be as fearless and faithful for the truth as was William Romaine.

Faith Cook

Preface

Considering the influence William Romaine exercised on evangelicalism throughout the eighteenth century, it is surprising more has not been written about him. The two main biographies were both published soon after his death, and it was not until 1949 — a gap of more than 150 years — that another full length study was attempted, an unpublished Edinburgh Ph.D. thesis by Donald Davis. According to Davis, Luke Tyerman attempted to write a biography of Romaine but his manuscript, held by Epworth Press, is now lost. J. C. Ryle included Romaine in his *Christian Leaders of the 18th Century*, but that account is taken mainly from the work of William Cadogan, Romaine's first biographer, and offers little new. Other short accounts have appeared, such as Peter Toon's biography, which prefaces a new edition of Romaine's *The Life, Walk and Triumph of Faith* (1970), but it is largely extracted from Davis.

Cadogan's work was published in 1796 at the request of Romaine's nearest relatives. The author found no documents among Romaine's papers that would furnish a biographer with useful material except one memorandum, which Romaine wrote when he was seventy years old, and which does not appear to have been for publication. Cadogan is right when he says that Romaine employed his pen 'not upon himself, but upon his God and Saviour'. The advantage of this work is that Cadogan was a close friend of Romaine's and so had ready access to him. He could therefore paint a picture of his subject in its true colours. Unfortunately, he makes no reference to Romaine's relationship with Selina Hastings, the Countess of Huntingdon — thus his work is incomplete.

Cadogan's omission was partly corrected by another friend of Romaine's, Thomas Haweis, in his work of 1797. Haweis was personally acquainted with Romaine for more than forty years. He had hoped that 'some person better qualified than myself would undertake the subject, with materials more abundant, and capable of adorning his memory with trophies of more excellent workmanship', but in that he was disappointed.[1] He collected every available 'fact of importance' and solicited information from those who knew Romaine. While in Portsea he received from William Kinsbury a parcel of Romaine's letters for the biography, first proposed by Romaine's son. He also used some papers in his possession. Uniting these sources he hoped to give 'a fuller and more explicit view of this distinguished veteran ... than could perhaps be drawn from any other existing documents'.[2] He wrote with the conviction that his memoir would 'afford to every gracious heart, matter of thankfulness and great joy; stimulate the ministers of Christ to imitate so bright an example, and all the people of God to be more diligent followers of those who through faith and patience inherit the promises'.[3]

D. G. Davis's thesis, *The Evangelical Revival in Eighteenth Century England as Reflected in the Life and Work of William Romaine (1714-1795)*, written with academics rather than the general public in mind, contains new information about Romaine, but it is only available to the determined researcher. It is a thorough, well balanced, chronological account, and, though it lacks the input of substantial unpublished manuscript material, it is a valuable source.

Perhaps one of the reasons why a modern biography on Romaine has not been forthcoming is that Romaine kept no diary, and his letters contain few personal details except when he wrote to members of his family. It is said that he resisted all attempts to persuade him to record his spiritual experiences.

Therefore one has to dig deep to be able to put 'flesh on bones' and to breathe into him the breath of life so that he becomes 'alive'. Thankfully, in the last fifty years, various unpublished letters have come to light and a good deal has been written on his contemporaries and the eighteenth-century religious scene, much of which has broadened our knowledge of Romaine.

One of the uplifting aspects of Romaine's letters is their spiritual content. The writer is often carried away by the glories of Christ as he fills the page with expressions of the loveliness of his Saviour. 'More of Christ' and 'Let Christ be exalted' are his themes. Such heart-felt praise of the Redeemer unveils more about Romaine's experience and life than many lines of personal comment. I quote three examples, all written to his sister to whom he freely expressed himself.

The first was written on 29 September 1764, the day before his Blackfriars' probation sermon. Romaine had just returned to London after visiting his sister, having preached at Bradford, Powsey and other places: 'Jesus has travelled with me, and been with me of a truth. O what have I experienced of his love since I left you! He has not only let me taste that he is precious, but he has made me also live upon his grace. He lets me have nothing but love, free, rich love; and my very physic is given by and tastes of his love, and always works greater love in me to him: so that Jesus is become exceeding dear to me.'[4]

The second is from an undated letter: 'The more I think and preach about the infinitely rich Jesus and his love, the greater still does he appear. My heart grows warmer to him. His cause grows more amiable; and nothing gives me pain, but that I do so little for him, and speak so poorly of him.'[5]

The last extract was written on 19 November 1768:

> He is the Prince of the kings of the earth, to whom all blessing is due. Yea, he is above all blessing and praise, and that for evermore; because he humbled himself, God was made man... O how I triumph in my inmost soul in his love! He loved me — I pay him homage — all

within me, all without me, blesses his holy name. He is
my King — my royal Saviour — I pay him my allegiance
with heart and hand. Not that he may be away — away
with that proud thought! — but because he is mine:
— therefore I would walk before him, without fear, in
holiness and righteousness all the days of my life.[6]

Throughout his ministry Romaine enjoyed an intimate fellowship with Christ. In contrast to recent writers, who seem content
only to emphasize Romaine's theology, especially his Calvinism, which was stricter than most of his contemporaries, I have
tried to give a more balanced view, highlighting the man and his
deep walk with God, as well as his theology, which of course is
vital if our study of Romaine is to be complete. My aim has been
to unveil the heart and soul of the preacher who was so greatly
used by God.

Romaine's life conveniently divides into three sections. The
first extends from his birth to the start of his London ministry
in 1747. The second extends from 1747 to his final settlement
at Blackfriars in 1766. Of this second period Ryle says, 'At no
time in his life, perhaps, was he more useful and popular. He
was in full vigour of body and mind, and enjoyed a reputation
as a bold and uncompromising preacher of evangelical doctrine
throughout the metropolis, which few other living men equalled,
and fewer still surpassed.'[7] The final period stretches from 1766
through his long ministry at Blackfriars to his death in 1795.

It is hoped that a close look at so great a champion of the
faith will encourage others to draw ever nearer to our blessed
Saviour, and that it will inspire them to serve the Lord of Glory
with a fresh zeal in these days of apathy and spiritual indiffer-
ence. If these objectives are achieved, then by the grace of God
the time and effort taken in compiling this work will have been
worthwhile. Before I close I must mention how much I have enjoyed researching the life and times of Romaine. The privilege
is one I shall always treasure. I hope my enthusiasm has been
transmitted to the printed page.

Christ's way to glory was humility: so is ours. His glory, indeed, was his humility; so is ours. He that humbleth himself shall be exalted, was true of the head as well as of the members. O that you and I may be in this conformed to him!

William Romaine.[8]

The subject of the following memoirs was a man eminent in the religious world, and deservedly held in the highest esteem and veneration. A life of great extent, and remarkable usefulness gave him a singular pre-eminence over most of his contemporaries. His abilities and learning were allowedly great, and in the connection in which he moved made him looked up to, as the first of his brethren. Unwearied activity — an uninterrupted state of health for sixty successive years of labour — early rising — and diligent improvement of his time — doubled in a measure the period of his mortal days, and proportionally increased the sum of his knowledge and experience. So that take him for all in all, we shall be long ere we look upon his like again.

Thomas Haweis.[1]

1
Early Years

William Romaine was highly regarded by his fellow evangelicals. John Newton, for instance, in a funeral sermon he preached for Romaine from John 5:35 ('he was a burning and shining light'), commented, 'Mr Romaine was fifty eight years in the ministry, an honourable and useful man, inflexible as an iron pillar in publishing the truth, and unmoved either by the smiles or the frowns of the world. He was the most popular man of the Evangelical party since Mr Whitefield, and few remaining will be more missed.'[2] Thomas Haweis, in the preface to his biography on Romaine, opens by saying, 'The eminence and usefulness of such a standard bearer fallen, cannot but make his memory dear to his surviving friends; and his reputation having reached to thousands, who never were blessed by his personal ministrations, all will be anxious to know something of a man so famous in his day and generation.'[3]

J. C. Ryle, in his preface to *Christian Leaders of the 18th Century*, in which he reviews the lives of eleven godly men, one of whom is Romaine, confesses that he is a 'thorough enthusiast about them'. He goes on to give them high praise: 'Excepting Luther and his Continental contemporaries and our own martyred Reformers, the world has seen no such men since the days of the apostles... There have been none who have preached so much clear scriptural truth, none who have lived such lives, none who have shown such courage in Christ's service, none who have suffered so much for the truth, none who have done so much good.'[4]

In comparing the ministries of Whitefield, Wesley, Grimshaw and Romaine, 'four spiritual heroes', he remarks:

> Whitefield and Wesley were spiritual cavalry, who scoured the country, and were found everywhere. Grimshaw was an infantry soldier, who had his head-quarters at Haworth, and never went far from home. Romaine, in the meantime, was a commander of heavy artillery, who held a citadel in the heart of a metropolis, and seldom stirred beyond his walls.[5] Yet all these four men were mighty instruments in God's hand for good; and not one of them could have been spared. Each did good service in his own line; and not least ... was the Rector of Black-friars, William Romaine.[6]

William Romaine was born on 25 September 1714 in Hartle-pool, a small fishing town on the north-east coast, with a popu-lation of less than one thousand. 'Fewer than a half dozen nar-row streets of houses lined the inner edge of a small peninsula jutting into the North Sea and surrounded on three sides by water.'[7] The house of Romaine's birth was situated at the south-west corner of St Mary's Street, just a few yards from the west end of St Hilda's Church in the High Street, where he was bap-tized. Some eighty years after his death, the house was used as a butcher's shop. It was demolished in 1937 and a modern building called 'Romaine House' erected on the site. The year 1714 was highly significant in the purposes of God, for it was in that year that several of the great future leaders of evangelical-ism were born, men such as George Whitefield, Howel Har-ris, Samuel Walker and James Hervey. These men exercised a profound influence on the Christianity of eighteenth-century England and Wales.

St Hilda's Church, Hartlepool.

Romaine remembered with affection the place of his birth and visited it annually. On many occasions, St Hilda's thronged with large congregations who eagerly listened to the words of eternal life that came from the lips of one of their own countrymen. On 4 July 1757 John Wesley wrote in his diary: 'The clouds and wind in our face kept us cool till we came to Hartlepool. Mr Romaine has been an instrument of awakening several here; but for want of help they soon slept again.'[8] When Romaine wrote to his mother on 5 August 1769, he said,

> When I look back to Hartlepool, and review the dealings of a precious Jesus with you and with yours, my debt increases: and when I consider his goodness to Hartlepool sinners, and Bishoprick sinners — how many of them he has called from darkness to light, O what a tribute of praise ought we to be continually paying to the Saviour of the North country! And if we particularly consider our relations, one by one, whom it has pleased our good God to work upon by his Holy Spirit, we should call

upon all within us to bless his holy name, and all without
us to join in showing forth his praise.[9]

On 27 February 1876, George T. Fox erected a tablet in St Hilda's to the memory of Romaine, saying:

> As a native of this country, I felt it was a disgrace to us
> that no recognition of his great services had ever been
> made in this town, and I resolved to give utterance to my
> own feelings and to show the high reverence I had for
> his character, principles, and work by erecting in this his
> native town a tablet to his memory.
>   It is not to glorify the man, nor yet to rescue his
> memory from oblivion, that I have taken this step, but
> from a sincere desire to honour God, and to engrave on
> the walls of [St Hilda's] church some of those precious
> soul saving truths which he proclaimed with such lucid
> Scriptural distinctness, and which, when read by you
> and those who follow you in future days, I pray God may
> be blessed to the spiritual good of many souls.[10]

Part of the tablet reads:

> A Christian of eminent piety, a ripe scholar, and a preach-
> er of peculiar gifts, mighty in the Scriptures.
> He was honoured of God to become a leading instrument
> in accomplishing that great revival of evangelical religion
> in the Church of England, which took place last century.
> In addition to his unwearied labours as a minister of the
> Gospel of Christ, and his faithful proclamation of the
> distinctive doctrines of grace, he greatly promoted the
> cause of truth, was the instrument of quickening and
> deepening vital piety in the hearts of thousands, and has
> bequeathed a rich legacy to posterity by his admirable
> Treatise on *The Life, Walk and Triumph of Faith*.[11]

The remainder of the tablet is inscribed with four quotations from Romaine's *The Life, Walk and Triumph of Faith*.

Romaine's father, William Romaine senior (1672-1757), was the son of Robert Romaine, who died six years before his son in 1751. Robert Romaine arrived in England from France with his family about the year 1682, soon after the relaxation in 1681 of English immigration and naturalization laws in favour of French refugees.[12] He was admitted a citizen of Hartlepool on 27 August 1683. William Romaine senior was a well respected corn merchant and a man who feared God, which is evidenced not only by the testimony of contemporaries, but by his dealings with others.

In 1741, when England was at war with Spain, the price of wheat rose sharply from six to fifteen shillings per measure. Upon this occasion the people rose and came in great numbers, a formidable mob, to Hartlepool. Mr Romaine went out to meet them, asked them their wants, and was answered that they wanted cheaper corn. He put an immediate and an effectual stop to these riotous proceedings, first by promising to sell all the corn he had at five shillings a bushel, and then by performing his promise; for he sold to all that came, while the other merchants refused to sell any.[13]

William Cadogan describes Romaine's father as a 'man of God and consequently of strict morals; a steady member of the Church of England, a constant attender upon her services, and so exact an observer of the Sabbath Day, that he never suffered any of his family to go out upon it, except to church, and spent the remainder of it with them in reading the Scriptures, and other devout exercises at home'.[14] Another describes him as a man of real piety and a genuine friend of the ministers of the gospel. He served the town as mayor on three occasions, in 1723, 1735 and 1745. He died in July 1757 at the age of eighty-five, and was still remembered with respect as late as 1816.

Romaine senior and his wife Isabella had nine children altogether, of which William was the second; they strove to raise their children under the influences of a happy Christian home and according to orthodox Anglican tradition. Romaine wrote to a friend on 30 July 1784, and gave a word of testimony about the faith of his parents and three surviving sisters:

> I have three sisters alive [Miriam, Dorothy and Eliza-beth], all in years, as well as myself; and we are to have a family meeting to take our leave, final as to this life. It has brought a great solemnity upon my spirit; and it would be too much for my feelings, if I had not all the reason in the world to believe that our next meeting will be in glory. Mr Whit[e]field used often to put me in mind, how singularly favoured I was — he had none of his family converted; and my father and mother and three sisters were like those blessed people — 'And Jesus loved Martha and her sister and Lazarus;' and, as they loved him again, so do we.[15]

After Romaine senior died, Romaine's mother and one unmarried sister continued in business at Hartlepool. They were respected and loved partly because of their attention to the needs of their customers, and partly because they used to read and explain the Scriptures to their neighbours, with the view of encouraging, comforting and edifying them.

Romaine, who was always loved and revered by his family, and his affection and care for them is obvious from his letters, often mentions his mother in the most tender terms. He was concerned that she lacked the assurance of salvation. 'My mother is waiting [on the Lord],' he said in a letter of 3 March 1764. 'She trusts in the Lord, but has not the comfort of believing. She shall not be ashamed. God will appear for her, and she shall rejoice in his salvation.'[16] Again, the following year: 'My duty to my dear mother; she is safe... Die as she is, she cannot perish — only she wants the present comforts of our salvation. She dares, she does, venture her soul in the hands of Jesus, who never did, nor can, lose anything committed to his care.'[17]

'My tenderest duty waits upon my dear mother,' he writes in another letter. 'I hope God will finish his work in her, before she goes hence.'[18] It is clear from these and other letters that he was deeply concerned about the spiritual welfare of his family and that they were the regular subjects of his prayers.

One of his sisters, Elizabeth, married Michael Callinder of Newcastle on 11 October 1760. Dorothy married one of Wesley's preachers, John Heslup of Hartlepool, on 24 June 1767. Romaine wrote to Mrs Heslup from Blackfriars on 19 November 1768, rejoicing in her news of 'poor sinners converted, and of believers settled and established in their most holy faith'.[19] In another letter to her, dated 26 June 1773, he said, 'My thoughts often run about poor Hartlepool. I believe the Lord has a people among you, and I wish he may honour Mr Heslup, by making him useful to gather them together, and to build them up in their most holy faith. My prayers are not wanting for him and them.'[20] Dorothy died on 26 July 1793, two years before Romaine's own death, and he wrote to her bereaved husband, exhorting him to exalt Christ in his behaviour and preaching, 'that Northumberland sinners may hear and live'.[21] Miriam, who was the only sibling to outlive him, married Thomas Parker of Sunderland on 23 March 1759 and then John Young of Sunderland on 30 January 1773. His elder brother Robert was a grocer in London. He died suddenly at the George Inn at Buckden in his thirtieth year. His two other brothers, James and Ralph, and two of his sisters, Elizabeth and Isabella, died when they were young.

Although the family were held in high regard and ran a successful business, they do not seem to have been particularly wealthy as there is no evidence that William Romaine received any considerable inheritance. His position as a servitor of Christ Church, Oxford, in which he laboured for assistance in tuition, suggests that he was not given a liberal allowance by his parents.

His parents, recognizing his gifts and abilities, sent him at the age of ten to Kepier Grammar School at Houghton le Spring, about fifteen miles from Hartlepool, which had been founded in 1557 by the rector Bernard Gilpin (1517-1583), the 'apostle of the North'. Gilpin was a 'tall, lean person, with a hawk like nose and charming, tactful manners', who has rightly been called the 'father of the poor'. 'He would sometimes strip his cloak off and give it to an ill clad beggar. Riding with his servants in the country on one occasion, he saw a poor husbandman's horse fall down dead in the plough. Immediately Gilpin told one of his servants to unsaddle his horse and give it to the poor man. His habit was on Sundays to feast all his parishioners, in three divisions, according to their ranks, at his table.'[22]

He was greatly respected, and sometimes feared, by many in the neighbourhood, even by those who did not share his beliefs. On one occasion, his horses were stolen. While others expressed the highest indignation at such an act, the thief rejoiced at his prize, but only until he found out to whom the horses belonged. 'Terrified at what he had done, he instantly came trembling back, confessed the fact, returned the horses, and declared he believed the devil would have seized him directly, had he carried them off when he knew they belonged to Mr Gilpin.'[23]

The grammar school was founded with the financial help of, among others, John Heath of Kepier, 'a man of large means and a great encourager of learning', who 'gladly fell in with Gilpin's ideas'.[24] As soon as it opened it flourished. Able

Kepier Grammar School, Houghton le Spring.

Bernard Gilpin,
the 'apostle of the North'.

masters from Oxford were placed in the school and many scholars were sent to the universities, where they 'proved great ornaments to the church and nation'. Some of the brightest pupils
Gilpin instructed in his own study, and when the number of
young people who wanted to attend the school became too
many for the town to accommodate, he fitted out part of his
own home for that purpose. He seldom had fewer than twenty
or thirty children boarding with him, and the poor he lodged
free of charge.

In the early part of the eighteenth century, the school was
known as a 'seminary of sound learning and religious knowledge'.[25] Romaine was educated there for seven years (his master
was Gilbert Nelson). After acquiring all the learning that institution afforded, he was sent to Hart Hall, Oxford (now Hertford
College). He matriculated on 10 April 1731, but soon moved
to Christ Church, where Charles Wesley had just become a tutor. His tutor may have been Fifield Allen, who was afterwards
chaplain to Bishop Gibson, archdeacon of Middlesex, subdean
of the Chapel Royal, prebendary of St Paul's and editor of the
Three Electras used in Westminster School.

He made great literary progress and showed unwearied
diligence towards his studies. It was not long before 'the bril-
liancy of his genius, a thirst for knowledge, and an aptitude to
acquire it', gained the respect and attracted the attention of his
superiors, and thereby he met some of the ablest scholars of
the university. His proficiency under his tutor may be inferred
from his early appearance as an author who had studied much
before he started to write, and who had particularly studied the
Scriptures in their original languages, as an effectual preparation
for a ministry in the church.

There is a story mentioned by his curate and successor in the
church at Blackfriars, William Goode, which shows the esteem
in which he was held at the university, as well as the disregard
he paid to his dress — a disregard that was noticeable in all his
future life. The anecdote, originally told by the Hutchinsonian

A panoramic view of Hertford College, where
Romaine first studied at Oxford.

Julius Bate, author of *Critica Hebraea*, to a friend, was related
by Goode in the funeral sermon he preached and published on
Romaine's death:

> Dress was never his foible, his mind was superior to
> such borrowed ornaments; and, immersed in nobler
> pursuits of literature, before consecrated to a still more
> exalted purpose, he paid but little attention to outward
> decorations. Being observed to pass by rather negli-
> gently attired, a visitor enquired of his friend, a master
> of one of the colleges: 'Who is that slovenly person with
> his stockings down?'
>   The master replied, 'That slovenly person, as you
> call him, is one of the greatest geniuses of the age, and is
> likely to be one of the greatest men in the kingdom.'[26]

Romaine was at Oxford University at the same time as other men who were to become well known. John Wesley was a fellow of Lincoln College, and he and his friends, George Whitefield, James Hervey, Benjamin Ingham and others formed, 'The Holy Club'. Because of their devotional exercises, they were nick-named 'Methodists'. However, in the words of Thomas Haweis, Romaine 'studiously avoided all connection with them and their meetings'. He was too engrossed in the pursuit of literature and had joined a set of scholars who began to be called 'Hutchinso-nians'. 'Having imbibed with them all their High Church princi-ples, he felt no relish for men of a spirituality of temper, which he had not yet learned to cultivate, and from whose reproach, as Methodists, he naturally kept aloof.'[27] Nor does it appear that he had contact with other men such as Samuel Walker or Wil-liam Talbot, who were also at the university at that time.

He enjoyed being with those who had adopted the philo-sophical, moral and ecclesiastical opinions of John Hutchinson (1674-1737), a High Church Anglican, who 'maintained that the Hebrew Scriptures embraced a complete system of natural philosophy as well as of religion. He laid especial stress on the typical sense, and held that all parts of the character and work of Christ are symbolized in the Old Testament.'[28] The *Dictionary of National Biography* describes Hutchinson as a 'half educat-ed and fanciful man of boundless vanity', who 'seems to have started from the opinion that [Sir Isaac] Newton's doctrines were of dangerous consequence'.[29] He was the author of *Mo-ses' Principia*, the first part of which appeared in 1724 and the second in 1727, and which was directly opposed to Newton's *Principia*, which he regarded as aiding the Deists to undermine the authority of the Bible, particularly the Old Testament. He denied Newton's theory of gravitation and his teaching is a typi-cal example of eighteenth-century anti-Newtonianism.

According to Hutchinson, the natural philosophy of New-ton and his associates subverts the central doctrine of the Christian faith, the doctrine of the Trinity. Hutchinson insisted that revelation is the only secure basis, not only for theological reflection, but also for natural philosophy. Acting upon this premise, he devised a 'Mosaic physics' based upon the Hebrew text of Genesis 1:1-17... He asserted that the oldest religion and natural philosophy are the genuine one and argued that the teachings of Moses, which are related to Christianity as type to antitype, stand first in the order of priority.[30]

With his mystical interpretation of Hebrew roots, Hutchinson laid out a complete system of philosophy and theology, which attracted men of greater eminence than himself. What drew them to his beliefs was his spiritual method of understanding Scripture, his intense reverence for it, and the way he applied its doctrines to man's everyday life. 'Scripture had been treated too much as a matter for mere intellectual discussion, and too little as the spiritual nutriment of the soul and the inspiration and guide for the deeper and more important activities of the spirit.'[31] Eleven years after his death, his works were published in twelve volumes, which helped to spread his notions more widely, notions that Wesley thought gave 'pain to those who believe the Bible, and diversion to those who do not'.[32] Julius Bate; Duncan Forbes, president of the court of session; John Parkhurst, the Biblical lexicographer; Bishop George Horne and William Jones of Nayland, Horne's chaplain, were among his followers.

The Hutchinsonians of Romaine's day 'were men who professed deep reverence for the Scripture; studied the Hebrew with peculiar ardour; were respectable for their strict moral conduct; and adopted the highest sentiments of the ecclesiastical hierarchy; with the bitterest enmity, joined to the most sovereign contempt of all separatists from the Church of England'.[33] According to William Jones, during the 1750s they were reproached and taunted 'as the most mistaken in their opinions and the most dangerous in their attempts that ever infested the Church', and by the end of the century much of this antagonism remained.

In the company of Hutchinsonians, the Old Testament became Romaine's favourite resource and he gained from his studies a treasure of knowledge that would serve him well when his 'new mind' united with a critical knowledge of the Bible. For the rest of his life he maintained a love for Hebrew language studies. When his *Hebrew Grammar* was published posthumously, the *Evangelical Magazine* commented: 'This Grammar has been long handed about in MS, among the friends of the late Mr Romaine, who was known to be an excellent Hebraean.'[34] John Ford, who attended Romaine's ministry at Blackfriars and St Dunstan's, was one of many instructed by Romaine to study the Hebrew language. He was also encouraged by his tutor to 'exercise his talents in expounding the Scriptures, where he had an opportunity of doing it to edification: which issued, at length, in his becoming a preacher of the gospel'.[35]

As Romaine's evangelical convictions deepened, and thanks to the influence of his friend Thomas Haweis, he was slowly weaned from Hutchinsonianism, although as late as 1755, some six or so years after his evangelical conversion, he was still unashamed to be called a Hutchinsonian. This is an example of a stubbornness he often displayed, commendable when fighting for the truth, but an arrogant trait when refusing to admit error. In the preface to a sermon preached at Christ Church, Newgate Street, on 19 May 1755, he writes:

> Let them [his opponents] ridicule it [the sermon] ever so much as Hutchinsonian Enthusiasm, yet since it is expressly taught in Scripture, and maintained in the clearest manner by our church, it will give me no concern to be reckoned an enthusiast, while the scripture is on my side, or an Hutchinsonian, while the church of England supports me; and if men will call the plain doctrines of Scripture enthusiasm, and will treat the articles, and homilies, and liturgy of our church as Hutchinsonianism, I hope I

shall live and die a Church of England Hutchinsonian Enthusiast.[36]

His complete separation from the Hutchinsonians is best confirmed by Haweis, who in his biography of Romaine compares his subject with 'the most bigoted Churchmen, and intolerant':

> They contend for the form, Mr Romaine for the substance, of religion. He pleaded ... for the application and enjoyment of divine truth in the conscience; they for bishops, priests, and deacons, and the two sacraments of sacerdotal administration, as essential to the being of a Christian. They exploded all personal experience of a divine witness by the Spirit of God in the heart, as rank enthusiasm. He maintained it as the essence of truth and Christianity... they differed from him in the boldness and zeal with which he endeavoured to propagate the peculiar doctrines of Jesus to others. Their zeal indeed attached to different objects, the opposition, contempt of, and endeavour to suppress, what they were pleased to stile [style] Methodism, wherever it appeared... the church of England had never a more dutiful, affectionate, and illustrious son, than Mr Romaine... there was a great gulf fixed between them.[37]

Haweis continues his comparison by mentioning the opposition that the Hutchinsonians showed Romaine 'all his life long'.

However, before Romaine rejected the form for the substance of religion, there was another decade of preparatory experiences for him. He had to turn away from knowledge and learning as the road to salvation and look solely to Christ, the Lamb of God who takes away the sins of the world.

Romaine was an able and learned young man, perhaps the ablest and most learned of all the early Evangelicals.

John Overton.[1]

As a scholar — his acquisitions were extensive, and his learning sound. He had a just and critical knowledge of the three learned languages, but especially of the Hebrew tongue, which he much cultivated, much delighted in, and pressed on others to acquire. He had a comprehensive acquaintance with nature, and natural philosophy; and if in this last he held some peculiar views, different from the present generally approved system, he had well studied the points, and stood, even in his peculiarities, in company with some of the brightest geniuses, and deepest scholars, of his time.

William Goode.[2]

2
A Man of Learning

Romaine graduated Bachelor of Arts on 13 February 1734. He was ordained deacon when he was twenty-two years old by the Bishop of Hereford, Henry Egerton, on 17 October 1736. He probably would have preferred to stay at Oxford for literary pursuits, but his financial situation meant he was obliged to take the first opportunity to enter the ministry of the church. However, he left the university a scholar and a well-read man, competent in Hebrew, Latin and Greek. Like many evangelicals, he would have gladly kept up his study of the classics, but after his conversion more important matters absorbed his time. In a letter written from Lambeth on 18 January 1763, while 'sitting at his Master's feet', he said, 'He has made me willing to hear his words; and I find his lips so full of grace, that I cannot spare a moment for my Homer or Virgil, my favourite Tully or Demosthenes. Adieu for ever to all the classics.'[3]

On leaving Oxford, he may have thought he could distinguish himself as a preacher. He had studied eloquence and to improve his elocution had watched the famous actor David Garrick, whose voice was described as 'clear, impressive, and affecting, agreeable though not harmonious, sharp though not dissonant, strong though not extensive. In declamation it is uncommonly forcible, in variation unaffectedly simple.'[4] His first curacy was at Lewtrenchard, near Tavistock in Devon. He travelled there

Benjamin Hoadly, Bishop
of Winchester.

with a friend, whose father lived at Lydford, with the intention that his friend would find him a ministerial position. He was duly installed at Lewtrenchard, where he stayed for six months. There is nothing remarkable about his ministry in that place.

He returned to Oxford to take his Master of Arts on 15 October 1737, but did not stay long. Twelve months later he was living in Epsom, Surrey, and on 15 December 1738 was ordained priest by the notorious Bishop of Winchester, Benjamin Hoadly, famous for his part in the Bangorian controversy and an aggressive leader of the extreme Latitudinarian party in church and state. For the next ten years, while living at Windelsham, he served the churches of Banstead, near Epsom, and Horton, Buckinghamshire, as curate to John Edwards, who held both livings.

It was from Epsom in 1738 that he first entered into controversy via a letter to the author of the famous work *The Divine Legation of Moses*, William Warburton (1698-1779). Warburton, who had a reputation for being 'excessively sarcastic and abusive' in dealing with opponents, was rector of Brant Broughton in Lincolnshire, and in 1760 became Bishop of Gloucester. He hated Methodism and took every opportunity to ridicule its leaders and denounce its teachings. Methodism, he claimed, was nothing more than 'the old Puritan fanaticism revived'. He said of Whitefield: 'Of his oratorical powers, and their astonishing influence on the minds of thousands there can be no doubt; they are of a high order: but with respect to his doctrines, I consider them pernicious and false.'[5] He regarded Lady Huntingdon as an 'incurable enthusiast' and bitterly opposed her preachers. Leslie Stephen, in *History of English Thought in the Eighteenth Century*, has this to say about him:

> Warburton led the life of a terrier in a rat-pit, worrying all theological vermin. His life ... was 'a warfare upon earth'... Amongst bigots and libertines we must reckon everyone, Christian or infidel, whose faith differed by excess or defect from that of Warburton, and add that

Warburton's form of faith was almost peculiar to himself... Probably no man who has lived in recent times
has ever told so many of his fellow creatures that they
were unmitigated fools and liars.[6]

In his 'mischievous book', *The Divine Legation of Moses*, published in two parts (1737 and 1741), he argued that

... because the sacred books of Judaism say nothing
respecting a future state of rewards and punishments,
it must be divine, since it did really accomplish the punishment of wrongdoers without such a doctrine, and no
other legislation has been able to do so without it. This
it could do because the foundation and support of the
Mosaic legislation was the theocracy which was peculiar to the Jews and dealt out in this life righteous rewards and punishments upon individual and nation. An
'extraordinary providence' conducted the affairs of this
people, and consequently the sending of Moses was divinely ordered.[7]

One critic comments that the 'theological system presupposed
in the *Divine Legation* is grotesque, and is the most curious
example of the results of applying purely legal conceptions to
such problems'.[8] Another regards it as the most 'astounding illustration ... of his lack of judgement, his devotion to paradox,
and his infallible instinct for seizing the wrong end of the stick'.[9]
The work is certainly defective in exegesis and limited to only
one line of argument.

In the letter Romaine wrote to Warburton (4 October
1738), described in *The History of the Works of the Learned* for
August 1739 as 'so rare an example of sincerity, candour and
politeness', he represented himself as a young student seeking
further instruction. He thanked Warburton for his 'excellent
book', which he had read 'with a great deal of pleasure', and
had ever admired his 'elegant style, great learning, and strength

of argument'. He then passed on various criticisms he had heard while in the company of several clergymen. He implied that he had defended Warburton, but when the disputants attacked the proposition which Warburton had promised to demonstrate, he, 'being no great proficient in divinity', was not able to answer their queries; hence he was sending them to the author of *The Divine Legation* with a request for help.

The tone of the letter is sickeningly servile, with Romaine returning his 'grateful acknowledgements' for Warburton's work, claiming, 'I would (if it was in my power) hinder the least fault from entering your finished performances, and could wish that ENVY ITSELF MIGHT BE DUMB.' He closes his letter by saying, 'I ... flatter myself that you will not think you act out of character, when you inform the ignorant, confirm the wavering, and oblige a SINCERE ADMIRER. If you would be so good as to think anything I have said worthy of your notice, and would condescend to write one word to fix my doubts, you will lay the GREATEST OBLIGATION on your constant reader, and most humble servant, W. Romaine.'[10]

Warburton, on receipt of the letter, despite all his inquiries, could not discover who 'W. Romaine' was, so he wrote a brief civil reply in which he stated that an important part of his argument was 'to prove that the fathers, patriarchs and prophets of the Jewish line had a knowledge of a future state, and the redemption of mankind by the Messiah'.[11]

In his zeal for the truth as he then understood it, Romaine returned to Oxford in order to oppose Warburton publicly. He preached before the university at St Mary's on 4 March 1739. The sermon, from the text Mark 12:24-27, was later published under the title *The Divine Legation of Moses demonstrated from his having made express mention of, and insisted so much on, the Doctrine of a Future State, whereby Mr Warburton's Attempt to demonstrate the Divine Legation of Moses from the Omission of a Future State is proved to be absurd and destructive of all Revelation.* Among his opening arguments was the statement that Warburton's design promotes that 'very cause which it

The University Church, Oxford (St Mary's).

Interior of St Mary's.

pretends to overthrow: because ... the very foundation upon which it is built is weak and false: for it is a matter of fact, that a future state is mentioned in Moses' writings, and is so far from not being to be found there, that it makes, if not the whole, yet a very great part of those writings, it being delivered there in such plain, literal terms, that he who can barely read, may read and find it there'.[12]

The proposition he was trying to prove was that if the 'doctrine of a future state could not be directly found in the law of Moses, yet there are many strong and unanswerable arguments, which suppose that it is, and prove that it ought to be there'.[13] He argued 'that future rewards and punishments were the sanctions of the Mosaic dispensation'; and showed in the first place, 'from the reason of the thing', and 'from the scriptures of the New Testament, that the doctrine of a future state was taught by Moses, and known by the Jews'.[14]

Towards the end of his sermon, in which he ably controverted Warburton's sentiments, he accused his opponent of assaulting Moses and of trying to defend his 'unchristian cause' with the 'foiled weapons of Sadducees, Infidels and Atheists'. With his parting shot, he referred to the articles and homilies of the Church of England, which 'assert that the fathers of the Jewish nation expected a future state of eternal happiness through the merits of Christ':

> We, who have subscribed to those articles and homilies, must believe this doctrine. And if men may disbelieve the articles and homilies, and yet subscribe to them — and after that subscription write directly against those very doctrines to which they have subscribed — and if they should be encouraged and countenanced by numbers who also have subscribed to them — and if that very church, which requires this subscription, should not censure such a manifest breach of her laws, which she maintains are founded upon the laws of God; this would be a most melancholy state of religion; and from such

persons and such proceedings will all Christians pray,
— 'Good Lord, deliver us.'[15]

Haweis infers that Romaine was provoked by Warburton's
stand against the doctrines he thought important, and by his
enemy's opposition to 'master Hutchinson' and his associates.
He then states: 'Intrepid courage always bore him onward, and
probably ... a desire to make himself of some consequence in
the university, by daring to attack so formidable an adversary;
whose insolence and asperity were ever ready to return double
measure to every antagonist.'[16]

After the publication of Romaine's sermon, when Warburton
discovered the identity of 'W. Romaine', spiteful correspondence began between the two, some of which was printed in
the London General Evening Post for May and June 1739.
Warburton had already written to his friend Thomas Birch on
23 April about Romaine's 'diabolical design to entrap me' with
his letter, and denounced his antagonist as an 'execrable scoundrel'. His principal complaints against Romaine, and in them he
was justified, were that he 'professed admiration for a work and
its author, which he did not mean, and put into the mouths of
others, in a private letter, what he afterwards published as his
own arguments against the plan of the divine legation'.[17] He declared that he no longer believed 'one word' of what Romaine
wrote about a conversation with some clergymen, but took it for
granted that he 'had no other meaning than to conceal his own
kind intentions under a false accusation of his brethren'.[18]

A few days later, stung into further action by Warburton's
response, Romaine wrote a letter which was published in the
London General Evening Post for 2-5 June 1739. He accused
Warburton of 'violating the rules of decency by publishing ... a
private letter of mine without my leave' and of diverting 'people's attention from the points in dispute to a personal quarrel'.
He says that his conversation was not 'false', 'but that there
are numbers of clergymen who understand the subject, and are
ready to defend it against him'. In his reply, he evades the main

point, but rightly claims that Warburton 'recanted his whole scheme' when he admitted that the Old Testament did have a knowledge of a future state and of Messianic redemption.

Warburton was furious and on 7 June wrote to Birch:

> [Romaine] has most amazingly betrayed the scoun-
> drel in his remarks on my publication of his letter. The
> owning himself a rogue so plainly as to confess he was
> not in earnest in the letter he wrote, is such a hard-
> ened confession of villainy as one seldom meets with
> out of Newgate [prison]... this fellow wears the mask of
> friendship, betrays his brethren, and is kindling a fag-
> got [bundle of twigs] for you, while he pretends to offer
> incense.[19]

He wrote to the antiquarian William Stukeley on 26 June: Romaine is the 'scoundrel I wrote to from your house. But the poor devil has done his own business. His talents show him by nature designed for a blunderbuss in Church controversy; but his attack upon me being a proof-charge, and heavy loaded, he burst in the going off; and what will become of him let those who made use of him consider.'[20]

Matters were made worse by a second sermon Romaine preached two years later on the same subject and from the same text (Mark 12:24-27), entitled *Future Rewards and Punishments Proved to be the Sanctions of the Mosaic Dispensation*. This sermon was preached before the University of Oxford at St Mary's on 6 December 1741 and printed at the beginning of the following year. In it, Romaine sought to prove 'That the doctrine of a future state actually is to be found in, and doth make a very great part of, the writings of Moses; the obligation to observe every law, rite, and ceremony, being enforced upon the sanctions of future rewards and punishments.'[21]

It was warmly supported by his Hutchinsonian friends and answered with sarcasm and invective by his Warburtonian enemies. The author of Romaine's biography in *The Evangelical*

Magazine (1795) notes at this point, 'Though he had not ...
an intimate experience of the efficacy of the gospel, yet his acquaintance with Hutchinsonian sentiments naturally led him
into clearer views of evangelical truth than most of the clergy
entertained.'[22]

In the whole affair Romaine showed more of the warmth
of youth and inexperience than the wisdom and temper of age,
and laid himself open to the most 'scurrilous effusions of malev-
olence, abusive language, and opprobrious [scornful] names'
from the flowing pen of Warburton. Although there is no excuse
for Warburton's vindictive response, Romaine was also to blame
for the underhand way in which he first approached his opponent, and for displaying the attitude of an upstart who dared
cross swords with 'one of the most powerful polemicists of the
century'.[23] John Watson, in his biography of Warburton, says,
'The matter certainly did Romaine little honour. If he did not
mean Warburton to take his praises as sincere, he was wrong
in praising him at all; and, whatever was the case, he should
have had sense and grace enough not to retract the commendation which he had bestowed.'[24] This bruising encounter taught
Romaine valuable lessons and persuaded him to be more cau-
tious before entering the battlefield of controversy. It is also another example of his obstinate refusal to drop an argument.

At Banstead, Romaine became acquainted with Sir Daniel
Lambert, who had a country house in the parish and who was
elected Lord Mayor of London for a brief period in 1741. On taking up that office he invited the young curate to be his chaplain
and in that capacity brought him forward to preach before the
city fathers at St Paul's on 2 September of that year — an opportunity that would have brought Romaine the recognition he
desired as a preacher. His sermon, published as *No Justification
by the Law of Nature*, was taken from Romans 2:14-15. In it, he
'displayed a far better view of the doctrine of justification than was
customarily held forth at that time in the churches, except from
the clergy, commonly called Methodists'.[25] Cadogan writes,

Though we do not discover in this sermon the same fertile experience, use and application of the truth, as are to be found in his later writings; yet we discover the same truth itself by which he was then made free from the errors of the day... We discover in it the reasoning of a logical head, the writing of a classical pen, the religion of a believing heart, and the preaching of a sound divine. The point evidently pursued in it is redemption from sin by the blood of Jesus, as it was revealed from God to Adam, and through him to the patriarchs; to Moses and the prophets, and through them to the Israelites; and as it was conveyed to the Gentiles before the preaching of the gospel among them, by tradition.[26]

Romaine set out to prove that God's creatures were never made to teach themselves but to learn from their Maker, and to hold forth his grace as the only remedy suited to their fallen condition, not as a human device, but as a divine revelation. He pointed his readers to the person and work of Christ and the 'necessity of our redemption by Christ':

The law of Moses, [he says, pointed out by its types and emblems] the person of Christ. Particularly it pointed him out by sacrifices, which typified what he was to do and suffer for us. The necessity of these sacrifices proved the necessity of Christ's sacrifice. And God's requiring them as necessary for redemption, proved also the necessity of our redemption by Christ; and therefore it is evident, that the law pointed out and proved the necessity of our redemption by Christ, and purification by blood.[27]

Considering he was only twenty-six years of age (he was not twenty-seven until 25 September), the sermon and its reasoning unveils a mature grasp of the doctrines of the Bible, and shows him already preaching 'Christ and him crucified'.

However, both Cadogan and Ryle are premature when
they write, respectively, 'The truth is, he was a believer — possessed of that unfeigned faith which dwelt in his father and his
mother before him, and we are persuaded that it was in him
also.'[28] And, 'The truths of the glorious gospel appear to have
been applied to his heart by the Holy Spirit from the days of
his childhood at Hartlepool.'[29] There is little doubt that he had
a sound understanding of biblical truth at this time, but it is to
be questioned whether this truth was a series of propositions
known only in the head, or rather a living reality in the heart
and experience. The tone of these early sermons, including a
sermon from Judges 11:30-31, *Jephthah's Vow Fulfilled and his
Daughter not Sacrificed* (1744), preached before the university
at St Mary's, is dry and scholastic, and without the 'life' of later
productions. In the last mentioned, he says:

> It has generally been supposed that [Jephthah's] daugh-
> ter was sacrificed. An action so contrary to the laws of
> God and man, and so inconsistent with the good char-
> acter which St Paul has given of Jephthah's faith, that it
> is not easy to conceive, how it came to pass, that such
> an opinion was ever entertained at all, much less how it
> became so general...
>
> This opinion ... [is] not defensible: because hu-
> man sacrifices were forbidden by the law of Moses,
> and Jephthah did not transgress this law: for he was
> directed by the Spirit of God in making his vow — he
> was never punished for it — he is commended for it by
> St Paul — and had success in consequence of it... The
> arguments brought to prove that she was not sacrificed
> [are]: the historian has neither included her in the vow,
> nor in the fulfilling it — and if she had been included, the
> law had provided a ransom, whereby the vow would be
> kept, and she not made a burnt offering... The true in-
> terpretation ... was settled beyond all doubt from certain
> passages in the history, which gave her the attributes of

a living person some years after her father had fulfilled his vow.[30]

This sermon brought a response from William Dodwell, rector of Shottesbrook, Berkshire, a keen controversialist and voluminous theological writer, who was made Archdeacon of Berks in 1763. In the preface of his *Dissertation on Jephthah's Vow*, occasioned by Romaine's sermon, he claimed that every real difficulty that Romaine proposed in the usual interpretation of the vow 'had long ago been considered and answered' by authors who had written on the subject. 'It must be an error of great inattention,' on Romaine's part, 'to pronounce so peremptorily that his own construction "is free from all the objections to which the common opinion is exposed". On the contrary, I should need no other conviction of the reality of the sacrifice than the complicated absurdities of this new evasive refuge.'[31] Perhaps Romaine was being deliberately provocative in his interpretation in order to gain attention.

It seems we have to wait until the close of the decade before Romaine moved away from this pedantic style, which was designed to impress his hearers and which raised few voices of discontent against its evangelicalism. When he became a new man, and preached evangelical doctrines with new authority and inspiration, his sermons caused great offence and were strenuously opposed by the enemies of true religion.

The small size of his parish at Banstead afforded him ample opportunity to study those points of doctrine which he held so tenaciously in later years. It also gave him the time to prepare for the press, with improvements and a preface, a new edition of the *Hebrew Concordance and Dictionary* of F. Marius de Calasio (d. 1620), a Franciscan friar and a learned professor of Hebrew at Rome. The work originated as the concordance of Rabbi Isaac Mordecai Nathan, published at Venice in 1523. A second and corrected edition was published at Basil in 1581. The third edition is Calasio's. It is a work of 'great erudition', but by Romaine's time was quite scarce — Romaine could only find a few copies and these mainly in Oxford and Cambridge universities.

In March 1745 he published a pamphlet entitled *Proposals for Printing by Subscription the Dictionary and Concordance of F. Marius de Calasio. In Four Volumes Folio with great additions and emendations.* In *Proposals* he gives a brief sketch of the author and his work. Calasio was born in Naples, studied Hebrew at an early age and was soon 'celebrated throughout Italy for his extensive knowledge of the Eastern languages'. Pope Paul V appointed him professor of Hebrew at Rome and Doctor of Divinity, but he died as he was preparing his work for the press. The pope carried on the impression at his own expense, but he too died before it was completed. His successor, Gregory XV, had it published in 1621 in four large volumes.

Romaine, who also wanted his work to be published in four volumes and 'no less than 2½ guineas for each volume', sums up the changes he made by saying, 'The chief omissions in Calasio will be supplied, all the particles of the Hebrew will be regularly digested into the body of the concordance, and every other word omitted by Calasio will be inserted in its proper place; and every passage where it is to be found will be observed.' These changes constituted the 'great additions' to the work. The 'emendations' were mainly of the errors that had crept in through the negligence of the press.[32] A Hutchinsonian admirer regarded the publication as the 'first remarkable and expensive effect of the revival of the *Hebrew* literature among us, and it ought surely to be the general wish and endeavour, that this first effort may succeed happily, and that its success may raise the hopes and animate the courage of others to the like undertakings'.[33]

Romaine's edition, which demonstrates his ability to write classical Latin, reflects a strong Hutchinsonian bias and was only truly appreciated by those who shared his views. The *Monthly Review*, in commenting on Julius Bate's *Critica Hebraea*, writes sarcastically, 'The followers of Mr Hutchinson's system will not fail to pronounce it a *Chef d'oeuvre* [a masterpiece]; while the

Rationalists will consign it to a peaceful place on the same un-
dusted shelf, on which the great Calasio reposes, undisturbed,
in the friendly arms of the Reverend William Romaine.'[34] He
received just criticism for omitting the definition of the word
for God, 'Elohim', substituting a word that reflected his own
opinion — an opinion which the majority of Hebrew scholars
rejected. In an address which he prefixed to the work, he drew
readers' attention to the change and made this apology: 'I have
endeavoured to perform the office of a faithful editor; you have
Marius himself not in the least diminished or added to, excepting only one place, and that of such great consequence that I
should have thought it a crime if I had neglected to amend it.
This I have done with the best intention, and only this once; I
hope therefore that it may be pardoned.'[35] He added that he
had marked the place with inverted commas.

It was a huge work, which 'procured him no small literary
fame', although in point of real usefulness it was inferior to Dr
John Taylor's *Hebrew Concordance*. Many great men had encouraged him in the undertaking and Oxford University also
assisted him. Lordships, archdeacons, bishops and many digni-
taries of the church generously subscribed to it. George Horne
at once possessed a copy and his *Commentary on the Psalms*
was a consequence. The first two volumes of the *Concordantiae
Sacrorum Bibliorum Hebraicorum* appeared in 1747, the third
in 1748 and the fourth in 1749. Thus the work took him the
best part of a decade to complete. The enormity of the task is
captured in Romaine's own words in his *Proposals*: 'I have ...
been persuaded to propose to the learned the publication of a
work, by far the greatest that ever was finished in the Christian
world, and which alone will supply the defect of most other
Lexicons and Concordances.'[36] Haweis explains that although
it was sought after, it was not a financial success:

The performance is great; sufficient in its nature and
magnitude to have deterred any other man from attempting it; and notwithstanding it was subscribed for by

every crowned head in Europe, and the Pope himself in
the front of the list, I do not apprehend that any considerable emolument repaid the immensity of the toil and
expense with which it was attended. And the edition, I
believe, has not been disposed of to this day [1797].
Indeed I have heard the bookseller failed, and a single
copy of the work was all he received for his labours.[37]

So Romaine was growing in knowledge and enhancing his reputation as a man of learning. The courage and doctrines that
marked him in later years were already part of him, as we see in
his daring to challenge and in many ways overcome the 'great
Colossus' Warburton. Furthermore, his ability as a preacher
was being recognized — but the vital spark was missing. The
house had been built but as yet it was not on fire. The passion
for Christ's glory and his labour for the souls of men were taking second place to his own ambitions. All that was about to
change.

The Evangelical party within the Church of England did not consist of 'disciples of Wesley and Whitefield' left behind by Wesley as 'a rearguard' within the Establishment... Walker of Truro and his circle of Gospel clergymen in Cornwall; Adam, Grimshaw, Conyers in the North; Romaine, Venn, Berridge, these men owed their conversion not to a Methodist sermon or tract but to the same overpowering sense of spiritual insufficiency that had driven the Oxford Methodists to their new faith.

John Walsh.[1]

O what am I, that such a sinner as I am should be thus highly favoured? A child of wrath by nature, even as others, and by practice, having sinned long with greediness against light and conviction, sinning and sorrowing, sorrowing and sinning, from year to year, a slave to the lust of the flesh, to the lust of the eyes, and to the pride of life, every moment fit and ripe for hell. O what a monument of infinite patience and longsuffering! spared from day to day, and at last called to the saving knowledge of Jesus.

William Romaine.[2]

3

A New Heart

London life in the eighteenth century was a 'swirling mass of contrasts', as one writer put it. 'A rowdy hedonistic, gin-swilling public rubbed shoulders with gentlefolk keen to do good work.' Gin-swilling was at its worst between 1720 and 1751, partly because the liquors were so cheap and intoxicating, and were 'retailed indiscriminately and in the most brutalising and demoralising conditions'.[3] Nearly every shop visited by the poorer classes sold spirits and thereby created an 'orgy of spirit-drinking', which not only added to the misery of the poor, but increased crimes of violence throughout the city, the drinkers often 'carried to a degree of outrageous passion'. Children who were left naked and to starve at home by their drunken parents were forced to beg and steal. One horrific example will suffice to show the suffering caused by gin-drinking:

> The scene is in St Giles where in 1750 every fourth house at least was a gin-shop. Its eighty-two 'two-penny houses' were also brothels of the lowest class and places for receiving stolen goods. Many of the crimes of the time bear all the marks of a gin-inflamed insanity. There is the case of Judith Dufour who fetched her two-year-old child from the workhouse, where it had just been 'new-clothed', for the afternoon. She strangled it

and left it in a ditch in Bethnal Green in order to sell its
clothes. The money (one and fourpence) was spent on
gin and was divided with a woman, who (she said) instigated the crime.[4]

It was the custom of the time for almost every man who had the
means to spend his evenings drinking or at some other place of
public entertainment. Along with gambling, these habits were
responsible for 'bad masters and bad apprentices, resulting in
bankruptcies, absconding debtors, runaway apprentices, and
deserted children, and leading by an inevitable sequence to
paupers, vagrants, and thieves'.[5]

In the middle of the century, deaths in London greatly exceeded births, many dying prematurely because of excessive
drinking. Children were abandoned on the streets and left to
the mercy of the parish; their fathers, if they were still alive,
were either too drunk to support them or in prison because of
debt. The duty of the parish was to send these children to the
workhouses, where, according to the ideal, they were 'bred up
to labour and industry, virtue and religion'. Sadly, the appren-
ticeship system was accompanied by many evils and large numbers died of neglect. Further, London communities faced the
constant danger of ruinous buildings collapsing; squalid living
conditions; the window tax, which induced people to block up
windows, which in turn reduced the amount of light and air in
their homes; the frequent wars and dislocating transitions that
had to be made from peace to war, and war to peace; the irregularity of many London trades; and the battle that was frequently lost against epidemics such as typhus, dysentery, mea-
sles and influenza — all of which meant that from the years
1730 to 1749 74.5% of the children christened died before they
reached the age of five.

On a brighter note, the advocates of the Methodist revival
had been actively propagating their views for some years and
had established themselves in the city. It was a convenient centre
for Wesley's followers and for those who looked to the Countess

The Foundery, Moorfields. This historical site was once
the capital of Wesleyan Methodism.

of Huntingdon. In 1740, after Wesley had severed his connexion
with the Moravians in Fetter Lane, he moved to the Foundery,
a large building in Moorfields, which became the headquarters
of Wesleyan Methodism in the capital until the opening of the
City Road chapel opposite Bunhill Fields in 1778. There were
other chapels, too, such as the French Protestant chapel in West
Street, Seven Dials, which Wesley took over in 1743. Whitefield
and the Huntingdonians had the Tabernacle in Moorfields and
the chapel in Tottenham Court Road.[6]

It was into this fractured society, where life was so uncertain
and insecure, and yet where Methodism had taken root, that
Romaine moved in 1747. The two most plausible reasons why
he moved to London are firstly, that he wanted to be nearer
the printers of the *Concordance* for convenience's sake and in
order to promote effectively the work; and secondly, he hoped
his 'occasional sermons would pave his way to farther notice,
and his abilities, which self-love had not depreciated, procure
him more rapid advancement in the great city, where superior
talents could hardly fail to engage attention, and noble patrons

be found proud of distinguishing merit in every line'.[7] In the memoir of Romaine in the *Evangelical Magazine* for November 1795, the writer comments that he came to London 'strongly entrenched in notions of his own exalted abilities, and flattering himself that he required no other recommendation to a rapid preferment in a city where talent was always admired and justly estimated'.[8]

However, in these self-centred aspirations he was disappointed. He was not noticed or applauded, and had little prospect of a church or any of the objects he coveted; and to make matters worse, the publication of Calasio was not proving a success. Feeling somewhat peeved no doubt, he told his friends that he had no intention of settling in London. Cadogan supposes, rather speculatively, that from the 'bent of his genius to the study of nature, of minerals, fossils, plants, and the wonders of God in creation, that a country life, so favourable to these pursuits, would have been chosen by him'.[9] So with a heavy heart he decided to move north, back to Hartlepool, but God intervened in a remarkable way:

> He had bid adieu to the Metropolis, and had sent his trunk on board the ship, where his passage had been taken; and he was on the pavement passing to the water-side, in order to embark for his distant native country, when he was accosted by a gentleman whom he did not know, who asked if his name was not Romaine. On his replying in the affirmative, he apologized for the abruptness of his address, informed him, that having known his father some years before, the striking resemblance he bore to him, had led him to put the question. Enquiries for his family having brought on a conversation, which led to his present views, and past disappointments of procuring employment in London — the gentleman informed him, the lectureship of the parish in which he resided, St George's, Botolph Lane [near London Bridge and which was united to St Botolph's, Billingsgate], was

then vacant; and he promised to exert his utmost influence to procure his election, if he would stay and wait
the event. Mr Romaine was startled; he consented on
condition he should not be obliged personally to can-
vass the parish: to which his high spirit thought it an
indignity to descend; and that it became not a minister
of Christ to solicit preferment. This being acceded to,
his trunk was disembarked, he returned to his lodging,
and his unknown friend secured his election, and fixed
the future scene of his life and ministrations in the city,
on which he was that very moment turning his back for
ever.[10]

He was elected in October 1748 and in the following month
the *Gentleman's Magazine* simply carried the notice: 'Mr
Romayne, editor of Calasio's *Dictionary*, chosen lecturer of the
united parishes of St George's Botolph-lane, and St Botolph's,
Billingsgate.'[11] The rector at the time was Thomas Woodford.
Botolph Lane, where Sir Christopher Wren is thought to have
lived while St Paul's was being built, was named after the 'vanished church', St Botolph, Billingsgate, described as a 'proper
church and hath had many fair monuments therein'. It was destroyed in the Great Fire of London, 1666, and never rebuilt.[12]
St George's stood on the west side of the lane on the south
corner of St George's Lane. It too was destroyed by the fire, but
Wren rebuilt it in 1671-4 using rubble from St Paul's Cathedral.
It was finally demolished in 1904.[13] Romaine's ministrations at
his first lectureship probably occurred only once a week, and no
record survives of how he was received.

In all this Romaine was moments from leaving the sphere
where he was to be greatly used as an upholder of the gospel,
and where his ministry was to be blessed to many. Haweis reflects on these providential circumstances and concludes:

Had not Romaine met this stranger — had he not instantly been struck with Mr R's resemblance to his father —

had he not accosted him with a curiosity, for which probably himself could give no reason — and which on no
other occasion perhaps he would have been disposed
to indulge in the street — addressing a man he had
never seen before. Had he passed a moment sooner or
later — had the lectureship not been then vacant — had
not the conversation led to the cause of Mr Romaine's
departure — in short, if a thousand unforeseen circumstances had not concurred just at that critical moment,
the labours of that great reviver of Evangelical truth in
the churches of London, [would have] been lost to the
Metropolis, and with it all the blessed consequences of
his ministry, which thousands have experienced, and for
which they will bless God to all eternity.[14]

Romaine was still unconverted and unable to enjoy the evangelical doctrines of the gospel of which he became such a champion.
His letters confirm that he was a stranger to the power of godliness
and that he had not yet entered into that knowledge of himself
and of God that are necessary for salvation. Like so many others
he grew clearer by degrees through reading the Word, prayer and
experience. This gradual change is apparent between the years
1739 and 1749. His education at Oxford and his Hutchinsonian
views had led him a little way, but it was in London that he was
brought into the full light and liberty of the gospel. The final crisis point was probably in 1749, although a letter he wrote to a
young candidate for the ministry from Lambeth on 3 December
1767 suggests his awakening began around 1745. In the letter,
he encourages the reader to study the Bible: 'Will you learn from
a poor penitent? Indeed I repent, and God forgive my misspent
time in sciences and classics. I saw my folly two and twenty years
ago, and have since studied nothing but the Bible.'[15] This could
simply refer to his commitment to the Word of God and not to
the time of his conversion, for surely he would have been more
specific if he had been writing about his salvation, which produced such a dramatic transformation in his life.

In a letter to Mrs Medhurst from Lambeth, dated 15 November 1766, he looks back to his conversion. Writing in the third person, he describes himself as an arrogant and ignorant young man, who learned 'very slowly' that the Holy Spirit, who 'will glorify nothing but Jesus', will 'stain the pride of all greatness and of all goodness, excepting what is derived from the fulness of the incarnate God':

> He was a very, very vain, proud young man: knew almost everything but himself, and therefore was mighty fond of himself. He met with many disappointments to his pride, which only made him prouder, till the Lord was pleased to let him see and feel the plague of his own heart. At this time my acquaintance with him began. He tried every method that can be tried to get peace, but found none. In his despair of all things else, he betook himself to Jesus, and was most kindly received. He trusted the word of promise and experienced the sweetness in the promise. After this he went through various frames and trials of faith, too many to mention.[16]

In the same letter, and still writing in the third person, he explains how he was 'brought to a clear conviction that all fulness of good is in Jesus'. 'You must go to him, you must go to him,' was the humbling lesson he had to learn. It was only the knowledge of his own nothingness and that Jesus is everything that crucified his pride. 'He has been attempting for many years to be something, to do something of himself, but could not succeed: disappointed again and again, yet he could not give it up, till God made him feel, in him, that is, in his flesh, dwelled no good thing: and now he writes folly, weakness, sin, on all that is his own; not only clearly convinced that all fulness of good is in Jesus, but is also ... content it should be in him.' He was now happy to go to Jesus for 'those very things of which he himself is empty, and which he cannot have anywhere else'.[17]

The change was remarkable. He was like a bird set free from
its cage to enjoy the blessings of freedom. Instead of fighting to
satisfy the lusts of his pride, his heart glowed and his countenance brightened as he talked of Jesus and his sufficiency. One
is thrilled at his words:

> O that you did but know what I experience in living upon
> the fulness of Jesus!... This subjection to his will is heav-
> en regained... I see myself in him perfectly accepted,
> perfectly justified, perfectly comely in his comeliness,
> perfectly happy in his love — all the desire of the soul
> satisfied with Jesus' person, and Jesus' work. This, this
> is the death of pride. Here free-will, self-righteousness,
> a legal spirit cannot work. The spirit and power of Jesus
> in this his glory makes them hide their heads.[18]

He never forgot the pit of darkness and degradation from which
he was rescued, and as late as 1795, the year of his death, he
was still amazed at and overcome with gratitude towards his
'compassionate Saviour':

> I was even as others once — by nature a child of wrath,
> and an heir of misery. I was going on in the broad way
> of destruction, careless and secure; and I am quite as-
> tonished to see the danger that I was in. I tremble to
> behold the precipice which I was ready to fall over when
> Jesus opened mine eyes, and by the light of his Word
> and Spirit showed me my guilt and my danger, and put
> it into my heart to flee from the wrath to come. O what a
> most merciful escape! I cannot think of it without adoring
> the compassionate Saviour who remembered me in my
> low estate, for his mercy endureth for ever![19]

But Romaine's experience went deeper than just a 'one-off conversion'. Each day he enjoyed the 'kindness of [God's] heart,
and the bounty of his hand' in such a way that he could not

describe. Whenever he went to Jesus, he was sent away with 'matter of thankfulness'. In short, he fell in love with Jesus over and over again, and described him as 'infinitely lovely' and 'everlastingly precious'.

In another letter to the same friend, dated 21 March 1767, after admitting that he had never found the freedom to share his testimony with anyone else before, he describes in more detail first the distractions and discouragements he encountered, and secondly, 'God's wonderful dealings with me' and how he could not look back without 'adoring my meek and lowly Prophet'. I give an extended extract from this important letter:

> When I was in trouble and soul-concern, he [God] would not let me learn of man. I went everywhere to hear, but nobody was suffered to speak to my case. The reason of this I could not tell then, but I know it now. The Arminian Methodists flocked about me, and courted my acquaintance, which became a great snare unto me. By their means I was brought into a difficulty, which distressed me several years. 'I was made to believe that part of my title to salvation was to be inherent — something called holiness in myself, which the grace of God was to help me to. And I was to get it by watchfulness, prayer, fasting, hearing, reading, sacraments, &c. so that after much and long attendance in those means, I might be able to look inward, and be pleased with my own improvement, finding I was grown in grace a great deal holier, and more deserving of heaven than I had been.'
>
> I do not wonder now that I received this doctrine. It was sweet food to a proud heart. I feasted on it, and to work I went. It was hard labour and sad bondage, but the hopes of having something to glory in of my own kept up my spirits. I went on, day after day, striving, agonizing (as they called it), but still I found myself not a bit better. I thought this was the fault, or that, which being amended, I should certainly succeed; and therefore set out afresh,

but still came to the same place. No galley-slave worked harder, or to less purpose.

Sometimes I was quite discouraged, and ready to give all up; but the discovery of some supposed hindrance set me to work again. Then I would redouble my diligence, and exert all my strength. Still I got no ground. This made me often wonder; and still more, when I found at last that I was going backward. Methought I grew worse. I saw more sin in myself instead of more holiness, which made my bondage very hard, and my heart very heavy. The thing I wanted, the more I pursued it, flew farther and farther from me. I had no notion that this was divine teaching, and that God was delivering me from my mistake in this way: so that the discoveries of my growing worse were dreadful arguments against myself, until now and then a little light would break in and show me something of the glory of Jesus; but it was a glimpse only — gone in a moment.

As I saw more of my heart, and began to feel more of my corrupt nature, I got clearer views of gospel-grace; and in proportion as I came to know myself, I advanced in the knowledge of Christ Jesus. But this was very slow work: the old leaven of self-righteousness, new christened holiness, stuck close to me still, and made me a very dull scholar in the school of Christ. But I kept on, making a little progress; and as I was forced to give up one thing and another on which I had some dependence, I was left at last stripped of all, and neither had, nor could see where I could have, aught to rest my hopes, that I could call my own. This made way for blessed views of Jesus.

Being now led to very deep discoveries of my own legal heart, of the dishonour which I had put upon my Saviour, of the despite I had done to the Spirit of his grace, by resisting and perverting the workings of his love, these things humbled me. I became very vile in mine own eyes; I gave over striving; the pride of free will, the boast of mine own works, were laid low. And as self was debased, the Scriptures became an open book, and every page presented the Saviour in new glory.

In the letter, he mentions seven truths that were explained to him and 'which are now the very joy and life of my soul'. The first was 'the plan of salvation', which was 'so ordered from first to last ... that he who glorieth should have nothing to glory in but the Lord'. Secondly, 'the benefits of salvation', which he calls all the 'free gifts of free grace, conferred without any regard to what the receiver of them is; nothing being looked at by the Giver but his own sovereign glory'. When he considered these benefits one by one, it was the 'very death of self-righteousness and self complacency', for 'all is of God', who 'humbles us that we may be willing to receive Christ', and who keeps us humble 'that we may be willing to live by faith upon Christ received'. This was the third truth. The fourth was the 'inestimably great benefit' of living by faith; for this is a 'life in every act of it dependent upon another. Self is renounced, so far as Christ is lived upon. And faith is the most emptying, pulling down grace,' because it will 'not let a man see aught good in himself, but pulls down every high thought, and lays it low in subjection to Jesus'.

Fifthly, he learned to see Jesus in all his works and duties, which are dead 'unless done in and by the faith of the Son of God. Against this blessed truth,' he admits, 'I find my nature kick. To this hour, a legal heart will be creeping into duties, to get between me and my dear Jesus, whom I go to meet in them. But he soon recovers me from the temptation, makes me loathe myself for it, and gets fresh glory to his sovereign grace.' A further humbling lesson was the unbelief, pride and impatience he found in his heart. 'I read the trial of your faith worketh patience; the trial of mine, the direct contrary. Instead of patient submission, I want to have mine own way, to take very little physic, and that very sweet: so the flesh lusteth. But the Physician knows better. He knows when and what to prescribe.' Finally, he learned the

importance of 'looking at nothing but Jesus' in life and in death.
'These all, who had obtained a good report in every age, died
in faith. On their death-bed they did not look for present peace
and future glory, but to the Lamb of God.'[20]

These are the lessons he was taught, not by man, but by
God. He fought against them until his Heavenly Teacher, with
kindness and gentleness, humbled him to receive them. In his
letter he writes on, as if caught up with the wonder of his Saviour
and unable to stop speaking of his praise:

> I have not learned them, as we do mathematics, to
> keep them in memory, and to make use of them when
> I please; no, I find in me to this moment an opposition
> to every gospel truth, both to the belief of it in my head,
> and to the comfort of it in my heart. I am still a poor de-
> pendent creature, sitting very low at the feet of my dear
> Teacher, and learning to admire that love of his, which
> brought me down, and keeps me down at his feet. There
> be my seat, till I learn my lesson perfectly... In heaven
> all is perfection. The saints are as humble as they are
> happy. Clothed with glory, and clothed with humility, with
> one heart and one voice they cry, 'Worthy is the Lamb'...
> My heart is in tune, and I can join that blessed hymn
> — looking at him as the Giver of grace ... as they look at
> him the Giver of glory. I can take the crown most gladly
> from the head of all my graces, as they do from the head
> of their glory, and cast it down at his loving feet: 'Worthy
> is the Lamb.' He is — he is — blessings on him for ever
> and ever!...
>
> Adore and praise him with me and for me. And learn,
> my dear friend, from what I have here related, to trust
> him more... Let nothing keep you from him; whatever
> you meet with, let it drive you to him; for all good is from
> him, and all evil is turned into good by him. O wondrous
> Saviour![21]

These letters express the genuine feeling of his mind and give an insight into the dealings of God with his soul. He was deeply humbled by God, seeing his own good works as nothing more than filthy rags, and led to rest wholly on Christ for salvation. The pride which had underpinned his desires was mortified as he saw the corruption of his own heart. The vain imaginations he had entertained were cast down, and the lofty thoughts of his own wisdom and ability, which had exalted themselves against the knowledge of Christ, were dissolved. Instead, he was ready to take refuge as a poor sinner at the foot of the cross and to yield himself to the obedience of his Saviour. From this point, the doctrines of the gospel were no longer theoretical truths to be preached as a matter of duty, dry and dusty, but experimental and living realities exploding from a heart on fire. The Word became like a sharp double-edged sword in his mouth, with which he struck the strongholds of Satan.

With the evangelists and pastors I was also much pleased; — with the wisdom and knowledge, and truly amiable temper, of the rector of St Mary Woolnoth — with the simplicity and watchfulness, and unblameable life and labours, of Mr Foster — with the admirable talents and eloquent evangelical preaching of Dr Peckwell — with the apostolical spirit, and abilities, and great grace of Mr Cecil — with my old friend and fellow-labourer, and a wonder of a man, who seems now drawing toward the end of his highly-honoured labours, Mr Romaine — with the ingenious and very useful Mr De Coetlogon, and Mr Herbert Jones.

Henry Venn writing to James Stillingfleet on 26 April 1783.[1]

4
Evangelicals in London

At the beginning of the eighteenth century, the religious and moral state of England was at its most depraved. Sexual immorality, corruption in high and low places, gambling, and robbery are just four examples of the degradation into which the nation had sunk. All the filth of society seemed to concentrate in London, 'the darkest spot of the land'. The church, supposedly a light of hope, was trapped in a 'spiritual paralysis' that had set in after many years of decline. The city's clergy, often dignified and respected men of learning, were mere rationalists who 'let alone the mysterious points of religion, and preached to the people only good plain, practical morality'. The result was an appearance of godliness on their part, but a faith and message that lacked reality and power, and that produced little or no effect for good in the communities they were meant to serve. 'We make no use of the high commission we bear than to come abroad, one day in seven, dressed in solemn looks ... to be the apes of Epictetus,' complained Bishop Hoadly.

At this time the celebrated lawyer Blackstone heard all the well-known preachers in London and announced that not one of the sermons contained more Christianity than the writings of Cicero. From all he heard, it was impossible to tell whether the preachers were followers of Confucius, Mohammed or Christ! The 'old Calvinist clergyman,' says another, 'was not merely an endangered, but almost a vanished, species'.[2] One of the most dreadful comments of the period is ascribed to Lady Montague, and it clearly links the depravity of morals with the loss of true Christianity: 'They ought to take the not out of the Decalogue and put it in the Creed.' Mark Pattison, in his essay *Tendencies of Religious Thought in England, 1688-1750*, summarizes the country's spiritual and moral collapse when he depicts the period 'as one of decay of religion, licentiousness of morals, public corruption, profaneness of language — a day of "rebuke and blasphemy"'.[3]

As the century moved on, God raised up an army of men to battle for the gospel — men who, if the Establishment closed its door on them, lectured weekly from many important city pulpits and ministered to large congregations in proprietary chapels. Romaine, for his part, was sincerely attached to Anglican doctrine and discipline, and was convinced that the most appropriate way of advancing the cause of Christ lay through the Establishment. He 'saw plainly, that to bring her [the Church of England's] authority into reverence, to make her services comprehended, and preach the truths contained in her Articles and Homilies, was the surest way of doing permanent good'.[4]

Above: Ten men drinking in a tavern.
Right: The Sleeping Congregation (1733). Engraving by William Hogarth.

He never depreciated the usefulness of itinerants, and supported many of them, but his role was to be played out within the confines of Anglicanism. He has rightly been described as the forerunner of the Evangelical party in the Church of England. Dissenters, for their part, treated him with great respect and honoured him as a voice of hope for the nation. Edwin Sidney, in *The Life of the Rev. Rowland Hill*, says, 'I have never met with a pious nonconformist who questioned the usefulness of Romaine's ministry in London, nor the value of his admirable writings.'[5]

Two views of the Thames River.

When John Newton arrived in the city in 1780, Romaine was still the only beneficed evangelical north of the Thames, with few who supported his forthright proclamation of the doctrines of the revival. Overton, in a colourful portrait of Romaine, remarks: 'There is something very striking in the thought of this one solitary figure rising up like another John the Baptist in the moral wilderness of London, and proclaiming, not for a brief space, but Sunday after Sunday ... what he believed to be vital but long-neglected truths; and the stern, reserved, self-contained character of the man adds force and vividness to the picture.'[6] In many ways he was like John the Baptist — fearless, uncompromising, rugged in appearance, severe in character — and in his way he owned the greatest power of all the early evangelicals.

However, for thirty years evangelicalism had been advancing within the church by means other than city incumbents, mainly through proprietary chapels and lectureships. Acknowledging this advance, Bruce Hindmarsh comments, 'Evangelicalism in London was thriving within the same ecclesiastical underworld as had Puritanism 200 years earlier, when the first lectureships appeared and "godly ministers" depended widely upon private patronage.'[7]

The proprietary chapels, which the bishops permitted to be built to meet the needs of the increasing population, were often erected in the suburbs by subscription and maintained by private individuals. No districts were attached to them and the lay proprietors were allowed to choose their own ministers; but it was not a good arrangement. The chapels were intended for those who could afford the high pew rents, so they inevitably excluded the less affluent, and the system lay open to exploitation by unscrupulous West End developers, who saw in it a means to commercial success.

> A property owner might erect a chapel as an inducement to those who were in search of new houses to acquire them on his estate, and at the same time with the hope of some profit to himself. The proprietors of these chapels, in order to attract congregations and fill the pews, were ever on the look out for some rising popular preacher, to whom a fixed stipend would be paid. Sometimes a cleric who fancied himself as a preacher would open such a chapel on his own account.[8]

In spite of their obvious weaknesses, these chapels were for a time often the only way an evangelical preacher could obtain a hearing and were the means employed to advance the gospel.

Lectureships exercised a greater influence than the proprietary chapels and in London they were held largely by evangelicals. The system can be traced back to the Puritans, who, because of their evangelical beliefs, could not easily obtain livings. Instead, they set up lectureships financed by parishioners or by wealthy patrons. In this way they increased the opportunity for religious instruction while keeping themselves independent of the incumbent of the parish and free to preach the doctrines of the gospel without compromise or fear of interference.

In the eighteenth century, parishioners elected a clergyman, whom the bishop would licence, and then invited him to lecture once a week at an hour outside the regular service times of the church. These men were usually good gospel preachers and, once licensed, not only possessed an independent authority, but also escaped the scrutiny of their Ordinary. Lectureships could be held in conjunction with livings, as was the case with Romaine, or with curacies or other appointments, as with Henry Venn and Thomas Scott. 'It was quite possible and even customary,' writes Elliot-Binns, 'for a clergyman to hold several such appointments if the times of the services did not clash.'[9] As can be imagined, these posts in London were eagerly sought by ambitious young clerics, and several well-known churchmen began their careers in this way.

Lectureships gave evangelicals a voice, which inevitably the enemies of the gospel tried to silence. In January 1759, for instance, a printed notice addressed to the 'Beneficed Clergy of the Diocese of London', from 'their (as yet uninfected) parishioners', urged incumbents to refuse evangelical lecturers:

It is well known, that since the introduction of lectureships, there have crept into our pulpits a set of very irregular teachers; utter enemies to decency and order, and propagators of most absurd doctrines; whereby they unsettle the minds of the laity, and allure them to forsake their lawful pastors: men, who despise all rule

and authority, and openly declare they know no superior
in the Church; who are puffed up with spiritual pride, and
proclaim themselves the only true gospel preachers: by
which device ... they are become the idols of the popu-
lace, and the vulgar herd from all quarters of the town,
dance after their summons...

By these disorderly crowds of their followers, we
your helpless parishioners are driven out of our churches, and deprived of the benefit of public worship...

That the enormities complained of may be speed-
ily cured, and that the reverend gentlemen in possession may never be ousted their churches by a fanatical
faction, but that we may long enjoy the benefit of their
orthodox ministry, is the hearty prayer of *their most affectionate parishioners.*[10]

Opposition, however, did not deter these men, who continued
to preach — Romaine lectured at St Dunstan's until his death
in 1795 — and, with the additional opportunities that chap-
laincies afforded, they reached large congregations across the
metropolis.

One early evangelical clergyman was Richard Thomas
Bateman, rector of St Bartholomew-the-Great in Smithfield.
He was a man of high birth and considerable natural talents,
who had been awakened under the ministry of Howel Davies
in Wales, where he also held a living. 'Being converted himself,'
says Tyerman, 'he, at once, with great fervour, began to pray and
preach for the conversion of others.'[11] He was a sincere friend of
the Methodists and allowed both Wesley, who he had known at
Oxford, and Whitefield the use of his pulpit, which involved him
in some unpleasant litigations with Bishop Gibson — litigations
that came to nothing when the bishop died. Romaine served as
Bateman's morning preacher at St Bartholomew's during the
last two years of his life. He died in 1761.

Another early London evangelical was Thomas Jones, 'the
seraphic Mr Jones' to his admirers. In 1753 he was appointed

St Saviour's, Southwark. Before the Reformation, the church was known as the Priory Church of St Mary Overy.

junior chaplain of St Saviour's, Southwark, where he was for several years the only beneficed evangelical in the London area. Romaine's acquaintance with him began about 1751, when Jones was first under 'soul-concern', and from that time, for the next eight or nine years, their intimacy and friendship gave Romaine 'a constant opportunity of being a witness of God's gracious dealings with his soul'.[12] In his funeral sermon, which was published the same year for the benefit of his widow, Romaine pays a glowing tribute to his friend:

> He told me in his last sickness ... that as a dying man he had nothing to trust to but the righteousness of Jesus Christ; and that his faith in it had been so strengthened in his illness that he had not one doubt or fear...
>
> You could not converse with him without being put in mind of the meekness and gentleness of Christ... In his behaviour, in his conversation, he showed that he had put on ... bowels of mercies, kindness, humbleness of mind, long suffering, ready to bear with others, and ready to forgive...
>
> His own flock, to whom the Lord had made him an overseer, was much upon his heart. How earnest have I often heard him in prayer for them!... There is an alms-house in the parish called the College, and some small stipend for doing duty in it. Mr Jones thought it

was not right to take the money, unless he did the duty. Accordingly he began to read prayers, and to expound the scriptures in the college chapel, and went on for some time. The congregation used to be very large, and the success was very great. Many souls were in this place first awakened who are now walking in the faith and fear of God, adorning the gospel of our Saviour. But here he was stopped, and refused the use of the chapel. After this he set up a weekly lecture in his church, but he had not preached it long, before he was denied the use of the pulpit. However, he was not discouraged, he went on giving away good books, some of which he carried in person to every house in the parish; catechising the children, who came weekly to his house for that purpose; and paying religious visits among his parishioners, when they used to talk freely of the state of their souls. By these methods he tried to win his people to Christ.[13]

Henry Venn described the sermon as giving 'a most pleasing account of Mr Jones's death. Most comfortable and animating are such scenes! In them we see how true the Lord our strength is, and that there is no unrighteousness in Him: we may see what manner of support and consolation He imparts in the dying hour.'[14] Typically, the *Monthly Review* was unimpressed: 'To read the senseless sermon before us were enough indeed to give the reader a surfeit of all religion. But it is really not more an object of ridicule than of indignation; and the author of it not less profane than stupid.'[15]

The loss that Romaine felt is revealed in a letter he wrote to Richard Hill: 'Sunday morning, this city received a most heavy stroke from the hand of God. That dear minister of the Lord, Mr Jones, was taken from us... My dear Sir, pray for me; this is a great shock to me. I am now alone, as I first set out; not one minister in any parish church to countenance me. Thank God,

I have One with me, whose favour is better than life. In Him I depend. He never failed me yet.'[16]

Romaine always spoke highly of Jones. From Lambeth, on 11 January 1763, he wrote a short account of his life in a recommendatory preface, which is prefixed to Jones's *Works* published the same year. Romaine wrote the preface 'because I should hereby have an opportunity of showing my gratitude to the memory of my dear brother, and also of doing some good to precious souls, and to the interest of our Lord's kingdom, which was his end and aim in preaching and printing these sermons'.[17] In the words of another, Jones was a 'gifted preacher, a fine scholar, and possessed a remarkably sweet and placid disposition'.[18] He was a tireless worker, whose numerous activities took up so much of his time that many of his sermons were criticized for being too hastily prepared. He sometimes began to compose his Sabbath sermons late on Saturday evening, which meant 'I can never find time to smooth my language, nor to embellish my discourses with pretty conceits, but am obliged to send them abroad into the world *in puris naturalibus* [stark naked].'[19]

His superiors continually opposed him. Balleine comments: 'Without his unfailing good temper he could not have stayed at his post. For nine years he had to endure a bitter persecution; his teaching was denounced, his sermons were caricatured, his personal character vilified in a never-ending stream of controversial tracts.'[20] He did have a few supporters: Romaine, of course; Lady Huntingdon, at whose London residence he often preached; and John Wesley, who wrote to him in March 1759 offering his friendship, which Jones gratefully accepted. But there were few like-minded men with whom to enjoy fellowship. His premature death on 6 June 1762, at the age of thirty-three, was a sad loss to the evangelical cause, and moved John Newton, who was 'greatly affected' by his removal, to think more seriously about entering the ministry. With the passing of his 'dear and honoured friend ... he felt he could no longer be silent'.[21] The inscription on his monument in Southwark Cathedral de-

Henry Venn.

scribes him as a 'painstaking minister, followed much for his doctrine'.[22]

Henry Venn, who had adopted evangelical doctrines 'in consequence of a faithful and diligent application to the Holy Scriptures',[23] accepted the curacy of Clapham in 1754, lecturing at the same time in three London churches: St Antholin's, St Alban's, Wood Street and St Swithin's, London Stone. With a workload of at least six sermons a week to prepare, he was the first London preacher to break through the custom of reading sermons and 'commenced a free address to the conscience'. In this regard he was even before Romaine, whom he heard at St Dunstan's on many occasions. At Clapham, Venn associated with the leaders of the Methodist revival. In 1755 he met Whitefield, who preached in his church — 'a momentous day for Venn, and he never ceased to feel the magnetic hold of the mighty preacher on his soul'[24] — and frequently attended his ministry at the home of John Thornton. He corresponded with John Wesley and was present at his Oxford conference in 1756. He itinerated with Martin Madan, the wealthy cousin of William Cowper and a controversial and eccentric figure, and stayed with the Countess of Huntingdon at Clifton.

In 1756, during a severe illness, which incapacitated him for more than eight months, Venn was able to examine his own beliefs in the light of evangelical doctrines. The outcome of these reflections transformed his ministry: 'His views of eternal things [became] clearer, his meditations on the attributes of God more profound, his views of the greatness of the salvation of Christ more distinct; and the whole of his religion ... received that tincture of more elevated devotion which rendered his conversation and his preaching doubly instructive.' After this time he used to observe that he was no longer able to preach the sermons he had previously composed.[25] His evangelical beliefs were further strengthened by his marriage to Eling Bishop ('Mira') on 10 May 1757 in Clapham Church. He had earlier introduced his fiancée to Romaine, who probably recognized in her a faith that matched his own.

With the help of George Whitefield, whom he accompanied on a preaching tour to the south-west of the country at this time, and the counsel of Lady Huntingdon, the change was complete. 'The divine light burst through the darkness in which his mind had been involved, and he now strenuously laboured to extend, by every means in his power, the knowledge which had been imparted to him.'[26] He experienced a deep burden for the salvation of souls and his prayer life was invigorated, so that before he left London he was fearlessly preaching the gospel from the city's pulpits. Whitefield, in writing to Lady Huntingdon in 1757, said, 'The worthy Venn is valiant for the truth — a son of thunder. He labours abundantly, and his ministry has been owned of the Lord in the conversion of sinners.'[27] It was another great loss to London when in 1759 he went to Huddersfield, where in the years to come Romaine was among his visitors.

At Clapham, Venn became very friendly with the philanthropist John Thornton, who was said to be the second wealthiest merchant in Europe. He was certainly a great friend of evangelicals and one of the first leading laymen to support the awakening. He was active in summoning support for Romaine's appointment to St Andrew by the Wardrobe with St Ann's, Blackfriars.

He was also John Newton's patron, allowing him £200 a year for charitable purposes, plus any extra he needed. Newton told Richard Cecil that he thought he had received from Thornton upwards of £3000 in this way while at Olney. Cecil himself paid a fine tribute to Thornton:

> He purchased advowsons and presentations with a view to place in parishes the most enlightened, active and useful ministers. He employed the extensive commerce in which he was engaged as a powerful instrument for conveying immense quantities of Bibles, Prayer Books, and the most useful publications to every place visited by our trade. He printed, at his sole expense, large editions of the latter for that purpose, and it may be safely affirmed that there is scarcely a part of the known world, where such books could be introduced, which did not feel the salutary influence of this single individual. He was a philanthropist on the largest scale, the friend of man under all his wants.[28]

It is said that he spent between £100,000 and £150,000 on works of charity. In a letter to the wife of John Riland, dated 14 April 1769, Venn exclaimed: 'I have this morning left Mr Thornton. Oh, that God would make me, in my sphere ... such a tree of righteousness as he is! Indeed, his humility can be only equalled by his bounty, and by his watchfulness and diligent use of the means of grace.'[29] In 1790, when Thornton was dying, his daughter, Lady Balgonie, asked the poet William Cowper through William Bull to write an epitaph for her father. Cowper immediately consented and composed a poem that expressed his thoughts on the great benefactor's life, part of which reads:

> Thy bounties all were Christian, and I make
> This record of thee for the Gospel's sake;
> That the incredulous themselves may see
> Its use and pow'r exemplified in thee.[30]

Romaine wrote to Walter Taylor on 10 November 1790: 'Mr John Thornton gone to heaven! O what a loss to earth!' And Henry Venn, in a memorial sermon for Thornton, said: 'Doing good was the great business of his life, and may more properly be said to have been his occupation, than even his mercantile engagements, which were uniformly considered as subservient to that nobler design.'[31]

Richard Conyers, Thornton's brother-in-law and nominee, held the living of St Paul's, Deptford, for twenty years from 1767. He had been converted to an evangelical ministry at Helmsley in 1758 after he had read in church, as part of the lesson for the day, Ephesians 3:8, and realized that the phrase 'the unsearchable riches of Christ' meant nothing to him. As far as he was concerned everything was very simple and he could discern no mystery in the gospel. For a time this ignorance plunged him into despair, until on Christmas Day he read Hebrews 9:20 and 1 John 1:7 and the veil was taken away. 'I went upstairs and down again,' he said, 'backwards and forwards in my room, clapping my hands for joy, and crying, "I have found him! I have found him, whom my soul loveth!" And, for a little while, whether in the body or out of it, I could hardly tell.'[32] The following Sunday he announced to his congregation the change that had taken place in his heart and the new doctrines he had embraced. Immediately he began to preach the gospel with power and authority.

At Deptford, Conyers converted his coach house and stable into a domestic chapel and established lectures four nights every week. Sadly, he made 'but little impression' in London, although from what Wesley wrote on 17 February 1783, his ministry was not entirely fruitless: 'I had an opportunity of attending the lecture of that excellent man, Dr Conyers. He was quite an original: his matter was very good, his manner very bad. But it is enough that God owned him, both in the conviction and conversion of sinners.'[33] On 23 April 1786, after preaching to a crowded congregation in Deptford church, and

Richard Conyers .

St Paul's, Deptford.

while pronouncing the benediction, his speech faltered. He was hurried home, where he died four hours later.

Another nominee of John Thornton's was Roger Bentley, who held the living of St Giles, Camberwell, from 1769. Among his congregation were the Brasiers, the Edward Venns and the Gambiers. He had been Conyer's curate at Helmsley and was one of London's first evangelical incumbents. He died in the same year as Romaine, 1795.

Romaine's friend, Henry Foster, 'a bluff Yorkshireman', was appointed his curate at St Andrew's in 1767, and stayed for about eight years. He eventually resigned, partly because the likelihood of an evangelical in London securing a benefice was nonexistent unless John Thornton bought one for him. He became morning preacher at St Peter's, Cornhill, and began preaching at Long Acre Chapel in 1780. He was one of the founders of the Eclectic Society, and for many years supplied the congregation which Augustus Toplady had established at Orange Street Chapel.

He has been called a 'somewhat prosaic character, though much respected as a pastor and a judge of character'.[34] He was certainly a popular preacher who attracted large crowds. When John Newton went to hear him open a new lecture at Christ Church, Spitalfields, in 1783, he commented that the large church could not hold all the people who wanted to attend, and many departed, unable to reach even the door. John Thornton was his greatest admirer and in his will he instructed that when Clapham, his most valuable living, became vacant, it should first be offered to Foster. When the vacancy occurred, Foster was unwilling to accept it. One plausible reason for this decision is given by Stillingfleet: 'He went over, made many enquiries and fixed in his own mind to accept it, that upon this determination he lost his peace of mind and could get no rest — when he came to the resolution to refuse, his peace was restored and he was happy.'[35] Others suggest that he was unwilling to leave his successful lectureships at Long Acre and elsewhere. John Venn

Richard Cecil.

became the rector of Clapham instead. In 1804 Foster became vicar of St James, Clerkenwell.

Foster was a great friend of Richard Cecil, a refined and scholarly man, who in 1780, on the strength of a bond from the evangelical aunt of William Wilberforce, assumed personally the lease at the proprietary chapel St John's, Bedford Row, where he exercised a long and successful ministry. As a result of his efforts, St John's became one of the chief centres of evangelicalism. In 1787 he became lecturer at Christ Church, Spitalfields and, for a short time, at Long Acre Chapel, which he shared with Foster. He also lectured at St Margaret's, Lothbury, in the early morning, and in the evening at Orange Street Chapel, which subsequently became a Nonconformist place of worship.

Unfortunately, delicate health curtailed his activities but he still managed to exercise a considerable influence on the movement, and many regarded him as the 'intellectual chief' of London evangelicals. Overton comments that there was a 'stately dignity, both in his character and in his style of writing, which was very impressive',[36] and thought him to be 'far more gifted than either Romaine or Newton for the post of a leading London clergyman. He had the culture without the reserve of the former, and the geniality without the ruggedness of the latter.'[37] He was a great source of strength and encouragement to other leaders on account of his godliness and powerful preaching. It is said that he was 'capable of riveting the attention of a congregation by the originality of his conceptions, the plain, straightforward force of his language, the firm grasp of his subject, and by a happy power of illustration which gave freshness and novelty to the most familiar subjects'.[38]

Romaine was not entirely alone in the early years, for in 1750 Madan started to preach at the Lock Hospital near Hyde Park. He had been trained as a lawyer, and was called to the bar in 1748. One evening he was with his friends at a coffee house when they begged him to go and hear John Wesley preach so that he could return and, for their amusement, mimic his style. On entering the chapel he heard Wesley announce his text,

Martin Madan.

'Prepare to meet thy God', with such solemnity that he was compelled to listen, and the Word of God penetrated his heart. He returned to the coffee house and was immediately asked by his excited friends 'if he had taken off the old Methodist'. 'No, gentlemen,' he replied, 'but he has taken me off.' From that time he withdrew from their company and prepared himself for the ministry of the church.

Romaine and others encouraged him in his desire for ordination, but his association with the Methodists proved a difficult barrier. Eventually, after initial disappointments and through the efforts of Lady Huntingdon, he was successful. His first sermon was preached at All-hallows, Lombard Street, where the novelty of a 'lawyer turned divine' drew a large congregation. He was then appointed the first chaplain to the Lock. At first, he preached in the parlour of the hospital and later in the adjoining chapel, which was opened in March 1762, with Romaine as the 'special preacher'. Romaine had also preached at the founding of the hospital in 1746, but his message would have been less evangelical on that occasion. Through Madan's faithful and powerful ministry, the Lock became a stronghold of evangelicalism in London and the most famous chapel in the opening years of the movement.

Madan was a man of learning who knew the original languages of the Scriptures, and his training as a lawyer undoubtedly helped him to present the gospel with sound and clear reasoning. He never held any benefice or accepted any salary in the church. He was nicknamed 'the counsellor' and Thomas Haweis, who knew him well, said that he was 'a man of the easiest and pleasantest temper to live with'.[39] Seymour describes him as

> ... rather tall in stature, and of a robust constitution; his countenance was majestic, open and engaging, and his looks commanding veneration; his delivery is said to have been peculiarly graceful. He preached without notes; his voice was musical, well modulated, full and

Lock Hospital, Hyde Park Corner.

powerful; his language plain, nervous, pleasing and memorable; and his arguments strong, bold, rational and conclusive; his doctrines were drawn from the sacred fountain: he was mighty in the Scriptures.[40]

Romaine and Madan were friends for about thirty years, often exchanging pulpits and travelling together, and leading many to a knowledge of the truth. So it was a test of their relationship when, in 1780, Madan published his controversial work *Thelyphthora*, in which he advocated polygamy as a means of protecting the rights of women. 'His argument was based on Old Testament passages, and his thesis was that outcast girls, such as those at the Lock [which had been designed for venereal patients only], might have happy lives if they were allowed to become the wives of their seducers, even though the latter were already married men.'[41] It aroused a 'storm of indignation, criticism and opposition', and led to his resignation of the Lock chaplaincy. He retired into private life at Epsom, where he died in 1790.

Thomas Haweis, a protégé of Samuel Walker, moved to London in 1762 after being dismissed from his curacy of St Mary Magdalene, Oxford, by Bishop Hume, for preaching evangelical doctrines. In the capital, Madan offered him the hospitality of his house in Knightsbridge, treated him as one of the family, and installed him as his assistant in the chaplaincy of the Lock Hospital, where he was the first of several notable assistants. At the time of his arrival, Romaine, 'this Boanerges', as Haweis called him; Jones, who was to die in June of that year; and Madan, were the only evangelical preachers in the city. Haweis, however, was undeterred, and endeavoured to declare the gospel of God as faithfully as he had done in Oxford. To identify further with the evangelical cause he published his Oxford sermons in 1762, and his catechetical lectures the following year. He also helped Madan to shape evangelical hymnody; 'exercised a considerable influence over John Newton at a critical juncture in his life', mainly through correspondence, and, it is said, by his wise counsel 'saved Newton for the Church of England';[42] and formed lasting friendships amongst the evangelical laity. He left London in 1764 to take the living of All Saints, Aldwincle, Northamptonshire.

In 1773, the 'stately' Charles De Coetlogon came to assist Martin Madan at the Lock Hospital, which by then had become the most important evangelical pulpit in the growing and fashionable West End. De Coetlogon soon became very popular and was acknowledged as the greatest of extempore preachers. When Henry Venn heard him in February 1775, he wrote: 'His discourses are all I wish to hear — judicious, doctrinal in a proper degree, very experimental, and faithfully applied.'[43] The *Dictionary of National Biography* states: 'Aided by a fine presence and great fluency of speech, De Coetlogon acquired a considerable reputation as a preacher of the Calvinistic school.'[44] Through his pulpit eloquence and published works, he became a tower of strength to the evangelical cause in London.

Thomas Scott by Joseph
Collyer the Younger, after
Laurence Joseph Cossé
line engraving, 1820.

Thomas Scott arrived in London from Olney at Christmas, 1785, to become joint chaplain with De Coetlogon at the Lock Chapel. He was a man of 'high character and earnest piety', whom the party regarded as one of its foremost leaders, but he lacked the popular gifts necessary to maintain the attention of his hearers. Soon the size of the congregations at the Lock dwindled, much to the disgust of the governors, who suggested he should change his style of preaching. He also lectured in the evening at St Mildred's, Bread Street, and every other Sunday, at six o'clock in the morning, at St Margaret's, Lothbury. He was fully conscious of his deficiencies, saying on one occasion, 'Some things requisite for popularity I would not have if I could; others I could not have if I would;'[45] and at a different time, 'Everything conduced to render me more and more unpopular, not only at the Lock, but in every part of London.'[46] 'His preaching,' says another, 'was not to the taste of his hearers, who thought his insistence on practical points had an Arminian savour; and the intensity of his conscientiousness made him angular.'[47]

Scott was not simply concerned about the spiritual welfare of his congregations, but also for the physical state of the patients at the Lock Hospital, which

... treated about five hundred girls annually for venereal disease, but provided no after-care, so that most
girls returned to prostitution. Scott raised the money, no
doubt mainly from Clapham pockets, to build a hostel
for the girls to stay till he had found them a job. While
this was being built he had several erstwhile prostitutes
lodging in his own house. He received no salary for this
work but had the satisfaction of seeing similar hostels
established in another part of London, and in Dublin,
Bristol, and Hull.[48]

However, it is not his preaching or works of charity but his writing for which he is remembered. While in London he wrote
a commentary on the Bible, which made him the best known
evangelical expositor of the eighteenth century, and which produced a profound influence on the religious life of the time. It
was originally published in weekly parts and took 'four years five
months and a day' to complete, costing the author 'unknown
sorrow and vexation' on account of the pressure he was under
to finish each week's work, the method of his exegesis, his state
of health and because of pecuniary anxieties. In every sense it is
a great work, which became a standard of reference and devotion among evangelicals. It was read aloud at family prayers in
almost every evangelical home, and touched deeply the minds
of many in the party. Thirty-seven thousand complete sets were
sold during Scott's life time, and its immediate success, according to Overton, was 'almost unparalleled in literary history, or at
least in the history of works of similar magnitude'.[49] Sir James
Stephen does not hesitate to speak of it as 'the greatest theological performance of our age and country'.[50] Scott left London in
1803 for the rectory of Aston Sandford, Buckinghamshire.

John Newton arrived in London from Olney in 1780, which
means that Romaine had been the only beneficed evangelical
incumbent in the city for the last fourteen years! In a letter to
his friend, William Barlass, a minister of the Secession Church

in Scotland, Newton speaks of the state of religion in the city's Establishment at the time:

> There are ... but two gospel ministers who have church-
> es of their own — Mr Romaine and myself... He is an
> eminent preacher, and has crowded auditories. But
> we have about ten clergymen, who, either as morning
> preachers or lecturers, preach either on the Lord's day,
> or at different times of the week, in perhaps fifteen or
> sixteen churches... There is likewise the Lock, and an-
> other chapel in Westminster; the former served chiefly
> by Mr Coetlogon, the latter by Mr Peckwell — both well
> attended.[51]

Soon large numbers of visitors came to hear Newton at St Mary Woolnoth, which was regarded as one of the most important of the city churches, and the parishioners complained that ei-ther their seats had been taken or they could not reach them because of the crowd in the aisle. This was the beginning of the remarkable ministry he exercised in London. Romaine wel-comed Newton and the two friends occasionally preached in each other's pulpits.

While it is true that Romaine was a better preacher and a more profound theologian, Newton's 'quaint illustrations, his in-tense conviction of sin, and his direct address to men's perplexi-ties, temptations, and troubles'[52] made his sermons extremely effective. Hindmarsh concludes his work on Newton with these observations:

> Newton's genius was not as an original theologian like
> Jonathan Edwards, a spectacular preacher like George
> Whitefield, or a theological synthesizer and organiza-
> tional leader like John Wesley. His achievement was
> rather as a broker of consensus, whose spirituality and
> manner of theological formulation represented an ide-
> al of evangelical catholicity... He was pre-eminently a

practical theologian whose concerns were those of the conscientious pastor, parish evangelist, and spiritual counsellor.[53]

With the publication in 1780 of *Cardiphonia*, collections of his familiar letters to twenty-four different recipients, Newton's most distinctive office in evangelicalism as 'the gentle casuist of the revival, spiritual director of souls through the post', was assured.[54] Hylson-Smith, looking at the wider picture, calls him 'a sole survivor among the great evangelical leaders of his generation, and a bridge between the pioneers and the new evangelicalism of the Napoleonic era'.[55] Skevington Wood speaks for many when he says, 'For twenty-eight years Newton delivered the evangelical message from this strategic pulpit [St Mary Woolnoth] and did perhaps more than any other to commend the cause.'[56]

In the same year that Newton arrived in London, William Cadogan, Romaine's first main biographer, embraced evangelical views, mainly through the persistence of William Talbot's widow, whom he spoke of 'not only as the best friend I ever had in my life, but as a mother to me in love, in every good office and in continual prayers for my person and ministry'.[57] He had been appointed to St Luke's, Chelsea, in 1775, a living he combined with St Giles, Reading. As the work in Reading prospered, he more and more left St Luke's in the hands of his curate Erasmus Middleton, and so did not influence London evangelicalism as much as he might have done. Romaine and Cadogan became good friends, often preached in each other's pulpits and exchanged visits, and maintained a regular correspondence until Romaine's death.

Two years later William Abdy was the first curate-in-charge of St John's, Horsleydown, Southwark, although he did not succeed to the living until the beginning of the nineteenth century. For thirty-nine years he lectured at Bow Church, and for twenty-three years at All Hallows. In 1785 Basil Woodd took over Bentinck Chapel, Edgware Road, and taught his people to support financially almost every good cause in the country;

William Cadogan,
Romaine's first biographer.

and John Eyre, one of Trevecca's 'most outstanding students' and Richard Cecil's former curate, came to the Ram's Chapel at Homerton. He became the founder and editor of the *Evangelical Magazine*, the first issue of which appeared in 1793. He was prominent in the founding of the London Missionary Society (1795), along with David Bogue and Thomas Haweis, and was involved in the Village Itinerancy Society, which he founded in 1796, and the Tract Society, which he served as a director from 1799. He died on 28 March 1803 at the age of thirty-nine.

At the end of March 1786 Romaine appointed as his curate William Goode, who succeeded him to the rectory of St Andrew-by-the-Wardrobe and St Ann's, Blackfriars. In 1789 Goode obtained the Sunday afternoon lectureship at Blackfriars and five years later the Lady Camden Tuesday evening lectureship at St Lawrence Jewry. The former of these lectureships he resigned in 1796 on his appointment to the lectureship at St John's, Wapping, which he retained until his death in 1816. On 2 July 1795, three weeks before Romaine's death, he was appointed secretary to the Society for the Relief of Poor Pious Clergymen of the Established Church residing in the Country, a society he had supported from its institution in 1788. He also helped to found the Church Missionary Society (1799). According to his express desire, he was buried in the rector's vault at Blackfriars, near the remains of Romaine.

Two years before Romaine died, George Pattrick came to London and proved to be one of the most effective evangelical lecturers. He had previously been chaplain of Morden College, Blackheath, but was dismissed in 1790 because his sermons were said to 'treat almost solely of faith and grace and such like controversial points'.[58] On 19 March 1796 he became lecturer of St Leonard's, Shoreditch, after being elected by 947 votes to 357, an indication of the support among the laity for evangelicalism. However, because of the opposition of the incumbent and church wardens, he had to wait until December to preach his first sermon. Late in 1797 he was chosen as Sunday evening lecturer at St Bride's, Fleet Street. He also lectured at six o'clock

on Sunday morning at St Margaret's, Lothbury. He was a popular preacher, whose voice was strong, with clear enunciation,
and wherever he went large crowds attended his ministry. His
obituary notice in the *Evangelical Magazine* for December 1800,
describes him as 'more of a Barnabas than a Boanerges'.

Time and space will not allow mention of every individual.
Suffice it to say that John Thomas was the incumbent of St
Peter upon Cornhill; Joseph Butler held the living of St Paul,
Shadwell; T. L. Barbault was at St Vedast, Foster Lane; and of
course in 1792 John Venn, later one of the original founders
of the Church Missionary Society, was presented to the valu-
able living of Clapham. Other lecturers that deserve notice are
George Dyer at St George the Martyr; Watts Wilkinson, who
drew huge congregations as afternoon lecturer at St Mary
Aldermary, where he ministered for sixty-one years, and at
St Bartholomew-by-the-Exchange; and William Gunn, John
Newton's curate, lectured weekly to large crowds at St Mary
Somerset and St Margaret's, Lothbury.

In January 1783 the Eclectic Society was formed, which
enabled several of the aforementioned men to meet on an in-
formal basis once a fortnight to discuss important religious subjects, and which was the chief means of bringing a sense of
unity to their scattered ministries. The four original members
were John Newton, Henry Foster, Richard Cecil and layman Eli
Bates. In February of that year, Newton wrote, 'Our new institution at the Castle and Falcon [hotel, Aldersgate Street, where
the society originally met] promises well. We are now six members, and voted in a seventh last night. We begin with tea [at
four]; then a short prayer introduces a conversation for about
three hours upon a proposed subject, and we seldom flag... I
think they are the most interesting and instructive conversations
I ever had a share in.'[59] After three years, the society moved to
Cecil's vestry at St John's, Bedford Row.

The three additional members mentioned by Newton were
probably William Abdy, Basil Woodd and the sculptor John
Bacon. By October, the Congregationalist John Clayton, who

had been awakened under Romaine's preaching, had joined the group, along with the Moravian La Trobe. As time went by others joined the group, including Thomas Scott in 1786 and Charles Simeon from the country. The design of this 'non-partisan' society had always been to include two or three evangelical laymen, evangelically minded dissenters, as well as the evangelical clergy. Newton comments on the advantages of this mixture:

> We are all unanimous and pleased with each other. We are one as to essentials, and our smaller differences of sentiment are such as only conduce to give the conversation a more agreeable variety, and tend to illustrate our subjects to greater advantage. The spirit of the design is kept up, and every member seems to find it well worth his while to attend punctually. I hope I find some real advantage, and have reason to number it among my chief privileges.[60]

The society was destined to play an important role in evangelicalism, not only in London, but nationwide. Matters of importance were frequently referred to it for consideration, and from the topics discussed many vital initiatives in the history of the evangelical party originated, including the establishment of the Church Missionary Society in 1799, various schemes for training qualified but indigent students for the ministry, and in 1802 the *Christian Observer* magazine, while similar associations of Anglican evangelicals in other parts of the country followed its lead. Alexander Zabriskie conjectures that the 'Eclectic Society furnished powerful leadership in keeping the evangelicals with the Church of England when the Wesleyans and the Lady Huntingdon Connexion withdrew'.[61] Zabriskie's comment cannot be proved, but in gathering together these men were anticipating the great age of organized religious society and were forming, albeit unwittingly, a clerical counterpart to the Clapham Sect.

The forerunner and commander-in-chief of these London evangelicals was William Romaine. With his conversion, a new hope was born in the heart of the city.

[Romaine] was a man of too intrepid a spirit to be intimidated or deterred from the zealous discharge of his duty. Through evil report and good report he persevered, and grew under the cross. The scene of usefulness from which he had been driven, but animated his activity in the remaining sphere of his labours, and St Dunstan's became truly a praise in the earth. I shall pause a moment before I begin the accounts of the mighty effects of his ministry in this centre of the Metropolis, to lift up my heart in praise to God for the inestimable blessings of his grace in that place, and for the amazing multitudes called to the happy experience of the salvation of Jesus by his labours there. In these 'he being dead yet speaks'.

Thomas Haweis.[1]

5

St Dunstan's, St George's and Gresham College

Until Romaine's conversion no lasting fruit from his labours had appeared, nor had a single soul been converted under his ministry. The only effects had been a 'barren admiration' from those who praised his eloquence. On one occasion, he had been applauded for his sermons by a dignitary in the church who expressed a high opinion of the preacher's oratory, but that boost to his ego was the height of his success. But since he had received a new heart, new desires had emerged. He no longer wanted to impress his congregation with 'polished performances from the pulpit', but to save their souls. To that end, he descended from the lofty perch of self-taught excellence and the enticing words of man's wisdom, to the plainness and simplicity of the Christian gospel. Now his single determination was to preach Christ crucified and to turn away from seeking the congratulations of men. The transformation was astonishing.

An important door of opportunity opened for him in 1749 when he was chosen lecturer of St Dunstan in the West, a church in an influential position in Fleet Street and in which several famous men had preached. In 1523 William Tyndale had proclaimed the doctrines of the Reformation in the church, and two or three of his sermons were heard by a wealthy cloth merchant,

St Dunstan's.

Humphrey Monmouth, who had become a 'Scripture man'. He took Tyndale into his house for six months, 'where he lived like a good priest'. In 1538 Robert Redman printed Tyndale's translation of the Bible. His print shop was next door to St Dunstan's.

The first living of the Puritan William Bates was St Dunstan's, then one of the richest in the church. On account of his eloquent preaching he was nicknamed 'silver-tongued'. He attracted so many listeners that the congregations overflowed into the street. The diarist Samuel Pepys records going to hear Bates twice in one day and on both occasions having to push his way through the multitude. On a separate visit, he complained that although he managed to squeeze into the gallery beside the pulpit, he 'stood in a crowd and did exceedingly sweat all the while'. Bates remained vicar until the Act of Uniformity was passed, when he joined the 'two thousand' of 1662.

In 1666 the Great Fire of London came within yards of the church, and on 18 August the following year Pepys 'walked towards Whitehall, but being weary, turned into St Dunstan's Church, where [he] heard an able sermon from the minister of the place'.[2] In 1701 the church was extensively repaired and the roof replaced. In Romaine's time the position was particularly important as the church was so near the law courts and

Samuel Pepys.

virtually opposite the entrance to Salisbury Square, where the Church Missionary Society would have its humble beginnings, and where Samuel Richardson already had his printing works. Samuel Johnson is another famous name who must have often passed the church on his way to St Clement Danes.[3] The church was demolished in 1830.

In the person of Romaine's predecessor Richard Terrick, bishop successively of Peterborough (1757) and London (1764), who Alexander Carlyle thought 'a truly excellent man' and 'a famous good preacher and the best reader of prayers I ever heard',[4] two lectureships were united, the one endowed by Thomas White for the use of the benchers of the Temple nearby, and the other a common parish lectureship, supported by voluntary contributions. Romaine, whom Terrick had known at Oxford and where he had honoured his learning abilities, was elected to both. Horton Davies in his *Worship and Theology in England* recognizes the importance of Romaine's appointment and goes on to say that evangelical Anglicanism began either with the conversion of William Grimshaw in 1742 or with Romaine's election as lecturer at St Dunstan's.

The lectureship was endowed with an annual salary of £18, for which two sermons were to be preached on Sunday and

Thursday evenings during eight months of the year. Thomas
Haweis comments that

> ... this was the chief preferment that during sixteen
> years he attained, and perhaps the sixteen most use-
> ful ones of his whole life, as he was during the great-
> est part of the time, almost, if not altogether, the only
> preacher in the established church from Hyde Park cor-
> ner to Whitechapel, where those who were acquainted
> with the pure Gospel of the grace of God, could then, I
> believe, hear it to their satisfaction and edification.[5]

The *Evangelical Magazine* (1795) says that in 1749

> ... there was no other like-minded with himself in all the
> established churches of London; so that he had to sus-
> tain the attacks of pharisaical and ecclesiastical oppo-
> nents; but his blessed Lord and Master made him stand
> as a brazen wall against all opposition, and gave him the
> pleasure of seeing nearly half the churches in the city,
> and more than half in the Borough, occupied in whole
> or in part, by ministers who preach the unsearchable
> riches of Jesus Christ.[6]

Haweis, who knew the deplorable state of the gospel in London
at the start of Romaine's ministry and the subsequent change
for better, blessed God for having 'raised up the first-fruits in Mr
Romaine's ministry'. William Goode, in his funeral sermon on
Romaine, stated that in his lectureship Romaine 'went through
the whole Bible by way of exposition once, and many parts
twice' in his evening exercises.

Helen Knight in *Lady Huntingdon and her Friends* paints a
colourful portrait of Romaine at about this time:

> Here comes one with quick, elastic step; his eye is
> keen; his thin, yet strongly lined face is surmounted by

a grey wig somewhat smitten by the hand of time; his plain, and certainly not polished manners, are perhaps in keeping with the blue suit and coarse blue yarn stockings, in which he is usually seen; he cannot stop for all the elaborate courtesies of life, for manifold cares and duties eat up his time, which he is bent on using wisely, as one who must give account. Behold Rev William Romaine, curate of St Dunstan's ... whose searching and pungent appeals were at once the scorn and the delight of multitudes.[7]

Romaine enjoyed great success at St Dunstan's and the people crowded to hear him, so much so that, as with William Bates, the congregation spilled onto the street. William Huntington attended Romaine's preaching at St Dunstan's for the first thirteen years of his ministry in London, and when Romaine died he lamented, 'There is no one now to hear in London.'[8] For nine years Romaine preached without interruption.

Soon after Romaine's appointment to the lectureship of St Dunstan's, on 8 February and 8 March 1750, earthquake tremors terrified the inhabitants of London, who were already alarmed because of a general fear of approaching judgements. The wickedness and callousness of society, the irreligious nature of people's lives, coupled with the rebukes and fearless denunciations of some of the city's preachers, heightened awareness in the public mind of an outpouring of God's wrath. So when the city began to tremble many panicked. Seymour says the 'earth moved westward, then east, the westward again, through all London and Westminster. It was a strong and jarring motion, attended with a rumbling noise like that of thunder. Many houses were much shaken, and some chimneys thrown down, but without any further hurt.'[9] On the day of the second quake Charles Wesley wrote to his brother, who was in Bristol:

This morning at a quarter after five, we had another shock of an earthquake, far more violent than that

of February 8th. I was just repeating my text, when it
shook the Foundery so violently, that we all expect it to
fall upon our heads. A great cry followed from the wom-
en and children. I immediately cried out, 'Therefore will
we not fear, though the earth be moved, and the hills be
carried into the midst of the sea: for the Lord of hosts
is with us; the God of Jacob is our refuge.' He filled my
heart with faith, and my mouth with words, shaking their
souls, as well as their bodies.[10]

To add to the drama, a soldier 'prophesied' that another earthquake would destroy half of London and Westminster on 4 April
between midnight and one o'clock in the morning. Thousands
believed him.

When the looked for night arrived, Tower Hill, Moorfields,
Hyde Park, and other open places, were filled with men,
women and children, who had fled their houses which
they expected to become a heap of ruins; and there,
filled with direful apprehensions, they spent long hours
of darkness, beneath an inclement sky, in momentary
expectation of seeing the soldier's oracular utterance
fulfilled. Multitudes ran about the streets in frantic con-
sternation, quite certain that the final judgement was
about to open; and that, before the dawn of another
day, all would hear the blast of the archangel's trumpet.
Places of worship were packed, especially the chapels
of the Methodists, where crowds came during the whole
of that dreary night, knocking and begging for admittance. At midnight, amid dense darkness, and surrounded by affrighted multitudes, Whitefield stood up in Hyde
Park, and, with his characteristic pathos, and in tones
majestically grand, took occasion to call the attention of
listening multitudes to the coming judgement, the wreck
of nature, and the sealing of all men's destinies.

> The scene was awful. London was in sackcloth.[11]

A month after the second tremor, and three days before the expected fulfilment of the soldier's 'prophecy', on 1 April 1750, with London 'holding its breath', Romaine was appointed assistant morning preacher at St George's, Hanover Square, an appointment that was made purely in recognition of his character, and not due to any personal friendship, and which brought him more prominently before the general public. It became the most important pulpit he ever occupied regularly. The church, built by John James in 1721-1724 for the popular new residential area, was one of fifty new churches that were erected under the Act of 1711.[12] It was situated in the heart of the West End and recognised as the mother-church of the most fashionable quarter of London.

Romaine's new office, which was not regularly endowed, depended entirely on the will of the church's first rector, Andrew Trebeck (d.1759), and the person procured by him at his own option, discretion and expense. J. C. Ryle is right when he says that Romaine was the man for the job: 'His undeniable powers

St George's.

as a preacher attracted attention. His well-known scholarship commanded respect even from those who did not agree with him. And best of all, his bold, uncompromising declarations of the real gospel of Christ, and plain denunciations of fashionable sins, were precisely the message which the Bible leads us to expect God will bless.'[13] Soon Romaine, with his usual earnestness, and no doubt benefiting from the population's fear of calamity, was preaching before ever-increasing crowds:

> His manner [says Haweis], his voice, and above all, the subject he treated, could not but excite attention from their dissimilarity to everything around him, and in the other churches. Though, I believe, he yet servilely adhered to a written sermon, he delivered it with pathos and energy, and the Gospel which he preached was so much another Gospel from what they had heard before, that great and small bore testimony to the power with which he spoke. The fame of his preaching soon awakened general attention. Multitudes thronged around him, eager to hear all the words of this life. The church began to be filled from door to door, and murmurs of disapprobation proceeded to complaint.[14]

It was at St George's that he first attracted the attention of Lady Huntingdon.

One of the complaints mentioned by Haweis was that the church was filled with 'poor people' attending the Word of Life and forsaken by the rich. The numbers of hearers were too many and seats reserved for local householders were being taken by 'low class visitors'. William Goode in *Faith Triumphant in Death* observes that a nobleman, who attended the church, said to some who were complaining at the crowd and the inconvenience occasioned by it, 'that he wondered such complaints should be made with respect to the house of God, by those who could bear to be much more incommoded at the playhouse without complaint'.[15] A friend of Romaine's, James Compton, the earl of Northampton, who may have made the above remark, rebuked the murmurers: 'If the power to attract be imputed as a matter of admiration to Garrick, why should it be urged as a crime against Romaine? Shall excellence be considered exceptional only in divine things?'[16]

There were many who came to Christ as a result of Romaine's ministry at St George's. One of the first was John Sanders, who afterwards became George III's state coachman:

> His going to hear [Romaine] was through the persuasion of his wife... He heard, as he used to say, 'to profit'; and received such a deep conviction of sin, and such a terror of the wrath of God due to it, that he was sometimes afraid even to sleep, for fear he would wake in hell. This work of the law upon his conscience followed him more or less for about six years... At last, by the gradual work of the Spirit of God, he was brought into the liberty of the children of God.[17]

He lived to the ripe old age of eighty-nine, and long adorned the doctrine of God with an 'exemplary and godly life'. He always retained the 'most affectionate regard' for Romaine. Haweis, in his biography of Romaine, exclaims: 'Good old man! whom for near forty years I have had the pleasure of knowing. If yet your faculties remain, if your eye can yet read, or your ear hear this faithful report of your dear departed pastor and father, it will awaken every remaining sensibility of your heart, and make you lift up your voice in praises, as you have done a thousand, thousand times, that ever Romaine preached at St George's Church.'[18]

It was the same John Sanders, who was one day in Exeter listening to John Cennick preaching on the streets, who stepped in to rescue the preacher from an unpleasant experience — not that Romaine would necessarily have agreed with his actions!

The preacher, who had already been ill-treated by the
mob, was expatiating on the blood of Christ, when a
ruffian butcher, exclaiming 'if you like blood, you shall
soon have enough of it', rushed from his shop with a
pail nearly full of blood, which he would have cast on
Mr Cennick had not Mr Sanderson [Seymour misspells
his name] calmly met him, and, suddenly catching the
pail, poured its contents over the man's own head. This
drew the attention of the mob from the preacher to Mr
Sanderson, who escaped with difficulty, and was obliged
to leave the city early in the morning.[19]

During the five years of his ministry at St George's, Romaine
preached occasionally at St Mary-le-Bow, a church famous for its
bells, in exchange with the rector Thomas Newton (1704-1782),
a one time curate of Andrew Trebeck. Newton had been chosen
lecturer of St George's in 1747 and in 1761 he was appointed
Bishop of Bristol, being consecrated on 28 December of that
year. Romaine also preached at Mayfair Chapel, Curzon Street
(demolished in 1899), in exchange with Andrew Trebeck himself,
who was the morning preacher there. Before the Marriage Act of
1753, Alexander Keith had performed illicit marriage ceremonies
without banns or licence in the chapel, and in 1742 over 700
couples were wedded in this way. It was in the chapel in 1752 that
the Duke of Hamilton married Elizabeth Gunning, 'a bed-curtain
ring being used in the absence of anything more suitable'.[20]

It was in 1750 that Romaine became friendly with James
Hervey, who was staying in London, albeit against his will, on
a kind of sabbatical leave to regain his health. Hervey's friends,
led by Stonehouse and Thomas Hartley, had been concerned
about Hervey's health and his need for a change of air for some
time. So they secretly corresponded with their London friends,
including Romaine, and with their cooperation

... conspired to abduct Hervey by gentle force and carry
him off to London, where they felt he could be looked

James Hervey.

> after more professionally and so have a better chance
> of recovery. Under the pretence of going for a short ride
> with Hervey, his friends collected him at Weston Favell
> and proceeded to take him to London. It was some time
> before Hervey realised what was happening though his
> protests were loud and long when he found out, but his
> friends remained immune to his pleas to return... Hervey
> arrived at Whitefield's house in Tottenham ... for what
> would be a two years stay.[21]

Romaine often visited him and occasionally accompanied him
to hear Whitefield preach. On one occasion, he joined Wesley to
have breakfast with Whitefield. Hervey was present along with
Gifford, Gill, Cudworth and Cennick. Romaine led the doctrinal
part of the service and Gill gave a short exhortation.

His London 'holiday' turned out to be a time of blessing for
Hervey as he was able to hear a growing number of true evangelical preachers who were being encouraged and instructed
by Romaine and his circle. In one letter, he wrote: 'On Sunday
I heard the admired Mr Romaine. His text was Romans 5:1;
his doctrine evangelical. The faith which purifies the heart, and
works by love; the imputed righteousness of Christ, compre-
hending both his active and passive obedience; the operation
of the blessed Spirit in producing this sound and lively faith,
were the substance of his discourse.'[22] On 7 November 1751
he wrote to Lady Frances Shirley, Lady Huntingdon's aunt, and
spoke of the strong meat he had received from Romaine's sermon on Romans 5:1:

> He spoke upon our Saviour's vicarious sufferings, and
> vicarious obedience, their absolute necessity, and their
> complete sufficiency for our justification. I think he
> touched upon the transcendent excellency of the Bible.
> I well remember, he directed us to the illumination and
> influence of the divine Spirit; in order to understand its
> heavenly meaning, and feel its sacred efficacy, — points

of the last importance to our happiness! I heartily wish him abundant success in explaining and enforcing them to his thronged auditories.[23]

Romaine came to love and respect Hervey. In 1757 when a group of London evangelicals, under Romaine's leadership, gathered to discuss how they could best promote true evangelical fellowship and the spread of the gospel, Hervey was one of the first they asked for support. Romaine called Hervey's *Theron and Aspasio* (1755) a 'masterly defence' of the doctrine of Christ's righteousness, defended the author against Wesley's attacks upon it, and wholeheartedly supported the posthumous publication of *Aspasio Vindicated*, Hervey's eleven letters against Wesley's criticisms. Sadly their friendship came to a premature end with Hervey's death on Christmas Day 1758. In a public tribute to his friend, preached at St Dunstan's on 4 January 1759, Romaine said:

> Mr Hervey had great experience of God's love to him, and therefore his heart was full of love to God; and out of the abundance of his heart, his mouth spoke. There was such a sweetness of heart-love upon his tongue, that he used to speak of the love of the adorable Redeemer like one who had seen him face to face in the fulness of his glory. He would, with all the power of language and dignity of sentiment, speak for a long time together, in praise of the ever-blessed Saviour... Having set the Lord always before him, he saw the love of God in everything; and therefore it is not to be wondered that all objects and events should give him occasion to speak of it. In his last sickness, it continued still to be his favourite theme...
>
> He watched like a shepherd over his flock... In the pulpit he was fervent and earnest with his people, and would often exert himself beyond his strength: for he preached the great doctrines of salvation as one who

had experienced the power of them...

His holy life was an excellent recommendation of his principles; for I never saw one who came up so near to the Scripture character of a Christian. God had enriched him with great gifts, and with great graces, and had made him humble.[24]

On 25 June 1751 Romaine was appointed to the professorship of astronomy at Gresham College, founded by Sir Thomas Gresham (1519?-1579), son of Sir Richard Gresham, Lord Mayor in 1537-1538, for lectures on 'the sciences of divinity, astronomy, geometry, music, law, medicine and rhetoric'. Gresham set up the college in his fine mansion at Bishopsgate for free public lectures, and in so doing aroused the jealousy of his own university at Cambridge. The professors, whose salaries were met from rental income from the shops near the Royal Exchange, were required to be unmarried men. The college, however, was not a success. By 1647 complaints of its management had surfaced, and with the Fire of London destroying the Royal Exchange, its source of revenue was cut off. There was further discontent in 1707, and sixty years later the 'building, then in a ruinous condition, was sold under the act of parliament to the government for an excise office'. The lectures were then delivered at the Royal Exchange until a new college was built in 1841.[25]

Gresham College.

Although in Romaine's day the college was on its downhill path, the new professor, with a godly zeal for the truth, began a course of lectures to overturn the Newtonian system of philosophy, then almost universally accepted, and to establish in its place the doctrines of the Bible as he understood them. Basing his comments on the Old Testament, he endeavoured to demonstrate that to adopt the Newtonian system, which was founded more on science and speculation than the Scriptures, was to militate against the account of creation in Genesis — religious and moral opinions that were contrary to the views held by others. As can be imagined, his lectures immediately attracted attention, especially since he delivered them with animation and deep conviction. It was not long before opposition arose.

On 15 February 1752 *The London Gazetteer* published a letter, addressed to the 'Lord Mayor of the city London ... and the worshipful aldermen of the said city, but especially to those on the Gresham Committee', condemning Romaine and his views. The writer, who calls himself 'Philalethes', which means 'scholar', claimed that Romaine's lectures 'consist of nothing but criticism on the lives of the astronomers, the usefulness of telescopes, the depravity of the minds of the astronomers, the nonsense contained in the words infinite space'. He goes on:

[He] converts all the improvements obtained in this science by the great labours of the learned, into (as he expresses himself) a state of certainty of uncertainties, and declares most of the learned therein are traitors to their God... This is the first professor, that in order the better to conceal his ignorance, ever attempted to derogate from the honour and use of astronomical learning... If, gentleman, during the professorship of this person, nothing by his auditors is heard but ignorance, accompanied with superlative audacity, and ludicrous, low, impertinent jests and sarcasms, it would be better to make the place a sinecure, and the salary given to the poor... In the church he preaches contrary to his actions herein;

but that attempting lure, and attractive magnet gold, attacks the man, and hastily obtains a conquest on this child of light...

I ... hope you will not suffer the late renowned Mr Machin's [Romaine's predecessor] place to be thus buffooned... You or any succeeding committee, have a right of expelling for the cause of neglect, or nonqualification.[26]

The following month, *The London Gazetteer* published an expostulatory discourse between a freeman of the city of London and Romaine, which has been summarized below:

The citizen said to Romaine, 'Your knowledge of science will gain you no credit with astronomers.'

Romaine replied, 'I do not burden myself with endless rules of geometry and numbers and there is no proof of my ignorance. My rules are religion and reason.'

Citizen: 'You ridicule both astronomers and science itself and I advise you to give up the place.'

Romaine: 'I suggest you have a design on the position yourself and are trying to frighten me into surrender. I am perfectly qualified to continue in office and I will not quit.'

Citizen: 'I advise you to speak in such terms that astronomers can understand, and to read in your next lecture a set of lectures from some geometrical astronomer.'

Romaine: 'Certainly not! I have publicly declared against using technical terms/words because they are useless and little understood. I do not want to be obliged to numerical astronomers because they seldom if ever come to church — they are so busy with rules, scales, sectors etc. If I had thought myself unqualified, I would have relinquished the post to other candidates.'

Citizen: 'I desire your thoughts on Bishop Wilkin's

and Dr Keil's astronomy.'
       Romaine: 'The bishop's results are all vague and
uncertain, and amount to nothing at all. Keil's works are
a confused chaos.'[27]

The enmity against Romaine came to a climax when one of
his lectures was printed in the *Gentleman's Magazine* for March
1752.[28] As will be seen, Cadogan is right when he says that he
'disputed some part of the Newtonian philosophy with a boldness and banter, which were not likely to be well received, when
derogating from the honour of a man, who was held little less
than divine'.[29] He opens the lecture, which was delivered to a
'very crowded audience', by saying,

In my former lectures I took notice of the difficulties
and absurdities that attend the modern astronomy, and
this I did in order to prepare the way for an astronomy
that should be obvious to common capacities: And, as
I therein all along rejected technical terms and math-
ematical gibberish, as unnecessary, and quite foreign,
to the nature of true astronomy, all the modern math-
ematicians and philosophers have spared no pains to
prejudice me in the opinion of the public; have run into
all kinds of reflections against me, because they consider me as dangerous to the honour of their study, which
they had taken so much pains to render and preserve
unintelligible. Everything they have said against me,
except what might affect my Christian character, and
that has always been left unattacked. All this have they
done, notwithstanding they are not only ignorant of what
I have to propose, but while the wiser and more moder-
ate think they may possibly be some truth in doctrines
drawn from Moses. These modern philosophers cannot
bear to hear it affirmed, that there was any astronomy
four thousand years ago, and think it greatly derogatory
from the honour of the divine Newton, to suppose that

there was any philosophy so long before his. But it is
from Moses that I pretend to draw what I have to offer,
and Moses had his astronomy from a great master, who
did teach more in one line than our modern astronomers
do in a whole folio.[30]

As he continues, the language grows steadily stronger and the
tone more mocking: 'To make a good astronomer, you must
first of all be fully acquainted with an abundance of this sort of
hard names, and then it is proposed for you to purchase a large
pair of globes, and a great telescope, and starve whole moon
shining nights in gazing at the stars, without being sure of gaining anything but an astronomical cold, and for which you may
expect a cure from the contemplation of Jupiter's belts.'[31] He
closes his lecture with further sarcasm and ridicule: 'The math-
ematicians and astronomers ... differ one from another in their
demonstrations, no less than one hundred and twenty-one millions of miles: and likewise, I will conclude with observing, that
the modern divinity brings you no nearer, than one hundred
and twenty-one millions of miles short of heaven.'[32]

When it is remembered that the men who opposed him were
in the audience, or at least read the lecture in the magazine,
it is hardly surprising that he did not remain long at Gresham
College. One of his biographers reports: 'The admirers of Sir
Isaac Newton not relishing the philosophy of Mr Hutchinson,
nor the spiritual remarks with which Mr Romaine's lectures were
spiced, soon deserted him.'[33] These 'spiritual remarks' incorpo-
rated into formal lectures, along with Romaine's ridicule and
sarcasm and the fact that he drew large crowds of 'the wrong
type of people', offended his employers, who pressured him
to leave. A month after the above lecture was published, on 9
April, he resigned. The following epigram, although dated 1754,
was probably composed soon after his resignation:

> Romaine may make the pulpit quake with heavenly
> eloquence,

As is his due, the poet-mob their facile praise com-
mence;
He's puffed with pride, disdained, hedged about by
many a friend,
Yet our professor's masterpiece soon meets its
destined end.
Pray, is this awe deserved by what our threatened
genius wrought,
For Newton spurns the threat'nings vain wherewith
the heaven is fraught?
And yet the load he cannot bear — 'Friends, you've
destroyed me quite,
Renown to me the earth has given, but not the
skies of night.'[34]

Professor of astronomy was a strange position for Romaine
to hold, especially since there was no fire burning in his heart
for the stars or mathematics. His passion was to preach Christ
to lost souls and to see lives conformed to the image of God,
which is why he asked questions such as, 'Were dying sinners
ever converted by the spots on the moon?' and 'Was ever a
miser reclaimed from avarice by Jupiter's belt?' Perhaps he saw
an opportunity to overturn the Newtonian system, or to share
the gospel with men of science. Whatever the reason he accepted the post, he was unwise to attack Newton's philosophy
with such strong language, and to use ridicule and sarcasm as
weapons to overcome his opponents. A softer approach may
have encouraged those who disagreed with him to listen more
impartially to his arguments, but Romaine never did anything
by half-measures. At least his professorship emphasizes his all-
round ability and knowledge, his intrepid spirit, and, for him to
be appointed in the first place, the respect with which he was
held by others. After his resignation he forgot about planets and
galaxies and concentrated on what God had called him to do.

A cold heartless scepticism about all the leading truths of Christianity prevailed widely among the upper and middle classes of society [in the eighteenth century]. Bishop Butler had complained not long before, 'that many persons seemed to take it for granted that Christianity was fictitious, and that nothing remained but to set it up as a principal object of mirth and ridicule'. That such principles naturally produced the utmost profligacy, recklessness, and immorality of practice, no Bible reader will be surprised to hear. In fact, the utter ungodliness of the age was so thorough that few living in the present day can have the slightest conception of it. Against this ungodliness Romaine boldly lifted up a standard, and blew the trumpet of the gospel with no uncertain sound. He was in the highest sense a man for the times, and he was exactly in the right place.

J. C. Ryle.[1]

6

A Widening Ministry

In 1752 Romaine wrote a recommendatory preface for a three-volume work (*The Spiritual Magazine*) by his friend John Allen, who in 1764 became minister of the Baptist church in Petticoat Lane. Allen's work, which was subtitled *The Christian's Grand Treasure,* and reprinted several times, was originally published once every six weeks at six pence a number and professes to contain a 'complete body of divinity'.

In his preface, Romaine, who thought highly of the work, encourages parents to put Allen's work into the hands of their children 'that they may be, through divine blessing, rich towards God. He encourages masters to give their servants one penny a week 'to buy a spiritual treasure for their immortal souls, that they who are poor in this world may be rich in faith, and heirs of the kingdom'. To unbelievers he says, 'In this *Spiritual Magazine* you will find the treasures of life, joy and peace divinely opened, to make you wise unto salvation by faith in Jesus Christ;' and for believers there is contained in it 'such a harmony of divine truths, that will prove a constant feast for your spiritual appetite, rays of knowledge for your understanding, springs of life for your refreshment, rivers of joy for your delight, and an ocean of happiness for your portion'.[2]

This is generous praise for a man who was later dismissed from his London church for 'bad behaviour' and from his next church at Broadstairs, Newcastle. He retired to New York, where he preached to large congregations until his death. 'It is to be feared,' comments the *Dictionary of National Biography*, 'that he was deficient in principle, or rather in practice'. According to his own opinion, he was a 'strict Trinitarian' and a high Calvinist, with 'an attachment for some of Hutchinson's opinions', and his works were held in high regard by supralapsarians.[3] In the area of Christology he strongly opposed John Gill, and his teaching caused havoc among nineteenth-century Strict Baptists. His work *The Spiritual Magazine* continued to be republished with Romaine's commendation, which probably played some part in its acceptance.

Less than a year later (1753), Romaine became nationally known for his opposition, both in preaching and in print, to the *Act to Permit Persons Professing the Jewish Religion to be Naturalized by Parliament*, which had been introduced into the House of Lords in April by Henry Pelham, chancellor of the Exchequer, and his brother Thomas Pelham-Holles, duke of Newcastle. Cecil Roth comments that the bill 'provided simply that Jews who had been resident in Great Britain or Ireland for three years might be naturalized upon application to parliament without taking the sacrament'.[4] The bill was read in the House of Commons for the first time on 17 April and again on 7 May, when it was debated and the motion to commit passed by 95 votes to 16. Between the second and third readings great opposition arose, and a petition against the bill was presented by the subscribing merchants and traders of the city of London, 'pleading that if the bill became a law, it would have bad effects upon the nation's Christianity and business'.[5]

Jews had been banished from Britain during the thirteenth century, and had only started to return in Cromwell's time, not to seek employment and a better standard of living, but to escape starvation and obtain charity. However, they did not enjoy full religious and civil liberties. In 1753 there were about 5000 Jews in England, and a minority thought it was time for them to be naturalized. Josiah Tucker (1712-1799), afterwards dean of

Gloucester (1758), and a 'very shrewd though a rather crotch-
ety and inconsistent writer', supported the bill. He had already
written some tracts, but it was through his pamphlets in favour
of the new measures that he first became known. His opinion
on naturalization was 'so unpopular that he was burnt in effigy
at Bristol along with his pamphlets'.[6] Romaine was one of his
warmest opponents.

The bill was read for a third time on 22 May and though opposed it was finally passed, which provoked a 'veritable storm
of protest propaganda... A flood of pamphlets on both sides of
the proposition almost inundated the public.'[7] During the inter-
val between the passing of the Act and receiving royal sanction,
Romaine published a pamphlet called, *A Modest Apology for the
Citizens and Merchants of London, who Petitioned the House
of Commons against Naturalizing the Jews*. The text he chose
as the foundation to his *Apology* was provocatively Acts 16:20:
'These men, being Jews, do exceedingly trouble our city.' With
strong and offensive language, which would not be acceptable
today but was the norm in the eighteenth century, he presents
twenty-one reasons against naturalizing the Jews, claiming that
if the bill was passed, 'then every vagabond Jew may purchase
all the liberties and immunities of free-born Englishmen'.[8] The
premise for his arguments is twofold:

> 1. We look upon the Jews, who lived in the time of Christ,
> as traitors, rebels against God. The act of rebellion was
> rejecting Jesus for the promised Messiah, and crucify-
> ing him for a malefactor...
>   2. The present Jews are guilty of the same treason
> by aiding and abetting traitors, for they defend their an-
> cestors' rebellion; they justify the crucifying of the Son
> of God, and if they had him in their power, they would
> crucify him again. Their books are full of the bitterest
> curses and blasphemies against Jesus Christ.[9]

He endeavours to prove that it is not God's will for the Jews to be naturalized and that it is against the prophecy in Deuteronomy 28:65. Naturalizing the Jews would make this and other prophecies impossible to fulfil:

> In what manner the naturalizing of the Jews will affect the authority of these prophecies is very obvious: for first, God cast them off for rejecting Christ, and we take them in; he drove them out of their own land, because of their unbelief, but we receive them as free-born subjects in our land, notwithstanding the same unbelief. God expelled them, they come to us expelled, and we naturalize them: so that, what he made their punishment, we turn into a reward, by doing which, we act directly against providence, for we take them into our communion, whom he had excommunicated, and we give them a better land to make them amends for losing that, of which he thought them unworthy.[10]

Some of Romaine's language is harsh, extreme and blatantly anti-Semitic: 'You know a Jew at first sight... Look at his eyes. Don't you see a malignant blackness underneath them, which gives them such a cast, as bespeaks guilt and murder? You can never mistake a Jew by this mark, it throws such a dead, livid aspect over all his features, that he carries evidence enough in his face to convict him of being a crucifier.'[11] Romaine's racism heightened the people's anger, so that, according to Thomas Birch, the 'rage of the people is ungovernable'.

Neither of the Wesleys nor Whitefield, who was saddened by Romaine's aggressive stance, entered the controversy. In a letter Whitefield wrote on 8 June 1753, he spoke of his fellow worker Romaine: 'God keep him and all others from further entanglements by fleshly wisdom and worldly policy, which I think have nothing to do with the work of the Lord.'[12]

In October, Romaine published a second pamphlet in the form of several letters, in which he again expressed his opposition to the bill. It was a reply to a reasonable and well-written pamphlet entitled *Considerations on the Bill to Permit Persons Professing the Jewish Religion to be Naturalized by Parliament*, which, according to Romaine, contained 'many notorious falsehoods, perverted many Scriptures, and has mistaken the plainest facts'. 'If the citizens and merchants,' says Romaine in the preface, 'had made no answer, then the Jews would have triumphed. They would have said that we could not answer; and therefore some reply became necessary. And it fell to my province to draw it up.' Romaine's objective was to overthrow the 'grand battery of the Jews' (i.e., the pamphlet), so that they and their 'advocates would not be in haste to erect another',[13] and to confute the opinion of the ministerial lawyers that the Jews were natural born subjects. If that could be done, believed Romaine, the whole piece would fall to the ground.

In a letter from Thomas Birch to Philip Yorke, Birch, no doubt alluding to Romaine's controversy with Warburton, comments on Romaine's pamphlet: 'It ... has all the distinguishing characters of that writer: impudence, buffoonery, virulence and insincerity... The chapter pretending to show from Scripture authority that we ought to have no commerce with that nation, is not to be matched out of the Church of Rome for falsification of the doctrine of the New Testament.'[14]

There is no doubt Romaine acted conscientiously, supposing the bill to be contrary to God's Word and an attempt to overturn the fulfilment of prophecy; but it must be admitted that the influence of Hutchinsonianism, with its view that the Rabbis had corrupted the pure Hebrew text of the Old Testament and the divine pattern of Jewish thought and life, affected his understanding of the problem. However, he had most of the nation on his side, which enhanced his reputation and popularity, and it is partly due to his opposition, along with the outburst of anti-Jewish feeling that was fostered by certain city interests, and for which he must take his share of the blame, that the bill was lost before the end of the year. His friends were so impressed with his arguments that they collected his various letters on the

subject into two pamphlets, and printed them, at the expense of
the London Corporation, in 1753.

In a biography of the Hutchinsonian George Horne
(1730-1792), bishop of Norwich from 1790, the writer, William
Jones, mentions the following anecdote:

> In the year when the Jew Bill was depending, and af-
> ter it had passed the house, he [Horne] frequently em-
> ployed himself in sending to an evening paper of the
> time, certain communications which were much noticed,
> while the author was totally unknown, except to some
> of his nearest acquaintance. By the favour of a great
> lady, it was my fortune ... to be at a table where some
> persons of the first quality were assembled, and I heard
> one of them [Lord Temple] very earnest on the matter
> and style of some of these papers, of which I knew the
> secret history, and was not a little diverted when I knew
> what passed about them. To the author of these papers,
> the Jew Bill gave so much offence ... that he refused to
> dine at the table of a neighbouring gentleman, where
> he was much admired, only because the son-in-law of
> Mr Pelham was to be there; he was, therefore, highly
> gratified by the part taken in that perilous business by
> the Rev William Romaine, who opposed the considera-
> tions dispersed about the kingdom in defence of the
> Jew Bill, with a degree of spirit and success, which re-
> minded us of Swift's opposition to Wood's Halfpence in
> his *Drapier's Letters*.[15]

Meanwhile, Romaine's preaching at both St Dunstan's and
St George's was attracting large crowds and the gospel was
spreading in London. Charles Wesley, writing from London on
4 February 1755, said, 'The Lord of the harvest is thrusting out
labourers in divers places. Mr Romaine, Venn, Dodd, Jones,
and others here are much blessed.'[16]

Seven days after this letter, on 11 February, Romaine married twenty-four-year-old Mary Price of Shoreditch, 'a pious lady of genteel fortune', whom William Grimshaw described in 1761 as 'a precious soul'. The ceremony probably took place at St Leonard's, Shoreditch. Under her husband's influence Mary grew to command a good knowledge of the doctrines of the Bible. The following anecdote, which Romaine told Augustus Toplady at Broad Hembury on 18 September 1773, illustrates her Scriptural competency. At Tiverton, she spoke with a local clergyman who was protesting with no little zeal against those who believed in 'irresistible grace', exclaiming that such grace was 'quite incompatible with free-will'. 'Not at all so,' answered Mrs Romaine, 'grace operates effectually, yet not coercively. The wills of God's people are drawn towards him and divine things, just as your will would be drawn to a bishopric, if you had the offer of it.'[17] It appears that some of her husband's intrepidity of spirit had rubbed off onto her!

Their first child, William, was born in London and baptized on 4 June 1756. In 1770 he apprenticed as a glassman and four years later on 15 April he matriculated in Trinity College, Oxford. He took his Bachelor of Arts at Oxford in 1778 and his Master of Arts two years later, and, like his father, became a clergyman. On hearing his firstborn expound the Word of God in family devotions, Romaine said to several friends a few days before his death, 'O what a marvellous mercy it is, that I should have a son who is a son of God!'[18] Two other children were born to the Romaines: Adam (born July 1758), who joined the army, was commissioned as lieutenant in the Eleventh Regiment of Foot in Ireland on 1 June 1778 and promoted to captain in the 98th Regiment of Foot on 28 December 1780. He died in Ceylon in 1782. A daughter, whose name has not been recorded, was also born. She married the evangelical Yorkshireman Robert Storry, who had been prepared for the ministry by Joseph Milner and ordained in 1774. The following year he became Thomas Adam's curate at Wintringham, where he lived for six years in the rectory, before he was appointed vicar of St Peter's, Colchester, in 1781.

A sermon that Romaine preached at this time was *A Method for Preventing the Frequency of Robberies and Murders*, delivered at St George's, St Dunstan's and several other places in London, from Matthew 15:19-20. His aim is to uncover the root of the problem and then to apply the remedy. 'The heart is the cause of all,' he says, 'and no act of parliament can touch the heart. It is out of reach of every human tribunal... The polluted fountain is still inaccessible to any authority but the great Creator's. He alone can give the almighty fiat, let it be clean, and it is clean.' And the remedy: 'The great purifier is Jesus Christ, whose blood has infinite merit to wash away the pollutions of the whole world... Nothing but the sprinkling of the blood of Jesus can dry up this fountain of sin, and nothing can carry the virtue of it to the heart but an almighty Spirit.'[19]

In commenting on Romaine and this sermon, Samuel Walker of Truro, writing to his friend Thomas Adam on 16 February 1755, says, 'Mr Romaine, no doubt you have heard of as a popular preacher in London: he has appeared with boldness, and was particularly so free in the time of the Jew act, that there was talk of his being taken into custody. Some time ago he printed a sermon upon the frequent robberies; wherein he showed, I thought, a very honest heart, though he seemed wanting in the Christian scheme.'[20]

Not long after his marriage Romaine published his first book of nine sermons, *A Practical Comment on the Hundred and Seventh Psalm*. His opening comments in the preface shed light on his style of preaching and the contents of his sermons:

> The following comment was not drawn up with any view to its publication. It was only intended for the pulpit, at the Thursday's lecture in St Dunstan's, and after it had been preached would have been thrown aside; for the author is obliged to make a sermon every week, besides the lecture; and he had no thoughts of sending such hasty compositions to the press... Their manner is unfashionably plain and simple; they have nothing

> studied or brilliant in their style, nor delicately nice in the
> method; no pretty turns of wit, nor striking antitheses
> to entertain the reader. And the matter is as opposite
> to the established taste as the manner of them... They
> are the plain honest truths of Scripture, of the Christian
> church, and of the Church of England... They are here
> laid before the world, as they were preached, without
> any alteration.[21]

He calls upon true ministers of the gospel to exert themselves
for their master's honour in these days of 'reproach and blasphemy; for we are sunk into the very dregs of the latter times'.
All the people, high or low, 'are totally corrupt, not only in morals, but also in principles'. The doctrines of the Reformation are
spurned and every clergyman who attempts to preach the truth
is immediately branded an enthusiast. In a turn around from
two years previously, he insists that 'instead of defending the
Jew-bill and the marriage-bill, I rather insisted upon the total
corruption of mankind by the fall, and the freeness and fulness
of redemption through Jesus Christ, and the necessity of the
grace of the Holy Spirit to change and renew our corrupt hearts'
— essential doctrines that 'are now dressed up by our great
men in a bear-skin, and baited under the odious nickname of
enthusiasm'.[22] John Newton, who had already heard Romaine
preach in March at St Dunstan's, read the book, along with a
sermon by Robert Leighton, and was moved to pray for a similar bold faith and temper in the light of the impending war with
France.

Unwisely, Romaine chose to attack the *Monthly Review* in
his preface:

> Let me give you a friendly caution against being misled
> by a set of infidel writers, who pretend to give characters
> of books which they never read, in a thing called *The
> Monthly Review*, in which I have seen every sound
> doctrine of Christianity ridiculed and blasphemed,

and every damnable heresy openly defended and maintained. I expect no favour from these men. I desire none. To be spoken of well by them would be indeed reproach; their abuses will do me service: and they may load me with enthusiasm; I will carry it patiently, and would suffer any infamy or torment upon earth rather than be answerable for their horrid blasphemies against Jehovah and his Christ.[23]

These comments instigated a lifetime feud with the periodical. James Hervey, in a letter dated 5 April 1755, expressed his concern: 'Mr R[omaine] has let fly upon them, in a manner that is, I think, more zealous than judicious; such as shows him to be galled by their invectives, though he professes the contrary; and such as seems to betray resentment, rather than display a calm and dispassionate concern for the truth.'[24]

The *Monthly Review* made no direct comment on Romaine's work, but instead published short reviews of two answers to it. Of the first, *An Answer to Romaine's Comment on the 107th Psalm*, the reviewers said, 'We have here a modest, candid, and sensible vindication of the literal sense and meaning of the 107th Psalm, in opposition to Romaine's wild and fanatical interpretations.'[25] The second work was written by John Douglas and entitled *An Apology for the Clergy*. The *Monthly Review's* response was predictable:

Romaine and other *Hutchinsonian* ranters, having grossly abused the clergy of our established church, in their sermons, in their pamphlets, and in newspapers, for *preaching morality*, and for other such like wicked *anti-Hutchinsonian* doings; this apologist offers some things in vindication of the said clergy, and likewise exposes the folly, and dangerous tendency of the principles and practices of our modern enthusiasts, or *popular preachers*, as they are by some styled.'[26]

In the same year appeared Romaine's *A Discourse on the Benefit which the Holy Spirit of God is of to a Man in his Journey Through Life*, which was preached at Christ Church in Newgate Street on Monday 19 May (1755) from Ezekiel 36:25-27. It was drawn up at the request of the executor of Miss Elizabeth Hill (of Falmouth, Cornwall), 'a charitable and pious lady'. Romaine, whose teaching always displayed an utter dependency on God, sums up the prophet's doctrine in these words:

> We cannot so much as set out upon our journey to heaven, until he [the Holy Spirit] cleanse all the faculties, by removing the blindness of the understanding, and the depravity of the will and affections. It is his office to give us a new heart and a new spirit, disposed to receive impressions of the divine law, and then to endue it with power to walk in the statutes of God, and to keep his judgments and to do them; so that every step we take from the first moment we set out, until we happily arrive at the end of our journey, is directed and supported by the Holy Spirit of God.[27]

As with most of what he preached, he was quite prepared for the hostile reception this sermon would receive, 'not only from the *Monthly Reviewers*, the avowed enemies of the established church and its established doctrines, but also from all mere nominal Christians'.[28]

This was followed by *A Discourse upon the Self-Existence of Jesus Christ*, preached originally in 1755 at St George's and at St Dunstan's from John 8:24, which several persons, who found great benefit from it, earnestly requested him to print. 'It is the produce,' writes Romaine, 'of a grateful heart, willing to make some return, how poor and small soever, for the numerous, great, and inestimable blessings received from his hands... I desire no greater honour than to be an humble instrument in his hands of magnifying and exalting Jesus Christ.'[29]

Even before the first edition was published, two anonymous authors were deeply offended by the bare title in an advertisement, and wrote bitterly against it. Not surprisingly, the *Monthly Review* called it 'an amazing rhapsody'. The Unitarian George Clark, in a letter to Walter Harper, accuses Romaine of labouring to frighten his hearers by saying that

> ... a want of belief in this self-existence is a damnable error... He is *absurd*, in having put a meaning on this passage, which it cannot possibly bear; and *presumptuously* so, in dealing out so abundantly the divine thunder, against heresies of his *own* creation... You will, perhaps, be of my opinion, that Mr Romaine's sermon, on *The Self-Existence of Jesus Christ*, recommends a system of divinity, as opposite to that contained in the Scriptures, as truth and error can be.[30]

With the controversy surrounding the sermon, it is easy to understand why it had to be printed several times to meet the demand.

The doctrine that Romaine expounded was, as the title suggests, the self-existence of Jesus Christ, which, he warns his readers, 'is not a mere speculative point, it is not an indifferent thing, whether you believe it or not; but your eternal salvation is so much concerned in it, that if you do not believe it, you will die in your sins, and will have every one of them to answer for at the tribunal of God'.[31] After declaring that 'our blessed Saviour is the great and eternal I AM', he pleads with his readers to believe the doctrine and not to damn their own souls:

> Oh! my brethren, if your souls be dear and precious in your own eyes, do not choose hell torments. Why will you die in your sins, and go deliberately into the lake, that burneth with fire and brimstone for ever? Might not one infer from your conduct, that you were in love with hell? For you cannot prove that Jesus Christ is not God.

It is impossible to prove it; and why then will ye deny his divinity, and with overt acts of high treason attempt to rob him of his essential glory? Why will you act such an absurd, such a wicked part, and destroy yourselves?[32]

It should be pointed out that Romaine was not fond of 'thundering out damnation' any more than his listeners were of hearing it, and he seldom had the word in his mouth; but there is 'certainly such a thing as damnation, and the Almighty has threatened to inflict it upon the deniers of Christ's divinity', he insisted.[33]

These sermons reveal Romaine to be a fearless preacher of the gospel who had experienced its truths in his own heart. He was prepared to declare the whole counsel of God and was undeterred by the oppositions of men, nor did he court their applause. He answered to God for the doctrines he preached. At the centre of all was the person and work of Jesus Christ, whom he loved with an undying love, and whose grace he freely and without hesitation made known. His ambition was to rescue men and women from darkness, to wash them in the blood of Christ, to make them servants of the most high God, and to rejoice with them as they entered life through the narrow gate — all by the power of the Holy Spirit, without whom he could do nothing.

It is hardly surprising, knowing the message Romaine preached, that during the summer of 1755 the resentment against him at St George's reached an all time high. Whitefield, just back from a trip to America, heard about Romaine's difficulties and wrote to William Cudworth on 7 June 1755:

It will rejoice you to hear that the glorious gospel of Jesus Christ gets round apace. Several of the clergy, both in town and country, have been lately stirred up to preach Christ crucified, in demonstration of the Spirit, and with power. This excites the enmity of the old Serpent. The greatest venom is spit against Mr Romaine, who, having

been reputed a great scholar, is now looked upon and
treated as a great fool, because he himself is made wise
unto salvation, and is earnestly desirous that others
should be. Methinks I hear you say, 'O happy folly!'
May this blessed leaven diffuse itself through the whole
nation![34]

The antagonistic clergy, who felt personally attacked by
Romaine, complained bitterly, and urged the rector Andrew
Trebeck to dismiss him without charge, the supposed offence
being that he publicly and from house to house refused to stop
preaching Jesus Christ to large congregations. When informed
that the crowds attending his ministry from different parts were
causing great inconvenience to the inhabitants, who could not
reach their seats safely, and that he was in danger of being dismissed by Trebeck as a result, he replied with the meekness and
gentleness of his Master, that he was 'willing to relinquish an office which he had faithfully performed, hoping that his doctrine
had been Christian, and owning the inconvenience which had
attended the parishioners'.[35] He retired from this office on 28
September 1755, 'under the glorious imputation of crowding
the church', as one writer puts it.[36] As he was reluctant to part
with many of his friends, who wanted to remain under his ministry, he met them weekly at the home of a Mr Butcher; for this
'irregularity', he was threatened with prosecution.

Ryle comments that 'a more discreditable affair than this
probably never disfigured the parochial annals of the diocese of
London. An eminent and godly clergyman was removed from his
post because he attracted too many hearers! And yet, at this very
time, scores of clergymen in London churches were no doubt
preaching every week to empty benches or to congregations of
half a dozen people, without anyone interfering with them!'[37]
Trebeck's son, speaking from firsthand knowledge of all that had
gone on, gave this testimony of Romaine: 'I shall be always ready
to attest his zeal, and in conversation with him during that time,
and occasionally afterwards, I found him mild and friendly.'[38]

In a similar vein, John Douglas, in his *The Destruction of the French Foretold by Ezekiel* (1755), satirizes Romaine by satirizing his own earlier work *An Apology for the Clergy*. He sarcastically calls Romaine 'that great, that inimitable man'.[39] 'Observe,' he goes on, 'how indefatigable this great, this good man is, in his endeavours to revive and propagate the knowledge of the true doctrines of Christianity, of which Christians are so shamefully ignorant. Warm with a holy zeal, he advanceth the glorious work, by every useful help; the Hebrew original concealeth no treasures from his piercing sight; and he can find great assistances from the translation.'[40] The *Monthly Review* took delight in further mockery: 'He [Douglas] makes a merry proposal for incorporating our modern decypherers of *Hebrew* enigmas, by royal charter, under the name of *The president and fellows of the college of state interpreters*, with ample salaries annexed; and he points out Mr Romaine as the properest person in the world for president.'[41]

Lady Huntingdon had been following Romaine's career with interest since his appointment to St George's, and on account of his sufferings and growing reputation, resolved at this time to show him support and kindness. Lord Northampton, who had married the Countess's relative, Baroness Ferrers of Chartley, had mentioned Romaine to her with high commendation, and informed her of the crowds that followed him and the rising opposition to his ministry. He spoke highly of the doctrines he proclaimed and of his ability to preach with fire and clarity. So the Countess opened her home in Park Street to him and his hearers:

Knowing that it would be below the dignity of the nobility to mingle with the ordinary citizens, two separate gatherings were established. For his regular hearers she encouraged Romaine to make use of her kitchens and ancillary rooms where his people could gather and hear him without any disturbance. And for the nobility his weekly ministry to her titled hearers [in her drawing

Lady Huntingdon, the 'Queen of the Methodists', was influential in promoting Methodism in eighteenth-century England. The larger portrait is by J. Russell.

room] became a feature of his life for a number of years. Not only was Romaine willing to preach in Selina's London home, he also began to minister in other pulpits where her influence gained him a hearing.[42]

She also opened her country residence, Donington Hall, to Romaine; and shortly afterwards she was able to erect or open chapels at Brighton, Ote Hall, Bath and Bretby Hall, in all of which Romaine preached for her with singular success.

Late in 1755 there was great anxiety in London, partly on account of an expected French invasion, but more because of news of the terrifying Lisbon earthquake, which struck in mid-morning on 1 November, reminding the inhabitants of the 1750 tremors that had rocked their own city. Shortly after the quake, three large tsunamis swept over Lisbon's harbour, killing thousands of refugees. A week later, after inextinguishable fires and incessant aftershocks, the whole city was in ashes, its people scattered, and perhaps half its population dead. The largest recorded wave to hit the coast of Britain was from the Lisbon tsunami of 1755, when twelve-foot waves pounded the coast of Cornwall.

The Bishop of London, Thomas Sherlock, responded to the crisis by urging the clergy to 'preach repentance', a letter Romaine quoted in his sermon *An Alarm to a Careless World*:

As to you, my brethren of the clergy, who share with me the care of the souls in these populous cities, let me exhort you ... to awaken the people, to call them from the lethargy in which they have too long lived, and make them see their own danger. Speak to them, persuade them, as knowing the terrors of the Lord. Speak to their hearts and consciences with such plainness as becomes the ministers of the gospel: tell them in season, and out of season, that unless they repent, they must perish. If the warnings we have had are a call to the people to repentance, remember they are still stronger

Scenes from the Lisbon
earthquake.

calls on us to preach repentance, and to discharge the duty we owe to God and his church, and to the flock of Christ over whom we are placed. May this work of God prosper in our hands![43]

On 30 November of that year Romaine addressed the people at St Dunstan's from Amos 4:12: 'Prepare to meet thy God.' The sermon, in which he painted awful pictures of the fate of the wicked, was published under the title *An Alarm to a Careless World*. In the preface, he answered those who blamed the earthquake on the wickedness of the Portuguese: 'Doubtless they were sinners, but not above all the inhabitants of the earth. We rival them in immorality, and we exceed them in infidelity. They were cut off in judgment. We are spared in mercy... Careless sinners may flatter themselves with notions of safety, but unless they leave their sins they cannot be safe.'[44]

He went on to show that 'God our Saviour, who once came in great humility to visit us, is now preparing to meet us in judgment;' and to urge his listeners to prepare their hearts for his advent, so that when he comes 'you may lift up your heads with joy, knowing that your redemption draweth nigh'.

Do you not suppose that the inhabitants of Lisbon thought themselves as safe as you may do at present? They had no apprehensions of an earthquake. They did not imagine that God was going to destroy them that morning. But you hear how they were surprised and overthrown with a great destruction. While they were speaking, peace, peace, unto themselves, they were called and hurried in a moment to judgment. One had his heart upon getting a handsome fortune, and was just sitting down to cast up his accounts, and he was cut off that moment, and called to judgment, with a soul full of the love of money. Another, intent upon his pleasures, was feeding his imagination with a vile scene of indulgences, and his filthy soul was taken in the midst of this impurity, and brought before the all-pure and holy God. One with an oath in his mouth was calling for damnation upon his soul, and it came, while the words were in his mouth, and down he sunk into the pit of hell. Dreadful it is to think of the manner in which they were surprised and cut off in their sins.

Suppose such a judgment should be sent to this city at the same time of day, how would it overtake sinners both high and low? The great, tired with diversions of the preceding day, would be surprised in their sleep, and would awake in the eternal world, full of hatred to Jesus Christ, and his people, and his holy faith. What can they expect from the Judge? And the lower people would be up, but at the devil's work, going on careless in their sins, lying and cursing, and swearing, and blaspheming God, and snatched away with some horrid imprecation in their mouths. Why may not this happen to you, as well as to the inhabitants of Lisbon?[45]

Romaine warned his congregation to flee from the wrath to come, and to seek, without delay, the love and friendship of the supreme Judge:

Cry aloud for mercy. The judge may still be entreated. Oh plead with him then, and be importunate, until he become your friend. Remind him of his love to sinners. Urge his bloody sweat, his bitter cross and passion, his cruel mockings, bufferings, and scourgings, endured all for sinners. Plead these with him, and lay before him the torments and the shame of the cross, and the piercing of his hands and feet, which are the engravings of his love to sinners, and be assured that tender heart cannot want love for them, which bled to death for their salvation. Hold on this plea until you find him gracious, and are enabled to place your whole trust and confidence in the sufferings and death of Jesus Christ. Then you will be safe.[46]

Two weeks later, on 14 December, he preached from Matthew 25:13, and entitled the sermon *The Duty of Watchfulness Enforced*, which was published the following year.

> Look around you, and consider your situation. You are upon the verge of eternity. The joys of heaven and the torments of hell are before you. And you are not sure of a day longer to provide for them. Time flies. Death approaches. Behold the Judge standeth before the door. The late extraordinary providences proclaim his near approach... In a moment you will meet him in judgment. And is all this nothing to you?... God has commanded you to watch, you do not watch. He has required you to be always ready, you are not ready... He has overthrown large and populous cities, which are now nothing but heaps of wide-extended ruin; all this makes no impression upon you. Although many thousands of their inhabitants be buried under the ruins, yet you neither feel for yourselves, nor for your fellow creatures, whom vengeance suffered not to live. Oh hardened, insensible sinners!...
>
> Go to the throne of grace with humility and prayer. Pray without ceasing. Be importunate. Knock at the door of mercy until it be opened. Hear and read the word of God. Frequent his table. Be found in all the ways of his ordinances, and he will be found of you. He will give you living faith working by divine love, and with these graces your hearts will be strengthened, and enabled to watch, until your Lord come.[47]

It was with these urgent appeals, making use of contemporary events, that Romaine called sinners to repentance. According to Cadogan, both sermons 'are not exceeded in any of his writings':

In both, and particularly in the preface to the former, there are some valuable antidotes against the prevailing philosophy of the day, which ascribed everything to second causes, and almost denied the existence of the first, excluding the God of nature from the works of nature, and refusing to acknowledge him as the author of judgments; and sin, committed against his divine majesty, as the cause of them. This, as he tells us in the preface before mentioned, was the philosophy of the year 175[5], when the 'learned accounted for earthquakes by changing their name into airquakes, and then they were explained philosophically'.[48]

Ryle comments on these two sermons that it is 'impossible to read them without feeling deep regret that the Church of England in the west end of London has not had more of such preaching'.[49]

If he does not make us a praying people, it may be feared that he will give us over to destruction; for look around you. See the troubles of Europe. Does not your heart bleed for the shedding of so much Christian blood? Examine the state of the Christian churches. What coldness and deadness is there in some! And how greatly are they, who have a little life, opposed and persecuted! Consider the danger that threatens the Protestant interest. Are not these so many loud calls upon you to use your interest with God, that he would put a stop to these general calamities. And then look around this kingdom, and see whether it does not stand in need of your prayers.

Romaine preaching from Acts 12:5.[1]

Will the metaphysician think of laying his reason and the light of nature? It is written, Jesus Christ is the foundation, and there is no other. Will the moralist think of laying a system of ethics, and the religion of nature? Jesus Christ is the foundation, and there is no other. Will the Arian, Socinian, and other infidels think of being justified without the merits of the God-man? Jesus Christ is the foundation, and there is no other.

Romaine preaching from 1 Corinthians 3:11.[2]

His ministerial career in the metropolis is a conspicuous example of the persistent and scandalous persecution which the earlier Evangelicals often encountered.

Sydney Carter.[3]

7
Prayer, Preaching and more Persecution

At the beginning of 1756, soon after he left St George's, Romaine became curate and morning preacher at St Olave's, Southwark, where he continued for three years. The church's burial registers record that Mother Goose was buried there on 14 September 1586, and on 24 July 1665, Mary Ramsay, who is said to have brought the Great Plague to London. Those who died from the plague have a 'p' after their name.[4] The area around St Olave's supported twelve dissenting churches, including John Gill's only a few metres away. Romaine took it in turns with Gill to visit the ailing James Hervey in Mile Lane. To the St Olave congregation he dedicated his sermon on Ezekiel's dry bones preached in the church on 24 October 1756 and published at their request.

For the first year he lived in the rectory house, and then early in 1757 he moved with his family to Walnut Tree Walk, Lambeth.

> Here he had a delightful retreat, in which he spent some of the happiest of his years. A little garden, which he dressed, kept and planted; and as he viewed the productions of it with faith, and received them with thankfulness, he converted it into another Eden. Here he

received his friends, particularly serious candidates for
orders, and his younger brethren in the ministry, admitting them to his early breakfast, and feeding them with
knowledge and understanding.[5]

Supported by his wife he kept an open breakfast table, where
others could join them and listen to Romaine's words of wisdom. Although only a forty-three-year-old curate, many of the
younger clergy looked up to him as a father in Israel. One of
these clergymen, who had the pleasure of breakfasting with
Romaine at Lambeth, gave this account of their conversation:

On taking the bread prepared, which I thought good,
he mentioned the circumstances of the late Dr John
Fothergill's having in some cases advised the not giving
to sick people, and especially to weakly ailing children,
preparations from London bread, on account of the too
frequent adulteration it underwent previous to baking. I
was then a young clergyman, and shall not easily forget
the manner (for I still feel the impression) of his turning the subject to the ministerial administration of the
bread of life to the people. He touched very clearly and
forcibly on a variety of modes by which the word of God
was perverted, and the ill-leaven and other ingredients
too often mixed with that heaven-imparted sustenance,
which was intended to be meat indeed; and this he
did in such familiar, easy, and yet pointed terms, and
with that paternal benignity of look, as left me equally
pleased, and, I trust, improved by the interview. It rendered bread to me of more value, both as a support and
as a sign. I have yet cause to thank him for the discussion it produced, and shall ever revere his memory for
so well-timed and happy an allusion.
        The same morning I remember well his men-
tioning it as in his opinion a fault, to preach censoriously,
sarcastically, or harshly of brethren in the ministry, or

of others, however remote from ourselves in matters of sentiment and persuasion. My friend, Mr George Whitefield, said he, one day told me very candidly, that there was a time in his life, when he thought he had never well closed a sermon without a lash at the fat, downy doctors of the establishment. 'At that period,' said he, 'I was not lean myself, though much slenderer than since. I went on, however, and seldom failed to touch pretty smartly upon the objects of my dissatisfaction, till one day, getting up into the pulpit in Tottenham Court Road, I found the door apparently narrowed, and moved in obliquely. The idea then struck me, that I was becoming, at least in appearance, a downy doctor myself; and from that time I never more made the downy doctors a subject of castigation.'[6]

In this matter Whitefield acted wisely, for it is better to preach up Christ than to preach down those with whom we differ.

One of the worst conflicts of the century was the Seven Years' War, which began in 1756. It was waged on several fronts — Europe and America, India, the coasts of Africa, and many islands — with the British mainly fighting the French. Romaine was deeply concerned with the crisis, and took part in services of prayer and preaching called by the government because of a threatened French invasion. At the onset of the war he organized a weekly hour of prayer. Some years later, because he was so encouraged in his prayer efforts, he sent a circular letter to every serious clergyman he knew, inviting them to set apart one hour in the week for calling on God, to implore his mercy on the Established Church that he would revive his work and send forth more labourers into that part of the harvest field. At the beginning of the letter he describes how the hour of prayer originated, and how he was moved to pray for 'our Zion', before mentioning his own 'clergy's litany':

In the year 1756, a weekly hour of prayer was agreed upon by several religious clergy and laity in order to humble ourselves under the mighty hand of God, till he should be pleased to put a stop to the calamities of that time. He did hear us, glory be to a prayer-hearing God, and he turned our supplications into praises. About that period it began to be laid very near my heart to pray earnestly and often for the prosperity of our Zion, for which I never fail to make intercession in all my addresses to the throne of grace. But once a week, on Friday, I have what I call the clergy's litany. In which, after general petitions for the out-pouring of the Spirit upon all the ministers of our church, I make mention by name of those my fellow-labourers, whom God has highly honoured in making them faithful and useful in the ministry. As I go over their names, recommending them to the care, and their people to the blessing of our Glorious Head, it is my custom to ask particularly for them, such things as I know or hear they want.[7]

Edward Vaughan says Romaine devoted two hours to this practice: 'He had their names written down on paper, and used to walk about his room, mentioning them one by one, and specifying their wants as far as he knew them.'[8] Romaine, in the letter, mentions seven motives that moved him to pray in this manner and some of the advantages he found in it. He also encourages his readers to meet him at a set hour, 'from nine o'clock on Friday morning to ten', and to pray 'for the brethren by name', an exercise that had been 'exceeding profitable' to Romaine for several years.[9]

In 1757 he printed *An Earnest Invitation to the Friends of the Established Church, to join with Several of their Brethren, Clergy and Laity in London, in Setting apart one Hour of every Week for Prayer and Supplication during these Troublesome Times.* Alongside the first edition was a sermon entitled *The Duty of Praying for Others* (Acts 12:5). It was printed anonymously, but its style and spirit are so obviously Romaine's, and it 'may be ranked among the best of his writings'.[10] At the close of the sermon he urges his readers to:

> Go to the throne of grace at the appointed hour, and use your interest with him that sitteth upon the throne. Do not spend your evening in talking of other men's matters, but mind your own duty. The less they mind theirs, the more you should pray for them. And instead of prating, as I hear many professors of religion prate, 'Oh that we might have more public fasts, more public meetings for prayer, more general reformations, &c.;' get thee into thy closet, and set about thy own reformation as soon as thou wilt. Pray and fast, as long as thou wilt, and the more thou growest in grace, the more wilt thou pray for others, as well as thyself. Let us all, then, with one heart and one voice now begin, and God grant we may pray without ceasing, as they did in the text, until we obtain the like deliverance.[11]

In the preface of the 1779 edition of *Earnest Invitation*, he acknowledges the power and efficacy of prayer: 'The cloud may be dark which hangs over our heads; it may threaten a destroying storm; it may spread blacker, and look more dreadful; yet prayer can pierce through the cloud; the prayer of faith can gain admittance into his presence who has his way in the whirlwind, and who presides over the storm.'[12] In the tract itself, he first examines the grounds and reasons for prayer and deep humiliation: 'We are altogether sinful in nature, sinful in life, a country professing Christianity, and yet abounding with sin, and hardened in it at this very time, when God is chastising and punishing us for our sins.' He then invites 'any person' to humble himself and pray

> ... for the preservation of the Protestant church, and all its members throughout Europe, and especially for the

peace of our established church, and for all orders and
degrees of its ministers, beseeching God to give them
his grace and heavenly benediction, that both by their
life and doctrine they may set forth his glory, and set
forward the salvation of all men. And to the end there
may never be wanting such persons in the church, let us
pray for all seminaries of Christian education, especially
for the two universities...

May the God of love dispose us also to pray fervent-
ly for all the Protestant dissenting congregations which
love the Lord Jesus in sincerity. May he shed that love
abroad in all our souls, which alone can effectually free
us from party spirit...

And as the hearts of kings are in the hand of God,
we must pray him to direct the heart of our gracious sovereign lord, King George, to do what will be for the glory
of God, and for the good of his people...

Let us also pray for the queen, for the prince of
Wales, and for all the royal family, that God would en-
due them with his Holy Spirit, and enrich them with his
heavenly grace...

And let us desire the Spirit of wisdom to direct both
houses of parliament, all the king's counsellors, and
judges, and all the magistrates throughout the kingdom...

Let us beg of God now to go forth with our fleets
and armies, and to give them success against our enemies.[13]

He closes with a final exhortation: 'Never be tired of such a
good work ... carry thy prayers into practice.'

The tract was printed again in 1795, a few months before
his death. J. C. Ryle calls it 'one of the most useful publications
that Romaine ever sent forth'. It was made 'eminently useful
when it first appeared and has led to an amazing succession of
supplications, intercessions, and prayers down to the present

day [c.1885]'.[14] In 1757, when the tract was originally written, Romaine only knew about twelve clergymen in the whole of England who were willing to adopt his scheme of prayer. By 1779 there were at least eighty evangelical ministers preaching the gospel up and down the country, and by the time of his death there were over 300 like-minded men in the Establishment.

This increase is confirmed by one of Romaine's biographers. Later in his life it was customary for him to preach an anniversary sermon on 2 March, the day of his election to the living of Blackfriars, in which he gave a short account of the progress of the gospel in the kingdom. In one of these sermons he 'mentioned that himself and three others agreed to spend one hour in the week, at a stated time, in prayer for the revival of the power of godliness in the established church'. His biographer continues: 'To so small a number were spiritual clergymen reduced, that out of twenty thousand, there were not twenty who preached the truth as it is in Jesus; but before his death he had, in his possession, a list of more than three hundred.'[15]

One who responded to the call was John Newton, who wrote to a friend in 1758: 'I thank you for Mr Romaine's book. I have endeavoured to observe his appointment, as likewise the Dissenters' hour on Wednesday mornings... The times are indeed dark.'[16] Another was James Hervey, who wrote from Weston Favell:

> My dear friend, I am much obliged to you for your donation of thirty shillings to purchase five hundred of *An Earnest Invitation to the Friends of the Established Church*, &c. I have put the money into the hands of one who loves the Lord Jesus in sincerity, and who will take care that the pamphlet is properly dispersed according to our desires. 'Tis an excellent design. I daily beg of God to bless it; for what he vouchsafes to bless, will be blessed indeed.
>
> Enclosed I send you a form of prayer, founded on the plan laid down in the *Earnest Invitation*, &c. 'Twas

transmitted to me last night by a pious clergyman, who,
I believe, was himself the author of it... Permit such persons to take copies, as you think will make a proper use
of it.[17]

Romaine was always encouraging ministers and the people of
God to devote a portion of their time to prayer for the exten-
sion of God's kingdom and for that revival that is so necessary
if the work of God's people is to be truly effective. With the
'list of more than three hundred' in his hand, he could testify
to the power of prayer, which, it must be said, was not only
instrumental in strengthening the Establishment in England, but
also Independent, Presbyterian and Anglican evangelistic work
throughout the world, and inspiring other denominations to
follow suit. The English Particular Baptists, for instance, had a
Prayer Call in 1784 which resulted in their overseas missionary
work, as well as sparking into life several denominational and
inter-denominational inner missions and foreign mission societies.[18]

At this time, Romaine occasionally preached before Oxford
University. On 11 April 1756 he preached two sermons from
1 Corinthians 3:11, entitled *The Sure Foundation*, one in the
morning at St Mary's, and one in the afternoon at St Peter's, in
which he considered four truths: 'Jesus Christ is the foundation
of all saving knowledge... He is the foundation of all acceptance
with God the Father... He is the foundation of all holy obedience... He is the foundation of all present and eternal happiness.'[19] In the midst of the first sermon, he cried out, 'Honour
Jesus Christ, and exalt him above all, and then his highest hon-
ours shall descend upon this university, and he will make her
very enemies to be at peace with her. Oh for that happy day,
when the honour that is of God shall be sought after as the
crown and reward of your studies!'[20] However, his message was
too direct, too strong, too evangelical for the leaders of the university and it was not well received.

On 20 March the following year things came to a head when he preached before the university two sermons on 'The Lord our Righteousness' from Isaiah 45:8. Again, the morning sermon was delivered at St Mary's and the afternoon sermon at St Peter's. At the close of his second sermon, he said:

> Whoever amongst us seeks justification through Christ's righteousness cannot be offended at what I have said — and I would offend those who seek for justification without Christ's righteousness. I would gladly stir them up and provoke them to examine their principles, and to try whether they can trust their eternity upon them. If they trust to their own righteousness, they are lost for ever... there is no righteousness but Christ's, wherein sinners can appear without spot of sin at the bar of justice.[21]

Romaine did 'provoke' his congregation and 'great offence' was caused by what he said, for they were 'anything but typical Oxford sermons'. 'Indeed,' remarks Skevington Wood, 'not since the voice of John Wesley had been silenced by "a mortifying neglect" after his discourse on "Scriptural Christianity" had St Mary's [and St Peter's] heard anything quite like it.'[22] A great ferment ensued among the staff of the university, and as a result the pulpit was closed to Romaine forthwith. Samuel Walker wrote to his friend Thomas Adam in April of that year, telling him: 'Romaine has been again in the University pulpit, where he preached imputed righteousness, but it is said will be allowed to preach no more there.'[23] Walker wrote again in October, this time to Lady Huntingdon: 'Mr Romaine has been preaching in the University pulpit, but his doctrine cannot be endured, and he will not be permitted to preach there again.'[24]

In response to his ban, Romaine felt compelled to publish the sermons with the following dedication to Dr Thomas Randolph, vice chancellor of the university and president of Corpus Christi

College, and supposedly 'a stout champion of orthodoxy as at that time understood':

> When I delivered these discourses, I had no design to make them public; but I have been since compelled to it. I understand they gave great offence, especially to you [and the heads of houses], and I was in consequence thereof refused the university pulpit. In justice, not to myself, for I desire to be out of the question, but to the great doctrine here treated of, namely, the righteousness of the Lord Jesus, as the only ground of our acceptance and justification before God the Father, I have sent to the press what was delivered from the pulpit. I leave the friends of our church to judge whether there be anything herein advanced contrary to the Scriptures, and to the doctrines of the reformation. If not, I am safe. If there be, you are bound to make it appear. You have a good pen, and you have great leisure. Make use of them; and I hope and pray you may use them for your good and mine.
>
> I am, with my constant and hearty prayers for the university's prosperity, Mr Vice Chancellor, your humble servant in Christ,
>
> WILLIAM ROMAINE.[25]

The vice chancellor did not respond to Romaine's challenge.

The above anecdote is a sad indictment on the low state of the church in which liberalism still reigned, and a necessary reminder of how important it was for men like Romaine to preach the unadulterated gospel without any thought of enhancing their reputations or gaining the applause of those in high office. G. T. Fox speaks for all who love the truth when he says, 'One cannot but admire the moral courage which enabled Romaine to confront such an audience and to proclaim in their unwilling ears truths so unpalatable, which he knew they repudiated and despised, but which,

like Jeremiah and other reformers, he felt constrained to declare.'[26]

Another who heard Romaine at Oxford and was deeply offended by his sermon was Thomas Bliss, son of a future
Astronomer Royal. After admitting that Romaine 'advanced,
with great earnestness, most of the principal gospel doctrines',
he describes, with honesty, his violent reaction: 'I was so extremely exasperated at this mode of preaching, that I could have
found in my heart to have torn him to pieces.' About ten days
later he heard a sermon by Thomas Haweis, during which 'my
views of divine things, my sensations, the objects of my love and
hatred, were all totally changed; and I cordially embraced and
relished those very doctrines which I before detested and ab-
horred'.[27] Bliss, perhaps in direct answer to Romaine's prayers
for the Established Church, joined the growing number of evangelical clergy. He first assisted William Grimshaw at Haworth
before becoming Curate of Broadwoodwidger and then in 1770
Rector of Ashford and Yarnscombe in Devon.

Thomas Haweis, then a student at Oxford, also heard
Romaine 'preach with delight' before the university in 1757
'those beautiful and truly evangelical discourses'. He was stirred
in his soul and 'enheartened in his own evangelical witness
by Romaine's fearless proclamation of an unadulterated gospel';[28] and he soon had the 'honour and pleasure of knowing
him'. Romaine preached in his church at Oxford, and in return
Haweis occasionally preached for him when he visited London.
In his *Life of Romaine*, Haweis gives an important portrait of
Romaine from the early days of their friendship:

> His stature was of the middling size, his visage thin and
> marked, the lines of his face were strong, and as he ad-
> vanced in age, deeply furrowed; his eye was quick and
> keen, yet his aspect benign, and frequently smiling; his
> manners were plain; I thought his address rather rough
> than polished: he dressed in a way peculiar to himself;
> he wore a suit of blue cloth always, a grey wig without

Thomas Haweis.

powder, and generally but a poor one; and I remember to have been struck, when I first met him, with seeing him comb it himself in the vestry at St Dunstan's before the service began — he latterly wore a better: his stockings were coarse and blue, as his clothes; I doubt whether they were yarn or worsted. He walked a great deal; never kept a carriage — rose early, and had a multitude of visitants.

The frequent interruptions of this kind to which he was exposed often broke in upon his time unpleasantly. And his temper was not always proof against impatience on these occasions, and subjected him to the imputation of rudeness. And perhaps his conduct was sometimes blameable in this respect... If he has sometimes shut the door too hastily, or spoken too sharply, I have known him bow before a kind rebuke, and grant what he had petulantly refused.

A person one day had brought him a petition, and solicited a favour, which he returned without looking at it, and was showing him to the door — 'Your Master, Sir,' said the person humbly, 'who knows my case, would have me treated with greater tenderness.' He stopped

short, took back the paper, examined its contents, and
procured for the petitioner the favour he had requested.
The multitude of obligations which he conferred on hundreds would be too many to relate. And if he was compelled often to refuse his assistance, no man took more
pains to serve those, whose interests he espoused.[29]

Haweis also states his admiration for his friend: 'Mr Romaine
has a record deeply engraved in the hearts of thousands... It
will be a pleasure to myself to leave behind me this testimony
to my friend; and to honour him dead, whom living I so highly
respected.'[30] And again: 'The cross in which he so nobly led
the way, to his dying day he manfully bore, and no minister in
the kingdom has more successfully laboured in the gospel, or
more zealously maintained those doctrines, that are branded
with Methodism, than Mr Romaine.'[31]

From the events at Oxford, Haweis dates 'the commence-
ment of [Romaine's] separation from his Hutchinsonian brethren', many of whom were in the university. His zeal for the
truth, his spirituality and work for the kingdom of God, along
with the increasing reproach of the cross, pulled him in a different direction. The Hutchinsonians, who called Romaine 'the
departed brother', were careful to avoid anything to do with
Methodism, looking instead 'to the preferments and good things
of the Church, unattainable in the course Mr Romaine was determined to pursue'.

And my preaching [Haweis continues] at that time in the
university having roused much enmity, and theirs in particular, as I was neither high Church nor Hutchinsonian,
his friendship with me, and preaching for me, probably
widened the door of their separation. And whatever occasional intercourse the similarity of their philosophical
opinions might have afterwards led to, yet every day,
like diverging lines, their tempers and pursuits were at a
greater distance from each other.[32]

However, Romaine never lost his love for the Hebrew Old Testament and derived great benefit from some of the Hutchinsonian teachings. Newton once wrote to William Howell, informing him that 'Romaine is much of a Hutchinsonian; but when he preaches in that strain I do not think his sermons so edifying as those which he delivers in the more usual and popular way.'[33]

Before his expulsion from the Oxford University pulpit, Romaine had published a sermon called *The Parable of the Dry Bones*, which he had preached on 24 October 1756. It is an urgent appeal to all who are dead in trespasses and sins that it is only 'the Holy Spirit and his work upon the heart that makes us Christians'. One young man who was convicted of sin through reading it was John Valton, later one of Wesley's lay preachers. 'One day,' he says, 'I met with Mr Romaine's Sermons. (Was not this book providentially put into my hands to show me the means to attain salvation?) I read the sermon on the Dry Bones but which I thought it impossible to live up to what was therein required, being amongst friends who would laugh at me, and would stigmatize me with the odious epithet of Methodist.'[34]

In the spring of 1757 Lady Huntingdon opened her London home twice a week for preaching services and Romaine was among the principal preachers. It was there that he first met Lord Dartmouth, who also opened his Cheltenham home for religious services. His chaplain, George Downing, was keen for Romaine to travel west, but it appears that Romaine did not respond to the invitation. Probably in the summer of that year, Lady Huntingdon arranged for Romaine and Madan to travel through several counties on a preaching tour. In Warwickshire they were joined by William Talbot and together they moved on through Worcestershire and Gloucestershire. It may have been during this tour that Romaine's father died.

During this period Romaine was on friendly terms with the Wesleys. On 21 September 1757 Charles Wesley wrote to his wife from London: 'Yesterday I dined with Mr Madan and Mr Romaine, and had much fellowship with them in prayer.

Both send greetings.'[35] In the same year John Wesley defended Romaine and others against the attacks of Robert Sandeman. Sandeman had taken exception to Romaine's question in his *Comment on the 107th Psalm*: 'When the blessed Jesus invites, when he presses you to accept health and salvation at his hands, what can tempt you to reject his gracious offer?' Sandeman, who opposed all direct calls for the unconverted to turn to Christ, replied: 'Thus it would seem our devotion must be animated by the consideration of the great goodness and condescension of the Deity manifested in sending us the precious person of a clergyman, as his representative, to waste his lungs for an hour or two upon us.'[36] On 1 November 1757 Wesley responded to Sandeman in a letter and ably defended the evangelical position.

In 1757 Romaine published another tract, *A Seasonable Antidote against Popery*, which was a response to Josiah Tucker,

William Legge
(Lord Dartmouth).

Charles Wesley.

rector of St Stephen's, Bristol, and his tract on the doctrine of justification. He opens by stating:

> The papists have their emissaries everywhere; and they are vastly busy at present. They have more interest in this kingdom, and their doctrines have more advocates, than people imagine. Some of their pretended enemies are their best friends, and do them the greatest service. While they cry out, popery! popery! and would make men believe that they are no Papists, they maintain the fundamental principles of the church of Rome. These were maintained openly in a little piece lately printed at Bristol, in defence of the popish doctrine of justification by works.[37]

He then printed the whole of Tucker's tract before answering it in the form of a dialogue between a true believer and an inquirer, who was a member of Tucker's church, to demonstrate the difference between the doctrine of the New Testament and the doctrine put forth by Tucker.

Romaine was not one who loudly and aggressively attacked Roman Catholicism. Occasionally he mentioned their errors, but usually in a restrained and respectful manner. In 1771 he wrote to his sister: 'I have done with names — great authorities — and living popes — for we have an English Pope. In opposition to whom, I am a Protestant. I protest against the merit of works, and all its long train of errors; but I will not dispute with any Pope. I will rather pray for him, as I do. God open his eyes, and turn him from darkness to light, from blind Popery, into gospel liberty.'[38] Nine years later he wrote to the Bishop of London and told him: 'There are no persons in my parish, who will confess to me, that they are papists.'[39]

A further publication of 1757 was William Mason's *Methodism Displayed and Enthusiasm Detected*, which the author, a justice of the peace at Rotherhite Wall, Surrey, addressed to his close friend Romaine. Mason sat for many years under

Romaine's ministry and wrote his pamphlet to explain and defend the evangelical doctrines.

At St Dunstan's, on the afternoon of Christmas Day 1757, Romaine preached from Luke 2:7, and again set forth the true doctrines of Christianity. A member of his congregation, claiming to have taken down the sermon in short hand, published it in the new year under the title *The Necessity of Receiving Christ in our Hearts*, and subjoined to it some critical observations by an anonymous writer, who accused Romaine of being 'very uncharitable' in his remarks and of 'misciting' text. The writer was particularly aggrieved at Romaine's doctrine of full assurance, calling it 'both false and pernicious'. 'And now, Sir,' he says to Romaine in signing off, 'if you should ever think of publishing your said discourse, I hope you will first make it conformable to the doctrines of our Church, as contained in her Liturgy and Articles; from which I observe you are much inclined to deviate; wherefore that you may be led into the way of truth.'[40]

It seems that by this time Clapham, under the leadership of Henry Venn and John Thornton, had become an important rendezvous for evangelicals. The names of Romaine, Venn, Jones, Madan, Downing, Maxfield and others are frequently mentioned in connection with religious services there. Whitefield, a regular visitor at Thornton's house, wrote to Lady Huntingdon on 15 January 1758, with encouraging news:

> Mr Romaine, Jones, and Venn are heard with surprising attention, and a mighty power seems to attend the word. All meet frequently at the Clapham Bethel for mutual prayer and edification, and our glorious Immanuel continues to smile on our feeble endeavours. How have we wrestled in earnest, ardent, outpouring of our souls in that noble mansion, for each other's spiritual growth — for the extension of the Redeemer's kingdom, and the conversion of ungodly ministers! These spiritual routs are blessed entertainments![41]

Thomas Mortimer, who was made English vice consul for the Austrian Netherlands in November 1762, wrote *Die, and be Damned* (1758), a criticism of Methodist beliefs, which was directed principally against Romaine and the 'modern practice of some divines, who preach eternal damnation, with as much eagerness and industry, as their heavenly Master, when on earth preached salvation; and who make no scruple publicly to declare, that unless you believe in Christ according to the singular principles of Methodism, you must infallibly die, and be damned'.[42] There is no record of any reply from Romaine, who generally ignored criticism of this nature.

While dismissing opposition from antagonists such as Mortimer and with the encouragement of having like minded men at his side, he wrote to his sister on 18 July 1758: 'There seems to be a great hungering and thirsting after the word in most parts of the country; I pray God some persons may be sent to break the bread of life, and to distribute the waters of comfort to them. The work of God still prospers in this city, which is the only token we have for good — for it shows that God, in the midst of wrath, remembers mercy.'[43]

The Tabernacle house was the resort of evangelical ministers of all denominations. On one occasion John Wesley, the celebrated Romaine, Dr Gill, Dr Gifford, Messrs Cudworth and Cennick, breakfasted with Whitefield and Hervey; and afterwards spent the morning in reading the Scriptures, prayer and exhortation. These meetings were seasons of holy joy to them; the Spirit descended with great power upon their souls; their faith was strengthened, their love quickened, their zeal stimulated, and their lives afresh devoted to the service of their Master.

Alfred New.[1]

8

Romaine and the Other Leaders of the Revival

On 22 January 1758 the Vicar of St Dunstan's, William Gibson, died. His successor, Alexander Jacob, who was not instituted until 21 July, strongly disliked Romaine's evangelical preaching, and, perhaps moved by jealousy at his popularity, saw fit to dispute his right to the pulpit, although he had been legitimately appointed lecturer. Romaine wrote to his sister, and spoke of Jacob's opposition and his efforts to hinder the preaching of the gospel: 'I have had sad troubles with the new vicar of St Dunstan's. He will let none preach for me without a license, which puts me to great inconvenience; but all is governed by One who knows what is best, and does what is best, for his own glory and his people's good.'[2]

However, Romaine was not deterred from preaching the gospel elsewhere and on 7 November 1758 he wrote to Lady Huntingdon with encouraging news:

> You will rejoice with me in hearing that the kingdom of our dear Lord spreads daily. In my late excursion in Northamptonshire, Bucks and Bedfordshire, I found great congregations, both in houses and in churches; and I met with numbers under awakenings, and several

who had received Christ Jesus the Lord, and had found
true joy and peace in believing. Oh what matter of
thankfulness is this! Let us praise the immense, infinite
love of Jesus Christ, and let us pray him to spread still
farther the glories of the cross.[3]

On 5 July 1759, Charles Wesley wrote to his wife and gave
her a glimpse of Romaine's predicament at St Dunstan's: 'On
Tuesday I breakfasted with Mr Romaine and his wife, who were
very loving and open. He expects to be thrust out of the churches soon.'[4] In the autumn of that year, at the height of his troubles over the lectureship, Romaine travelled to Cornwall to seek
the advice of another evangelical whose views he respected,
Samuel Walker of Truro. It was a surprise visit for both men.
Walker had no idea he was coming and Romaine had only decided to make the journey the day before he set out. In a letter
to his good friend Thomas Adam of Wintringham, written on
11 October 1759, Walker mentions how Romaine had been
prevented from using the pulpit during the long vacation and,
to make matters more difficult for him, how his 'too hot friends
have been, he says to a man, pressing him to come out [of the
Establishment], engaging him to build a chapel':

> Between the both his trial was not small [comments
> Walker]; and the rather, because none in London will
> permit him to preach in their pulpits. Hence, he was al-
> most ready to conclude, that were he turned out of St
> Dunstan's, he should get no employment in the estab-
> lishment. In these uncomfortable circumstances, he told
> his friends he would come down and consult me, be-
> cause he knew I was in his opinion for sticking to the
> Church... We talked over the matter fully. He is deter-
> mined to stick fast, and to wait. He sees his friends are
> in a bad spirit. He will not engage in a lawsuit against the
> vicar and vestry; if his friends will, they may. He will not, I
> hope, publish his case, which he had resolved to do.[5]

After a stay of two days, Romaine returned home 'in pretty good spirits', and with a rough copy of Walker's *Hints for a scheme more effectually to carry on the work of reformation at this time begun in divers parts of the kingdom, under regular ministers of the Church of England* in his pocket. Nothing, however, came of the *Scheme*.[6] Thomas Adam wanted Walker to advise Romaine to stand fast: 'His road is waiting and patient suffering; and desertion of the Church, of which he has otherwise a good opinion, on account of hardships, will be nothing but resentment, and can never have a good issue, or give him comfort on cool reflection.'[7] Romaine was indeed encouraged by Walker to stay within the confines of the Establishment and to fight for the freedom to preach. G. C. B. Davies, commenting on Romaine's conversation with Walker, says that the 'effect of Walker's judgement and persuasion were of incalculable value to the whole cause of enlightenment within the Church of England. Had Romaine seceded at this stage, it is not too much to say that the result might have been disastrous to the Evangelical movement.'[8]

Meanwhile three tracts appeared, two in defence of Romaine, one against him. The latter, which greatly helped Jacob's cause, was entitled *An Apology for the Parishioners of St Dunstan's* and was written by 'one of the inhabitants', who maintained that when a clergyman undertakes a lectureship, he is '*thrusting his sickle into another man's corn*; that he invades a province which does not properly belong to him'.[9] He goes on to describe the crowds that attended Romaine's ministry and the subsequent problems encountered by the parishioners:

> Little order or decency can be observed in an assembly, consisting of a promiscuous crowd of people, pushing, squeezing, and shoving forward, riding on one another's backs, and tearing their clothes to pieces, with eagerness to get within hearing of the preacher; some panting for breath; others sweating and staring, with their eyes staring out of their heads; others, not able to bear up

against the press with which they are thronged on every
side, fainting and falling to the ground, where it is almost
impossible to prevent their being trampled to death...

The parishioners [cannot] attend the divine worship
in that peaceable quiet manner they used to do, being
prevented by that tumultuary accession of people from
all quarters that crowd our little church whenever you
ascend the pulpit. It is with the utmost difficulty that we
are able to get to our pews, and we are forced to struggle through a ragged, not to say, unsavoury multitude,
at the hazard of our clothes, and not unfrequently, of our
pockets.[10]

The churchwardens also voiced their disapproval of this 'scrum
in church'. Their affidavit for May 1760 reads: 'Great crowds of
people, not parishioners, have been accustomed to assemble
about the church every Sunday afternoon more than an hour
before the opening of the doors, when Mr Romaine was expected to preach, and to fill the aisles and pews as soon as the
doors were opened, preventing the parishioners getting to their
seats, and this crowd for two years past has been continually
increasing.'[11]

The vicar and churchwardens, on examining the founder's
will, discovered that the endowment that financed the lectures
only provided for sermons to be preached while the law courts
were sitting. Romaine had been preaching all year round. So
on the first Sunday of the long vacation (1759) they met him
at the door and told him he could not lecture again until the
courts sat in the autumn. On the first Sunday of the autumn
term, expecting to be able to resume his lectures, he found
the pulpit door locked, the vicar occupying the pulpit, and
the beadle sitting on the stairs. He was told that the time of
his lecture had been moved to seven o'clock in the evening.
Nevertheless, he appeared constantly in his place to assert his
claim to the lectureship as well as his willingness to perform the
office. His friends were not happy with the new lecture time and

eventually carried the affair before the King's Bench, asking for a mandamus to restore the lecture to its usual hour and to allow it to continue throughout the year.

The court decided that the vicar and churchwardens had acted within their legal rights and deprived Romaine of the parish lectureship, but confirmed him in the lectureship endowed by Thomas White. He was allowed to use the church for lecturing, but only at seven o'clock in the evening, according to Lord Mansfield's decision, and only when the courts were in session. The churchwardens, seizing the opportunity for further mischief, refused to open the church until exactly seven o'clock, leaving the preacher and a congregation of hundreds, if not thousands, waiting in the street until 'the wooden giants on the tower had beaten out the hour of seven'. The churchwardens also refused to warm or light the church in winter, so Romaine frequently read prayers and preached by the light of a single candle, which he held in his hand, while his shivering congregation sat or stood in darkness. In this way the persecutors hoped his followers would lose patience and self-discipline, and act in a way that would lay their leader open to a charge of misconduct, with which they might dismiss him, but they were disappointed, for both lecturer and hearers acted with restraint and peaceableness.

This deplorable state of affairs continued for several years until one particular evening, when the congregation was assembling outside the church waiting for admission, Romaine's predecessor in the lectureship, Richard Terrick, who knew Romaine to be 'a man of approved abilities, of untainted morals, and a warm advocate for the established forms of worship',[12] happened to be passing St Dunstan's Church. Observing the huge crowd and the church doors locked, he inquired into the cause of such a large gathering. He was told that they were Romaine's people who were waiting to hear him preach. After further investigation, he concluded that Romaine's opponents were unreasonable in their conduct and demanded that the service of the church should begin at six o'clock, that the doors should be opened in proper time, and that lights should be provided for the winter season. The unpleasant affair ended and Romaine was established in his ministry at St Dunstan's, where he continued till his death, and which became 'the rallying point for Evangelicalism in London'.[13]

During the early part of the St Dunstan's conflict, he published *Twelve Sermons upon Solomon's Song*, which he dedicated to his 'St Dunstan's parishioners'. In the dedication he says,

> Ever since you were pleased unanimously to choose me your Lecturer, I have endeavoured to discharge my duty as one who must give an account... Knowing therefore the terror of the Lord, I have not shunned to declare unto you the whole counsel of God. He knoweth my heart; and he has seen how honestly I have preached the word, and how earnest I have been with him in prayer for a blessing upon it... You have heard me for some years, and chiefly upon the same subject. I hope you are not tired of hearing of the love of Jesus to poor helpless sinners: I am sure I am not tired of speaking upon it.[14]

He made the sermons public to remove men's prejudices and to reconcile their minds 'to this sweet portion of God's holy word'. He also thought it was 'quite providential' that these sermons on the love of God should be published at a time when he was 'furiously attacked by a nameless writer, and charged with preaching nothing but hell and damnation'. 'It would have been as true a charge,' he says, 'if he had said I always preached in Hebrew. This volume shall answer for me. Here my doctrine is: Believe, and thou shalt be saved: love God, and thou shalt be happy.'[15]

The *Christian Magazine* for 1790 described these sermons as 'excellent discourses' and cordially recommended them to its readers. Surprisingly, the *Monthly Review* was not as critical as usual: 'Those who think, with Mr Romaine, that *Solomon's Song* can afford a foretaste of those pleasures which "are at God's right hand for evermore", may find abundance of consolation in the perusal of these right godly discourses; which, however, we can by no means recommend to the carnal reader.'[16]

Throughout this troubled period, Romaine enjoyed a deepening fellowship and ministry with many of the leaders of the revival. In February 1759, after Britain had suffered various military setbacks in the Seven Years' War, Romaine joined in a fortnight of intercessory prayer and preaching meetings with Lady Huntingdon at her Park Street residence, along with Whitefield, the Wesleys, Madan, Thomas Maxfield, Venn, John Fletcher and others — all of whom 'shared in preaching, exhorting and conducting sessions of prayer'.[17] At these meetings a 'deep sense of the Divine presence seemed to penetrate every soul in attendance'.[18] The following Thursday morning (29 February), after the preaching, Romaine 'concluded with a short Scriptural prayer and the usual benediction'. At the prayer meeting on Friday evening Charles Wesley preached, while Whitefield, Downing, Venn and Romaine conducted the other parts of the service. The Lord's Supper was administered on Tuesday 6 March by Whitefield, who was assisted by Romaine and Madan, the former praying before the elements were distributed. On that occasion all were 'touched to the heart and dissolved in tears' by Whitefield's solemn and impressive address to the communicants.[19]

Whitefield and Romaine shared a deep regard for each other, and often united in ministry at places like Brighton and Bath. Romaine 'honoured Whitefield's character, gloried in his friendship, and cheerfully associated with him in his labours', and on his death in 1770 paid his co-worker a glowing tribute. In the letter he wrote to Lady Huntingdon on 7 November 1758, Romaine said: 'Mr Whitefield is come to town, full of love and zeal, and burns still clearer and brighter. What a wonderful instrument is he! When I look at myself compared to him, I think what is a glow-worm in moonshine? It is totally eclipsed; and

George Whitefield, the most popular evangelical of the
eighteenth century.

yet the moon and the glow-worm shine by the same borrowed light. Oh for more of Christ, and less of self!'[20]

Whitefield in return spoke enthusiastically about the 'spiritual routs' at Lady Huntingdon's house and particularly mentions Romaine. He points to the usefulness of Romaine's ministry in her chapel at Bath, and in a letter to John Gillies, says how Romaine preached at Tottenham Court Chapel and raised £100 for his work among the Stockbridge Indians. In 1767 Whitefield counted it a privilege to preach the gospel at the door of Romaine's mother's house in Hartlepool. Seymour, in comparing the two men, says: 'In point of popular eloquence and commanding oratory, Mr Whitefield was certainly his superior, as indeed he was to every other man of his day ... but in erudition and critical knowledge of the Scriptures, Mr Romaine far excelled him, and, indeed, most of his contemporaries.'[21]

Romaine's relationship with Wesley was not so harmonious or affectionate. Although they ministered together on a number of occasions, their doctrinal differences kept them from enjoying a truly close relationship. Wesley could not differentiate between Romaine's strict Calvinistic position and antinomianism. On one occasion, he wrote a word of warning to John Fletcher of Madeley (20 March 1768), who was 'sick of the conversation' of Calvinists:

> I do not wonder at it at all, especially considering with whom you have chiefly conversed for some time past — namely, the hearers of Mr Madan and Mr Romaine (perhaps I might add of Mr Whitefield). The conversing with these I have rarely found to be profitable to my soul. Rather it has damped my desires, it has cooled my resolutions, and I have commonly left them with a dry, dissipated spirit.
>
> And how can we expect it to be otherwise? For do we not naturally catch their spirit with whom we converse? And what spirit can we expect them to be of, considering the preaching they sit under? Some

aged 38

aged 63

John Wesley, one of the
eighteenth century's leading
evangelicals.

happy exceptions I allow; but, in general, do men gather grapes from thorns? Do they gather constant, universal self-denial, the patience of hope, the labour of love, inward and outward self-devotion, from the doctrine of absolute decrees, of irresistible grace, of infallible perseverance?[22]

However, Wesley freely admitted that Romaine was an instrument raised up by God.

John Berridge, vicar of Everton, a small village in Bedfordshire, was another good friend of Romaine's. After he had 'fled to Jesus alone for refuge, 1756', to use his own description of his awakening that is inscribed on his tombstone, he began to preach with great power and his sermons deeply affected the people of Everton and others, who travelled twelve or fourteen miles to hear him. Whitefield, on his way to Scotland in July 1758, wrote: 'Mr Berridge ... promises to be a burning and shining light.'[23] Wesley too was impressed. He went to Everton the following year at the request of Lady Huntingdon, and reported back: 'His word is with power; he speaks as plain and home as John Nelson, but with all the propriety of Mr Romaine and tenderness of Mr Hervey.'[24]

In a letter to Wesley (16 July 1759), Berridge describes the extraordinary effects of his ministry: 'The word is everywhere like a hammer, breaking the rock in pieces. People fall down, cry out most bitterly, and struggle so vehemently, that five or six men can scarcely hold them down. It is wonderful to see how the fear of the Lord falls upon unawakened sinners.' Berridge closes his letter by referring to a 'wonderful outpouring of the spirit of love amongst believers', which affected them so dramatically that they fell to the ground unconscious and were not able to work for several days.[25] Concerned about these strange manifestations, the Countess of Huntingdon wrote to Romaine and asked him to take Madan with him to Everton to 'examine minutely into the circumstances'. The two men were accompanied by John Walsh. On their arrival in Bedfordshire they were

John Berridge.

warmly received by Berridge and Hicks, vicar of Wrestlingworth, situated four miles from Everton.

At Potton, they spoke to John Keeling and others, who related their experiences:

> Ann Thorn, another native of Potton, spoke of depression after her visions, but stated that she was still visited 'with such overpowering love and joy, especially at the Lord's Supper, that she often lay in a trance for many hours'. As they were speaking they were called into the garden, where another young woman, Patty Jenkins, had entered a trance. She appeared asleep with her eyes open uttering praise in a low voice and when words failed, 'she frequently laughed while she saw his glory'. Mr Madan did not know whether it was of God or the devil. [According to Wesley, Romaine was filled with solemn awe.] Walsh sat down beside her, whereupon he himself entered into an ecstatic state. When it was time to depart to hear Mr Hicks preach at Cockayne Hatley, a village a short distance away, Patty Jenkins regained her strength and they all walked together, sixteen in number, 'singing to the Lord as they went along'.[26]

Hicks's sermon was excellent and there were no unusual occurrences.

The following day, Friday 13 July, Romaine and Madan, still uncertain as to whether or not the 'signs' were from God, accompanied Berridge and Hicks to Tadlow, a short distance east of Wrestlingworth. 'Great numbers, feeling the arrows of conviction, fell to the ground, some of whom seemed dead, and others in the agonies of death; the violence of their bodily convulsions exceeding all description. There was also a great crying and agonizing in prayer, mixed with deep and deadly groans on every side.' At Everton the following Sunday about two hundred persons, chiefly men, 'cried aloud for mercy; but many more were affected, perhaps as deeply, though in a calmer way'.[27]

Walsh claims that Romaine and Madan were convinced after hearing the testimonies of two children: Alice Miller, aged fifteen, and Molly Raymond, aged eleven, who had been converted on 20 May. While these two girls may have helped to ease their concerns, it was probably the ministries of Berridge and Hicks, along with the testimonies of other converts, which proved the work to be a genuine move of God. Seymour says they were initially astonished and doubts filled their minds, but after they had 'conversed with several of those who had fallen in violent convulsive fits, and had accompanied Mr Berridge and Mr Hicks in some of their itinerant excursions, and witnessed the effects of their preaching, they were filled with a solemn awe, and felt fully convinced the work was of God, though occasionally mingled with the wild-fire of enthusiasm'.[28] Invigorated and inspired by what they had witnessed, Romaine and Madan returned to London.

After this visit Romaine and Berridge became good friends, and took every opportunity to support one another in the ministry. On 1 August 1763 Romaine relieved Berridge at Everton so that his friend could go to Lady Huntingdon's new home at Ote Hall and then on to London. On 16 January 1766, on account of the financial problems Berridge was experiencing, Romaine, in a letter to a friend, appealed for assistance:

> Yesterday I dined with Mr Berridge. He was making great complaint of his debts, contracted by his keeping, out of his own living, two preachers and their horses, and several local preachers, and for the rents of several barns, in which they preach. He sees it was wrong to run in debt, and will be more careful. But it is done. My application is to Lady Margaret. Will you stand, my friend, with her, and tell her Berridge's case? If she pleases to assist him, I should be glad to convey her charity to him.[29]

St Bartholomew-the-Great,
West Smithfield.

Little else is recorded of their relationship. Berridge died in
January 1793. 'Poor dear old man!' said Romaine. 'Thou art
gone to thy rest. I shall be happy to sit down at thy feet in the
kingdom.'[30]

In 1759 Romaine gave up his curacy of St Olave's and became morning preacher at St Bartholomew-the-Great, West
Smithfield. The rector, Richard Thomas Bateman, was also a
chaplain in the Royal Navy and his duties in that sphere meant
he was away from London for long periods. Consequently, the
principal responsibility for the church fell on Romaine. Early
in 1761 Bateman died and on 15 June John Moore, a man
obviously opposed to evangelical truth, was appointed his successor. He immediately dismissed Romaine. Four days later,
on 19 June, Romaine wrote to 'the Friday night society', with
whom he could no longer meet, and recommended to them
two things:

> The first is, that you would consider the present afflict-
> ing providence as the work of God. Men can do noth-
> ing but what God pleases; therefore murmur not, nor
> repine at second causes; for it is a reflection upon God.
> Remember, God does all things well... In the second

place, God takes away very often from his people all
their props, that they may lean more upon him... Look
then, my dear friends, at the God-Man, Christ Jesus;
make him your all in all, and then you will want means
less, because you trust more to the God of all means.[31]

He concludes the letter with these words: 'I [further] recommend to you these three things:— Submission to God's will
— Living in Christ — and Living to Christ; — and while you
do these things you shall never fail. The Lord comfort you, and
carry on his work in your hearts. To his mercy I commend you,
who am bound by many ties, to be your faithful and loving pastor, though dismissed for a time.'[32]

In the same year that he went to St Bartholomew's, he advised John Newton, perhaps surprisingly, that because of the
difficulties surrounding his ordination, it was plainly not God's
will for him to enter the Church of England; instead, he should
accept the invitation of an Independent congregation. Newton,
however, was not deflected from his goal, for some five years
later, on 29 April 1764, he received deacon's orders, and on 17
June the same year he was priested.[33]

During his time at St Bartholomew's he travelled and
preached for Lady Huntingdon, and experienced the revival
that was taking place in Yorkshire. He was always enthusiastically welcomed at Aberford by Lady Margaret and her husband,
'dear brother [Benjamin] Ingham', whose 'chapels he constantly attended, whose friendship he cultivated, and whose ministry
he so highly esteemed'. Ingham sometimes joined him on his
preaching tours into the county of Durham — Romaine preaching in any 'open' church and Ingham in the Methodist chapels
and private houses. During these visits he enjoyed 'many opportunities of conversing with Mr Batty and Mr Allen, and other
preachers amongst the Inghamites, occasionally preached in
some of the chapels, and attended several of their meetings for
the regulation of the order and discipline of the churches'.[34]

In September 1760 Romaine accompanied Lady

Huntingdon to Aberford to visit Ingham and his wife, who was the Countess's sister-in-law and who had been instrumental in her conversion. They were present at the general meeting of the ministers and members of the societies held at Wheatley on 27 September when the church officers were chosen by lot. After the meeting Romaine visited several of the societies in Yorkshire and Lancashire, taking it in turns with Ingham to preach almost daily in some of the chapels. They stayed several days at Thinoaks, where there was a large crowd and two elders were ordained.

Romaine was highly impressed with what he found in Ingham's societies. About 1780, when in the house of David Parker in the King's Mews, London, he looked back to that time and made the following comment about Ingham's connexion in the hearing of George Burder, pastor of the congregational church at Lancaster, and a man who had been converted through the preaching of Romaine and Whitefield: 'If ever there was a church of Christ upon earth, that was one. I paid them a visit, and had a great mind to join them. That was a blessed work of God among that people.' Sadly, the societies were devastated by Sandemanianism, 'that horrid blast from the north' that 'destroyed all'.[35] Romaine, along with Whitefield and the Countess of Huntingdon, tried to reconcile the warring parties, but to no avail.

Romaine was also impressed with Lady Margaret, who often provided for his necessities when his poor stipend was wholly inadequate to meet the needs of his family. Soon after her death in 1768 he wrote to a friend:

> I got a good advancement by the death of Lady Margaret, and was led into a sweet path of meditation, in which I went on meditating and contemplating till my heart burned within me. Methought he had given a noble display of the riches of grace in his dealings with her, and had made her a happy partaker of that life which he came to give unto this world... Many a time my spirit

William Grimshaw.

has been refreshed with hearing her relate, simply and feelingly, how Jesus was her life. And in consequence of this, having peace with God, through Jesus Christ her Lord, she had an attachment to his person... She was certainly spiritually alive; and he who made her so kept her so.[36]

Another man with whom Romaine became very friendly was William Grimshaw of Haworth. Faith Cook lists Romaine, along with Wesley, Whitefield, Venn and the Countess, as the people Grimshaw 'loved best in the world'.[37] It is certainly true to say that between these two men, who shared much in common, a 'peculiar friendship subsisted'. After 1755 Romaine occasionally travelled to Haworth, sometimes arriving with his wife without prior notice, but he always received a warm welcome. In September 1760, while Romaine was visiting the Inghams at Aberford, Grimshaw rode across from Haworth and engaged Romaine to preach for him. The crowds gathered quickly and overflowed into the churchyard. Grimshaw read the prayers in the church and then announced, much to the surprise of Romaine, who was averse to open air preaching, that after the service in the church his brother Romaine would 'preach the glorious gospel from brother Whitefield's pulpit in the church-yard'.[38] Romaine complied and 'preached most powerfully'. Mr Whitaker of Ringway in Cheshire, who was born in the parish of Haworth, said, 'I did not hear Mr Romaine preach, and was too young to have made any observations, yet I have often heard the people speak of it with the greatest satisfaction and thankfulness.'[39]

Romaine repeatedly asked Grimshaw for a written state-ment of his beliefs and eventually, on 8 December 1762, he received a copy of his creed, which is 'infused with a sense of the greatness and mercy of his God and the smallness and in-significance of man even at his best'.[40] Its final words, addressed to Romaine, summarize the desire of both men:

> I think, we are both agreed to pull down man, and when we have the proud chit down, to keep him down. For this is the main. And never let him recover so much as his knees, till with a broken heart and contrite spirit, the dear REDEEMER raise him... When I die, I shall ... have my greatest grief and my greatest joy. My greatest grief, that I have done so little for JESUS; and my greatest joy that JESUS has done so much for me. My last words shall be: 'Here goes *An Unprofitable Servant!*'[41]

The high regard Romaine had for Grimshaw is seen in com-ments taken from a sermon Romaine preached at St Dunstan's from one of Grimshaw's favourite texts, Philippians 1:21, on 17 April 1763, ten days after Grimshaw's death:

> Mr Grimshaw was the most laborious and indefatigable minister of Christ that I ever knew, and I believe one of the most so that ever was in England since the first preaching of the gospel. For the good of souls he re-jected all hope of affluent fortune, and for the love of Christ cheerfully underwent difficulties, dangers, tribula-tions. He preached Christ and Christ alone... 'I cannot

do enough for Christ, who has done so much for me' [he would often say]. He was the most humble walker with Christ I ever met with; insomuch that he could never endure to hear any commendations made to him upon his usefulness, or anything which belonged to him.[42]

After Grimshaw's death, Romaine returned to Haworth. He took as his text Acts 11:23: 'Who, when he came, and had seen the grace of God, was glad, and exhorted them all that with purpose of heart they would cleave unto the Lord.' The distress of the people at losing so great a man was indescribable, but Romaine's sermon, striking and impressive as it was, urged them to pray for the continuance of their spiritual privileges. He showed the same faithful optimism in a letter to his sister:

> I dare not ... think one hard thought of his taking dear Mr Grimshaw to himself. His work was done. The Lord took him to rest; and, as to his people, they will be well looked after. Their Shepherd will see to it, that they lack nothing... I verily believe that Mr Grimshaw's death will be as useful as his life; and the work is not yet come to its height in Yorkshire. No it will spread farther, and deeper still; ministers' removals, yea, the most useful of us, shall tend to spread it. For all things work together, under God, for his glory and his people's good.[43]

Romaine's optimism was well-founded; for, in answer to prayer, John Richardson and John James Charnock, two evangelical and pious men, were raised up to succeed Grimshaw.

In 1760 Romaine published *Twelve Discourses upon the Law and the Gospel*, a series of sermons, originally preached at St Dunstan's, in which he 'endeavoured to distinguish and precisely to settle the difference between the law and the gospel' — a difference that is often dangerously confused. Some of the principles upon which he proceeded are summarized as follows:

1. The Lord God, the Almighty Creator of all things visible and invisible, has an unalienable right to make laws for the government of his creatures...

2. The law of the Lord God ... is unalterable...

3. The moral law, which the Lord God revealed to Adam in paradise, required of him perfect uninterrupted obedience...

4. The law given to Adam being unalterable, all his descendants are bound to keep it; for they are all under law, as God's creatures...

5. All mankind have sinned and broken the moral law...

6. The law has made no provision for pardon of the least transgression...

7. The law brings [all men] in guilty, and condemns them, and divine justice is bound to inflict the deserved pains and penalties; so that there can be no possibility of justifying them by the law...

8. There can be no salvation by the law.[44]

1. The gospel is salvation from the law...

2. The gospel sets forth to the convinced sinner salvation from guilt and punishment, by giving him freely as perfect a righteousness as the law demands...

3. In order to receive this righteousness the gospel requires no previous qualification...

4. But how is Christ's righteousness received, and the sinner made righteous by it at God's bar? By faith and not by works...

5. With respect ... to the sinner's acceptance and justification before God, the law and the gospel ought to be distinguished...

6. The law is [not] repealed by the gospel...

7. The law [is not] made void by faith.[45]

These sermons are good examples of his preaching at this time. Ryle regarded them as the 'best and most valuable work he ever sent to the press'. But not everyone was so complimentary. William Felton, rector of Wendon Lofts, Essex, wrote to Romaine from Highgate on 26 February 1761, criticising his *Discourses*, with the motive of helping all rightly 'understand the means of obtaining salvation'. He says he was moved to answer Romaine's work by a 'real concern I feel for those who are taught to deny, that any righteousness in themselves is required as a condition of their justification, and a desire of convincing them of their error, as I am not able to distinguish their principles from Antinomianism, whatever their practice may be.'[46] On several other occasions Romaine was accused of Antinomianism. Once a clergyman of not very good repute followed him and called him an Antinomian. 'Romaine merely replied he was sorry to be called an Antinomian, and especially by *him*.'[47]

On 3 January 1761 Romaine was officially appointed Lady Huntingdon's chaplain, although he had been acting in that capacity since 1755. Later in the year he took part, with Venn and Berridge, in the opening of her chapel at Brighton, from where he wrote to Mrs Thomas Medhurst on 20 July: 'We go on sweetly in this place. Christ is indeed exalted, and reigns glorious in many a heart, as I wish he may in yours.' A couple of days later he wrote again, with this comment: 'Strange doings... A party for me, another against me. Violent on both sides. Alas, alas! What's all this about?'[48] Later in the month he was in Kippax, with Wesley and Venn, where he 'read prayers'.[49]

It is evident that in the autumn of 1761 he was experiencing some difficulties with Ebenezer Blackwell, a banker in Lombard Street. Romaine, apparently accused of spreading a false report about Blackwell, wrote to him on 30 September, saying, 'I find Mrs Knipe and Miss Bishop have been at your house, and have asserted the very same things for which you were so angry with me in your letter. I heartily wish God may lead you into all truth, and keep you clear of that bane of true godliness a *party spirit*.'[50] However, rather than pacifying his correspondent, the letter seemed to inflame the issue, for Blackwell wrote back on 2

October obviously upset. This extract is taken from a draft copy of the letter:

> I was not *angry*, but I am sure I was *truly grieved* for you, and I beg of you to tell me who savours most of a *party spirit*, the person that shall take pains to relate a story upon hearsay only which is greatly to the disadvantage of another who differs from in some points of religion or one who shall in a friendly manner without mentioning names make a strict enquiry after the unkind report and when found false shall inform the other of it advising him for the future if not on his own account yet for the sake of others, to be cautious how he spread such unkind reports.
>
> I do not think if twenty people was to assert the *same things* it would in the least lesson your unkindness, any more than it would my guilt if I was to spread abroad the many false storys that have been told of W. Romaine, even tho' I had heard the same things from twenty different persons before.[51]

Although this appears to be an isolated incident with Blackwell, it does highlight Romaine's tendency to provoke rather than appease those who disagreed with him. His zeal for the truth led him to attack his opponents, whereas, on many occasions, a more conciliatory approach would have served his purposes more effectively. Nothing further seems to have come of the correspondence, so in all probability an opportunity to be reconciled to a Christian brother was lost.

Looking back over Romaine's long and useful life, Haweis notes that if he had collected a register of ministers and people converted under his friend's ministry the 'names, and anecdotes attending them, would fill volumes... I know, indeed, a great cloud of witnesses to the benediction of the Spirit of God, upon Mr Romaine's labours of love... He was eminently blessed in propagating [the doctrines of the gospel], and seeing thousands the fruit of his labours.'[52] Unbeknown to Romaine, he had another thirty-three years in which to add names to this 'register of souls'.

There is [an] urgent need of calm and prayerful study of the word of God. That word, blessed be its Author, is like a rock amid the ocean of human thought. There it stands unmoved, notwithstanding the raging of the storm and the ceaseless lashing of the waves. And not only does it thus stand unmoved itself, but it imparts its own stability to all who simply take their stand upon it. What a mercy to make one's escape from the heavings and tossings of the stormy ocean, and find a calm resting place on the everlasting Rock.

C. H. Mackintosh.[1]

9

Stalwart for the Truth

Ever since Romaine had been engaged as one of Lady Huntingdon's preachers, he had been busy making the most of the opportunities she presented him, especially as he had no parish responsibilities. In the spring of 1758 he preached at her London residence, and the following summer he was in Brighton proclaiming Christ before crowds of eager listeners. In 1761 he preached at Ote Hall, where his labours were crowned with success. After one visit he wrote enthusiastically to the Countess:

> Such a time I scarce ever knew as we have had at Oathall [a variant spelling of Ote Hall]. I met the society twice and had spoken with them one by one for two Sundays before we had the sacrament; we were about one hundred communicants at the Lord's table. It was a feast indeed; he not only made us welcome to the bread and cup of salvation, but also vouchsafed his divine presence, and gave us blessed foretastes of the marriage supper. Surely Oathall is a highly favoured place, where the Lord himself delighteth to dwell.[2]

The Countess herself, writing to Howel Harris, said: 'Dear Mr Romaine [is] so blest in Sussex that I dare not remove him and no hearts [are] ready to engage in this work and yet it shall be well taken care of.'[3]

On 10 August 1762 he attended, along with the Countess, Madan, Venn and Whitefield, Wesley's nineteenth annual conference at Leeds, with a view of achieving closer collaboration between evangelicals and the Wesleys. The only record of the proceedings is Wesley's comment: 'We had great reason to praise God for his gracious presence from the beginning to the end,'[4] and that George Story was appointed a lay preacher. On 12 August, Romaine was back in London before he preached several times at Harrogate. Then on 21 August, after breakfasting with Sir Charles Hotham, he wrote to the Countess:

> I have managed my matters as to be able to set out for Brighthelmstone [Brighton] on Monday morning next: and, God willing, shall stay there till Michaelmas. O! join your prayers with ours, that the Lord of the harvest would be with us, and bless our labours in this part of his harvest field. By all accounts the desires of the people are very pressing for my coming down to help them, which I hope is of the Lord's doing, and is a good token for us. But be that as it will, it is ours to sow the seed, to rain and shine upon it and to give the increase is God's part. To him we must leave it.[5]

When he arrived in Brighton, Romaine was kept busy trying to sort out the problems caused by John Wesley's doctrine of Christian perfection. Some of these notions, which had caused such mischief in London, had filtered into the society at Brighton and threatened to disturb its peace. Romaine's visit and the effects of his ministry there were 'peculiarly useful at this time' as he endeavoured to combat the workings of Satan.

In September he returned to London, where news of his ministry was beginning to spread. Howel Harris, for instance, on 1 November 1762, wrote in his diary that he had heard of 'a great work' done by Romaine and others in London. Two months later, on 17 January 1763, he went to hear Romaine at St Dunstan's 'to past 8. Had great love to him,' he wrote, 'in seeing the faithfulness the Lord gives him in the face of the whole land in the midst of London. I spoke to him and said this must raise hatred to him.'[6]

Romaine at this time promised to undertake the duty of the Lock Hospital and so allow Haweis to preach for the Countess. Ten days after Harris's first diary entry, he again wrote to Lady Huntingdon from Lambeth, giving her more details about Brighton's battle with perfectionism:

> The enemy has begun to attack them, and has in part succeeded... The temptation with which at this day he disturbs them, is to hinder them from living upon Christ, as poor needy helpless sinners, and from finding by faith all they want in his fulness. This exalts the Saviour too much, and makes them too safe and happy; therefore Satan would persuade them to get riches, strength, and a clean heart, quite without sin in themselves; so that then they may look inward with complacency and delight, and look outward on others of supposed smaller attainments with a STAND BY — I AM HOLIER THAN THOU, and look upward with a *God, I thank thee that I am not as other men are.* Thus you see pride enters in and Christ is thrust out.[7]

Lady Huntingdon was keen for Romaine to renew his services at Brighton, so she invited him to proclaim the 'unsearchable riches of Christ' to a rapidly growing congregation. His reply is dated Lambeth 28 December 1762:

> My heart and prayers are with you; but the Lord does not make a way for me to visit you. To him I submit in this (although it be a great self-denial), as well as in other things. His will is always good, and it is always good for us to be resigned to it... I am a poor dull scholar, but

> he is a kind Master, and through him I get on, though
> halting and slowly. Such am I and such is he, that I can
> be telling of nothing else but of his salvation all the day
> long.
>   I cannot forget the dear little church. I think they
> must be better for my fervent prayers. The Lord Christ
> keep them all, and add to their number.[8]

He wrote again to Lady Huntingdon on 5 February 1763 and told her that he was still hoping 'some kind providence will soon send me amongst you. Madan you know is refused preaching for me by an order of vestry made some years ago; and Haweis has no licence from any bishop, nor has Tynley.'[9]

In March, Wesley wrote to Lady Huntingdon — an undated letter she received on 21 March 1763 — complaining of the lack of support he had received for his doctrine on perfection from Whitefield, Madan, Haweis and Berridge. 'Their voice seemed to be rather down with him — down with him; even to the ground.' He then praises Romaine in a way that suggests Romaine supported his peculiar doctrine: 'Only Romaine has shown a truly sympathizing spirit, and acted the part of a brother. I am the more surprised at this, because he owed me nothing, only the love which we all owe one another. He was not my son in the gospel, neither do I know that he ever received any help through me. So much the more welcome was his kindness now. The Lord repay it seven-fold into his bosom.'[10]

Five days later, from Lambeth on 26 March 1763, Romaine, who had seen Wesley's letter, wrote to the Countess, a little perplexed, explaining to her in no uncertain terms his view of perfectionism. It is interesting to note, contrary to his younger days, how unwilling he is to preach anything other than Christ:

> Enclosed is poor Mr John's [Wesley] letter. The contents
> of it, as far as I am concerned, surprised me; for no one
> has spoken more freely of what is now passing among
> the people than myself. Indeed I have not preached so

much as others whose names he mentions, nor could I. My subject is one, and I dare not vary from it. The more I read and preach upon the all-sufficiency of the adorable Jesus, the more I am determined to know nothing but him, and him crucified. But whatever stands in my way of exalting him I would tread upon it as the merest dross and dung. A perfection out of Christ, call it grace, and say it is grace from him, yet with me it is all rank pride and damnable sin. Oh! Madam, we should be careful of his glory, and not give it to another, least of all to ourselves. Depend upon it, man cannot be laid too low, nor Christ set too high...

I pity Mr John from my heart. His societies are in great confusion; and the point which brought them into the wildness of rant and madness is still insisted on as much as ever. I fear the end of this delusion. As the late alarming providence has not had its proper effect, and perfection is still the cry, God will certainly give them up to some more dreadful thing. May their eyes be opened before it be too late![11]

Romaine was concerned about Wesley's problems and the effect perfectionism was having on his people, but he never expressed any sympathy for this doctrine — a doctrine that Luke Tyerman, Wesley's biographer, mistakenly claims Romaine did not understand.[12]

While he expressed no sympathy for Wesley's beliefs, his heart went out to Lady Huntingdon, who was visiting him in London when news came from Ote Hall that her twenty-five year old daughter Selina was seriously ill. Later, after Selina's death on 12 May 1763, Lady Huntingdon gave Romaine a detailed account of her last days. Romaine, who himself experienced bereavement when his son Adam died in 1782, wrote to Mrs Medhurst of Kippax, one of the Countess's nieces, and passed on many of the particulars of Selina's death, closing the letter with the words: 'Although my Lady bears this so well, yet

The Countess's younger daughter, Selina, 1762.

she feels it. She is but a woman, and though a gracious one, yet grace does not destroy nature. She is a parent and at present incapable of writing.'[13] Romaine showed Lady Huntingdon's letter to the Earl of Dartmouth, and his own letter to Henry Venn, both of whom wrote letters of consolation to the Countess.

During this period of Romaine's ministry, when he had no stated employment in the church apart from St Dunstan's, he welcomed the opportunity of preaching charity sermons in many London churches, which drew vast congregations. On one of these occasions, so the story goes, he 'found that he had been locked in the pew in which he sat during the prayers, so that he could not get out, and the rector impertinently ascended the pulpit. The people rose in a mass to depart, but Romaine begged of them to remain for the sake of the charity.'[14]

Occasionally, he preached at the Lock Hospital and again his preaching was remarkably well attended. He continued to serve the Countess in her Sussex chapels and to travel, arriving in Everton on 1 August 1763, before moving down to Brighton, from where he wrote to Mrs Medhurst on 1 September:

Since I left you, all has been hurry, travelling from place to place, till kind providence has brought me to Brighthelmstone, where I hope for a little rest — not so much to my soul; blessed be the grace of sweet Jesus, I have that — but rest from distraction, hurry, dust, heat, and want of sleep. This is a kind of haven after the storm. Not that I expect a continual calm here: it would be a sad place indeed if there were no enemies, no warfare, no trials and troubles in it. These I must have wherever I go; because they grow in my constitution, and are nourished in the body of sin — and because without them I should not know how to prize Christ. But I find my retired and private times are the best for my own soul, as more public times are for others: and yet that sweetest blessed Jesus, when I am in his work, takes care of me; and when I am watering others, he does not leave me unwatered myself.[15]

He also assisted at Lambeth in the parish church on the first day of the month, mainly because of his acquaintance with Archbishop Thomas Secker, who constantly attended and administered the Lord's Supper. Secker has been described as a 'favourable specimen of the orthodox eighteenth century prelate', and was on friendly terms with many leading dissenters such as Doddridge and Watts.[16] At this time Romaine rarely passed the Lord's Day without preaching twice and sometimes three times.

Several tempting opportunities opened up for Romaine in 1763. Lord Dartmouth offered him the living of West Bromwich, but 'I refused,' said Romaine, 'never intending to burden myself with such a heavy charge. Since that time I have frequently refused the like offer.'[17] George Whitefield, returning from America with a commission to secure a suitable minister for St Paul's Episcopal Church in Philadelphia, with a salary of six hundred pounds a year and the prospects of great usefulness, wanted Romaine to resign his lectureship and move abroad. Whitefield reasoned that as he was persecuted in one city he should flee to another; he therefore repeatedly urged him to accept the offer. But Romaine was adamant — he did not want to leave the place where God had set him. His abilities and zeal were suited to this station and he could not imagine being more useful in another sphere. Besides, if he left, his removal would open a vacancy that would not be supplied to the glory of God. Nor did he want to leave his many friends, whom he loved, but to stay and support them. However, in a letter to his sister, probably written in 1763, he mentions his willingness to follow God's lead:

> I have strong applications to go to America, to a church
> in the city of Philadelphia. The Lord must determine. I
> would not have one wish against his will. Being bought
> with an infinite price, all I have and am should be at his
> service... But I shall not be in any hurry. Waiting is good
> — on the Lord. I will tarry his leisure, and look at his

providences. My friends, in general, are for my staying in London; and so am I in my own mind. But I dare not choose, till my choice is made plain to me.[18]

In all he was determined to take his stand for the defence of the gospel in London unless the Lord clearly directed otherwise. In this connection, he lived to see many who had travelled to America, expecting to enjoy a utopia of religion and liberty, gladly return to England.

Extracts from three other letters further express his sentiments on this issue. The first is taken from a letter he wrote to Lady Huntingdon from Lambeth on 5 February 1763: 'For my part I am quite fixed, and every day more so, in my present work. I am called to it, and commanded therein to abide with God. People say to me, you might be more useful here — or, what a great deal of good you might do there. Alas! they know me not.'[19] The second is taken from a letter he wrote to a friend from Lambeth on 14 May of that year:

As to what you write about, I know not what to say. It is in the best hands. He knows what to do. Let him alone. Remember he is the head of the church, and he will look after his own matters, and well too. At present I see not my way clearly from London. Here my Master fixes me, and here I must stay till he call me to some other place. When he would have me to move, he will let me know his will. Besides, what am I? What does it signify where I am? A poor dumb dog, the vilest, the basest of all the servants of my Lord.[20]

The last is from a letter written four months later, from Brighthelmstone, on 26 September 1763:

Would — be worthy my acceptance? The worth of it does not come before me, but what my Master expects of me. His will must be my rule; and it has been a long

time as plain to me as that two and two make four. I am
stationed by myself. I am alone in London; and while he
keeps me there, I dare not move; as, when he has a mind
to remove me, my way will be as plain from London as it
is now to abide in it. If I hearkened to self, and wanted to
run away from the cross, I know of no place so snug as
— ; but would you have me such a coward as to fly, and
such a one to stand by me — one who has kept me in
many battles, and one who, I trust, will presently make
me more than conqueror.[21]

So Romaine would not depart for distant shores, but remained
in London and waited for God to increase his measure of usefulness as he saw fit.

In the same year, 1763, a chapel in Broadway, Westminster,
variously named Broadway Chapel, Westminster Chapel and
New Way Chapel, became vacant in July on the death of the
incumbent, Francis Bryars. His widow, who had the disposal
of the living, was willing to present it to Thomas Haweis, who
was then serving at the Lock, and whose friends encouraged
him to apply for the vacancy in order to enlarge his sphere of
usefulness. He was referred to Zachariah Pearce, the Dean of
Westminster, then bishop of Rochester, but was 'most ungra-
ciously refused' by him. Romaine, however, determined to
put the chapel to good use. He had a licence in the diocese
of London, and so probably hoped he would not be opposed.
He opened the chapel for a while and laboured with great success. He preached twice on Sundays before taking a coach to
St Dunstan's for his six o'clock service. But before a year was
up, the bishop's mandate and the threat of the spiritual court
compelled him on 2 February 1764 to leave the congregation
he had collected.

Thomas Wright, in his *Life of Augustus M. Toplady*, mentions an amusing anecdote, which is followed by his comments
on Romaine's departure from New Way. It concerns Thomas

Wilson of St Margaret's, Westminster, who was also prebendary of Westminster and rector of St Stephen's, Walbrook. Wilson, who only preached a 'fashionable morality', was not satisfied with his lot and had his heart set on a bishopric. One day he met the king:

> 'What news from your parish?' enquired King George ... of Wilson.
>
> 'Why, your Majesty,' was the reply, 'that fellow Romaine, who has got a chapel in the New Way, draws all my parishioners from the church.'...
>
> 'Humph!' replied the king, 'we will make him a bishop; that will silence him.'...
>
> The popularity of Romaine increased by leaps and bounds. As the result of it, so many persons gathered regularly to hear Jesus Christ preached, that the Dean and Chapter became seriously concerned; and seeing no other way of putting an end to the distressing state of things, they withdrew their patronage from the chapel, and prevented Romaine from continuing to preach there. Toplady, who was one of Romaine's most enthusiastic hearers, owed more to him than to any other clergyman of the Church of England, and by the time of Romaine's removal from Westminster, they had become staunch friends.[22]

In a letter that Augustus Toplady wrote to the Dublin banker William Lunell, there is a reference to Westminster's closure. Some of the words in the letter are illegible, so they have been reconstructed: 'You have heard, I doubt not, of dear Romaine's success in Lond(on. This) eminent man two or three years ago attempted to get possession of a chapel (situated in the) New Way, Westminster, within a few doors of my mother's house, but the (dean and) chapter ordered it to be shut up, and so it has continued ever since. (Subsequently), at Mr Romaine's request, I tried for it myself, but could not succeed.'[23] The Westminster

Chapter Book simply says that Romaine 'is hereby forbidden to preach or otherwise officiate in the New Way Chapel in the parish of St Margaret he having no licence from their commissary or consent of the minister of the said parish.'[24]

Romaine's labours at Westminster may have been short, but many had 'reason to bless God for them, having been in that chapel called by him to the knowledge of his grace and faith in him'.[25] In a letter written a month after he had left (3 March 1764), he noted how he counted it an honour to suffer for Christ's sake:

> I have got more preferment, God be thanked I am turned out of my little chapel. Rejoice with me, that I am counted worthy to suffer shame for his dear, dear, dearest of all names, Jesus. I do love him more for this mark of his love. 'Tis worth more than a thousand a year. I find to lose for Christ is vast gain. Who would not part with farthings for guineas? Oh I cannot tell you, words fail, how he has made up this loss to me, and how he has won my heart by it, and endeared himself beyond measure to me.[26]

There were other disappointments. In 1754 some of the parishioners of St Helen's, Bishopsgate, had wanted Romaine to have use of the church for reading prayers and preaching once a week, but it came to nothing. Eight years later it was agreed by the inhabitants of St Alfege parish (Greenwich), in the presence of the rector Mr Wynne, to appoint a Sunday afternoon lecturer. The election was to be held on the first Thursday in October. On the previous Sunday (3 October 1762) notice was given in the church with the rector's consent and printed notices distributed to every housekeeper in the parish. There were three candidates: Iliff, curate of the parish for Mr Wyatt, the late incumbent; Lloyd and Romaine, who was elected 'by a great majority'. The rector, however, refused to allow Romaine to preach. About fifteen months later twenty-nine of the parishioners signed a memorial

to Richard Osbaldeston, bishop of London, in which they asked
for his intervention:

> Mr Romaine being so chosen waited upon the rector
> for the use of his pulpit which the rector has absolute-
> ly refused him, at sometimes alleging that the said Mr
> Romaine was not fairly chosen, at other times saying fair
> or not fair he should not have his pulpit on any account
> whatsoever; by which means the parishioners of Saint
> Alphage [St Alfege] are entirely deprived of an afternoon
> sermon so very useful to some of them and to many of
> their servants who cannot go to church in a morning.
>
> Wherefore your memorialists humbly pray that your
> Lordship would give us an opportunity of proving be-
> fore you the lawfulness of our election in the presence
> of the Rev Mr Wynne and if that be allowed we hope
> your Lordship will hear and judge for us, whether Mr
> Wynne does upon good ground refuse us the liberty of
> having the clergyman whom we have chosen to be our
> lecturer.

The memorial was presented to the Bishop of London on
Wednesday 15 February 1764 by Samuel Saville vestry clerk
and others. The bishop told Saville he could not say anything
as to the contents of it, as Mr Wynne was not present with him,
and he could not license a lecturer until the rector had signed
the certificate of election. Once again a pulpit was closed to
Romaine.[27]

Early in 1764 Romaine brought out that 'excellent treatise' *The Life of Faith*, which had an 'exceedingly rapid and
extensive sale'.[28] He had been planning the work for a while.
From Lambeth on 26 March 1763 he wrote that for the sake of
'weak believers, and to save myself great trouble in continually
conversing with these persons, I resolve to write a little treatise
upon the subject' of the life of faith. He asks his friend, 'Forget
not me nor my book. Beg of the Lord Christ to bless it. If he

smile upon it, it will be useful to his people. That is my highest wish.'[29] In December 1763, he was busy from morning to night transcribing the book for the press. He admits it is a 'deep subject and depends much on experience', thus he let his friends Madan and William Mason of Rotherhithe read it before letting it go. The former 'approves of it', he told his sister in a letter (27 December 1763). Just before publication he wrote again to his sister (3 March 1764) and urged her to pray for it. 'Let it be a book of many prayers. Beg it may be a means of increasing faith in the hearts of all that shall read it.'[30]

After it was published, he said in a letter to a friend, dated Lambeth 17 April 1764, 'May my ever dear Jesus shine upon every page as you read it, and strengthen your faith, and warm your heart with his heavenly love. I beg your prayers for a blessing on this book.'[31] On the same day he wrote to another friend: 'Look unto him, and you shall be saved — this is the truth, which, if the Lord please, he can make my little book the means of establishing you in. I most heartily wish it, and beg of Jesus to bless you as much in reading, as he did me in writing it.'[32] In the preface of a later edition, written on 24 April 1793, he told his readers that the design of his treatise 'is to display the glory and all-sufficiency of the Lord Jesus Christ, and to encourage weak believers to glorify him more, by depending and living more upon his all-sufficiency'.[33] The subject of the work he explains in this way:

> Whatever grace he has promised in his word, he is faithful and he is almighty to bestow; and they may receive it of him freely by the hand of faith. This is its use and office, as a hand or instrument, having first received Christ, to be continually receiving out of Christ's fulness. The apostle calls this living by faith; a life received and continued, with all the strength, comforts, and blessings belonging to it, by faith in the Son of God; and he also mentions the work of faith, its working effectually in the hearts and lives of believers, through Christ strengthen-

ing them, and its growing in them, yea, growing exceedingly from faith to faith, by the power of him who loveth them.[34]

Not everyone was impressed with Romaine's work. In September 1764 the *Monthly Review*, in regard to *The Life of Faith*, and expressing their Latitudinarianism, said: 'There is a certain class of readers which, no doubt, will look upon this as a *sweet* treatise, a *comfortable* treatise, a *precious* treatise, a *soul-reviving, soul-refreshing* treatise &c. To us it appears a *silly* treatise, a *stupid* treatise, a *nonsensical* treatise, a *fanatical* treatise.'[35] Another reviewer condemned it as the 'death of all reason, all piety, all humility, all meekness'.[36] John Wesley, after he had read the work, wrote on 20 January 1765: 'I looked over Mr R — 's strange book on the *Life of Faith*. I thought nothing could ever exceed Mr Ingham's; but really this does; although they differ not an hair's breadth from each other, any more than from Mr Sandeman.'[37] Wesley again attacked the work in a letter to Philothea Briggs on 13 July 1771, saying it is such 'a hotch potch as I have ever seen and is brimful of Antinomianism (as are all Mr Romaine's writings)'.[38] Such comments from Wesley are predictable on account of Romaine's Calvinistic bias.

The Life of Faith has since been published many times, and, combined with the two volumes *The Walk of Faith* (1771) and *The Triumph of Faith* (1795), which were published in later years, it 'may fairly be described as an evangelical classic'.[39] Francis Bumpus in *Ancient London Churches* is right when he says the work contains 'many passages full of tender and passionate devotion';[40] while *The Baptist Magazine* describes it as 'experimental and devotional' and 'designed to stir up the pure mind, by way of remembrance'. Faith, it says, is 'appealed to as a principle, holy in its nature, and of heavenly origin, which requires to be sustained and nourished by divine truth'.[41] Joseph Owen, in the preface of the 1856 edition, writes:

Chiefly, indeed, it is intended for those who have been
convinced of sin and of righteousness; to whom the
word of God has been made effectual, by the application of the Holy Spirit, to teach them the nature of the
Divine law; and who, upon comparing their hearts and
lives with it, have brought themselves in guilty...

He who desires some practical help in the way of
discovering how he stands with God, and sound counsel and encouragement in furthering his progress in the
spiritual life, cannot fail, by the same blessing, of being
greatly edified by the perusal of these pages.[42]

Many in London and the north, who waited expectantly for his
summer visits, held the work very highly, as did others. William
Cowper, for instance, had a copy in his library, and George III
regularly read the works of evangelicals such as Romaine and
John Newton. All of this enhanced the respect in which Romaine
was held. Rowland Hill (1744-1833), son of Sir Rowland Hill of
Shropshire, expressed his opinion of Romaine to his sister Jane:
'I have many obligations to the great Mr Romaine, who has
often invited me and my companions to his house, where we
often meet by eight in the morning. O how sweetly does he pray
with us, teach us and exhort us. Every word that comes from his
mouth ought to be writ in letters of gold upon our hearts.'[43] So
great was his admiration of Romaine that he had his portrait in
his rooms at St John's, Cambridge.

So Romaine continued to write, travel and preach for the
glory of God. Little did he know as he was preparing *The Life
of Faith* and preaching in different parts of the country, that God
was about to open another door of usefulness — right in the
heart of London.

I have heard, in my heart, a voice say, 'Whom shall I send?' And I have been compelled to say, 'Here I am, send me.' Trusting then, sweet Jesus, to thy grace and power, depending upon thine arm and blessing, out I go, not only unfit, but also averse to the work. It is thine, Lord, 'to work in me both to will and to do'.

William Romaine, from a letter to his sister dated Lambeth, January 1766.[1]

10
Elected to Blackfriars

On 7 July 1764 Romaine was in London but 'poorly in health'. The weather was so hot and his congregations so large, that he was 'quite faint'; but as 8 July was his last day before the long vacation, he was hoping 'a little air and exercise' would set him up again. 'But it matters not,' he says. 'Christ is mine and he knows how to order my affairs. He can bless sickness as well as health; nay, he does bless all things to his people.'[2] He went to Brighton before travelling north in the first week of August to spend some time with his family and old neighbours. From Hartlepool he wrote to a friend on 7 August, with encouraging news:

> My sweet Jesus hath contrived so much work for me in these parts, and he is so evidently and powerfully with us, that I cannot leave my neighbours, who crowd to hear far more than ever, and they are to me as my own soul. We are, beyond all description, happy in our loving, lovely Lord. Such meetings I never knew — and twice a day — and many churches open. O that I could but stay! I am so knit in heart to my neighbours, and the most of them come and sit quietly to hear, that I know not how to leave them. But it must be.[3]

He continued his tour into Yorkshire. On the 27 September, Richard Hart, vicar of Kingswood, Bristol, wrote from St George's to Howel Harris at Trevecca, noting that 'Mr Romaine has lately been at Bradford, preached there twice on the Lord's Day; then came incog[nito] to Bristol, stayed a night or two, and slipped away.'[4]

He was certainly back in London by the 29 September because he wrote to his sister from Lambeth on that day: 'I have been about my Master's business, preaching at Bradford, at Powsey, &c.; and being now returned to London to preach three times tomorrow, I could not help giving you an account of ... my dear Jesus' great goodness to me. He has travelled with me, and been with me of a truth.'[5] While on his preaching tour in Yorkshire he picked up a newspaper and read that his name had been put forward for the vacant living of the united parishes of St Andrew-by-the-Wardrobe and St Ann's, Blackfriars.

St Andrew-by-the-Wardrobe, first mentioned in about 1244, derives its name from its proximity to the King's Great Wardrobe, a mansion built by Sir John Beauchamp. After Beauchamp's death in 1359, King Edward III purchased the building and moved his state robes and other effects there from the Tower of London. The church was repaired and beautified in 1627, but destroyed in the Great Fire of London. Sir Christopher Wren rebuilt it in 1685-95, with a south west tower of four storeys reaching to a height of eighty-six feet, and at a cost of £7,060 16s 11d. 'It is a plain brick rectangular church with a plain tower and was the last of Wren's city churches.'[6] The rectory house, in St Andrew's Hill, was built about 1766, the year Romaine became the rector.

The monastery at Blackfriars was dissolved in 1538 and mostly destroyed. During Mary's reign Sir Thomas Cawarden, Keeper of the Royal Tents and Master of the Revels, had to provide the parishioners with a new church, which was St Ann's. The roof of St Ann's collapsed in 1597 and a more substantial church was built, which was also destroyed in the Great Fire and not replaced.[7] It was united to St Andrew's in 1670.

The playwright William Shakespeare worked nearby at Blackfriars Theatre for at least fifteen years and would have known the church well. He eventually bought a house in Ireland Yard in St Andrew's parish. One of Shakespeare's contemporaries, the famous lutenist, singer and composer, John Dowland, is buried in the churchyard of St Ann's; and the Puritan, William Jenkyn, was chosen lecturer at the time of William Gouge's rectorship. Gouge, a member of the Westminster Assembly, was offered several so-called 'higher' positions in the church, but he always replied that it was his ambition to go from Blackfriars to heaven.

The right of presentation to this living was vested in the crown and the parishioners alternately, and in 1764 it was the parishioners turn to choose. Romaine's predecessor was Phocion Henley (1728-1764), a nephew of the then Lord Chancellor Sir Robert Henley, first Earl of Northington, and an intimate friend of Lady Huntingdon. He became rector in 1759 but died on 29

St Andrew-by-the-Wardrobe.

August 1764 of a 'putrid fever', which he had caught from one
of his parishioners. Cadogan describes him as a 'man of excellent spirit, and of great piety', who 'promised to be very useful
in the church'.[8]

Romaine was still just a curate and lecturer, and would
probably have finished his course in those offices if his friends
had not seized the opportunity of obtaining for him a settlement in the Church of England. One of these friends was Lady
Huntingdon, who exercised her considerable influence on
Romaine's behalf. 'It was immediately impressed on my mind,'
said the Countess, 'that Mr Henley's vacancy was to be filled
by dear Mr Romaine.' She spoke to the lord chancellor about it
and suggested to Thornton and Madan that they talk with the
parishioners.[9] Ryle says that the Countess 'saw clearly the immense importance of such a champion of Christ's gospel being
settled in a prominent position in London; and she left no stone
unturned to secure his success'.[10]

At first they had little hope of success, as some parishioners
on whose votes the outcome depended were wary and uncom-
mitted, knowing Romaine's links with Methodism, while others
feared an influx of visitors from other parishes. But the more
they canvassed, the more they were encouraged, and soon
found that at least two thirds supported him. At first all this was
done without his knowledge or consent. When his friends eventually conferred with him, they enthusiastically urged him to solicit the parishioners' votes, but he refused, which lead to the
rumour that he was 'above' such a menial task, 'while the other
candidates in canonicals were bowing from door to door'.[11] It
was at about this time that he wrote to his sister and expressed
his peace of mind concerning Blackfriars and his willingness to
submit to the Lord's will, whatever it may be:

> You have heard of my being a candidate for a church
> in the city. My friends put me up; and I am as if I were
> not a candidate, for I have scarce a thought about it.
> One wish I am sure I have not, but that Christ's will may

be done. Would he employ me in a larger field than I have at present, 'here am I, Lord, send me'. If he would have me to stay, and work where I am, I am content. Be thou, Lord, but with me, then I shall be and do what thou pleasest. Thus have I cast all my care for this and all other things upon the Lord, knowing that he careth for me. You will suppose then that I am happy; and so I am, very, very happy. I have got the pearl; let them take the field that will. For one end and purpose only do I now live. I see in this pearl of great price, the infinitely rich Jesus, far more wisdom, righteousness, holiness, strength, and blessedness, than I have yet attained; and I hunger and thirst for more, still more.[12]

The day of his probation sermon was 30 September 1764. Many of his friends who had been in the habit of hearing him, including Lady Huntingdon, stayed away in case they crowded the church and occupied the seats of the inhabitants, which, in that day, would have caused offence and been a hindrance to his election. In his sermon on 2 Corinthians 4:5 — 'We preach not ourselves, but Christ Jesus the Lord, and ourselves your servants for Jesus' sake' — he stated the doctrines he intended to preach and the practices he meant to pursue, and included a close application to each particular hearer. He also saw fit to give the reasons why he had not solicited their favour as was normal:

In this ordinance of preaching, and in all our ministe-rial labours, we are not lords but servants, servants to our great Lord and Master ... and servants also to you, bound to perform every good office, ready to every work and labour of love, which may promote your spiritual and eternal interest... But in whatever case one or both these ends cannot be promoted, we are acting quite out of character, if we engage in it. And for this reason I have not been able to behave towards you in the common way of soliciting for your favour. Some have insinuated it was from pride, that I would not go about the parish from house to house canvassing for votes; but truly it was another motive. I could not see how this could promote the glory of God. How can it be for the honour of Jesus, that his ministers, who have renounced fame and riches and ease, should be most anxious and earnest in the pursuit of those very things which they have renounced? Surely this would be getting into a worldly spirit, as much as is the spirit of parliamenteering. And as this method of canvassing cannot be for Jesus' sake, so neither is it for our honour: it is far beneath our function: nor is it for your profit. What good is it to your souls? What compliment to your understandings? What advantage to you in any shape to be directed and applied to by every person with whom you have any connexion, or on whom you have any dependence? Is not this depriving you of the freedom of your choice? Determined by these motives, when my friends of their own accord put me up as a candidate, to whom I have to this hour made no application, directly or indirectly, I left you to yourselves. If you do choose me, I desire to be your servant for Jesus' sake; and if you do not, the will of the Lord be done.[13]

The sermon was well received by the parishioners and published at their request.

On 14 October the Blackfriars' parish clerk decided that a public vestry would be held to reduce the three standing candidates to two. A second public vestry would then be held in order to choose the successful candidate. At the first vote John Warner and James Smith, who seems to have been curate to the deceased rector, both received 78 votes, with Romaine polling 73. A scrutiny was demanded by Romaine's friends, which produced the following result: Warner 77, Romaine 71 and Smith, who had had nearly 40 votes rejected, 36. Naturally, Smith was unhappy with the proceedings, and Warner contested the right of the churchwardens to reduce the number of candidates to two. As he had received the majority of votes he wanted them to present him to the Bishop of London 'as being duly elected rector in order that the bishop might induct' him to the living. In view of these disagreements the election was postponed until 22 January 1765.

At the second election Warner refused to stand, claiming he had been duly elected the previous October. Smith stood against Romaine, who received 'a great majority of votes'. On 26 January 1765, magistrate William Mason, a convert of Wesley's and a good friend of Romaine's, wrote to Lady Huntingdon with the precise figures: 'Our dear Mr Romaine is elected to Blackfriars, 134 against 105.'[14] However, Smith obtained an injunction, forbidding the bishop from inducting Romaine until the matter had been sorted in the court of chancery, where it remained for more than a year. By this time, some of the parishioners, caught up in the whole affair, were violently opposed to Romaine.

On 14 February, Romaine wrote to Mrs Medhurst with the latest developments, which in no way had dampened his zeal and love for Jesus:

I am nothing but a miracle of his goodness — the most astonishing that ever was! All, all from my first breath to this I am now drawing is mere mercy and grace, and so it will be for ever and for ever. My ministry is wonderful, that such a dumb dog should speak — such a very devil in flesh should feel what he says of that eternally precious Jesus, and be the means of making others feel it, and should have no doubt of feeling it blessedly to eternity. O what delightful views do these things give me of my sweetest Lord and dearest Jesus!

He seems willing I should preach more, and have a church in the city: but he will not let it come too easily, lest we should have whereof to glory. We are at law about it, and are like to be a great while, but in the meantime he is doing all things well. The very moment all things are ready, the church will be opened: and if it never is, he does not want me there, with which I am satisfied.[15]

He also wrote to his sister to keep her informed of the election and the state of his mind: 'My election is not ended about Blackfriars. Law goes on. But I am quite out of it. My mind is at peace... It is my one desire to please him; but how or where is not my business. He must look to that... If he want me to feed his sheep at Blackfriars, I shall go. If he does not, I trust I shall not go from him. Forbid it, Lord!'[16] Although he was trusting wholeheartedly in the Lord's leading, he was not completely 'out of it', for in one of his letters to Lady Huntingdon he asks for help with two Quakers named Webb, who had great power with the voters. He then mentions how his friends accuse him of being too easy. 'But I think not,' he says. 'Blackfriars' Church is desirable, but we cannot tell whether Jesus wants it or not; if he does, he will bring it about; if not, his will be done.'[17]

During this period of uncertainty he preached for Martin Madan at the Lock Chapel, where on 25 November 1764 Lord Dartmouth heard him preach 'an excellent sermon' from the words 'Adam, where art thou?', and apply its message in 'a very heart-searching and edifying manner'.[18] He also preached for Lady Huntingdon at Brighton, Ote Hall and at Bath after the chapel was opened in 1765, and travelled to Yorkshire to meet the Countess, preaching on his way at Bretby, Derbyshire, and other places. Romaine's connection with Lady Huntingdon provides an interesting picture of two strong individuals striving together in the common goal of glorifying God — the former by his zeal and diligence and the latter by her wealth and influence. It must be said too that Romaine was happy to preach in her chapels without any thought of remuneration. In fact, all he ever received from her was barely enough to pay his travelling expenses. This is not to say that the Countess was mean, quite the contrary, but the point has to be made to annul rumours that Romaine profited financially from his friendship with her. Haweis comments that neither Romaine nor Whitefield 'were ever a shoe-latchet the richer for any service done for her Ladyship'.[19]

In this connection it is worth mentioning that several of Romaine's letters at this period refer to Lady Buchan's legacy. Lady Isabella Erskine had died on 14 May 1763 and had left £800 for Romaine to distribute among the poor. The recipients were all to be of the Church of England and Romaine was bequeathed twenty guineas for his trouble. In one of his letters he speaks of how his heart ached when he was unable to help a poor prisoner, or a dissenter, with a wife and several children, because he was confined to church people. A rumour began to circulate that Romaine himself had inherited a 'very large legacy' from Lady Buchan. John Newton, who had first heard Romaine preach about 1750, wrote to Captain A. Clunie from Olney on 3 November 1764, at the height of the Blackfriars' election. Part of the letter concerns this rumour:

> You said that the Countess of Buchan left Mr R — ne a very large legacy. I doubt not but you was told so, and had reason for believing it. But as this report, if not true, may be in many respects to Mr R — ne's prejudice, I think it my duty to let you know that I have very good authority from a lady who is intimately acquainted with his circumstances, to believe it was otherwise.
>
> The money left him was wholly for charitable uses, except twenty pounds as a legacy for his trouble of distributing it; and that so far from being sole executor, he is not executor at all. If this is indeed the case, you will be glad to discountenance the other report, as it might deprive Mr R — ne of those assistances which I believe his family needs.[20]

Newton's main objective was to make sure that Romaine's much needed financial support was not suddenly cut off, but he may also have wanted to stop any rumours that could have proved detrimental to his election.

In April 1765 Romaine was in Brighton, being helped by Howel Davies and Peter Williams. On account of her son's illness in 1757 the Countess had left her house in Park Street, where Romaine had preached for several years, and travelled to Brighton. During her stay she had become seriously concerned for the spiritual welfare of its inhabitants and for those who visited the resort. Four years later (1761) she built a small chapel in North Street, which was opened by Martin Madan. She called her chaplains there, and Romaine spent his summer holidays in her ladyship's service. His ministry there was greatly blessed and large crowds, many of whom were converted, attended the chapel, which soon became too small to accommodate the people.

Many farmers and countrymen from Sussex were drawn to the chapel to sit under Romaine's ministry, and some were converted. Those who were born again urged the Countess to arrange for the gospel to be preached nearer to their homes. Just at that time an old gentleman and a justice of the peace by the name of Warden, who owned and occupied the mansion at Ote Hall, near Wivelsfield, which had formerly belonged to the Shirley family from which her ladyship descended, heard of her desire to carry the gospel into the wilds of Sussex. He waited on her in Brighton and offered his house for that purpose. She accepted and soon fitted up the large hall for a chapel and furnished the upper rooms for her own residence and for her ministers. By the end of 1761 it was open for worship. Romaine preached for her there and his ministry was 'blessed with some singular tokens of the divine favour'.

Early in 1765 the Countess, who was eager to introduce the gospel into Lewes, where her Brighton chaplains had already reaped fruit, obtained for Romaine one of the pulpits, and he preached from Galatians 6:17. Here his preaching gave 'great umbrage'. He 'afterwards preached in a large room and ultimately in the open fields'. Her ladyship said, 'All gave earnest heed while he applied those solemn words, "Behold the Lamb of God that taketh away the sins of the world." I did not see one careless or inattentive person, and there is reason to think that many poor sinners were cut to the heart.'[21]

In an undated letter to his sister, probably written in the summer of 1765, he mentions the continued success he was enjoying on the south coast: 'I am at Brighthelmstone, in Sussex, and shall not be gone till November. The Lord has been wonderfully with us here, and many souls are awakened. Some walking rejoicing in the Lord, and vast congregations.'[22] In 1774, the chapel was taken down and a larger chapel built, which was dedicated to God on 24 July and on which occasion Romaine preached in the morning from 1 Kings 8:11 and in the evening on John 1:14.

There is one occurrence at Ote Hall around 1765, possibly before, that is noteworthy. A captain in the dragoons by the name of Jonathan Scott, who claimed descent from the Scottish King John Balliol, was providentially led to hear Romaine preach. He was already, at least outwardly, a religious man — he read the Psalms on a daily basis and the lessons of the day, and strove to make himself righteous by his own works — but he had never experienced the saving grace of God.

Captain Scott happened to be quartered somewhere in the neighbourhood of Oathall, and ... being out on a shooting party, was driven by the rain for cover into the hovel of one of the peasants. There he found several labourers, who had taken shelter in the same cottage. He entered into conversation with them, and as religion was the subject in which he found them engaged, he put to them several questions, and heard them speak on divine subjects in a way that astonished him. This naturally produced the inquiry, where they had collected

Jonathan Scott.

their information and the sentiments they expressed;
they told him at the Hall yonder, where there was now
a very famous man, a Mr Romaine, preaching for Lady
Huntingdon, and they invited him to come and hear for
himself. This he determined to do the following Sunday.
Thither he accordingly repaired, and there the Lord met
him with the blessing of his grace. From that time the
happy change commenced, for which hundreds have
since reason to bless God, who have been called under
his ministry.[23]

Captain Scott was particularly struck with the solemnity of the
congregation and the impressive manner with which the service
was conducted. The words of Romaine, who preached from
John 14:6, were exactly suited to his case.

After being so impressed with Romaine, the captain was
anxious to talk with him:

He rode with him from preaching — was with him in the
house where he took some refreshment after preaching
— put himself at different times in his way — and made
use of all the means he could devise to bring about a

free intercourse. But all his attempts were ineffectual. Mr Romaine continued shy and distant...

Soon after this, Mr Scott was induced to visit his native place, Shrewsbury; and having to pass through London, a thought struck him, that he would wait upon Mr Romaine, to see (to use his own expression) whether there was any difference between the air of London and that of Brighthelmstone. He did so; and, to his great surprise, Mr Romaine received him with the utmost affability. He conversed with him in a very sweet and profitable way; and prayed most affectionally with and for him. Thus a most cordial intimacy commenced between these two eminently great, good, and useful men.[24]

On the captain's departure, Romaine asked him to deliver a letter, detailing his conversion, to Thomas Powys of Berwick in Shropshire. Powys, a friend of Lady Huntingdon's, was a rich and influential man, who was zealous for the cause of God and truth. At the time of Captain Scott's arrival in Berwick, he and his wife were enjoying the company of Henry Venn. They had just finished breakfast and family devotions, when they spotted the captain 'dressed in his uniform and riding his military horse'. Powys, who feared the captain would interrupt their time of fellowship, said, 'I am determined not to see him if I can avoid it.' And they quickly withdrew. However, the servant, who knew nothing of his master's reluctance to meet Scott, called Powys, who welcomed his guest 'with an air of distant civility'.

But after he had read Mr Romaine's letter, which he received with considerable agitation, giving an account of Mr Scott's conversion, he caught him in his arms, embraced and rejoiced over him as over one raised from the dead. In this position, with an elevated voice, he cried out, 'Mr Venn! Mr Venn! Mrs Powys! Mrs Powys! Come, come quickly! Here is Captain Scott, a convert to Christ, a new creature in Christ Jesus!' They both came, and

being informed of the contents of Mr Romaine's letter,
all three, in the joy of their hearts, embraced the penitent, and, in imitation of the angels in heaven, rejoiced
over him who had been dead, but was alive again; and
had been lost, but was found.[25]

Captain Scott remained in the army for some time, where he
proved 'a bold soldier of Jesus Christ'. John Fletcher, on meeting the captain, wrote to Lady Huntingdon, and said, 'For some
months he has exhorted his dragoons daily; for some weeks he
has preached publicly at Leicester in the Methodist meet-house,
in his regimentals, to numerous congregations, with good success... God keep him zealous and simple!'[26] His desire was to
preach the gospel, so in 1769 he sold his commission and went
to live in his wife's home in Shropshire, 'where he gathered an
Independent church, and from his base at Wollerton went out
on evangelistic tours which contributed to the founding of twenty-two Congregational churches in Shropshire, Staffordshire,
Cheshire and Lancashire'.[27] According to one admirer, he was
'the most pertinacious and successful of itinerant preachers' in
that part of the kingdom. He was also one of Whitefield's supplies at the Tabernacle for over twenty years, and it should be
'noticed, to the praise of Mr Romaine's liberality, that he not
only gave him encouragement to preach, but was particularly
active in bringing him to that place'.[28]

In 1765, Romaine sent to the press a short treatise entitled *The Scripture Doctrine of the Sacrament of the Lord's
Supper*, which was drawn up at the request of a charitable
lady, and published for the benefit of the poor. Its aim was to
open the nature and use of the sacrament in a short and simple
way so that it might be easily understood and remembered. In
the same year Romaine wrote a recommendatory preface for
William Mason's *A Spiritual Treasury*, a work that consists of a
meditation for each day of the year taken from selected texts of
Scripture. Mason was a Christian businessman and magistrate,
and a loyal supporter of Romaine throughout the Blackfriars'

William Mason.

affair. In his preface of 13 June 1765 Romaine wrote: 'I have found a sweet savour of Jesus' precious name, free grace and perfect salvation, in these meditations; and therefore I am persuaded it will be doing thee great service to recommend them to thy perusal.'[29]

Romaine wrote forewords to several of Mason's publications, including *The Christian Communicant*, in which he says, 'Very heartily do I agree with my friend Mason ... where he wishes for an increase of that Gospel spirit which makes less of outward things and more of Christ... The subject here treated of is one of the deep things of God, of which none can write as Mr Mason has, unless he be in his heart alive to God.'[30] Mason's pamphlet *Methodism Displayed and Enthusiasm Detected*, intended as an 'antidote against the delusive principles and unscriptural doctrines of a modern set of seducing preachers, and as a defence of our regular and orthodox clergy from their unjust reflections', is addressed to Romaine; and in the memoir of Mason in *The Evangelical Magazine* (1794), the author says that Mason had the 'happiness to class among his dearest friends the Rev Mr Romaine, for whom, to the day of his death, he ever expressed the most sincere regard, having sat for many years under his ministry'.[31]

The Countess of Huntingdon continued to look for new opportunities to spread the gospel and during 1764 she decided to erect a chapel at Bath. While it was being built, she accepted the offer of Lord Chesterfield to occupy his house and chapel at Bretby Hall, in Derbyshire, for the sake of the gospel. She called Romaine, but he could not go straight away. Instead, Joseph Townsend of Pewsey, William Jesse of West Bromwich and later Whitefield preached to large crowds in the chapel and in the open air. Meanwhile, on 13 July 1765, Romaine wrote to a friend from Lambeth about the Blackfriars' delay: 'My cause has been to be heard from day to day, before my lord chancellor, but put off, and yesterday was put off to the next term.'[32] At about the beginning of August, while in Hartlepool, he was

St Werburgh's Church.

alarmed by news from London that 'Dr Griffith thought my wife was sick unto death, and he had no hopes of her recovery.' He set out immediately and did not stop until he arrived in London, where he 'found things as bad as I had been made to believe; but Dr Griffith gave her something, to which the Lord gave his blessing; and it abated the fury of her distemper, God having mercy on her and on me also'.[33]

When his wife was better and with her blessing he journeyed to Derby, where the people 'flowed in from every quarter, and filled the chapel and court', but he refused to be a 'field preacher', so the crowd only heard what they could gather from the pulpit. Writing on 20 August he mentioned other opportunities: 'We had ... a most refreshing time. Fifteen pulpits were open [including at the great church and St Werburgh's]. Showers of grace came down. Sinners in great numbers awakened and believers comforted.' He stayed to preach all week and especially on the Sunday was 'much opposed by the mayor and the churchwardens, and the Arian party; but the Lord stood by me'.[34]

These 'fifteen pulpits' were not open to Whitefield, for he was too 'irregular' for the Derbyshire clergy, but he had 'roused their people so, that it became good policy to admit Romaine'. It was also a novelty to find Lord Chesterfield 'patronizing religion; and therefore wise to make the most of his sanction whilst he was in the humour. Romaine did well in continuing regular. But for that, he would have been less useful. It enabled him to introduce the gospel into churches, where there was no leaven in the whole lump.'[35]

It may have been as a result of Romaine's visit to Derby in 1765 that the following conversation took place:

A gentleman from London [Zachary Shrapnell, a pious man and a great friend of Lady Huntingdon's] visiting the peak of Derby, in his rambles fell upon a cottage, where he accosted a good woman, and being himself zealously attached to Mr Romaine's ministry, under which ... he was called to the knowledge of the truth, he entered into conversation with her, and was surprised to find her vastly intelligent in the things of God, and happily informed of all the characteristic doctrines of the gospel. He inquired if it was preached in the neighbourhood, and if there were many professors around her.

She said, 'Alas, no. I have not a creature of the same mind to converse with; am quite alone: those I hear and converse with seem to know nothing of the grace of God in truth.'

'And pray,' said Mr S[hrapnell], 'how came you to know it?'

'Why, sir,' she replied, 'some time ago there was a famous man down in this country called Mr Romaine; he preached some miles off, and many of the neighbours went to hear him: so I thought I would go too. Accordingly, away I trudged. And he had no sooner begun his discourse, but it seemed all directed to me: he opened the depravity of my heart and nature, con-

vinced my conscience of the sinful condition in which I
had been living, showed me the wages of death which
was due to me, and the truth of it I felt in my own soul.
He then opened the fulness and glory of Christ, described his sufferings and passion, and the design of
them, displayed the riches of his grace to the miserable
and the desperate, and invited them to embrace it and
be blessed. Sir, you cannot think the instantaneous and
wonderful effect it had upon me. I was convinced of sin,
justified by faith, and came home rejoicing: and from
that day to this have never lost the sweet savour of the
truths I there embraced. How I should long to hear the
gentleman. Do you know him? I think they said he came
from London.[36]

No doubt Shrapnell's heart leapt for joy as he heard this account
of the far-reaching blessing that rested on Romaine's ministry.

In the meantime, the Countess had been recalled to Bath
to attend to Judith Wordsworth, the sister of Joseph Townsend,
rector of Pewsey, and for many years the close friend and correspondent of Romaine. In January 1771 she married Thomas
Haweis. In one of Romaine's previously unpublished letters
to Miss Wordsworth, written from Lambeth on 27 September
1764, at the start of the Blackfriars' saga, he mentions the ef-
fectiveness of the 'medicines of the Lord':

We have a very distressing time of it, and were it not
for the many rich cordials suited to such a time, what
should we do? That ever adorable physician, whose
skill is matchless, has given us a receipt for every distress, and you know he is infallible. Did you ever follow
his advice, and fail of relief? Never, no never will you.
His medicines have such a divine effect that it's worth
being sick to have the pleasure of taking them! He mix-
es them up with so much judgment, that they have the
wonderful property of turning pain into happiness, and

> when they do not effect this presently, yet they are most
> surely bringing it about: which makes us bear the bitter
> taste in the mouth, yea and perhaps a little sickness at
> the stomach, because we know that this good physic
> will make us perfectly and eternally whole.
>
> You may have heard of my having tried in my day
> some of these bitter draughts, and I give it you under my
> hand and am ready to take my oath of it, that they never
> once failed of curing me.[37]

As in all his letters he extols the wonderful name of Jesus: 'One
day you'll see all his dealings with you pure mercy, free grace,
rich love. Oh that you may by faith see it more every day!...
Truly it's lost time to talk of anything but that dearest Jesus — oh
... love him — There's enough in him to make Brother Joseph's
[Townsend] heart leap for joy. I wish him all usefulness to live,
to preach, to think ... to do all to Jesus glory.'[38]

While in Bath, Lady Huntingdon invited her ministers to
participate in the opening services of her chapel. Romaine was
willing to attend, but many pulpits were available to him in
Yorkshire and he was enjoying equal success at Ote Hall and
Brighton, so he wrote to her ladyship on 11 September 1765,
saying,

> We have very sweet meetings, and a great revival of
> work, especially at Oathall. The hearers there are very
> hungry, and the bread of life has a delightful relish. On
> Sunday night, although it rained fast till about twelve
> o'clock, the congregation was very large, and the chapel
> and porch were quite full. I stayed to converse with the
> society, and preached again in the afternoon to them, and
> I verily think there are many truly awakened souls among
> them. Last Sunday was very fine, and the congregation
> far more than I had ever seen it at Oathall...
>
> I could wish, now that I am among the people, to stay

as long as I can with them. This is a very awful time. We have had four sudden deaths, which have greatly alarmed the careless. There is much stir, both among the gentry and the common people, and they crowd to hear. Our constant congregations are as numerous as they used to be on Sunday nights, and I find my own heart much in the work and more strongly attached than ever to this place; and the society most earnestly entreat you, if Mr Madan should come down to Bath, that I may be suffered to stay here with them. Why should we both be there at the same time, to stand in one another's way? Why should Bath have all, poor Brighton none?[39]

Madan could not attend so Lady Huntingdon wrote again to Romaine, pressing him to attend. He replied on 1 October 1765: 'I must openly tell you that my very heart and soul are now in this work; inasmuch that I have not minded going to Oathall wet to the skin, for the joy that was set before me.'[40] Lady Huntingdon did not insist, so Romaine remained at Ote Hall. Five days after Romaine's letter, the chapel at Bath, crowded with both aristocracy and ordinary citizens, was dedicated to God. Whitefield, who preached in the morning, reported: 'The great Shepherd and Bishop of souls consecrated and made it holy ground by his presence.'[41]

On 1 November 1765 Romaine was back in Brighton 'among a sweet people', with whom he was 'exceedingly happy'. 'The work of dear Jesus prospers among us,' he reports. 'His person grows more beloved, his work more precious, fellowship with him more close and intimate, and therefore more happy. Our hearts, warmed with his love, are warm with brotherly love; stirring up one another to press forward for the prize of our high calling, that is, to win Christ, and be found in him at the hour of death, and at the day of judgment.'[42] Five days later, in a letter to his sister, he shares the latest news about Blackfriars and his attitude towards it:

You ask about Blackfriars; the cause stands still. It was to have been heard the first day of this term, but the lawyers were not ready. They begged for more time, and my lord chancellor granted it to them. When it will come on now I cannot tell. But I can tell much of Jesus' goodness to me. He does not let all this waiting time be lost. He is teaching me to make up all my happiness in himself, and is kindly cutting off one and another view of rest short of him, who is our only rest... What he takes from me, I gain most by. For I am an immense, yea, an eternal gainer, when he fills up with himself the want of that which he takes away. Whatever brings me this blessing, I can welcome it. Welcome the loss of Blackfriars. Welcome every cross which brings me nearer to my Jesus, and makes me live in stricter fellowship with him.[43]

On 25 November he was enjoying the blessing of God at St Dunstan's:

Last night St Dunstan's was a very Bethel [he wrote to a friend]; it was like the dedication of the temple, when the glory of Jehovah came down and filled the house. I was preaching on these words: 'My meditation of him shall be sweet.' And so it was indeed... O what a seal did he set to this preached gospel! He made it the power of God. The meditation of his goodness yesterday has still a relish and delightful savour; today it is sweet, very, very sweet indeed.[44]

He had a similar blessing at Christmas, when he experienced 'a most remarkable time ... of his grace and love. I have scarce an acquaintance,' he enthuses to a friend, 'who has not been favoured with blessed visits from him. O how great is his goodness! How great is his beauty! Incomparable both! May your dear heart, my friend, feel what I did at the Lock on Innocents'

Day [28 December] when I was preaching on these words of
Psalm 87: "All my springs are in thee."'[45]

Romaine wrote to a friend on 16 January 1766, saying,
'Nothing is yet done at Blackfriars: but Jesus does all things
well, he times all things for the best; I am sure of it; therefore I
wait my Lord's time, and blessed waiting it is.'[46] At last on 28
January Lord Chancellor Henley decreed in favour of Romaine.
'It was the opinion of the court, that the inhabitants had no right
to reduce the number of candidates at the first election, which
of course made it void; and on the second election, in which
the only candidates were the Rev Mr Romaine and the Rev Mr
Smith, the former had the majority.'[47] Romaine immediately
wrote to his sister, informing her, with great humility,

> ... that this day my cause about Blackfriars was finally
> determined, and in my favour. I have retired and been
> alone this afternoon to abase myself. This is to me an
> amazing event. That such a one should be made a pas-
> tor; one that is plagued to death with his own heart, to
> make him a watchman over others! What is the Lord
> doing? With the utmost abhorrence of myself, and of my
> being unfit to be minister of a great parish, in the midst
> of this great city — I have been forced to leave it to the
> Lord...
>
> I give you this notice, to pray your Master and my
> Master to fit me for this new work. He knows my heart, I
> never had one desire for this new work, but that I might
> have more room to glorify Jesus... Beg of him to help
> me to exalt him, and to keep me down.[48]

He also described his thoughts and feelings at the enormity of the
task and responsibility in a letter to Lady Huntingdon on the decision in chancery:

> My friends are rejoicing all around me, and wishing me
> that joy which I cannot take. It is my Master's will, and

I submit. He knows what is best, both for his own glory, and his people's good. And I am certain he makes no mistakes in either of these points. But my head hangs down upon the occasion, through the awful apprehensions which I ever had of the care of souls. I am frightened to think of watching over two or three thousand, when it is work enough to watch over one. The plague of my own heart almost wearies me to death; what can I do with such a vast number? Besides, I had promised myself a little rest and retirement in the evening of life, and had already sat down with a SOUL, TAKE THINE EASE. And lo! my fine plan is broken all to pieces. I am called into a public station, and to the sharpest engagement, just as I had got into winter quarters — an engagement for life. I can see nothing before me, so long as the breath is in my body, but war — and that with unreasonable men — a divided parish, an angry clergy, a wicked Sodom, and a wicked world; all to be resisted and overcome. Besides all these, a sworn enemy, subtle and cruel, with whom I can make no peace, no not a moment's truce, night and day, with all his children, and his host, is aiming at my destruction.

When I take counsel of the flesh, I begin to faint; but when I go to the sanctuary I see my cause good, and my master is Almighty — a tried friend, and then he makes my courage revive. Although I am no way fit for the work, yet he called me to it, and on him I depend for strength to do it, and for success to crown it. I utterly despair of doing anything as of myself, and therefore the more I have to do, I shall be forced to live more by faith upon him. In this view I hope to get a great income by my LIVING — I shall want my Jesus more, and shall get closer to him. As he has made my application to him more necessary and more constant, he has given me stronger tokens of his love. Methinks I can hear his

> sweet voice — *Come closer, come closer, soul! Nearer yet; I will bring you into circumstances, that you cannot do one moment without me.*[49]

These were the views with which he entered into this new work.

On 25 February 1766 he finally took possession of the living of St Ann's Blackfriars, accompanied by the officers of the parish, and with the usual ceremonies of locking the pulpit and ringing a bell, after which he read prayers. The following day he was inducted and was observed 'to tremble much during the whole ceremony of his admission'. His actual service did not begin until Sunday 2 March. He had served the Church of England for nearly thirty-four years without a benefice. Now at last he had his own church, and large were the numbers that attended his ministry — the communicants on his 'first Good Friday rose to the unprecedented number of five hundred, and on Easter Day there were as many as three hundred'.[50]

There was great rejoicing at his appointment, particularly from Lady Huntingdon, who had worked so hard for his success. 'Through the gracious hand of God,' she says, 'my dear and excellent Romaine has at length succeeded, and the decision of the lord chancellor has put to silence the evil clamours of his unreasonable opponents.'[51] William Jesse of West Bromwich, who was then at Ote Hall with the Countess comments, 'We have had quite a little jubilee on the confirmation of the validity of our dear brother Romaine's election. Never have I seen more heartfelt joy and gratitude than was expressed on that occasion by her Ladyship. I verily believe that if Mr Romaine had not gained his election the disappointment and vexation would have well nigh killed her.'[52] Another who had fought strongly for his election was a certain publican. *The Evangelical Magazine* goes as far as to say that his election was 'principally owing to the influence' of this man. When Romaine found out about his support he went to thank him and received the following reply:

'Indeed, Sir, I am more indebted to you than you to me; for you have made my wife, who was one of the worst, the best woman in the world.'[53]

Romaine knew that the task ahead was not going to be easy. On 15 November 1766, after nine months at Blackfriars, he complained,

> A temper directly contrary to the Christian is spreading among professors. I see the delusion grow, and I am a witness to the baneful effects of it. How many have you and I heard of who want to be something in themselves, and, rather than not be so, will be beholden to Christ to set them up with a stock of grace! They would gladly receive a talent from him, that, by being faithful to grace given, and trading well with it, they may look with delight on their improvements, and thereby hope to get more grace and more glory. This is the Popish plan, the Arminian — very flattering to nature, exceedingly pleasing to self-righteousness, very exalting, yea, it is crowning *free will*, and debasing King Jesus.[54]

But with God's help he was going to be a light in the darkness and a voice of truth in the wilderness, to 'preach not ourselves, but Christ Jesus the Lord'. His appointment was a turning point, not only in his own ministry, but in the revival itself in London, where the Establishment now had an evangelical clergyman with his own church. Davis rightly says, 'Blackfriars Church became a rallying centre for the evangelicals in London, and from it Romaine's influence emanated to every part of England.'[55]

As rector of a London parish, Romaine became a rallying point for all in London who loved evangelical truth in the Church of England. Man after man, and family after family, gathered round his pulpit, until his congregation became the nucleus of a vast amount of good in the metropolis. His constant, unflinching declaration of Christ's whole truth insensibly produced a powerful impression on men's minds, and made them understand what a true clergyman of the Church of England ought to be... The good that he did, as rector of Blackfriars, though less showy, was probably more solid and permanent than the good that he did all the rest of his life.

J. C. Ryle.[1]

11

'A Single Eye to his Glory'

A new and larger sphere of usefulness was now open to Romaine at Blackfriars, where his popular talents and godliness filled the church with a congregation that listened to him with uncommon reverence and attention. Even the parishioners who did not attend church were blessed by his conduct and zeal for the gospel, and those who opposed him were less vocal. His undeniable learning made him a clergyman who demanded respect and an adversary few wanted to challenge. The geographical position of Blackfriars also gave him 'peculiar advantages', as Ryle notes. 'Almost within sight both of St Paul's and Westminster Abbey, he held a post from which he was always ready to go forth and do battle, either with tongue or pen. If error arose rampant, he was on the spot prepared to attack it. If truth was assaulted, he was equally prepared to sally forth and defend it.'[2]

The parsonage house into which he moved and which had been turned into a warehouse some time before needed wholesale repairs to make it fit for the residence of a pastor. So in the same year as he was instituted to Blackfriars he demolished the old premises and built for himself a new rectory house on St Andrew's Hill close to the church. In 1768 he moved in. The church itself, when he took possession of the living, was surrounded by a high 'dead wall', and the paths leading to it were very narrow. His parishioners were prevailed upon to make all the necessary repairs and alterations: to pull down the high wall so as to give the church more light and air, and to widen the paths leading to it. In 1774, they built a substantial gallery at the west end to accommodate the large congregation, and Blackfriars became one of the grandest places of worship in London. Romaine, who never asked any favour for himself, urged his friends who attended the church to present the united parishes with a token of their gratitude. This request was eagerly complied with, and the total collected towards defraying the expenses of erecting the gallery, and other improvements, was £500, which the parishes acknowledged with an inscription over the west door:

> This church was repaired and beautified Anno Dom:
> 1774,
> at the great expense of the united parishes, and the
> generous
> contribution of the congregation.
> The Rev William Romaine, M.A. rector
> of St Andrew-by-the-Wardrobe
> of St Ann's Blackfriars
> Charles Griffiths
> John Holton
> Thomas Cook
> John Davis
> Church wardens.
> Love as brethren.[3]

Romaine was concerned with the 'bricks and mortar' of his new parish, but he was more interested in the individuals who lived in it. The poor especially found in him a father and a friend. Large sums of money from the communion offerings, collections and other donations were distributed among them. The annual collections for the schools in the ward and the under-privileged in the parish, made at the weekly sacraments, which he instituted, and after charity sermons, which he preached, amounted on average to £300 a year. When he first came to the church, two pew-openers were employed in the church; when he died, the number had risen to eight, each able to live comfortably on what was given them by the congregation, without any further assistance from the parish.

Within the first few months of his Blackfriars' ministry he was calling his parishioners to support Eleaser Wheelock's Christian missionary school at Lebanon in Connecticut, which needed the money for both missions and poor relief. King George III subscribed £200 and Lord Dartmouth became the principal trustee for the British funds. Whitefield was a great supporter and in one of his letters he mentions how Romaine 'has preached and collected a hundred pounds'. Not everyone was so enthusiastic, however. The editors of the *Gentleman's Magazine* were unhappy that the money was going abroad and not helping the needy at home. In April 1766 they wrote: 'It is said, the Rev Mr Romaine, after one sermon only, collected £1001 12s 5d for an American charity; and were that pious divine, as well as others, to turn their thoughts to the increase of a fund for providing for the orphans of their poor deceased brethren, the good resulting from it would be its own reward.'[4] Such criticism did not deter him, for in the following year he was in Leeds, Huddersfield and Kippax advocating the school's cause.

He also gave liberally to various charities, such as the *Humane Society*, for which he preached annually for seventeen years. From a conviction of the usefulness of this institution he preached a voluntary sermon for them at Blackfriars in 1771. He observed 'that not only the lives, but the souls of some of his parishioners had been saved by the means of it; that their miraculous recovery made them serious; that their seriousness brought them to church; that the Lord of the church met them there, and gave them the spirit of faith, while they were hearing of his name'.[5] His sermons usually raised £30, and enlisted two or three new annual subscribers.

In addition, he supported the *Bible Society*, an institution
that distributed the Word of God among soldiers and sailors. He
preached on its behalf in his own and other churches in London,
and in different places in the country during his summer travels.
By this means he was a great benefactor to it every year. He
was also keen to provide for individuals who did not belong to
the Church of England. Thomas Wills, in *The Dying Believer*,
mentions that when Romaine was entrusted with a sum of money for distribution among poor debtors in prison and limited
to those of the Establishment, it 'cut him to the heart, when
he saw any dissenter in the same situation, with large families
also, and was prevented from assisting them in like manner'.[6]
When the clergy were asked to collect in their own parishes
for the 'unfortunate victims of the bloody Republic of France',
he was touched by their distresses and did all he could to support them. He preached at Blackfriars and made a collection
for them — actions that were heavily condemned by those who
claimed that 'to relieve the distresses of a papist was to encourage the errors of popery'.

Rarely was there an occasion when he did not call on his
hearers to contribute to the cause of the needy. He helped the
unemployed and distressed Spitalfields weavers by preaching
a sermon for them and collecting £109, which he paid into the
fund raised for their relief. After the fire on Ludgate Hill (1793),
which consumed several houses in the Blackfriars' parish, the
poor received several hundred pounds from Romaine, who was
an eye-witness to the tragedy. At half past three in the morning,
when the fire was raging, and again at nine o'clock, he called on
one of his wealthy parishioners, anxious to know what could be
done for the sufferers.

> He commissioned his friend to give them something
> for their immediate relief; and accordingly two guineas
> were given to each sufferer, to the amount of about
> ninety guineas... Mr Romaine made himself responsible
> for this sum. [The next day he went from house to house

— to his parishioners and private friends — in order to reimburse his wealthy parishioner the amount he had lent.] On the mornings of the Sunday and Tuesday following he pleaded from the pulpit for his poor parishioners, who had been burnt out of their houses, and lost their all. The sum raised upon this occasion, added to a donation of fifty pounds from his Royal Highness the Duke of York, amounted to upwards of three hundred pounds, which, together with a collection made by the inhabitants of Ludgate Hill, enabled Mr Romaine to distribute to the poor sufferers from ten to eighteen pounds a piece.[7]

With all that has been said, it is not surprising that one of Romaine's friends asked, 'What minister of this day, or for forty years past, has laid out himself more for the support of public charities of every kind, by preaching sermons for them, and by using his influence in various other ways, than he has done?'[8]

At the beginning of each year Romaine usually preached a sermon from a single Hebrew word, such as *Shiloh* or *Hosannah*, or from a 'motto' text, on which his congregation could meditate throughout the year. On Whitsun Monday he addressed the youth of his congregation and on Tuesday the aged. Both were 'very affecting seasons'. He also remembered the anniversary of his election to Blackfriars, when he reported on the progress of the gospel throughout the kingdom, and on the increase of evangelical ministers and their respective congregations. When he considered the spiritual state of the church, he gave thanks to God, who had 'made [him] the instrument of setting up the standard, and enlarging the circle of evangelical light and truth'.[9] In addition to the above, he set up a weekly lecture at Blackfriars on Tuesday mornings, which was well attended, and which was sometimes taken by other preachers, such as Thomas Haweis. His communion services, which brought delight to many, were also crowded with people from all over London, who, because of the numbers, had to be served by four ministers.

In order to encourage his hearers to adhere to the doctrines and discipline of the Church of England, and to continue in her communion, he preached a course of sermons on the Thirty-Nine Articles, during which he received a petition from his church wardens and parishioners to print and publish them 'for the interest of religion in general, and for our benefit in particular'. The petition, which was found among Romaine's papers, was signed by twenty-nine men and women. Unfortunately, for reasons unknown, it was not complied with.

It seems that his ministry at Blackfriars, from the outset, was peculiarly blessed. From Lambeth in 1767 he wrote to his sister: 'Through mercy, I am going on very well... He is very near me, and he makes himself very dear. He still smiles on our meetings, and is in the midst of us. Blackfriars is owned by him. He has set to his seal that God is there.' And again, on 21 February of that year, he reports: 'Here is good news of the increasing kingdom of Jesus. More ministers, especially, are raised up. We have more awakenings among us. More refreshing times. Things wear a very promising aspect. Thanks for these blessings! May they bring down more!' And yet, in spite of these blessings, he yearned for a deeper experience of God: 'I want nothing but more capacity to praise and to enjoy Jesus... Oh for more of his presence to fill the ordinances with life and power.'[10]

The work of his parish and pulpit absorbed much of his time and attention, but in the summer months, with many of his parishioners out of London, he had the opportunity to preach elsewhere. In the summer of 1766 he travelled to Brighton, where he became friendly with Thomas Powys of Berwick, Shropshire, who was visiting. He also spent time at Ote Hall and later with Richard Conyers at Helmsley in Yorkshire, before he moved on to Bath, where he supplied Martin Madan's place for October and the first part of November, preaching alternately with Whitefield at Lady Huntingdon's chapel to 'very numerous and attentive auditories'. Henry Venn was just one of those who heard him on his travels. Writing to Miss Wheler of Kippax in November 1766, he mentions how he had heard

Romaine at Bath, 'in that most plain but elegant chapel of Lady Huntingdon. He was very well attended on the week-days; but on Sundays the chapel is crowded.'[11] In a letter he wrote from Lambeth, 15 November 1766, Romaine says, 'I have been in a more preaching way this summer than I ever was in my life, and travelled much more, and have had with me a sweet savour of Jesus' dear name. O he is precious to my soul.'[12]

On 26 March 1767, Romaine wrote to Lady Huntingdon, informing her that he was present 'in spirit' at the re-opening of her Brighton chapel. He could not be with her because his curate had left and he was 'without an assistant'. 'The parochial duty tires me quite, and I would not go through it, but that I am perfectly satisfied it was the will of God I should have this church.' He goes on to mention his work at Blackfriars and how the appointment made it more difficult, but not impossible, for him to preach for her ladyship:

> As sure as ever any man had a call from heaven this was one. I have been long satisfied of this: and, therefore, I may not reason nor now complain. My time is short; I must up and be doing; for I have a home prospect, bounded in very narrow limits. I must go briskly on with my work, leaving it to my Lord to find me strength for it, and success in it; his blessing I expect here, and for ever; not for anything done at Blackfriars; and yet I would labour as hard as if heaven were to be the reward of my labours. When I was allowed more time and liberty, I gladly laid them out in your part of the vineyard, and what I can spare so I hope to do again. The people are very dear to me at Brighton and Oathall, having been so much with them, and personally acquainted with most of their experiences. I shall be amongst you in all your meetings, and shall keep up with you the communion of saints. May much life and power be with ministers and people, and may the chapel be consecrated anew by the presence and glory of the Lord Jesus which have so often filled it.[13]

Romaine's first responsibility was to his parishioners in London, so it is understandable that he could not preach for her lady-ship as frequently as before; although, during the early years of his Blackfriars' ministry, he continued to preach for her in the chapel near London and elsewhere. Lady Glenorchy, who, like the Countess, founded preaching places in both England and Scotland, was deeply influenced by his preaching. Seymour states that the 'excellent advice and heart-searching conversa-tion of the Countess, united with the preaching of Mr Madan, Mr Romaine ... contributed to establish and confirm her in the faith and hope of the gospel'.[14]

On 24 June 1767, Romaine's sister Dorothy, who was con-verted in 1762, married John Heslup of Whorlton, Yorkshire. The ceremony seems to have been hastily arranged, for three days after the wedding Romaine wrote to his sister, saying, 'As to your own connections, you are of age, and the best judge. Whatever you do, my prayers and best wishes shall attend you, married or unmarried.'[15] John Heslup was one of Wesley's lay preachers, who, according to Telford, incurred the wrath of Wesley, for 'paying attention to a lady' at Yarm. Wesley wrote to George Merryweather on 26 September 1768, 'I desire John Heslup may preach at Yarm no more. Quietly let him sink into nothing. And the less he preaches in other places the better till he comes again to his senses.'[16] The following month he wrote to Christopher Hopper and said of Heslup: 'The poor man is an incorrigible coxcomb. His last exploit with Mr Oastler's niece has pinned the casket. I cannot imagine what can be done with him or how he can be trusted anywhere.'[17] In his letters to his sister, Romaine always remembered Heslup, and offered advice concerning his walk with God.

There were many others who were converted through Romaine's ministry or instructed in the ways of God more perfectly by him, who afterwards went into the ministry them-selves. Many of his curates, whom he employed to assist him at Blackfriars, were carefully guided by him in spiritual things. One of them, Erasmus Middleton, well known as the author of

Lady Glenorchy.

Erasmus Middleton.

Biographia Evangelica, most of which he wrote while working for Romaine, followed Romaine in 'reintroducing the old evangelical spirit of the pre-Laudian Reformed Church of England into the post-Restoration church'. He worked closely with the leaders of the revival and was always willing to acknowledge, 'with great pleasure and gratitude', the 'kindness of my ever-valued and respected friend and rector', William Romaine,[18] whom he served from 1777-1785. William Ley, John Moore, Christopher Bassett, Henry Foster and John Foss were also Romaine's curates, and his last, William Goode, became his worthy successor (1795-1815). Goode's successor was Isaac Saunders (1815-1836), and he was followed by John Harding (1836-1851), all three of whom were Oxford evangelicals.

Initially, it seems that finding a settled curate was not easy. He complained to his sister on 27 June 1767 that he had been 'disappointed of three curates. At present I am without one; and I know not when I shall get one to my mind.'[19] By August the situation had been resolved, for he wrote two letters to his new curate Henry Foster, to whom he gave a title for orders. Both letters express succinctly Romaine's idea of his own situation and the duties incumbent on a candidate for holy orders. The first is dated Lambeth, 4 August 1767:

> In this whole affair I have desired simply to follow what is right, and to aim at the divine glory; and if I know my own heart (which is not easily known), my eye is single in your coming to me. I desire your good, and not mine own... I would have my church a nursery, where such as you may grow, till you are fit to be planted out, and when fit, I would not keep you a day, but rather use my interest to provide some preferment for you. This is my plan, my title, and my pulpit, and what I have in consequence of the Lord's sending me to Blackfriars. I have them for the Lord, and I beg grace of him that I may employ them so as shall be most to his glory...

Henry Foster.

I hope you will not forget me in your addresses to the throne of grace, and if I may give my advice, it is needful for you at present to be much in prayer for these graces:

First, for the right knowledge of yourself — your vileness.

Secondly, for the right knowledge of Jesus — his glory.

Thirdly, for a single eye to his glory in your taking upon you to be his minister and servant in holy things.

Fourthly, for a love to souls. When you know much of his love in saving your soul, that will make you labour much for Jesus, in trying to set forward the salvation of others.

And lastly, you should beg of God, and be always begging as long as you live, for an entire dependence upon the Lord to bless you in his work. We toil all night and day, and catch nothing, till the Lord bless the gospel net. The Lord bless it in you and by you, so prays your real friend and servant,

WILLIAM ROMAINE.[20]

Foster had expected to be ordained on Trinity Sunday, but was disappointed and had to wait until September. In the meantime, he received a second letter from Romaine in which his rector shared some of his own struggles and the faithfulness of God towards him:

> It was not without good reason that the Lord would not suffer you to be ordained last Trinity. He had much to teach you in these months, and I hope you have been a good scholar. He wanted to teach you your absolute un- fitness for the work of the ministry, and thereby to bring you to an entire dependence upon him. You cannot love the work, nor be successful in it, nor, upon succeed- ing, give him all the glory, but through his grace... It is very hard to learn, for I am still at it every day, and get but little ground. Self, proud self is such a dull scholar, and has such a bad memory, that though I am satisfied today Christ must do all for me, and all in me, and all by me too, yet I soon forget, and soon want to be some- thing in the work myself; but I do know, and, blessed be the name of Jesus, I do experience that his grace is sufficient for me; chiefly in the pulling down of my pride, and in making me willing to be nothing, that Christ may be ALL. May he pour out upon you and me more of his Spirit, to lay self very low, and to exalt the Saviour.[21]

In another letter that Romaine wrote on 11 August 1767 to an unidentified recipient seeking ordination, he again focuses the attention on the Lord. 'If the great Lord and head pleases, here is a door given for you into the Establishment, and may it be effectual. I hope your eye is single in this matter. Jesus' glory is your end and aim — episcopally ordained, or not. Keep that in view — let him send you how and where he pleases. It is good to go, to run his errands. He pays well. I never lost anything by him.'[22]

On 30 April 1768, Ingham's wife, Lady Margaret, died. Romaine, in a letter to Mrs Medhurst in May, wrote about the times his spirit had been refreshed by Lady Margaret's lively faith. These times of 'refreshment' were fairly common in Romaine's experience, for even as he was putting pen to paper, he exclaimed, 'O what a sight and sense had I of the incomparable grace of life giving Jesus! While I am writing, he makes himself, beyond what any words can describe, lovely to my eyes, and precious to my heart. He is my life; I find it, enjoy it in him.'[23]

In the same year that Lady Margaret died, Romaine, along with Whitefield, Wesley and Madan, was on the receiving end of a satirical work by James Murray of High Bridge Chapel, Newcastle, called *Sermons to Asses*. In his dedication to 'the very excellent and reverend Mess G. W. [George Whitefield], J. W. [John Wesley], W. R. [William Romaine] and M. M. [Martin Madan]', Murray says, 'There are no persons in Britain so worthy of a dedication of a work of this kind as yourselves. Some of you have preached for many years to the members of congregations that these sermons are designed for — and all of you, as far as your influence can reach, wish well to asses.'[24] Murray goes on in the preface to say that they will 'perhaps be offended at the author, for interfering in their employment, and preaching to their congregations. But this much the author may say for himself, that he has not preached after their manner; — and to make them some satisfaction, has given them the honour of a dedication.'[25] Romaine was far too busy to answer such ridicule.

Romaine and Lady Huntingdon were still interactive at this time. When the Countess was considering establishing a college at Trevecca in Wales to train men for the ministry, Romaine was very much in her initial plans. He was one of the ministers, along with Whitefield, Wesley and Venn, who drew up and approved the proposals for the examination of young men who might be suitable candidates for the college. Later, as the students were sent out to preach the gospel, the Countess often reported to her London friend the results of their tours. One of

Trevecca College.

these reports included an account of how Joseph Milner had been convinced of the 'great necessity he was under of securing an interest in Christ' after hearing Trevecca students at Hull.[26] Milner's conversion was 'one of the most important factors that led to a widespread work of God in that city'.[27]

In the summer of 1768, after the Countess had travelled to Brighton, Romaine, on the 11 June, wrote in support of her work: 'Our dear fellow soldier, Lady Huntingdon, fights bravely... She is happy in the adorable Emmanuel, and lives to him and for him. Her only view in Sussex is to carry glad tidings to a wretchedly ignorant people. He has hitherto prospered her design, and while he smiles upon it I believe she will never give it up.'[28] In the first three months of 1769 he often assembled with Venn, Whitefield and the Wesleys at Lady Huntingdon's London home for preaching and Christian fellowship. At their last meeting the doxology was sung 'with uncommon fervour and devotion, and all separated with a deeper sense of their mercies, and of their infinite obligations to the Lord Jesus Christ'.

During the eighteenth century there was a daily fight against diseases such as smallpox, which in turn led to a serious debate on the pros and cons of inoculation. Smallpox, it is said, increased in London after 1770, 'because inoculation, though a protection to the inoculated, spread the disease owing to ineffective isolation'.[29] According to Howlett, in villages and provincial towns inoculation had the opposite effect. Writing in 1781, he says, 'When an epidemic appears inoculation takes place at once... Where two or three hundred used to be buried in a few months, now perhaps not more than twenty or thirty.'[30] In a letter written from Blackfriars, 2 May 1769, Romaine gives his opinion on inoculation by relating the case of a doctor of divinity and his wife, who disagreed about inoculating their only son. 'The doctor said he could not do it in faith; the wife said she could do it, because she believed it to be for the best. Neither side would yield, so they agreed to put it off till the one or the other should give up their opinion, and both be of one mind. The child was thus left in God's hands: he got the smallpox in the natural way, and did well.'[31] It seems Romaine was in favour of trusting in the providence of God, rather than in using 'unnatural remedies'.

In the summer of 1769 he travelled with his wife nearly 800 miles preaching the gospel in various parts of England. After he had preached at St Chad's Church, Shrewsbury, the minister William Adams followed him into the vestry and said angrily, 'Sir, my congregation is not used to such doctrine, and I hope will never hear such again.' Several people were present, but Romaine simply replied, 'Sir, this surely is neither a proper time nor place for disputes.'[32] Two weeks later in St Chad's, Adams preached against Romaine's sermon. On 5 August, Romaine told his mother that he had enjoyed a 'good time at the Assizes, and preached to a vast congregation'. He also said that his journey from Hartlepool was the most pleasant in all his life, 'so many gracious providences, and so many outward mercies, besides the peace in my own soul'.[33]

He returned home 'self abased', as he puts it, 'ashamed and confounded at his mercies to me and mine; and yet to pour my praises to his grace, so mean my services in his own work, that

I am forced to cry for mercy on my best sermons and labours'.[34] By November, his lecturer had gone and he was forced to perform the duty himself, 'for fear a false prophet should get in. I did not seek it; but I hope the Lord, now he has called me to it, will give me will and power, and if it please him, success.'[35] This state of affairs did not last long, for by February the following year his curate, Henry Foster, had become the lecturer of St Ann's, Blackfriars.

In 1770 Romaine was as busy as ever travelling and preaching. On New Year's Day he preached in the evening at Lock Chapel, where Lady Huntingdon was among the congregation. 'I am just returned from the Lock,' she writes, 'where I heard a profitable sermon from dear Mr Romaine, on that awful passage — "This year thou shalt die."'[36] Towards the end of the month he was at Ote Hall, where he stayed for some time before returning to London early in March. On 5 March he travelled with Lady Huntingdon to Reading and then on to Bristol, where he preached twice on Sunday the 11th. The next day he went to Bath and the following evening preached in the chapel to a 'very large and serious congregation'. On Wednesday, 14 March, he arrived at Cheltenham. Being refused the use of the parish church he 'addressed a numerous body of people in a large school room', where Martin Madan and others had preached some years before. He preached for William Talbot on the following Sunday.

During these excursions away from London he was engaged in some personal struggles. In a letter he wrote from Blackfriars on the day he travelled to Reading he complains of 'the workings of a legal and self righteous temper, apt to nurse guilty fears, and to cherish misgivings and suspicions of [an] interest in the great salvation'. These, he says, 'are daily disturbing my peace, and are the very plague of my life'. The only remedy against them, as he knew, 'is to look well to the conscience, where they have their rise, and to use all appointed means for establishing it in the peace of God... A holy walk, and successful warfare, depend entirely on the testimony of conscience.'[37]

Early in 1770, William Adams was persuaded to publish his sermon against Romaine's doctrines under the title *A Test of True and False Doctrines*. In the preface, he says that his discourse was occasioned by a sermon 'so contrary to the sentiments of religion ... that I thought myself obliged on the first opportunity to give my testimony against it'. He acknowledges Romaine to be 'a person of known learning, and ... a principal leader among those who are called Methodists', but does not mention the 'particular tenets which gave this offence and the rash, unguarded terms in which they were expressed'.[38] He goes on:

> When the first principles of religion seem to be deserted, and the first duties of it superseded as fruitless and unnecessary, when the goodness and moral attributes of the deity are indirectly arraigned, and this with an undoubting confidence, and an air imperious and decisive, tending to blind the minds and surprise the credulity of the vulgar ... it cannot be unbecoming me to warn those with whom I am concerned, against being deceived with vain words.[39]

Sir Richard Hill, who was instrumental in bringing Romaine to St Chad's in the first place, was not slow in supporting his man. He wrote to Adams and reminded him that what Romaine taught was in accordance with the doctrines of the Church of England. Appended to Hill's pamphlet was a letter Romaine wrote to Adams:

> As you have in the most public manner, both from the pulpit and the press, personally traduced me, as a setter forth of strange doctrines, tending at once to surprise the vulgar and to mislead the credulous; the most exceptionable of which doctrines you tell us you forbear to mention; you cannot think it unbecoming my office as a minister of Christ, to join the author of this letter, in

Augustus Toplady.

calling upon you to explain your meaning; since it must
be allowed to be a very hard case to be so severely
condemned in general terms, without giving me an opportunity of vindicating — not myself, for I desire to be
out of the question — but the doctrines delivered in my
sermon, — doctrines which I am persuaded in my conscience, are not only contained in the word of God, but
are the very basis of that apostolical Church, in which
you and I have the honour to be ministers.[40]

John Green, bishop of Lincoln, replied in a letter to Romaine
and defended Adams. He says Adams had every right to caution his flock against error, and did so according to his 'constant principles of candour and politeness' by not mentioning
Romaine's name. Some of Romaine's comments, writes Green,
'shocked every serious and rational Christian who heard them'.
He then challenges Romaine to publish his sermon in order to
vindicate himself.[41] There is no record of Romaine's response.

Romaine invited many of his ministerial brethren into the
pulpit, among whom was his close friend Augustus Toplady. In
the early 1760s, while he was waiting to be ordained, Toplady
heard Romaine, Whitefield and the Baptist John Gill preach
on many occasions. His diaries note how he used to dash
from hearing Gill in the afternoon to an evening service with
Whitefield or to one of Romaine's mid week lectures. On one
Sunday, Toplady heard Romaine preach in Broad Hembury
Church, after which he told Romaine that their friendship was
one nothing could sever. Romaine replied, 'The reason is because God is not left out of it.'[42]

Toplady strongly opposed the Arminianism in the revival
movement. In a sermon preached at Blackfriars on 29 April
1770 from 2 Corinthians 3:12, he called it 'the gangrene of
the Protestant Churches and the predominant evil of the day'.
Romaine too had some strong things to say, but on the whole he
avoided the Arminian/Calvinism debate that was raging within
Methodism, even though his name was often mentioned by

participants and he himself was a committed Calvinist. Seven years before, on 26 March 1763, Romaine had written to Lady Huntingdon and made clear his attitude towards controversial issues:

> Things are not here [in London] as at Brighthelmstone. We have many precious souls, but we really want LOVE. The Foundry, the Tabernacle, the Lock, the Meeting, yea, St Dunstan's, has each its party, and brotherly love is almost lost in our disputes. Thank God, I am out of them. I wish them all well, and love them all; and where we differ, there is exercise for charity. But I condemn none that will not subscribe to my creed. By the grace of God I am what I am.[43]

Although Romaine avoided controversy whenever possible, he was nevertheless outspoken on issues he felt strongly about. For instance, when Archdeacon Francis Blackburne published his work, *Proposals for an Application to Parliament for Relief in the Matter of Subscription to the Liturgy and Thirty Nine Articles* (1771), Romaine, who deeply valued the Church of England's Articles and Prayer Book, vowed never again to enter a pulpit if the proposals were implemented. Thankfully, the king was strongly opposed to the petition and the House refused to receive it.

Towards the end of 1770, Henry Crooke, the Vicar of St Mary's, Kippax, died and a Mr S — was appointed to the vacant living, which caused great concern among those with Methodist sympathies. Mrs Medhurst, Lady Huntingdon's niece, was particularly alarmed, so she consulted Romaine, who knew the parish well from his annual visits.

The news was a 'blow' to Romaine, who 'was grieved sore, and began to complain and murmur', until he confessed that the Lord 'can make no mistake in his government'.[44] In an effort to help, he breakfasted with Baron Smythe, Venn's friend, on 27 November, who thought that Edward Buckley, curate from 1767 and an enthusiastic evangelical, would soon be vicar of Kippax. Smythe kept the living at Kippax vacant until a provision had been found for Mr S — , and then Buckley was duly presented. Romaine was thrilled and saw it as a direct answer to prayer: 'If ever there was an answer to prayer, this is,' he wrote. 'Oh that God may make it an encouragement to all ... to pray without ceasing! I am sure it has done me good, and opened mine eyes to see more of the glory of a prayer hearing God.'[45]

On 13 December he was rejoicing that everything had 'ended favourably'. He then gave this advice to the newly installed Vicar of Kippax: 'I wish he may lie low in the dust, as unworthy, utterly unworthy, of this great trust committed to him. But there is grace sufficient in Jesus; I wish he may live on that, and do all in his parish in a settled dependence on the assistance of the great Head of the church.'[46]

On 30 September 1770, there was an event of much greater significance than anything at Kippax. George Whitefield, the 'most brilliant and popular preacher the modern world has ever known', died in the home of Jonathan Parsons, pastor of the Old South Presbyterian Church at Newburyport, Massachusetts. In a letter to a friend on 13 November, Romaine paid tribute to his memory:

> Look at the public loss. O what has the church suffered in the setting of that bright star which has shone so gloriously in our hemisphere! Mr Whit[e]field's preaching is over: now he is praising. We have none left to succeed him, none of his gifts, none anything like him in usefulness. But the same glorious Jesus who gave him to us has taken him away. If he wants another such, he can make him out of a stone. Well, then, let us submit; let him alone, let him alone. His interest at K[ippax], his interest in England, is as dear to him as the apple of his eye. He is managing all for the best. May you and I bow the knee, and say, 'Thy will be done.'[47]

Five days after this letter (18 November), John Wesley delivered Whitefield's funeral sermon in which he summarized the great preacher's life, character and doctrine to an overflowing congregation at the Tabernacle. He described his character as consisting of 'unparalleled zeal, indefatigable activity, tender heartedness to the afflicted, and charitableness toward the poor, the most generous friendship, nice and unblemished modesty, frankness and openness of conversation, unflinching courage, and steadiness in whatever he undertook for his Master's sake'.[48]

He then went on to sketch Whitefield's doctrines, and it was his comments under this heading that caused many Calvinists to protest. Wesley portrayed Whitefield as a man who, from his earliest days as an Oxford Methodist, had proclaimed the same 'grand fundamental doctrines' as Wesley himself, which he 'summed up ... in two words, the new birth and justification by faith'. There was no mention of Whitefield's covenantal theology, with its emphasis on election and the final perseverance of the saints. Instead, Wesley chose to reiterate the view that Christ's righteousness, seen in his passion, was the sole meritorious cause of justification.[49] Heitzenrater rightly comments: 'This point was at the heart of the controversy of the previous decade and was part of the very issue that had sparked the original controversy between the two in 1739.'[50]

One of the protesters aired his displeasure in the *Gospel Magazine* (February 1771). He complained that it was improper for the words of a mad prophet — Wesley's sermon had been based on Numbers 23:10 — to be applied to so faithful a minister as Whitefield. He also pointed out that Whitefield's main doctrines were:

God the Father's everlasting, unchangeable love to sinners — his election of sinners by his grace to salvation — the everlasting covenant which was entered into by the holy blessed and glorious Trinity to save men. And in consequence of this everlasting love, election and covenant, that every believing member of Jesus shall cer-

tainly persevere in holiness to eternal life, as 'being kept
by the power of God, through faith unto salvation'.[51]

Without the fundamental truth of 'the everlasting, unchangeable covenant love of God to us', Wesley's doctrines on the new
birth and justification by faith are only a

> ... defective, precarious scheme, which may, which
> does, and which certainly will prove abortive as to sav-
> ing purposes. For, according to his avowed tenets, a
> soul may be justified by faith, and be born again of the
> Spirit, and yet never enjoy eternal life, but be eternally
> damned; unless the sinner does more for himself, to
> make his own salvation effectual, than the blood and
> righteousness of the Son of God hath done FOR him,
> and the Spirit of God hath effected IN him.[52]

Wesley's lengthy reply in a published letter to the editor of
Lloyd's Evening Post (26 February 1771) was 'controlled and
factual', but it did not bring the parties together, especially as
he falsely accused Romaine of writing the review. The letter
opens: 'The editor of a monthly publication pompously called
the Gospel Magazine, Mr Romaine, has violently fallen upon
one and another who did not knowingly give him any provocation.' Romaine's name occurs six times in the letter, with Wesley
finally asking, 'After asserting this, can Mr Romaine ever take
the name of catholic love into his mouth?'[53]

However, Romaine was neither the editor of the *Gospel
Magazine* nor the author of the review. In June 1771 the periodical responded to Wesley's accusations by reporting: '1. That Mr
R. was not the author of that review. He had not the least hand
in writing it. 2. That he is not the editor of our magazine... Now,
how Mr Wesley can answer to God, to the world, and to his
own conscience (to use his own words) for "so violently falling
upon Mr R. without provocation" ... must be left to himself.'[54]
Romaine also denied Wesley's charges. Richard Hill states that

'Romaine declared, that so far from being the author or inserter of the strictures, he did not so much as see them till after their publication.'[55]

Romaine and Wesley had never seen eye to eye and this latest skirmish was another in a list of difficulties between the two men. In his Journal for 14 September 1789, Wesley notes that he 'spent an agreeable hour with Mr Ireland and Mr Romaine, at Brislington'.[56] Perhaps a measure of reconciliation had taken place by then.

Romaine did not mourn excessively at the passing of great men, but used such solemn occasions to turn his eyes heavenward and to find hope and consolation in God. Whitefield had crossed the river to his eternal reward, but the Lord of heaven and earth was still working out his purposes in the wilderness of London and elsewhere. All Romaine desired as he approached the twilight of his days was to follow his own advice and to live each hour with a single eye to God's glory.

Both in his character and in his writings, Romaine approached more nearly than any of the so-called Puritans of his day to the typical Puritan of the seventeenth century. He was like one born out of due time. One can fancy him more at home with Flavel, Howe and Baxter than with Whitefield, Berridge and Grimshaw. Did we not know its date, we might have imagined that *The Life, Walk and Triumph of Faith* was written a hundred years before it actually was. Its very style and language were archaic in the eighteenth century, Romaine, indeed, thoroughly won the sympathy of the generation in which he lived, or at any rate of the school to which he belonged.

John Overton.[1]

12
An Eighteenth-Century Puritan

At the end of 1770, Thomas Haweis travelled to London to prepare for his marriage in January 1771 to Romaine's friend, Judith Wordsworth. Romaine offered his curate, John Foss, as a supply to Haweis's parish at Aldwincle and to accept his friend as an assistant during his stay in the metropolis. For a wedding present he gave Judith, who shared his love of Hebrew, an inscribed copy of the *Critica Hebraica* (1767) of Julius Bate, a learned Hutchinsonian friend. On the first leaf was a beautiful commendation of the Word of God. Later, Haweis gave the book to a South Seas missionary, but, much to his disappointment, forgot to copy the commendation. Thankfully, he received a letter of Romaine's written in the first leaf of a Bible sent to Mrs Gordon, a lady of his acquaintance, with a very similar commendation, which made up for the loss. The letter is dated 17 December 1778:

> Madam,
>   I herewith send you the Bible of which I was speaking to you, a book of inestimable value, containing the great character of grace, by which the Lord God has granted you under his hand and seal, a full discharge from sin and misery, and a full title to eternal life. This blessing he has given to you in his Son, and therefore

the record of God concerning his Son is the chief subject of the book — what he is in his person as God-Man
— what he has done — what he has suffered — his
complete righteousness — his prevalent intercession
are largely treated of, and because we cannot understand these things, nor believe them, nor make use of
them ourselves, therefore the Spirit who inspired the
book, still accompanies the hearing of it and reading it:
the means of knowing Jesus, of believing in him, and
of enjoying the Father's love in him. When you grow in
this knowledge, in this faith, in this love, how is this ordinance of God prized. His almighty power is still in the
word: hear, read, meditate, pray over it, and you will find
it able to make you wise unto salvation...

It is my privilege to be any ways useful to you in this
most noble design, and whatever prayer can do ... I shall
not cease to use for you, imploring the teaching of the
Spirit upon all your hearing, reading, the word of God;
may you find it profitable, every day more profitable for
those gracious purposes for which it was revealed. Yet
a little while and it shall be perfectly fulfilled, and more
than you can now conceive, fulfilled in your everlasting
glory.[2]

When Haweis left London with his wife, Romaine's warm and
cordial congratulations followed them.

On 15 February 1771, Romaine's mother Isabella died at
Hartlepool aged eighty-eight. 'She is gone a little before, and I
shall soon follow. The goodness of God to her was very great all
her life, but extraordinary to the moment of her death: so that
we sorrow rejoicing.'[3] In nearly all his letters to his sister he referred to his mother with the deepest affection, and was always
concerned about the state of her walk with God. Each summer,
while on his travels, he visited her in Hartlepool. Although she
was a good Christian woman, it appears that she had no assurance of salvation. 'Her case is safe,' says Romaine in one letter.

'I only wish her more happy in believing it.'[4] As indicated in the last quotation, her son had 'not the least uneasy thought about her [salvation]. She has God's promise.' 'My dear mother,' he writes from Lambeth on 29 September 1764, 'I am sure, will not be wanting when the Lord counteth his jewels.' And again the following year: 'I have no doubt of seeing her in heaven and rejoice with her in the goodness of the Lord to her soul.'

Shortly after her death he wrote to his sister and shared with her some reflections that, despite 'great bodily pain and indisposition', had quietened his mind and produced a willing submission to the Lord's stroke:

First, my mother's true conversion to the Lord. She knew in whom she had believed; and she was in Christ. Christ was her gain, both in life and death...

Secondly, she died in faith. O what a mercy to finish all well!...

Thirdly, we are not to mourn as those who have no hope. Our dearest friend is with her Lord, with whom we expect to be soon. We have only parted a moment, that we may meet for ever. It looks to me, in my near view of death, only like my taking leave of my dear mother, to go yearly to London. I shall go to her — blessed, truly blessed prospect! and I do not wish her to come back to me: — because,

Fourthly, I do indeed find that the Lord supplies the want of all creature comforts with his own presence. When he takes them away, it is to make more room for himself in the heart...

She had lived to a blessed time — even speaking after the manner of men — she died in a good old age, full of years — and was gathered to her people, to whom I am going. Now it is my turn...

I shall love you, my dear sister, as long as I live, for your attention to my dear mother. You have done your part... My kind love to Mr Heslup. He has been tried

with his attention to my mother; the good Lord repay his
kindness a thousandfold. Mine eyes overflow with tears
while I am thinking of both your goodness to her — God
bless you both — God bless you. [Since their marriage
in 1767 Romaine's sister and Mr Heslup had lived with
Isabella, looking after her in her old age.]...

Poor Hartlepool! Few know this loss. It is the greatest the town could have.[5]

At the end of March 1771 the first part of Romaine's treatise
The Walk of Faith was published, followed six months later by
the second volume. This work was a companion to his book
The Life of Faith which had been published in 1764 and which
had been well received. In 1795, not long before his death, the
final part of the trilogy *The Triumph of Faith* was published.
Romaine's design in *The Walk of Faith* was to 'bring the great
and leading points of our religion into use and practice, and to
show how necessary the doctrines of grace are for the well gov-
erning of the Christian walk. Everything needful is promised,
and by faith is received, which can make it even and regular,
holy and happy.'[6]

In a letter he wrote to a friend on 27 November 1770, he
mentions how *The Walk of Faith* was meant to be about the size
of *The Life of Faith*, 'but is already got much larger. My friends,
who have seen it, will not let me abridge it, but say I must add
a little more, and it will be two small volumes. My dear friend,
pray for it. May God make it a sweet savour of his adorable
name! It is a book of many prayers.'[7] Again, in a letter written
on 13 December, he calls his book a 'child of many prayers; I
scarce ever sit down to write, without asking a blessing upon
every line'. Then, with a sense of urgency, he asks for prayer:
'Beg it may come out with the unction of the Spirit, and carry,
wherever it goes, a sweet savour of the precious name of my
Lord and my God.'[8]

After he had finished the work, in a letter of 20 August 1771,
he tells how he was daily begging God 'that he would go out

with it and own it to the hearts of his dear people. My design ... was for the glory of God and their good. The plan is simple. It was to show that Christian principles are sufficient for all the purposes of Christian practice; so that whenever we fail in practice, we have first failed in principle.' In the second volume there are two chapters on the outward and inward crosses that Christians have to bear. They are the longest chapters 'because I felt what I wrote, and because all God's children carry these two crosses to the grave'.[9]

Opinions differ as to the value of Romaine's trilogy. William Huntington, a friend of Romaine's, regarded it as one of his 'best books', and Thomas Haweis says it gives the 'purest specimen of his manner of preaching and teaching; uniting plainness, pure evangelical truth, and deep experience'.[10] George M. Ella calls it 'a mighty demonstration of Reformed doctrine',[11] 'a Christian classic',[12] and claims that Romaine was one of the authors who 'transformed the English written language, making it available to all classes and purifying it in its subject matter'.[13] His work certainly influenced thoughtful men throughout the country.

George T. Fox, writing over a hundred years after its publication, calls it an 'immortal work, which is still so highly prized that a secular publisher has shrewdly seen his advantage in bringing out a cheap popular edition... [It is] a book which I would strongly urge everyone to buy.'[14] J. C. Ryle, in comparing the 'new doctrine' with the old, says, 'I am ... content with such teachings about sanctification as I find in ... *The Life, Walk and Triumph of Faith* of William Romaine.' John Overton thought of Romaine's trilogy as 'undoubtedly a strong book, perhaps the strongest that the Evangelical revival produced' — a book that possessed the strengths as well as the weaknesses of early Puritanism. 'To find its equal we must go back to the previous century.'[15] Thomas Chalmers, in his introduction to Romaine's treatises, wrote:

> [The] doctrine which is so frequently reiterated in these
> Treatises [is] 'that Christ died for our sins, according to
> the Scriptures'... He never ceases to make mention of
> Christ and His righteousness — and it is by the constant
> droppings of this elixir that the whole charm and interest
> of his writings are upheld... In despite of that literary na-
> kedness which they may exhibit to the eye of the natural
> man, who possesses no spiritual taste, and no spiritual
> discernment, let such a man have his eye opened to
> the hidden glories of that theme which of all others was
> dear to the bosom of their author; and whether from the
> press or from the pulpit, was the one theme on which he
> ever loved to expatiate... a purifying as well as a pleas-
> ing theme.[16]

True to form, John Wesley thought that most of Romaine's
work, *The Walk of Faith*, was deeply coloured with 'antinomianism'. In fact, Wesley thought *all* Romaine's writings were
'brimful of Antinomianism'. On 28 December 1773, he wrote
to Samuel Sparrow, with his usual suspect logic, 'We agree, too,
that preachers who "relax our obligation to moral virtues, who
decry holiness as filthy rags, who teach men that easy, palatable
way to heaven, of faith without works", cannot easily fail of
having a multitude of hearers; and that therefore it is no wonder if vast numbers crowd Blackfriars church and the chapel at
the Lock.'[17] This is a further example of the differences that ex-
isted between Romaine and Wesley. In a letter to his sister dated
Blackfriars, 27 October 1771, Romaine urges her husband to
avoid disputes. 'Desire him, from me,' he says, 'to read his Bible
more, and not busy himself about opinions.' He then asks:

> What has he or I to do with Mr Wesley? Let him go on in
> his way; and let us go on in ours. But let us be as diligent
> as him — our lives as exemplary — our good works as
> many. And let us beat him all to nothing in charity. If he
> revile, let us pray. If he be dogmatical, let us be meek

and lowly. I cannot give any account for my writing about him; for I do not love to have anything to do with him; but it came upon my mind, and I let it stand.[18]

Wilberforce, in an entry in his journal for 1795, remarks, 'Dined with old [John] Newton, where met Henry Thornton and Macaulay. Newton very calm and pleasing. Owned that Romaine has made many Antinomians.'[19] It seems probable that Thomas Scott, when he spoke of 'great names sanctioning Antinomianism', had Romaine in mind. But Romaine was no antinomian, far from it, although it must be conceded that his teaching could be perverted to fit in with antinomian thinking. In a letter he wrote to his sister on 22 December 1772, he makes clear his position:

If we do much for him, we have nothing to boast of; for he worketh in us both to will and to do. I am for good works as much as any of them; but I would do them to a right end, and upon a right motive; and after all, having done the best that can be done, I would not lay the weight of the least tittle of my salvation — no, not one atom of it, upon them. It all rests on Christ — he is my only foundation — he is my topstone: and all the building, laid on him, groweth up into a holy temple in the Lord. He has done all for me: he does all in me: he does all by me.[20]

Romaine's letters, which overflow with practical advice on how to walk with and serve the Lord, clearly demonstrate that his whole approach to salvation and the Christian life was: 'To God be all the glory for ever and ever.' God is everything and man is nothing, and he would not allow anything to undermine this Scriptural foundation. That is why his letters and other writings are full of the language of self-abasement on the one hand, and the exaltation of Christ on the other. He raised up Christ to push man down, and he pushed man down to raise up Christ.

In one of his letters, written at the beginning of 1772, he said, with straightforward honesty, 'It's high time I was turned out of the vineyard, and any other master, but mine, would have had nothing to do with me long ago. I loathe myself, and stand wondering daily at his kindness. Never was self lower, and his loveliness higher, than in this new year.'[21] In another letter of about this time, he goes even further:

> I was invited to preach in Buckinghamshire, where we have had the Lord with us of a truth. O what am I, that mine eyes should see such things as I see! I, who am the veriest filthy dunghill-sinner, that ever God suffered to live; that I, even I, should partake of his grace, as well as preach it: O it is astonishing! Surely, if I ever get to heaven (and I must not doubt of getting thither) I shall beat Mary Magdalene, and Paul, and Peter, and Manasseh, all to nothing. They had not half the pardon that I have; and yet, glory, glory, glory be to Jesus, I am among his pardoned ones. Who, then, shall sing his praises in such a high note as I can? None, no, not one of them all. I am the most indebted to free grace of all that ever were saved out of hell.[22]

Romaine was more Calvinistic than most of the evangelicals, that is true, but at no time did the doctrines he embraced cause him to break with Christian charity, as was the case with many. In fact, the role he played in the reformation of doctrine in the eighteenth century has been underestimated by modern evangelicals, especially his robust defence of justification by faith. Thomas Chalmers, in his introductory essay to Romaine's *Select Letters*, opens by reminding his readers that the 'great and unceasing topics on which he delighted to expatiate were the atoning blood and perfect righteousness of Christ, as forming the great and only foundation of his hope and of his confidence towards God'.[23]

About the middle of June 1771 Romaine was in Bath, where

he stayed until the end of the month. He then visited Frome, Pensford, Shepton Mallet, Warminster, Bradford and many other places in Somerset and Wiltshire, where several were converted under his ministry. He preached frequently in these places, 'sometimes in the churches, and sometimes in private houses, to very large auditories'.[24] On 15 July he travelled with Lady Huntingdon to Brislington, near Bristol, and they enjoyed the hospitality of James Ireland. During the summer he also visited his sister at Hartlepool, where he was kindly received, and went to Newcastle and Sunderland, where he was 'never so highly honoured ... as to be suffered to speak for my glorious Jesus'. At Yarum in July, 'Mr O' tried to stop all he could from going to church to hear 'that heretic Romaine'.

It was probably during the summer of 1771 that Romaine was first allowed the use of the church in Derby, having been refused on many previous occasions. He also preached several times at Ashbourne, Duffield and Belper 'with great acceptance and success'. At Shottle and other villages near Belper, 'considerable attention was excited, and great numbers crowded to hear the preaching of Mr Romaine, Mr Powley, Mr Jesse, and others, who from time to time visited those places, under the patronage of Lady Huntingdon'.[25]

By the middle of August he was enduring 'very great' spiritual and physical trials. 'I have the old burden very heavy indeed — a vast body of sin, under which I groan, and great bodily pain, hard to bear. I have been to the sea for relief; but my Lord thinks proper to refuse it. When I had other trials he spared me, and never let me know what bodily pain was: but now outward trials are in a great measure removed, this is my cross. He is merciful in all his dealings; blessings on him for his kind rod!'[26] With such a submissive attitude towards the providences of God, it is easy to see how he could be true to his motto: 'Cease ye from man.'

He had travelled from place to place for 'near three months', but by September he was back at Blackfriars and already planning his next visit to Hartlepool early in the spring. As always he was ready to yield to God's will: 'Our will must bow to his sovereign will; and, in submission to it, we always speak of tomorrow, not knowing what a day bring forth.' He yearned for more prayer to cover the preaching of the gospel, and for preachers to be dependent on God to bless the word to their congregations. 'O that fervent effectual prayer was but ascending more and oftener to the throne of grace, we should have more showers of blessings come down.'[27]

To combat the rampant errors and heresies that are always ready to attack the church, he recognised the importance of reading the Bible more than other books: 'I am sure God the Holy Ghost is the best writer; and I find him the best expositor upon his own writings... I repent of years wasted in fruitless study, and am, just as my studies are over, got to be right in them.'[28] He used to say: 'In books I converse with men; in the Bible I converse with God,'[29] and his advice was: 'Be a Bible-student, and a Bible-Christian.'[30] The stress he laid on God's Word is demonstrated in the fact that he is one of the few ministers who completed a commentary on the whole Bible in a course of evening lectures in one place.

It had been his custom for many years to preach a sermon on New Year's Day from a single Hebrew word, or more usually from a text that would be a 'sort of watchword, something very short and striking, and which may serve the believers to feast upon a twelvemonth. I have found this very useful to myself, and so have others.' On 1 January 1772 his text was 'Christ is all', and the following month he passed on the substance of his message to a friend:

> Christ is all light and life and love and joy, and that without ceasing; an infinite and everlasting fulness of all blessing. I would lead you to him in the direct road, which is to lead you out of self entirely. Christ is the way — look more at him and less at self; trust more to him and less to your faith or comforts; live upon nothing in yourself, but live every moment upon him; do not eye his gifts so

much — fix your heart upon the Giver; be always thinking of his fulness whenever you feel your own empti-
ness: whatever you are, or do, or suffer, let all things
bring you to make ... use of Christ. Read about him.
Go to your closet to converse with him. Go to church to
meet him. Make him your companion. Accustom your
mind to meditate upon him. Pray without ceasing to him
as your bosom friend. Do not be shy of him; he hates
shyness. Draw near; he bids you come with boldness,
vile, unthankful, unprofitable as you are: his dear heart
is always open to hear your complaints, and to relieve
your distresses, be they what they will...

You may walk in his light and enjoy his comforts.
You may take him for your righteousness and your holiness; you may live on him for grace and glory. He is
yours, and all he has is yours also, and for your use
today and for ever.[31]

He never grew tired of speaking about Christ, and with these
words he told his friend how he and his London congregation
intended to live throughout the year.

Romaine's ministry to a London surgeon and chemist, Mr
Baker, further illustrates his Christ-centredness. Mrs Baker had
heard Romaine occasionally at Blackfriars and when her husband was very ill, she asked him to visit. On his arrival, he took
the sick man by the hand and without any other introduction,
said:

You are, sir, a perfect stranger to me, and I to you. I ask
not what may have been your former character, or your
habits and course of life. I know all about it. I know that
you, like myself, are a sinner against God; that you were
born under his wrath and curse, and have gone astray
like a lost sheep, having transgressed that law which is
holy, just, and good, in thought, word, and deed; and
that you have no power in and of yourself to effect your

deliverance from this state of condemnation and misery.

Nevertheless be not discouraged. I bring you good
news, glad tidings of great joy. The God whom you have
offended is full of mercy and compassion. He willeth not
the death of the sinner, but rather that he should repent
and live. He has provided for your escape by the gift,
mission, meritorious obedience, and atoning sacrifice
of his incarnate Son. The work which he undertook he
has gloriously finished; and his righteousness, freely imputed to the penitent and believing sinner, will infallibly
justify from all the charges and liability to condemnation. He is able to save to the uttermost all that come
unto God by him; and him that cometh, you have his
own word, he will not cast out. He is willing at this very
moment to save you; only believe. Look unto him and
be saved.

Then, with great affection and earnestness, he pleaded with the
dying man: 'Sir, this is my message; were I to remain with you
till midnight, I have nothing more to tell you. Can you receive
it? I again ask, can you receive it? Look and live.' After he had
prayed, he said goodbye.[32]
Baker died shortly afterwards, but his widow started to attend Blackfriars regularly and was soon converted. When her
younger brother John Clayton came to live with her, she took
him to Blackfriars, and he was converted on his very first visit!
He describes his salvation as 'almost instantaneous, and could
compare it to nothing but a flash of lightning, which discovered
to him, as in a moment of time, the only method of reconciliation, the only ground of hope for ruined man.'[33] From that
hour he was a new creature. Not long afterwards he made Lady
Huntingdon's acquaintance and became one of the earliest and
most notable of the Trevecca students. After some years as an
itinerant preacher, and being refused episcopal ordination, he
became the minister of the influential Weigh House Independent

Church in London from 1778. The following year he was married by Romaine at Blackfriars to Miss Mary Flower. Their son and grandson both became preachers.

In a letter to his friend Zachary Shrapnell (29 October 1772) Romaine again overflows with a desire to glorify Christ as he urges his friend: 'Exalt higher and higher still — exalt our precious Jesus. You'll never be blamed for making too much of him.' He then rejoices in the One he loves: 'I am living upon my Jesus, and he is become my all. He of mere grace stepped in, and plucked me from hell... He made me to see his loveliness, and draws out my heart to him. It is from himself that I esteem his word and ways, and that I find walking with him a very heaven, a real paradise on earth.'[34] His genuine love for and intimate relationship with Christ is why he was such an effective minister of the gospel.

In the above letter to Shrapnell he also emphasises his dislike of controversy. Referring to the dispute occasioned by Wesley's doctrines in his minutes, he exclaims: 'God be thanked! I have nothing to do with it. For more than twenty years my dear master has delivered me from a spirit of controversy; and I trust he will deliver me to the end. Let others *dispute* about salvation, I will leave them and seek to *enjoy* it. And I do — glory be to my God. I am getting my harvest, while they are only sowing the seed.'[35] His attitude to controversy, formed from personal experience, is summed up in the advice he passed on to Mr Heslup via his sister on 26 June 1773, 'to avoid controversy as he would the plague'.

If he would be kept entirely, I will tell him how I am kept. The doctrines which others are disputing about, I am living upon. They have ceased to be with me a matter of controversy. I have brought them into experience. By which means, I not only am certain of their truth, but also receive from it great profit. Doubting and disputing are at an end; for what room can there be to question any doctrine, while it is really practical, and brings in a

great revenue? Thus a man gets to be settled. Others
quarrel about the shell, he feeds upon the kernel, and
often feasts upon it.[36]

He practised what he preached in 1775, because he avoided
becoming embroiled in the controversy over the American War
of Independence, which began in that year and which caused
feelings to run high in London; instead, in typical fashion, he
called his brethren once more to prayer for the nation.

There are only a few snippets of information on Romaine's
life over the next two or three years. On 13 January 1773 from
Blackfriars, he wrote a recommendatory preface to the third edition of Henry Dorney's *Contemplations*, which shows how keen
he was on the practical and experiential side of religion, and not
just on the dry bones of theology. Before it was reprinted he had
been trying to buy a copy but without success. In the preface he
calls the work a 'much desired publication'. 'It is ... very seasonable, and contains a sound and savoury experience.' He looked
on Dorney as 'a great Christian', who was 'taught the truths
of God very clearly and lived upon them practically'. He was
also impressed with how unweariedly the author used every
appointed means 'for an increase of divine knowledge, of faith,
of hope, and of lively communion with God in Christ... Reader,
may the doctrines of grace be made as evident to thy understanding, as enlivening to thy heart and as operative on thy life
as they were to Mr Dorney.'[37]

Lady Huntingdon wrote to Romaine on 29 July about the
death and funeral of Howel Harris, and thanked him for some
'hints' he had passed on concerning the Trevecca students.
'They shall be attended to, and any suggestions which may further the cause, will be most gratefully received. I am happy you
approve the plans I have adopted. The salvation of souls is my
one object upon earth, and my greatest earthly happiness and
joy.'[38]

In September, Romaine was in Tiverton and while there he
received a letter from Toplady, who was looking forward to hav-

ing him preach in his church on the 19th. 'God's Holy Spirit come with you,' said Toplady, who was happy to accommodate Romaine and his wife during their stay, 'and speak by you, and bless you to his people. You will sow on ploughed ground: and cannot offend the generality of my hearers, preach free and finished salvation as strongly as you will. May you be enabled to reach their hearts.'[39]

Early in 1774 Romaine's ministry was blessed to a student at the Royal Academy, George Burder, who often heard him at Blackfriars and St Dunstan's and found his preaching 'really useful to me'. Burder himself became a useful preacher. On 2 March, William Talbot of Reading died. Romaine, who had itinerated with him years earlier, regarded his death as a blow to the evangelical cause. 'Poor Reading!' he wrote. 'It is the worst day that town ever saw.' In that same year he assisted Thomas Pentycross, whom he had patronised at the beginning of his ministry and who had occasionally officiated for him with much acceptance, in obtaining the living of St Mary's, Wallingford.

On 1 July 1774 he was in Tunbridge Wells, and three weeks later he was preaching in Brighton at the dedication of Lady Huntingdon's rebuilt chapel. Later in the summer he travelled to Yorkshire and in September he was in Bierly, just south of Bradford, visiting Richard Richardson. It was at Bierly that he met the evangelical clergyman David Simpson, whose licence had recently been withdrawn by the Bishop of Chester for promoting 'Methodism'. Charles Roe, the owner of a silk mill in Macclesfield, was wanting to build a church for Simpson in the town, but episcopal consecration was proving a problem. There were other offers of livings open to Simpson, but he was undecided. Romaine wrote to him from Bierly on 5 September and gave him this advice:

> It seems to me worth your while to wait a little upon the Lord. Don't hurry: you may take a hasty step, and repent it all your days. Wait, I say, upon the Lord: he may teach you why he silenced you. You may see it was

David Simpson.

for your good. He wanted to teach you submission, to break your own spirit, and curb your self-will; perhaps he intended to humble you, and so to fit you for more usefulness; that having done his work at Macclesfield, you might rely more upon his grace in labouring for him elsewhere...

You are not shut out of the Lord's vineyard, but only called to labour in another part of it, where the door is open for you. Providence, in such cases, speaks as plain as Scripture... May our Divine Head bless you abundantly and give you a large Yorkshire harvest.[40]

Simpson, however, remained in Macclesfield and preached at Roe's church, which after some delay was consecrated in 1779.

Just before Christmas (11 December), he wrote to the bookseller Fisher of Rochester, who had asked for Romaine's advice on the appointment of a gospel minister. In replying he recommended a man by the name of Shepherd, 'a tried minister, and of some years standing, but at this time is un-provided for... He had a regular education, was brought up at the university, took his degree, and has been curate ever since he was ordained in and about Bath. He will come to you well recommended, and with proper testimonials.'[41] On Monday 30 January 1775 he preached in the afternoon before the Leather Sellers' Company.

On 13 April 1775 a young man named Joel Abraham Knight, while walking at Hyde Park Corner, overheard part of a conversation that was to change his life. 'I heard one of them say to the other, "I hope Mr Romaine will not have taken his text before we get there." "What," said I to myself, "is Mr Romaine going to preach hereabouts this morning! Then I will go and hear him too." I followed them to the Lock Chapel' and there experienced 'one of the most important turns of my life'.[42] Knight was ordained at Spa Fields and served in Lady Huntingdon's connection and at Whitefield's Tabernacle until his death.

In 1775 Romaine produced an unintentionally controversial work entitled *An Essay on Psalmody, with a Collection out of the Book of Psalms, Suited to Every Sunday in the Year*, which was a defence of the exclusive use of Psalms (in the Sternhold and Hopkins version) in church services. It was compiled for use in the sung liturgy, and in the hope that it would improve congregational singing. Each Psalm had its own short introduction and devotional application. In his preface to the *Essay* he gives the reason for writing: 'I have been persuaded to try to make the subject of these divine hymns plain and clear, and to restore the singing of them in the congregation to their primitive usefulness.'[43]

The book of Psalms, he says, 'treats of Christ, and contains the praises of the Father's love, and of the Spirit's grace, as they were manifested in the person and work of Jesus Christ'.[44] Its design is to record 'the wonderful love of the ever-blessed Trinity in saving sinners through Jesus Christ, and to keep it fresh and lively upon the hearts of believers'[45] — to thank and to praise the Lord God of Israel. With this in mind he encouraged people to sing the Psalms with the heart, for 'the heart makes the best music'. 'When they have met together, understanding the subject of the Psalm, and singing it with melody in their hearts, then the Lord has accepted their praises, and increased their joy in him.'[46]

He then endeavoured to remedy some abuses, such as the general ignorance of the subject of the Psalms, the lack of respect shown to the 'divine ordinance' of Psalm singing, the choice of improper portions, and the total neglect of them by some congregations: 'Human compositions are preferred to divine. Man's poetry is exalted above the poetry of the Holy Ghost.' On this last point, he writes:

> The value of poems above Psalms is become so great, and the singing of men's words, so as quite to cast out the word of God is become so universal (except in the Church of England), that one scarce dares not speak upon the subject...
>
> I blame nobody for singing human compositions... My complaint is against preferring men's poems to the good word of God, and preferring them to it in the church. I have no quarrel with Dr Watts, or any living or dead versifier. I would not wish all their poems burnt. My concern is to see Christian congregations shut out divinely inspired Psalms, and take in Dr Watts's flights of fancy; as if the words of a poet were better than the words of a prophet, or as if the wit of a man was to be preferred to the wisdom of God.[47]

To support his proposition for singing the Psalms in church and not 'human compositions', he presents six arguments, at the conclusion of which he boldly asserts: 'Experience demonstrates, that God does bless the singing of Psalms in the church, and does not bless the singing of men's hymns.'[48]

Before we examine several reactions to Romaine's *Essay*, it is important to understand that Romaine's zeal for the Psalms was principally directed towards upholding and, where necessary, re-establishing biblical theology in the church. He wanted the pure Word of God read, preached and sung by Christian

Dr Isaac Watts, commonly considered the father of
English hymnody.

congregations. Nothing, in his view, should be countenanced
that threatened the supremacy of Scripture. He strongly opposed hymns on the ground that they were man's creation and
not God's, and that they lowered worship to the level of entertainment. He saw hymn singing as a 'substitute for true worship
and a grave departure from the Scriptural norm. Wherever there
was a lack of "vital religion", he thought, people left off praying, singing the Psalms and hearing the Word, and descended
into singing Watts's "flights of fancy", along with other flippant
pastimes. The words of man had become more important to a
backsliding church than the word of God.'[49]

Before he wrote his *Essay* he had studied Watts's comments
on the imitation of the Psalms, where the hymn writer argues:
'Where there are any dark expressions, and difficult to be understood in the Hebrew songs, they should be left out in our
psalmody, or at least made very plain by a paraphrase. Where
there are sentences, or whole Psalms, that can very [with] difficulty be accommodated to our times, they may be utterly omitted.'[50] He also selects various expressions, such as Psalm 84:3,
6, and claims that they 'were hardly made for Christian lips to
assume without some alteration'.[51] Although Watts's design
was to brighten up worship, it was his language and tone that
caused some to question his doctrine of the inspiration, authority and perfection of Holy Scripture, which in turn helps us to
understand Romaine's opposition.

Romaine was especially antagonistic towards church choirs.
He wrote of the London churches, complaining that among
them psalmody is 'performed by some few, set by themselves
in a singing gallery, where they sing to be admired for their fine
voices, and others hear them for their entertainment'.[52] This
caused a congregational passivity, which was not the pattern for
corporate worship. One way to counteract this 'indolence' was
to get the congregation to stand while singing, which was no
easy task. In his *Essay on Psalmody* he wrote that the 'posture
generally used in singing' is a 'great impropriety and to me
very offensive'. 'When subjects go upon any joyful occasion to

address their sovereign, is it a custom in any nation of the world to do it sitting? Does the person who pays homage sit, or he who receives it?'[53] Then, in a conciliatory tone, he adds, 'But if you think otherwise, and prefer sitting, lolling, or any lazy, indolent posture, I will not unchristian you. We may differ and not quarrel.'[54]

Among those who differed from him were John Newton, Augustus Toplady and Lady Huntingdon, all of whom wished he had not expressed his opinion so forcefully in print. On 3 August 1775, Newton wrote to John Thornton and shared with him his thoughts on Romaine's *Essay*:

> I wish he had treated [Psalmody] in a different manner...
> I am afraid it will hurt some weak well meaning peo-
> ple ... to be told, that whatever comfort they may think
> they have received from singing hymns in public wor-
> ship was only imaginary... Some of us here, know that
> the Lord has comforted us by hymns, which express
> Scriptural truths, though not confined to the words of
> David's Psalms. And we know by the effects we are
> not mistaken. I believe Dr Watts's hymns have been a
> singular blessing to the Churches, notwithstanding Mr
> Romaine does not like them.[55]

According to Seymour, his reference to Isaac Watts's 'whims' 'gave considerable offence'. Lady Huntingdon and others remonstrated with him and it was altered. Toplady, who 'argued that singing a hymn in church was as much a work of the Spirit as preaching the word', whereas for Romaine preaching the gospel was the only God-ordained method of bringing sinners to Christ and the New Testament held no other view, wrote to the Countess from Brighton on 22 September 1775:

> Has your Ladyship seen the corrected copy of dear Mr
> Romaine's treatise on Psalmody? If you have, you must
> have perceived that the very exceptionable passages,

which laid that great and good man open to much just reprehension, are happily expunged. I asked him for a copy soon after my arrival in London; he answered, that in its present state, he did not acknowledge it for his; but I should have one as soon as published. He was as good as his word, and shortly after gave me his book. I examined it very carefully; and find that the faulty pages have been cancelled. We now no longer read of Watts's Hymns being Watts's whims, nor of the Holy Spirit's being present where the Psalms are sung. I am glad that my valuable friend was under the necessity of striking out these and such violent and unguarded positions. I never met with so much as one spiritual person who did not censure them most severely; but as he has been so humble and so just to truth as to displace them from his essay, I hope he will meet with no further slight and mortification on their account.[56]

One of the criticisms Romaine received was that he was happy with 'the scream of charity boys, led by a parish clerk, whose inharmonious notes grated the ears of the worshippers'. This statement is harsh, especially in view of what Romaine said in his *Essay*: 'There are many in our congregations, who seem to think they sing best, when they sing loudest. You may see them often strain themselves with shouting till their faces are as red as scarlet. The worst singers commonly offend this way.'[57] And again: 'We have many good psalm tunes, excellently composed and fitted for public worship. These should be studied, in order that they may be well sung, and properly applied.'[58] Having said that, it is true that few would have preferred the singing at Blackfriars to that of many other congregations.

While he would not introduce hymns into the service, there is no doubt that he enjoyed the poetry and concurred with the sentiments expressed in them, often quoting them in his sermons. Thomas Wills, in his funeral address, says, 'How have I seen his cheeks glow, and his eyes sparkle, when I have heard him repeat in the midst of a sermon from his pulpit those sweet words of one of our hymns, which was, as well might be, a great favourite with him:

> Jesus, thy blood and righteousness,
> My beauty are, my glorious dress;
> Midst flaming worlds in these array'd,
> With joy shall I lift up my head.
>
> When from the dust of earth I rise,
> To claim my mansion in the skies,
> E'en then shall this be all my plea,
> Jesus hath lived and died for me.

Wills goes on: 'Often with inexpressible exultation he could not refrain addressing Christ after sermon, in the words that begun one of his favourite hymns.'[59]

Regardless of his most valiant efforts, he was unable to stop the ever-increasing flow of hymnody that was spilling over from Methodist ranks and affecting every part of the evangelical revival. Nevertheless, in what he wrote on the subject, his motives were pure and his conscience clear. All he was trying to do was to give the Word of God its rightful place in the church service, knowing that it is only the Word that exalts Christ sufficiently and leads a sinner safely to God, and to prevent a theatre-type worship from invading the sanctuary. If he did err, he erred on the side of caution, for he preferred to please God by taking his stand on the foundation of Holy Writ, rather than pander to the fancies of men.

With the controversy behind him, Romaine was ready to enter the last years of his life with renewed vigour and zeal for the kingdom of God. In the words of the apostle Paul, he was 'forgetting those things which are behind and reaching forward to those things which are ahead'.

Read the word, there is his character; pray over it, there you will meet his Spirit; live on it by faith, there you will have graces and comforts; and go on, your time is short, improve it all you can. Grow ever so fast, and much, in the knowledge of Jesus, yet still there are worlds of science and experience before you. May you grow in grace and in the knowledge and love of God-Jesus.

William Romaine.[1]

13

A Man After God's own Heart

Romaine entered the last twenty years of his life as committed as ever to furthering the gospel in whatever way he could.
He believed that the reading of good books was essential to
Christian growth and understanding, and was always ready to
bring to the attention of the public a worthwhile work. Towards
the end of 1775 he recommended Elisha Coles's *A Practical
Discourse of God's Sovereignty*, which mirrored his own strong
belief in the doctrines of grace and their practical importance for
everyday life. In the preface to the fifth impression, he says:

> Our author has defended them [the doctrines of grace]
> in a masterly manner. He has not only proved them to
> be plainly revealed in the Scriptures, but has also shown
> that they are such constant use to the children of God,
> that without the steadfast belief of them, they cannot
> go on their way rejoicing. It is from these doctrines only
> that settled peace can rule in the conscience, the love of
> God be maintained in the heart, and a conversation kept
> up in our walk and warfare as becometh the gospel. It
> is from them that all good works proceed, and that all
> fruits of holiness abound to the praise of the glory of the
> grace of God.[2]

He then adds a word about his own experience: 'Until I received [these doctrines] I could not enjoy the blessings and comforts of the precious gospel.'

Romaine published nothing controversial on the American War of Independence, although the spiritual darkness over that land deeply troubled him: 'I keep on praying, but the cloud does not disperse. It is still thick, black and lowering. The storm gathers, and threatens a wide-spread ruin. This makes me pray more earnestly. I would be found among the holy mourners, deeply concerned not only for mine own sins, but for theirs also, which have brought down the just wrath of heaven.'[3] It is clear from his letters that he believed the Americans to be wrong both spiritually and politically. In the letter quoted above, which he wrote on 5 May 1777 to his friend Ambrose Serle, who was then in America with the British forces, he says:

> Judgment is gone forth, and if there be no turning from sin, judgment will continue: yea, if there be hardness in sin under judgment, it is not only the forerunner of greater misery, but is also a part of the sentence executed. O what a prospect does this give me of American misery! What can be worse, than they be, left as they are to themselves? God seems to let them alone. He has done with them. Hence they are given up to blindness and hardness. They see not, they fear not their certain ruin. There is not a word in all the book, so fearful in my view, as what I see now fulfilling — Ephraim is joined to idols, let him alone.
>
> Thus dark is the prospect looking at America.[4]

Then, in contrast to America's woes, he highlights how the Great King over all the earth 'is manifesting wondrous care for England'. 'His church flourishes. Many young ministers come out, more coming. A great awakening still all over our land. Some successful attempts towards a general reformation. Much prayer and supplication for our turning as a people to the Lord.

Signs of the good will of God to his church and people, and earnests, I hope, of better things provided for us.'[5]

At the beginning of August 1777, Mary Newton's father, George Catlett, who had resided in Olney since the beginning of the year, died 'in the hope of the gospel'. John Newton, writing to Mrs Cunningham, informs her of Romaine's 'providential' visit just days before his death:

> Mr Romaine came hither on Sunday. My father[-in-law] was much rejoiced to see him, and expressed himself to him very comfortably. Mr Romaine conversed and prayed with him two or three times, and was one of the last persons to whom he spoke on Friday evening. I thought it providential that the only gospel minister whom he knew, and had formerly heard, should be sent, as it were, on purpose to close his eyes, and receive his dying testimony.[6]

Mary Newton had recently been in London and had heard Romaine give 'a sweet discourse'. Thomas Charles of Bala also heard Romaine at this time and from Olney on 8 August 1777 he wrote to Watts Wilkinson: 'With no small pleasure I inform you that Mr Romaine stopped here two days, and gave us two excellent sermons on Christ's glory in his person and offices, and on his preciousness to a ruined sinner, when he is enabled to lay hold on him through faith.'[7] During this summer Romaine suffered a rare illness, but after relaxing under sunny skies on the beach at Weymouth his 'health, spirits and thankfulness' were restored. For the first time it seems travelling was a burden to him.

Romaine was always ready to counsel others in spiritual things and to instruct them on how to live more for Christ. In a letter he wrote on 7 April 1779, possibly to Thomas Eyre senior, a farmer, he first answers an inquiry on how to live as a Christian and glorify God. He opens by setting down the 'great principle and leading truth': 'A Christian is one who lives in Christ and

John Newton, a close
friend of Romaine's and
author of the English
hymn 'Amazing Grace'.

upon Christ. He is quickened by the Spirit of Life and made one with Christ; he lives and performs all the acts of spiritual life by the same way that he was made alive. He who lives most in this manner is the best Christian and will bring most glory to God.' He then deals with the second point: 'to know yourself while a son of the first Adam, although a son of the second Adam, who is the Lord from heaven. If you leave out this truth, you will be puzzled at every step, because you will always find some things in your actions against faith. Remember then, the animal man lives an animal life; the spiritual man lives a spiritual life; and you have both these in you.' Finally, from the stores of his own pastoral wisdom and experience, and with sound practical advice, he urges his reader to look to Christ for all things:

Trust in him night and day — summer and winter. Trust in him when things go wrong — in weakness — in adversity. That is the time to trust him for most grace, when you want most. Trust, and you shall have it; for the word cannot be broken... Little matters require his directions, and call for his assistance as well as great, because without him you can do nothing. By leaving Christ out, believers oftener miscarry in little things than in great. He leaves them to themselves, and then they blunder; as it is fit they should who neglect such a guide. He offers himself to you to be your wisdom; and he would give you his counsel in all your matters. You cannot think till you try, and by constant trial prove, what a happiness it is then to live upon Christ as your teacher. He would keep you from a thousand scrapes, and guide you through difficulties, bless you under troubles; yea, he would give you a spiritual use of all temporal things.

Resolve upon something of this kind, and will the event. In your family — in your fields — in buying and selling, consult Christ about all. Don't cut your grass, nor reap your corn — don't buy a cow or sell a horse — but look up to him, that he may bless you in it. Improve this

> hint: eat and drink — lie down and rise up — do all eye-
> ing him and then all will prosper.
> I commend you and your family to him. May he make
> you a spiritual farmer![8]

For some time Romaine, as Lady Huntingdon's chaplain and adviser, had been prepared to itinerate for the Countess on the supposition that, as peeress of the realm, she had a legal right to employ her chaplains in her own chapels. But when the Spa Fields judgement of 1779 settled matters in her disfavour and she afterwards licensed her chapels and preachers as dissent-ers under the Act of Toleration, Romaine, along with Henry Venn, William Jesse and other parochial clergy, felt compelled to withdraw from formal union. Such a separation undoubtedly hurt Romaine, for he had worked closely with the Countess for many years, and it was mainly due to her influence that he had secured the living at Blackfriars. However, he 'continued in the most cordial intimacy, and showed the same fraternal regard to ministers in the Church who laboured for her',[9] although a short note he wrote on a scrap of paper, the precise context of which is not known, suggests tensions were growing: 'Madam, I ... do not know, nor desire to know, one single step you are taking in this matter. I wish to mind my own business and not to interfere in the least with yours. It would be better for you if you heard more truths and fewer lies. I still pray for you and am your obedient servant.'[10]

An example of Romaine's tolerance is found when Lady Huntingdon in her will made Thomas Haweis, who had also withdrawn from her Connexion, one of her trustees and execu-tors, bequeathing to him, with others, her numerous chapels, and entrusting him with the charge to ensure that the gospel was preached in them. This news 'burst on him like a thun-der-stroke', to use his own words, for the Countess had never even hinted at such an appointment. Haweis was 'deeply op-pressed by the consciousness of the weight of this charge, and the opposition he must encounter in a faithful discharge of it'.[11]

He prayed earnestly about it and imagined all sorts of problems arising from it, more than he actually endured; but he did not want to decline so important a trust. In his dilemma he consulted his friend Romaine at Blackfriars. He shared with him the bequest and all the difficulties he envisaged, and asked Romaine if he was in his friend's position, what he would do. Romaine paused and then said that, taking everything into consideration, 'he ought' to accept the bequest, as he would do if he was in a similar position.

Haweis was happy with Romaine's reply and asked him if he could say that Romaine gave him that advice. 'With my free leave,' was Romaine's immediate response, 'and more than that, I will vindicate the step, persuaded your matters will be better conducted than if they devolved upon other hands.' He added, 'You will always find me the same, and though I may not give you my help, you will always be welcome to my pulpits, and receive every token of my fraternal regard and approbation.'[12] Romaine kept his word, for whenever his friend was in London he was asked to serve at Blackfriars, as was Thomas Wills, even when the latter was minister of her ladyship's chapel in Spa Fields. Sadly, others, who at one time reverenced Romaine's word as 'oracular', turned away from him and allowed the spirit of bigotry to blind their judgements.

It is clear from his letters and other writings of this period that the burden of prayer still lay heavy on his heart. Psalm 63 was especially important to him. It begins: 'O God, you are my God, early will I seek you. My soul thirsts for you, my flesh longs for you in a dry and thirsty land where there is no water.' He was always urging others to pray and to seek a closer communion with God. In 1779, as if to underline his determination to call the nation to prayer, he reprinted *Earnest Invitation to the Friends of the Established Church*, first published in 1757 at the beginning of the Seven Years War. He sent this tract to many of his friends, including Mrs Medhurst, to whom he said: 'I send you enclosed a little token of respect. You had it in the last war, and it is now again expedient, yea, necessary. I hope for your helping hand in this good work. Some must fight, and others pray. One is as much wanted as the other. If Moses does not pray, Joshua does not conquer. Prayers gained the victory.'[13]

He then begs his friend to join him and others in calling on God to restore peace to the land, for France had joined forces with the Americans, and Spain and Portugal were expected to follow suit:

> May God give you the spirit of prayer, that you may join
> the goodly company throughout the land, who will be on
> their knees next Sunday at eight o'clock. It is your duty.
> May you esteem it your privilege! and I wish you grow-
> ing communion with your God; more delight daily in ap-
> proaching the throne of his grace, and more blessings
> coming from him on you and yours. We have already
> many hands lifted up to engage the Lord of Hosts on our
> side. Mine are engaged, and I trust will not hang down
> till peace return.[14]

This hour of prayer from eight to nine on Sunday evenings for the nation was still going strong in 1784, when Romaine was in dread at what he thought was coming on the land. 'If nobody stands in the gap, vengeance will find its way. We have pleaded and prevailed. If we cannot this time and the measure of our in-iquities be full, it will however be well with them who are on the side of the Lord and his Christ.' And again: 'May we mourn and pray for our sins and others' — sigh for the dishonour offered to our almighty Jesus, and to the Spirit Jehovah, and to the word of his grace. Let us do what we can in the way of prayer.'[15] Comments such as these show how seriously Romaine took the godlessness of the nation, and uncover his fear that God's wrath would soon be poured forth.

The principal motivation behind Romaine's reluctance to debate controversial issues was his knowledge of the sheer fruit-lessness of 'civil war'. He was for laying aside 'those meetings which provoke disputations'. The way forward was not to argue, but to pray. 'The self-righteous spirit of Arminianism,' he says in a letter (10 October 1781), 'is fond of wrangling and altercation. Prayer will do more good in opposing it than a thousand arguments. And when the cause is removed in God's way and time, things may return to their old establishment. In the mean season a prayer meeting seems to be the best and most seasonable meeting.'[16]

In every department of his life prayer was an integral part. His greatest privilege was to spend time with his Father and to enter his courts. He was familiar with God but not too familiar. He knew he was a vile sinner saved by grace and that God was the Lord of glory before whom he must bow in humble adoration; and yet the 'King of kings,' he says, 'is extremely gracious to me, and admits me into his presence, and sometimes into his cabinet, when he vouchsafes me such a favourable audience'.[17] He was a man raised up, not simply to pray for his part of the vineyard, but for the nation as a whole.

In his memorandum book for 1779 he lists some of the answers to prayer for that year, which were also encouragements for him to pray on in 1780. Some of them are given in a letter at the end of 1779 to Ambrose Serle, now back in England from America. These notes were expanded into an eight-page article that was published in the *Gospel Magazine* for February 1780 under the title *Encouragements to Continue Praying for Church and State*. He opens the article by remembering how God had answered their united prayers during the Seven Years War, and urges people to pray for the American war in a similar manner: 'O for another army of such suppliants! What cannot they do! calling for, and trusting to, the help of the Almighty?... And now the host is gone forth against the enemy, may we at home follow them and aid them with our prayers! never ceasing, until God restores peace to the earth, and good-will between us and all our enemies.'[18] Then he lists the answers to prayer:

The providences in our favour in [England] 1779:
   1. After the high wind, with which the year began,

we had settled weather for several months, and the finest spring that ever was known: many days without a cloud, which is very uncommon in our island.

2. A very plentiful harvest, and got in well all over the kingdom.

3. A delightful autumn, abundance of grass, and a good feed time.

4. Our camps were remarkably healthful this year, as well as the last, although they broke up late.

5. Invasions threatened and attempted all the summer [at Guernsey and Plymouth], but without success.

6. Our fleets have arrived safe from all parts of the world, notwithstanding the boasted superiority of the enemies' navy.

7. The enemies' trade ruined — several of their ships taken, some dispersed by storms, some sunk. Visible providence was against them.

8. Our successes have been so great in the East Indies, that the French have no footing left there upon the continent.

9. Our East India ships as signally preserved this year from the Spanish fleet sent out to take them, as they were the year before from the French.

10. England and Ireland have been most happily united; to the great disappointment of our foreign and domestic enemies, and to the great joy of all good subjects.[19]

Romaine lists various providences against the French, Spaniards and the Americans, which he also views as answers to prayer. 'We humbled ourselves before our God, and he graciously inclined his ear, and heard us,' he says in the *Gospel Magazine*. 'We pleaded for mercy for our land and people, and he gave us evident proofs of his being on our side... All that wish well to their country are invited to join with us in praying for peace, and for the blessings of the Prince of peace.'[20] He closes his

St Mary Woolnoth.

letter to Serle with the words: 'I have a brighter view to give of God's answer to prayer in spirituals... Surely God is on our side. He does great things for us, without our fleets and armies. To him be all the glory. Prayer and praise must go together the next year. Much prayer will afford matter for much praise.'[21]

This 'sounding of the trumpet' was on the back of a real breakthrough in London and for Romaine personally, and which may have been a direct answer to his prayers, for in January 1780 John Newton left Olney and moved to the living of St Mary Woolnoth in the heart of the town. Now the capital had two beneficed evangelical clergymen to fight for the cause of the gospel.

In 1779 Lord George Gordon organized and led the Protestant Association formed to secure the repeal of the Catholic Relief Act of the previous year. This Act relieved Roman Catholics in England from certain penalties and disabilities imposed during the reign of William III. Gordon, 'an eccentric, fanatical Scotsman', as well as a member of parliament, led a huge mob to the houses of parliament on 2 June 1780 to present a petition against the Act. The confrontation exploded into violence and for several days Gordon's supporters went on

Scenes from the riots.

the rampage, causing widespread damage to property and the loss of many lives. Gordon was arrested and charged with high treason, but was later acquitted on the ground that he had no treasonable intentions.

Romaine was in London at the time of the riots and on 19 June he wrote to Ambrose Serle: 'The effects of the late troubles begin to be felt: Mrs P. died of the mob last Saturday. I am obliged at her request, to stay to preach her funeral sermon. Perhaps somebody may soon preach mine; my house and life are both threatened: but my Lord ruleth over all... If I am permitted to see you in the flesh, I can tell you of persons and things, at which both your ears will tingle.'[22] Although his curate Erasmus Middleton was a member of the Association's committee, Romaine not only refused to sign the petition, but actually burned it. This infuriated many of its supporters. Charles Wesley, not one to miss an opportunity, picked up his pen and wrote a poem entitled *The Protestant Association*, in which he impersonates the mob. Of Romaine, who had become 'an object of popular vengeance', he says:

> But O what death doth he require,
> Who cast our names into the fire,
> Repulsed and treated us with scorn?
> He, and his house and church, shall burn.
> That rogue *Romaine*, we soon shall have him;
> Nor *Mence's* tuneful voice shall save him;
> (Who would not the Associates join,
> Or list beneath a madman's sign).[23]

Romaine 'and his house and church' survived the rage of the rioters.

Alongside prayer, and equally dear to Romaine, was reading the Bible. As soon as he had finished his St Dunstan's lectures, his custom was to read from Genesis to Revelation 'without stopping or interruption', an exercise he always began with prayer and continued with a 'settled dependence on the spirit of prayer'. All the profit he received, he readily ascribed 'to the praise of his glorious grace'. In a letter to William Cadogan (3 September), he says: 'I have just finished my reading of the Bible for 1783. It has been a season of great teaching; I never went through it with more delight or with more profit. My soul has found it more precious than gold, and it is really sweeter than honey. But still I see much more before me to be learnt and to be experienced.'[24] Writing to Serle from Southampton on 14 October 1783, he exclaims: 'O what a treasure — what unsearchable riches are there in this golden mine! I never dug deeper, nor found more precious jewels, than upon this last perusal.'[25]

In his 14 October letter he wrote down some of the observations that arose from his Bible reading of that year. He saw afresh that one of the first things to be noticed and expected is 'the actual fulfilling of the promises to this day, namely, that the Holy Spirit is still in the word: he works in it and by it' to save the lost. Secondly, he was convinced afresh of the 'divine and infallible truth of the Holy Scriptures', that every line and word is according to the mind of the infinitely wise God. Thirdly, that what the Word reports, the Spirit has realised. And fourthly, that there is more to be received out of Christ's fulness than anyone upon earth has yet enjoyed. 'God has humbled me,' says Romaine, 'and has made me feel more of mine own poverty, and has thereby led me to live more upon Christ's everlasting treasury.'[26]

The following year, after reading through the Scriptures, he saw more clearly the 'uniformity of the Scripture plan' and how all parts 'perfectly harmonize'; when they are compared together, 'each illustrates and beautifies the whole'. He received another confirmation of the truth of Scripture, that it is the revelation of God, which was heightened by finding the power of God accompanying it. All this increased his love for the Bible: 'As I dig deeper, the mine becomes rich, and the treasures of grace are greatly enhanced by their being the earnests of glory. O what a book is this! What, is any way like it? I cannot get enough of it... I have just done reading, and yet I want to begin again: my appetite is keener.'[27] To help satisfy his appetite it is said that he read Psalm 121 every day.

Such revelations were undoubtedly aided by Romaine's spiritual approach to reading and studying the Bible. He studied to know it as a Christian, not as a metaphysician. He sought, 'not so much to comprehend it, as to believe it'. In all, he submitted his reason to God's reason, and kept praying that God would make his Word like the light of the sun, 'clear in my head and fruitful in my heart'. He would read his Bible, not to discover some new truth, but to be established in what he already knew, and to attain more practical confirmation in it. 'This I would chiefly seek for, that I may get growing experience of the wisdom of God, and of the power of God in his word, and may thereby enjoy the blessings of his love promised in it.'[28] In giving advice to a friend, he summed up his own attitude to the Bible: 'It is by continual dependence on the teaching of the Spirit, in and by the word, and by mixing faith with it, that we come to find its value, and to taste its pleasures.'[29]

The substance of his prayers as he read the 'Book of God' is given below. It is not a form but a directory, and he never confined himself to the exact words; but he did regard them as containing everything a Christian is warranted to ask of God concerning the profit he has promised to all who mix faith with his Word. It is a good example of Romaine's desire, not simply to study the Word academically, but to feed his soul on it and to live daily by it.

O thou Spirit of wisdom and revelation, be with me whenever I read thy holy word: testify to me in it, and by it, of Christ Jesus, who he is, and what he is to me; and glorify the Father's love in him. Open thou mine eyes to see the wondrous things revealed in it upon these subjects, that I may understand them in thy light, and that my judgment of them may be the same with thine: I beseech thee also to enable me to mix faith with what I

do understand; and what through thy teaching I am enabled to believe aright, that help me to receive in the love
of the truth. O God fulfil thy promise — put thy blessed
word into my inward parts: write it upon my heart. And
what I am taught to love, grant me power to practise; that
thy new covenant promise may in me have its full effect,
and I may be in heart and life cast into the mould and
form of thy word — thus becoming a real living edition of
the Bible. Make it my daily study. Render it my constant
delight. Let my meditation of it be always sweet. O thou
holy and eternal Spirit, witness thus to thine own record
— and let me experience it to be the power of God, as
well as the truth of God. In this dependence upon thee
in the use of it, let me be daily growing — until, by the
will of God, I shall have served mine own generation;
and then let it be the last act of my life, to seal the truth
of thy testimony concerning Jesus. Let me find thy witness true in the hour of death, and beyond death all the
promises made good to me, through Jesus Christ, in life
everlasting. Amen and amen.[30]

Romaine's love for and dependence on God; his practical belief
in the divine promises, from which he enjoyed daily succour; his
experiential knowledge of the Bible, which he constantly urged
his parishioners to imitate; and his faithful life of prayer, so precious in times of need, were all about to be severely tested. For
Romaine, a man after God's own heart, like King David, was
about to walk through the valley of the shadow of death. And
in that darkest hour the words of his favourite Psalm would no
doubt be a shelter from the storm and a comfort to his soul.

I will lift up mine eyes unto the hills,
from whence cometh my help.
My help cometh from the LORD,
which made heaven and earth.
He will not suffer thy foot to be moved:

he that keepeth thee will not slumber.
Behold, he that keepeth Israel
shall neither slumber nor sleep.
The LORD is thy keeper:
the LORD is thy shade upon thy right hand.
The sun shall not smite thee by day,
nor the moon by night.
The LORD shall preserve thee from all evil:
he shall preserve thy soul.
The LORD shall preserve thy going out
and thy coming in from this time forth,
and even for evermore.
(Psalm 121).

My system begins with 'the Lord reigneth'. It goes on, every step, with 'the Lord reigneth'. And whatever opposes it, must come down; for he has all power in heaven and in earth: 'the Lord God omnipotent reigneth for ever and ever'. In such times as the present, nothing can quiet the spirit, or settle the mind in perfect peace, but that this Lord is my Lord: under his care he has me and mine. Come what may, all is safe in his hands.

William Romaine.[1]

14
The Trials of 'An Old Man'

Romaine's son, William, married Miss Martha Roberts of St Sepulchre Church on 2 April 1782, and the happy couple set up home in Reading, where William had a curacy. Later in the year Romaine wrote to his son from Brislington:

My very dear son,
   Our letters were in opposition, although they were friendly. They met on the road. Passed each other. And left each party in suspense. However, all is well. We received yours yesterday, which stilled all our fears and apprehensions. We are made easy and thankful. You may rest assured of our partaking in your happiness, and of our rejoicing in your joy. May it be growing and lasting. You and Mrs R. the more you know of each other still happier. And giving us fresh reason to pray for you, and also to praise. For this I shall not cease to be your willing advocate. Having all my heart could wish in your present and in a pleasing prospect of everlasting blessedness. So be it...
   Mrs M R [Mary Romaine] is sitting by. She wishes everything kind and loving to you and to your dear partner.[2]

This joyful occasion was quickly followed by Romaine's se-
verest test. He was tenderly affectionate to his children, loving
them dearly, yet he knew that the Lord, who had given them to
him, had the right to take them whenever he saw fit. His most
trying affliction was the death of his second and youngest son,
Captain Adam Romaine, who was in the East Indies on duty
with the 98th Regiment of Foot. He was only twenty-four. In
May of that year Romaine had made one of his few references
to his son in a letter to Mrs Medhurst, when he spoke from personal experience:

> I hear you have a present exercise; namely, your young
> and beloved Isaac to be parted from you. There is grace
> sufficient even for this. You do not love your son more
> than I did mine [when he left home]. It cannot cross your
> will more than it did mine: but my son went into the army,
> and I do not repent; it was his choice. He has been kept,
> as far as I know, from army sins: and the same good
> God may also keep your son. Trust him in his loving and
> careful guidance; and the Lord will do what is best both
> for him and for you.[3]

In the above letter to William, which is dated 24 August, he tells
his son that he had received 'a good account of your brother
[Adam]' from Mr Maxwell, purser to Commodore Johnson, 'till
they parted beyond the Cape'. At that time he still did not know
that Adam was dead. He received the tragic news later in 1782
— news that was to shake his faith in 'the Lord[, who] will do
what is best both for him and for you' — in a letter from his
son's commanding officer:

> Sir,
>   It gives me great concern to be under the disagree-
> able necessity of communicating to you a melancholy
> event, in which you are nearly interested. Captain
> Romaine was seized about a fortnight ago with a disor-

The Trials of 'An Old Man'

der in his bowels, which terminated in a flux. I am sorry to add that the consequences have been fatal to him. Every attention has been paid to his memory which our situation permitted. I will not add to the distress which this misfortune must occasion, by describing how much he was beloved, and how much was expected from him by every person in the regiment.

I have the honour to be,

Sir,

Your most obedient and very

faithful servant, &c.

Trincomaley, June 4, 1782.[4]

Romaine was deeply humbled and shocked by the tragic news. His wife pressed him not to go to St Dunstan's that evening, an entreaty that would have convinced many to stay at home, but he replied that he must not leave his Master's concerns for the souls of men unattended on account of his own bereavement, and he went and preached as usual.

At the end of the year Romaine was still sorely afflicted, yet willing to submit to God's sovereign will. The struggle was hard and the pain deep, but God's grace was sufficient. His poor wife, too, experienced the most exquisite feelings over a 'child who never offended her in his life', and for several months was not able to see anyone. Her constant prayer during these dark days was to be delivered from a spirit of murmuring that would displease God. 'In the midst of her greatest floods of tears, she would cry out, "Lord, keep me, Lord, save me from thinking or speaking anything contrary to thy holy will." And he was very good to her, her faith was supported.'[5] She was greatly helped by a letter from Mrs I —: 'It sounded a concord; it met the very sentiments of her heart, and became, not a prescription, but an effectual medicine to her wound. It was not a letter about the balm of Gilead, but it brought and administered the healing virtue.'[6]

In a letter of 13 December 1782, he gives further details of his response to this 'very heavy affliction' and of God's goodness towards him:

> He [Adam] was cut off by a violent flux at Trincomalee in the island of Ceylon. I feel as a parent; I am no stone: but grace has got the better of nature. God supports. God comforts... I can, from my heart, say, 'Not my will, Lord, but thine be done;' whereby I have the advantage of finding that my faith, being put into the furnace, is true gold. It is, glory be to grace, proved and improved.
>
> When I first saw the letter which brought us the account, I knew the general's seal to it, and, fearing the contents, I looked up for the presence and for the support of my good Master and my old Friend; and he answered me in the words of a great believer, 'The Lord gave, and the Lord hath taken away.' He has a right to do what he will with his own. Then he enabled me to reply, 'Blessed be the name of the Lord;' and I do praise him for giving me some of Job's resignation, that I could use his words with the same spirit.[7]

The following day Romaine wrote: 'I could wish he would have spared my son; my soul delighted in him: he was a sweet youth. The remembrance of his person and manners and behaviour; his dutifulness, for he never offended me but once in his life; his conduct since he was in the army — these draw tears from mine eyes while I am writing.'[8] Romaine was no stoic, he felt deeply, and went continually to God for support, relief and strength to endure.

In a letter of consolation he wrote to a bereaved friend on 19 December 1794, just a few months before his own death, he used his own experience to impart advice and comfort:

> None of your friends can sympathize with you more on this melancholy occasion, than we do. I have wrote to

your brother by this day's post, directing him, where to look for supports and comforts. When I was in the same situation, by the loss of a son in the East Indies, I found the consolations of God, not a few, nor small. I hope and pray, that he may find the same, and in patience possess his soul. A parent, and Mr G. had much of a parent's feeling, cannot but grieve at the loss of an only son: yet there is grace promised sufficient to help to bear it quietly, yea to profit from this affliction.[9]

There were other trials that Romaine had to face during this period. In 1783 his wife was 'very much out of order — feverish — a sore throat'. The doctor was called and he expressed a hope that there was no danger, although the 'symptoms are not so good as he could wish'.[10] Thankfully, his wife recovered. His own health was not always good. While it is true he never missed a Sabbath through ill-health, there were times of sickness. On 13 August 1781 he wrote to a friend: 'I have not been at all well since I left you: a giddiness follows me constantly, and sometimes I am ready to fall.'[11] Earlier in the year he had complained of a sore finger that prevented him from writing for 'some months'. The following year he travelled to Southampton for health reasons, hoping the southern waters would assist his recovery. In a letter to his sister he unveiled his spiritual priorities: 'I have been very poorly a long time, but thank God, I find sickness better for me than health; and I am sure, when the Lord sees best, I shall be restored to my former state. The main thing is to be secure of our eternal health.'[12]

Romaine submitted to the sovereign hand of God in his personal afflictions, and acknowledged that the Ruler of heaven and earth is always worthy of praise. He entertained no doubts in the promises of Scripture and was fully persuaded that all things 'work together for good to those who love God, to those who are called according to his purpose'. He looked upon pain as a 'standing memorial of the exceeding sinfulness of sin. Happy for us,' he says, 'if every pain led us to loathe ourselves, and to admire Jesus' — two lessons he admits he was learning slowly, 'for they are both mysteries. Yea, I press on, though I know I cannot learn them perfectly till I get into the upper school.'[13] It is significant that his word for 1783 was 'Jehovah Shalom', Jehovah is our peace, as if he wanted to publish not only that the war with America was over but what God had done for his own soul.

With the comfort he received, he was able to comfort others. His constant advice was to trust all to Christ. 'Your one business is to trust your all in the hands of Christ; having received him, then to live upon him. Remember, he is to answer every purpose, body and soul; you and yours; earth and heaven. You are not living up to your privilege, if there be any person or thing that you keep back from Christ, and do not leave to his absolute management.'[14] In August 1777 he wrote to a 'very poorly' friend and passed on this advice: 'You are kept low for very good reasons. He ... has your best interest in view, and never loses sight of it. Could you look into his loving heart, as it is opened in the Scriptures, you would see the tenderest mercy in all your sufferings: yea, you would believe and rejoice under them.'[15] Just over a year after Adam died, on 22 September 1783, he wrote to a friend who had recently lost his mother.

> Our good Lord would not have you not to feel for your loss, but to mourn as one that hath hope. We cannot doubt but your mother is with the Lord... All is safe in his hand... Sorrow not, therefore, so much for her, as to hinder your gratitude to God for his special kindness to her living and dying. You have lost a mother, a good mother, and I have lost a friend; but neither you nor I would wish her back again... Blessed be his holy name, he supported her faith to the last.[16]

In a further letter of consolation (26 November 1785), he not only comforts his friend, but openly expresses his own feelings:

The church and people in R — have a great loss, and none more than yourself; for she really was a mother to you in love, in every good office, and in continual prayer for your person and for your labours. The poor will feel her loss. Her long experience made her wise in the things of God, by which she could teach the ignorant, with a meekness quite her own. Her natural temper, sanctified by grace, enabled her, frequently to check the spreading of furious zeal and wild separations...

My eyes are running down with tears, while I am writing, I do not resist his will. Oh no, I kiss the rod, but I do feel the smart, and shall for some time. God sanctify it! May the Comforter take the things of Jesus, and with them help us to improve this visitation.[17]

In one final example he turns a sad loss into a reason for praise:

He has taken away a sister — but she is with him. You have lost a friend, but he has found her. She is dead, but she liveth. O most blessed change. She is gone from sin and suffering to live with God for ever. I am ready to say, notwithstanding she will be so much missed in your family, from my very heart I praise and worship him, that he has taken her into his heaven and glory. He did it too in a way which was singularly kind to her surviving relations.[18]

There were times of blessing and encouragement as well. On 2 August 1783 he wrote from Reading, where he agreed to be a subscriber and collector for the gallery William Cadogan was building in his church: 'I never felt his goodness more in all my life, than in worshipping him at my Oratory: there I set up my Ebenezer afresh.'[19] On 30 July 1784, he penned these comments: 'The Prince of Peace was very much honoured in this city [London] yesterday. I scarce ever felt so much of his

presence in ordinances any day of my life. There was also great
outward reverence paid by all, except Quakers.'[20] Four and
a half months later verses from Isaiah (40:1, 2, 3, &c.) were
brought home to his heart 'to my unspeakable joy. I have trod
upon John the Baptist's heels, and have been favoured with
some of his views of the Lamb of God.'[21]

There were not so many occasions for him to travel during these years, and in 1781 he spoke of London as 'my prison'. However, we do find him in places such as Southampton,
Reading, Weymouth, Bristol and Bradford in Wiltshire. When
he was at home there were good opportunities to develop his
ministry and to share his opinion on various important topics.
He was a strong supporter of Sunday Schools, and expressed
his delight in how the Lord had used them for good in Yorkshire
(1784), where several persons, laity and clergy, had gathered a
group of unruly children to teach them to read, write and learn
the catechism.

> The Lord God has marvellously favoured the plan. He
> has inclined vast numbers of children to come; the par-
> ents in general are thankful; and the schoolmasters and
> mistresses have given great satisfaction. I know not
> of anything more promising for the rising generation,
> especially as it is made an indispensable part of their
> Sunday's employment, that they attend the church regu-
> larly with their masters and mistresses. Mr T. informs me
> of one good effect, that it has been the happy occasion
> of many conversions, by bringing poor people to see
> their children at church, who never before came to any
> place of worship. Others have also been won over to let
> their children attend by the little presents made to the
> neighbours' children, and by seeing their improvement
> in reading and writing.[22]

Romaine had a custom in Lent of catechising the children, and
whenever there was a new child, he would ask, 'What is your

name?' He would then explain to them what it meant and beg them, with all importunity, to remember the definition and apply the lesson of it to their lives. 'If they do not live up to it, not only I will witness, but also their very name will rise up against them.' This method often made a lasting impression on the children and on others too who came to listen. 'I knew a woman,' reports Romaine, 'who came in on Friday, into our church, and God made this simple way (the speaking to the children) the means of her conversion.'[23]

One of the wonderful aspects of Romaine's ministry, from the time of his conversion to his death, is his delight to speak of the Lord Jesus Christ and the things of God. In his sermons, letters, and other writings, hardly a line goes by without some mention of Christ and his finished work of salvation, or a piece of sound practical advice on how to know and love Christ more and the blessings that follow. A previously unpublished letter, written to Lady Hill of Hardwick (near Shrewsbury) on 2 January 1784, will suffice as an example of this Christ-centredness. He opens with thanks to God for bringing her ladyship 'by singular providences to the knowledge of the truth, and I hope to a sound experience of its power. These are the only two things worth living for... He has taught you to know Jesus and to be wise unto salvation.' Then he comes to the desire of his heart:

I hope and pray, that in this new year you may become better acquainted with your Lord and Saviour. For the more you know of him, the better you will trust him. And be assured, the more you trust him, you will find him such a faithful, such a bountiful friend that you cannot help growing more in love with him. And by degrees your love will teach you to become intimate with him. You will delight to be much with him in private, your heart in prayer will hold sweet converse with him. He will speak to you in his word, and will open the secrets of it... No friend can converse more familiarly with another, than he will with you. This heavenly fellowship will bring on,

The pulpit in St Mary-
le-Port Church, Bristol,
where Romaine frequently
preached.

as all friendship does, a growing conformity to him. And
this is being in heaven upon earth. For you will only have
to change the degree of your love, but not the object.
Sense will take the place of faith. But it will be the same
enjoyment of Jesus only improved and perfected. You
will see him soon face to face, as He is — you will be
with him, where He is — And like him, which is heaven
of heavens.[24]

During this period he was on friendly terms with William Tandey,
the curate in charge from 1784 of St Mary-le-Port in Bristol.
For several weeks in the summer Romaine would take charge
of Tandey's flock, teaching them the truths of the gospel. T. T.
Biddulph relates that on 26 September 1787 Romaine opened
the Wednesday morning lecture at the church. As in all his re-
lationships, he was never slow to impart spiritual advice to his
friends: 'You feel sin,' he wrote to Tandey on 27 January 1784,
'that is right, but it should lead you to Jesus. You feel remaining

sin: still the blood has almighty virtue to pardon and to subdue.'[25] On another occasion he said: 'You will honour the free
Giver by coming to him for fresh grace, and for more grace.
Go to him as I come to you. I have no doubt of your readiness
to grant *my* requests, and you can have no reason to doubt of
his to grant *yours*.' And again, perhaps remembering his own
affliction: '*He* keeps you in the furnace. It is *his* will. He means
you good. When you have no dross he will not use the furnace
any longer.'

From Southampton on 17 October 1785, he wrote to
Tandey, in typical fashion:

> I heard a dying friend of mine exhorting a minister who
> came to see him, *'Preach Christ, sir, preach Christ. You
> cannot preach too much, nor exalt him any way equal
> to what he is; for his name alone is excellent, and his
> praise above heaven and earth.'* I thank God that you
> do preach him, and I pray God that you may do it better
> every day... Neglect no opportunity... exert yourself in
> magnifying him; and doubt not that he will give you both
> strength and success, as will be most for his own glory
> and for your good.
>
> Take me for an example. Consider my years. What
> a miracle of love! Yesterday morning I was able to
> preach and assist at the sacrament, and in the after-
> noon to read prayers and preach again, to very crowded
> congregations. This morning I am quite well, and fit to
> go to my delightful work again. Blessings on that dear,
> dear Jesus, who loadeth me with seventy years' mer-
> cies... Mr Tandey, trust him and be not afraid. Look at
> him. Read what he promises, and give him full credit.
> He will be better to you than you can ever think.[26]

It is regretted that Romaine never kept a diary and that he did
not commit many of his autobiographical thoughts to writing,
except a piece entitled *An Old Man*, which he wrote on his

seventieth birthday (25 September 1784). It is given in full below:

> Through the gracious hand of my God I have this day arrived at the age of man: I have therefore set it apart for meditation, prayer and praise. May the Holy Spirit help me to improve it, that I may spend the little of my remaining time with more faith and unceasing gratitude.
>
> When I look back, I would be all adoration. As a creature I worship the Creator. Once I was nothing, and he brought me into being. O, what distinguishing favour to make me a rational creature! And as I was a ruined man, a sinner guilty, helpless, miserable! O, what sovereign grace to make me a new man! Who can tell (I cannot) how great the love was which provided a Saviour for such a rebel! What patience, how infinite! To spare me through childhood, through youth, through manhood, when every day, and everything in the day, were calling aloud for vengeance. I might have been many years ago in hell, and most justly; and now I adore the long-suffering of God, which kept me out of it. He had purposes of love toward me, which he made known in his own time and way. It was sovereign love which brought me to know myself, and to know Jesus. His own Holy Spirit begun and carried on the work. He opened mine eyes to understand the Scriptures. He gave me to believe the truth, and to feel their power; and now I set my seal to every word in them; finding God to be true and faithful, true in the promise, faithful in the fulfilment. Receive Christ — one with him — live by him — live on him — worship him — do all on earth as well as I can, till he enable me to do it better in heaven.
>
> In this believing view of things, I acknowledge that I have lived to a blessed time. All that is worth enjoying has been freely given to me. By the quickening grace of the Spirit, brought into oneness with Jesus, and to

partake of the Father's love in him, all is mine. Glory be to Father, Son and Spirit in the highest, the covenanting Trinity is mine. These are the prospects which faith, looking back, opens to the Christian with delight; and thereby renders my present condition a subject of praise and thankfulness. My time is almost run out, and what is short is now also but labour and sorrow. So says the oracle. And I feel it. The infirmities of age, the decay of the faculties of mind as well as body, consequently usefulness in one's place and station dying daily, these are always giving warning that the house made with hands must soon be taken down. It begins to be very troublesome to keep it up. One prop falls after another, and repeats the lesson — you must soon be turned out. Look after the house not made with hands, eternal in the heavens. Blessed be God for giving us the earnest of his Spirit, to enable us to look forward with a pleasing hope, when mortality shall be swallowed up of life.

It is by this same faith that God has reconciled my heart to his providence. He is my Father, my portion, and my exceeding great reward; my God and my Keeper. It is my privilege that he is to manage for me. He knows what is best for me, and to him I leave it. To be richer or greater, in more health, or in more honour, would be no addition to my happiness. I have enough of this world's goods. I am content with my place and station, and ask for nothing but more thankfulness for what I have. O what calm does this bring upon my mind! Looking back I can see his gracious dealings with me in all the events of my life. And he has brought me and settled me in the very condition in which I ought to be. What has God done? What has he not done to make me satisfied? Indeed I have all the reason that ever man had to adore him for his providence, and to bless him for his dealings with the children of men.

This day such are my views of his goodness to me in the time past, both in temporal, and also in spiritual mercies. All is well; and blessings on his name, the prospect before me, notwithstanding the infirmities of age, is comfortable. The promises in the Word afford exercise for faith, and never ceasing dependence; not only general promises, but also particular, suited exactly to my present circumstances. Our God has made gracious provision for old age, and has enabled me to make use of it, that through patience and comfort of the Scriptures, I might now have hope. He has given me a general warrant for my security. I have committed myself into his care and keeping; and he has declared, 'I will never leave thee nor forsake thee.' This is a continual cordial, and extends its heart-felt influence to the special promises, such as Isaiah 46:3, 4. This is spoken to the whole Israel of God, who have not only the life of the body from him, but chiefly the life of the soul. He creates them anew by the Spirit of life in Christ Jesus. He is the Author — he is the carrier on — he brings that life to its full perfection. It is every moment supported by his power, and blessed with his paternal affection. Age may come, hoary hairs may appear, the vigour of the faculties may decay, but his love is the same. He reveals it. He applies it. The old man feels it, and he turns it into the prayer of faith. O my Father, I do hearken unto thee; thou hast supported, thou hast carried me from birth to this moment; and I doubt not but now in mine old age, and in my hoary hairs, thou wilt still carry me and bear me, until thou hast finally delivered me. Amen. I believe, Lord, it shall be done unto me according to thy Word.[27]

Jesus is matchless beauty — and mine. He is all perfection, and I am perfect in him. The wonder of heaven, and soon I shall see him face to face. This hope makes studying the word, believing, growing up into him, very sweet and improving. Every fresh view of his heavenly person begets some conformity to him, and wishes for more.

William Romaine.[1]

Consider his nature, his essential glory, or his offices — his mediatorial glory, from what he saves us freely, and to what he brings us perfectly, even to life eternal: surely he is matchless Jesus. And he wants only to be known, that he may win our hearts, and we may admire and adore him...

Every fresh look to him confirms the reality, and increases the blessedness of living by faith upon him: and thus daily communion with him nourishes spiritual life, and renders it more easy, and more delightful.

William Romaine.[2]

15

'Looking to Jesus'

Back in 1780, Romaine's reputation had suffered when his friend Martin Madan had advocated polygamy as an answer to the social problems of homeless women who had been seduced by married men. In his *Thelypthora*, published in that year, Madan said that a man 'should be able to have two or more wives'. As can be imagined such a statement by one of his best friends stained his own name and gave his opponents an opportunity for slander.

Romaine, however, did not allow the smear tactics of his enemies to interrupt his own fellowship with God; for he began the last decade of his life as he had finished the previous decade — with praise and thanksgiving in his heart for God's goodness and grace. In a letter written on 9 January 1786 to his friend Walter Taylor, a blockmaker to the Royal Navy, whose house he frequented when in the vicinity of Portswood Green, Southampton, he opens with the comments: 'I begin with thanks. Blessed be his name who has spared us another year, and is still magnifying his mercy to us and ours.' He then urges his friend to try and add up all the mercies and benefits that God has given to him. 'I believe it will puzzle all your skill in arithmetic to give the sum total.' He had tried himself, but had failed and thought it best to 'end the trial with fresh praise... It is the right working of divine grace to be willing to ascribe all to grace. And instead of getting out of debt by praises, we are more indebted for our praises, and should be more thankful for more thankfulness.'[3]

In the same month, writing to a friend in Montpellier, who was enjoying the Mediterranean climate, he enthuses that there is something at Blackfriars 'far beyond the south of France... I live in an element, and when my sky is clear and my sun shines bright, and I feel some of its warm beams and I breathe its pure ether — these are real blessings; they come down from the Father of lights — gifts like himself.'[4] His letters often mention how grateful he is for the felt influence 'of those enlivening beams' of God's grace that make the everlasting day. 'All the honey in the world could not sweeten my tea this morning, as receiving it from my Lord's grace, and using it to my Lord's glory,' he wrote on 4 March 1786.[5]

Erasmus Middleton left Romaine early in 1786 to become curate of St Luke's, Chelsea, the living of which belonged to William Cadogan, who spent most of his time in Reading. As a result of Middleton's departure, the parochial duty lay heavily on Romaine until March of that year when a mutual friend introduced him to William Goode, who had recently given up a curacy in Hertfordshire. Initially Goode was reluctant to accept Romaine's offer of the curacy of Blackfriars, perhaps because the salary was only £40 a year, a big step down from what he was used to. At the end of their first interview, Romaine, noticing Goode's uncertainty and never one to give up easily, said, 'Well, do not say you *will not* come; but say, you will consider it.'[6] After careful consideration, and with his objections removed, he became Romaine's curate at the end of March. In a letter written several years later he acknowledged the guidance of divine providence in his decision when he wrote of the 'remarkable steps by which he was brought there'.[7] He stayed with Romaine until his death, when he became the rector of Blackfriars.

Romaine was as busy as ever during this time, preaching four or five times every week and visiting the sick from Hyde

Park Corner to Mile End. He frequently walked the ten minutes to St Dunstan's along Ludgate Hill and down Fleet Street, and then back to his rectory. He never expressed any desire for preferment, happy as he was to serve God in the place to which he had been called. This singular contentment he passed on in a letter of 23 May 1787:

> My judgment is singular perhaps: I am married to my parish: called by Providence; fixed; I do not look out, 'should I be better off — more useful, — would it not be of God, if the king should send and offer me the bishopric of London?' I have nothing to do with preferment: it is my honour, my profit, my pleasure, to preach at Blackfriars as long as I do preach. Here the head of the church placed me, keeps me: it is my charge. He can do much or little, as it is his holy will, by me: and the being in his will is my paradise. But I quarrel with nobody who thinks differently from me.[8]

At the end of 1787 (12 November), with his usual enthusiasm, he urged Tandey

> ... to admire and to adore the love of our Jesus. What cannot he do? How is it that Mr Tandey has preached the Wednesday lecture [at St Mary-le-Port] ever since I began it [there]? Surely, it is our Lord's doing — And may it be very marvellous in your eyes. My good brother, thank him — Bless him — And still trust. Hide not what he has done for you. Creep up, if you cannot run up into the pulpit, And speak a word for Him, who giveth power to the faint, and to them, that have NO might, *increaseth strength*... Prepare, pray in your chamber — pray in the pulpit — But make the Spirit of Jesus your one hope for matter and for success. Then all will be well.[9]

Romaine's chief desire was to glorify Christ and to encourage others in their Christian walk, which is evident from the mottoes he chose during the last ten years of his life. In 1786 his choice was 'I am Alpha and Omega ... Christ is the Beginning and Ending, and all between, from first to last. He is all in all ... the God of truth, who is, and who was, and who is to come, the great I AM, from everlasting to everlasting, the Almighty, Jesus the God of nature, the God of grace, the God of providence, the God of Glory.' He goes on to say that all who look to Christ are blessed, for they will find in him everything they need to save them from sin and misery, and to make them truly holy and eternally happy. 'We are come together this morning to devote ourselves afresh to his service, and to begin the year [1786] as we hope to end it, in the faith of the Son of God. He is our Alpha and Omega.'[10]

His word for the year 1788 was 'Looking to Jesus', a sight 'that would do an angel good, and much more a sinner; for his name is Wonderful. There is none like him in heaven or earth.'[11] A look to Jesus would make the year 'much better entitled to *annus mirabilis* [a remarkable year], than either the victory over the Spanish Armada or the Revolution. They are gone and past, but ours is altogether wonderful; in its duration, an endless year; and in its blessings, more and greater than any heart can conceive.'[12] For 1789 he chose '"The Lord reigneth," Jehovah Jesus, over all the worlds and over all creatures; and to him every knee shall willingly, or unwillingly, bow.'[13]

In 1790 his watchword was 'Trust in him at all times.' The word 'trust', he explains, means 'to lean upon anything which you think will support you; and you will do it with more or less confidence, as you are persuaded it is able to keep you from falling. This is a beautiful idea of faith, as it respects the word of God — our ground to lean upon.'[14] In June of that year, he wrote: 'It would be better with us, if we leaned more upon the Lord, and less upon other props. I have found that they have not only failed me, when I trusted most to them, but then generally hurt me most. Men, means, outward dependencies withdraw the heart from feeling the supplies of the Spirit, and the comforts of his grace; so that the affections grow cool and indifferent to the spiritual life.'[15]

Two years later his motto was 'Grow in grace,' and with it he wished his people a 'growing year': 'May much of the rain and shining of heaven upon the good seed, make it bring forth an hundred fold in London ... to the praise of the sower, who is the Son of Man.'[16] In 1794, partly as an 'infallible antidote' for his friends, who were uneasy about 'what was coming upon the earth', his word for the year was 'The God of hope', from whom 'believers in Christ may hope for all possible good, and to be saved from all possible evil... May he render this year famous for the exercise of Christian hope: well-grounded, sure and certain, built upon immutable things, and bringing the words before us into happy experience; even that the God of hope may fill us with all joy and peace in believing, that we may abound in hope by the power of the Holy Spirit.'[17] Writing to his sister, he summed up his thoughts on all the annual mottoes with the words: 'Christ all, I nothing.'

Although Romaine was as concerned as his friends about the 'signs of the times', he managed to turn his eyes heavenward and look at the dangers from a Biblical perspective. At the end of 1788, he comforted Walter Taylor, who could see 'a black cloud gathering' over the land and was fearful of what might happen 'when it bursts in all its vengeance'. He reminded him that 'the Lord reigneth' and that his subjects have 'nothing to fear in the worst of times; for their King is almighty, almighty to save'.

> My good Sir, this is the time for faith, to exercise it — aye, to improve it. What of fair weather, and sunshining faith? How can one tell whether it be true or genuine? But to put to sea in our little boat in the midst of a storm, the waves dashing over our heads, and threatening to swallow us up every moment: then to be able to say and feel, 'My Christ is with me in the boat, therefore I will

trust and not be afraid.' This is the proper working of the
faith of God's elect.[18]

According to Romaine, the 'spirit of the times runs strong against
all subordination', with the commandment 'Honour thy father
and thy mother' daily losing its authority. In a letter he wrote on
12 April 1790, he unveils his state of mind:

> In these troublesome times I find it good to follow
> Habakkuk's example, which is all the politics I wish to
> know: he prayed, he got into his watchtower, waited for
> an answer, and he received it, and praised God for it. I
> am doing the same for the public — at prayers for the
> church, groaning under an oppression harder than the
> Chaldean bondage. I pray on, but am still in my watch-
> tower. I can get no answer. One can see no end of the
> present troubles. The cause is not removed; therefore
> they continue; they increase, as if so many fiends of hell
> were let loose, and suffered to do all the mischief which
> Satan himself could wish. We know where to lay the
> blame: unbelief is the provoking sin; it has brought ruin
> upon many great kingdoms; so that we can trace the
> vengeance of heaven against it from age to age, down
> to the present miseries of Europe...
>   O my country, my country! I fear for England. We
> are not much unlike the kingdom of France, very near
> her in her sin, and may not be far from her in her punish-
> ment. Therefore I keep me in my watchtower, praying
> and pleading for mercy, begging our Lord to spare us for
> his own name's sake. This is my only plea.[19]

He longed for the Lord to pour out upon the nation a spirit of
prayer and supplication, with repentance, so that the approaching day of prayer and fasting, instituted for the 19 April of that
year (1790), would cause God, for his own glory, to work a
general reformation, that 'iniquity may not be our ruin'. In July

he exclaimed to Taylor, 'O what a to do is here! A great nation
mad and drunk with electioneering. I am pressed today to go
down to Durham, almost 300 miles, to vote... But I have other
work in hand, and go not.'[20] He was more concerned for the
souls of men than in supporting the political ambitions of the
country's rulers.

Two years later nothing had improved and Romaine wrote:
'Black clouds and great storms are gathering... Infidelity triumphs,' he complained, 'the fancied rights of men usurp the
rights of God, republicanism throws off subjection to God's ordinances, and every unbeliever is a king.' His only consolation
was that the government was on God's shoulders.[21] Later in the
year he wrote to Taylor: 'O my friend, we are as bad, as ripe for
destruction, as Jerusalem was; we have great reason to mourn
before the Lord, and to pray that he would spare this guilty
land.'[22] In December he prayed: 'O spare Great Britain! Lord,
spare us, and give not thine heritage over to confusion.'[23]

In the middle of 1793 the burden of prayer was as strong
as ever. 'I pray, but with trembling, for our own land, lest national iniquity, should be nationally punished.'[24] He was still in
his watchtower, looking for the 'discovery of the Lord's mind
and will in his present dispensations'. He continues:

> Indeed they are alarming: to me more so, because they
> do not alarm. The public is still thoughtless and secure,
> as if no storm was abroad and no danger near them;
> though for certain, some of the heaviest judgments of
> God are in the earth, calling aloud for repentance. And
> the professing few, with whom I converse, are not hum-
> bled and pleading earnestly with God for mercy, as the
> necessity of the times require... [After lamenting his own
> lack of Christian sympathy for the 'affliction of Joseph',
> he says:] Things grow darker and darker.[25]

Some of his most bitter complaints about the state of the nation
and church were made in 1794, the year before he died. He was

alarmed by 'philosophy, with its vain deceits; infidelity, with its natural children, a swarm of most profane practices, destroying all subordination to God's ministers, and to God's magistrates... These evils are growing worse and worse, especially as none can tell when they will stop, or how.' Such darkness kept him in his watchtower, looking to God 'for his gift of repentance and reformation to a guilty land, that iniquity may not be our ruin; and thanking him for his special favour, that there is a sanctuary out of the reach of all dangers'.[26]

During these troubled times there was hardly an hour when Romaine was not seeking the face of God, particularly for the salvation of sinners. In March 1786 he said, 'I very seldom go into any company, and when I do I return to my study, blessing God that I am once more alone.'[27] It was as if he could not wait to enter God's presence again. He longed to be found among the humbled, mourning for the lost, and crying and praying to the Lord of mercy for himself and for a guilty land. He was 'grieved for my Lord's glory, grieved for those who rob him of it, and praying earnestly to him, that he would grant them repentance unto life'.[28] When he saw the greatness of God's mercy towards him, his heart melted over the sins and sufferings of others. 'Then he makes me plead with him for my fellow-sinners, and very thankful, more than I am, or can be, for myself.'[29]

In a letter dated 2 February 1793, he writes: 'I see daily greater necessity for keeping in my watchtower; as it is my office to be found waiting upon God, humbled for my own sins, and praying and pleading for those who cannot read his present judgments against sin, and against the greatest of all sins — unbelief.'[30] Three months later he says: 'I am forced, which ever way I look, still to be humbled in prayer; in which I hope to be instant, and without ceasing, as long as these troubles continue; and it is not unlikely but they may continue as long as I live.'[31] Early in 1794 he is still on his knees, 'not so much in praying against the French (poor things!) as against sin, mine own, the nation's sin — infidelity — with all its infernal fruits; imploring, for mercy's sake, that God, our God, would not suffer iniquity to be our ruin'.[32]

The times were indeed tempestuous and the poor church was tossed on the waves like Noah's ark, but Romaine knew that not one 'embarked with Christ shall ever perish'. Nor was he alone in the chamber of prayer, for the Lord had 'poured out a very remarkable spirit of prayer, and multitudes, multitudes through the land are on their bended knees, lifting up holy hands, crying for mercy. I hope he will hear and answer, by granting us a national reformation, that iniquity and infidelity may not be our ruin.'[33] For Romaine, the only hope for the nation was for God's people to cry earnestly to him.

Surprisingly, perhaps, in view of what has been said, there were times when Romaine was quite upbeat about England and London. In 1789 he regarded the nation's privileges as 'uncommonly great'.

> We have religion in its purity, God's word in our hands, men sent of God to open and to explain it, and they are owned of him in their labours. Nowhere in the world is the gospel in its truth, and in its power, as it is with us. O what a rich incense of praise should go up to the throne of grace from us this day! O what superlative thankfulness do these favours of God require of British believers... The gospel runs and is glorified, and yet the times are quiet. The government is on the side of our most holy faith. Our king, God bless him, is himself a defender of it.[34]

These reasons were among those that caused Romaine to regard England as 'the peculiar favourite of heaven'. 'Our privileges as free men, and as Christians, set us far above the nations of the earth. It is my office to plead with the Lord and governor of church and state, that we may not be suffered to sin away our distinguishing blessings.'[35] Writing to a friend on 8 October

1793, he says, 'May God's favourite land be your favourite;'[36] and again in April 1794, he wrote: God 'can make England a very Paradise; so it is to me — all but heaven'.[37]

In the last decade of his life he made the most of any opportunity to preach the gospel outside London. In the summer of 1787 he travelled through England and in the next two years he is found in places such as Reading, Tiverton (Devon), Plymouth and Bridgwater (Somerset). Two years later he was again in Plymouth, where he preached in the Church of King Charles the Martyr. He spoke on the 'depth of human depravity and the sovereignty of divine grace'. In the afternoon the vicar, Robert Hawker, obviously disturbed by Romaine's sermon, tried 'to controvert or qualify the bold assertions or unguarded expressions which the morning preacher had advanced'.[38] Apparently, Romaine's visit helped many Plymouth clergymen to embrace a more biblical theology, including Hawker, who admits to having certain 'imperfect conceptions' cleared up by Romaine, in whose pulpit he preached with honour and delight in 1803:

> I found my mind [says Hawker] impressed with a more than ordinary solemnity, when I recollected the venerable character of that faithful servant of God, who had so often occupied it; when I called to mind the labours of so great a man in this place; and when I considered this very pulpit, in which I now stand, is the highly honoured spot, on which dear Mr Romaine stood, who is now with Jesus; a certain indescribable emotion passed over me, and induced sensations I had never before experienced.[39]

In 1791 Romaine again visited Reading as well as Salisbury, Bradford, Brislington, Southampton and other places. When in Sunderland he felt 'favoured with an opportunity of recommending my dearest Jesus in the oldest church in England, called Monk Weremouth, which belonged to the venerable Bede, a very favourite pulpit of mine, and from which his pre-

Robert Hawker.

cious name has been often, like ointment, poured forth'. From
there he travelled to Northumberland. But with the infirmities of
old age he was just not able to cope with the schedule of earlier
years.

He continued to resist the controversies that arose within the
church, avoiding the 'party spirit' that was prevalent in many of
his day. Writing to a friend on 4 March 1786, he exclaims: 'O
what times do we live in! Parties, disputes, quarrels, contentions,
who shall be the greatest — yea almost hatred itself in the family of love. We have much hearing and little doing. The apostle
James would be frightened to see the professors of the day, all
ears, without hands or feet — nothing about them active, but
a gossiping tongue. For these things I mourn and preach and
pray.'[40] However, he was prepared to stand his ground in the
face of opposition and frequently spoke out against those who
differed from him: 'Proud Arminians may laugh at *Why me!*' he
writes in 1788. 'But they, in whom Jesus will be admired, can
now see no reason in themselves: their true Spirit is self-loathing
and self-abhorrence. Their one song is *Worthy is the Lamb*.'[41] A
few years earlier he had written:

> I would not be an Arminian for the world; because I am
> not only willing, but happy in getting more and more into
> Christ's debt. They are only pensioners in heaven; they
> take all from him in use, and carry all back to him in
> praise. God teach us this heavenly lesson. Although I
> have learned but little, yet I would not be saved in any
> other way, than by sovereign grace; for only by this can
> I find employment in oneness with God, or happiness in
> God — All is grace, all is debt. The sense of this keeps
> one humble.[42]

In 1789, he strongly opposed Samuel Johnson's philosophy
'that a man of genius may force himself to write whatever he

pleases', on the grounds that the 'activity of our nature is a perpetual temptation to look upon ourselves as something'. Romaine's view was

> ... that every exertion of mind and body depends upon the grace of Another — life and breath and all things... The soul is as much dependent on the fresh supplies of the Spirit as the body is upon breath; so that the feeling of my poverty is my only riches, and the sense of my weakness is my only strength. If I write a letter, if any good accompany it, I wish ever to ascribe the praise to him, without whom 'we ... even we are not sufficient of ourselves so much as to think one good thought.' What possibly can be more humbling? And what can be more opposite to the doctor's spirit? Let him, and such, plume themselves upon their self-exertions; but we have learnt Christ better. In his school we know, that the humblest is the highest; and he does most for Christ, or rather Christ does most in him, who is sensible, that without Christ, he can do nothing.[43]

Such a response was typical of Romaine, who based his opinion, not on the deceptive philosophies of the age, but firmly on the Word of God. 'I am a man of one book and of one sentiment,' he used to say. 'The word of God and faith in his word make up all my learning, and enter into all my life, private and public.'[44] As late as 1790 he says, 'A body of sin and death like mine wants an almighty Saviour, and I am learning to put more honour upon his word and work daily. I find more need of him than ever, and it is some true joy that he is most exactly suited to my desperate case; having no hope but in his blood, not one ray but in his righteousness, no strength but in his arm, no happiness but out of his fullness.'[45] 'Things go quite right,' he says, 'when Christ is exalted, and self is brought down and kept down.'[46]

It was this daily dependence on Christ that enabled him to submit to God's will without complaint and to be so mightily used in the pulpit. At the beginning of 1786, when he was in want of a curate, he simply said, 'The great head of the church will send me one of his ordaining. I wait for such a one.'[47] He was not disappointed, for in the same year God sent him William Goode. Two years later, he preached the gospel to at least 2000 children, and the Lord was 'with us of a truth'. In a letter dated 12 May 1788, he summarises his sermon:

> Our nature is defiled — the fountain is pollution; so are the streams. Thoughts vain — play foolish — tempers rebellious and headstrong — end in destruction. Our Jesus is almighty to save us. He can teach the ignorant, wash the filthy, pardon the guilty — subdue every bad temper, and set in, and keep in, the way of life and salvation. He invites young people to come to him: promises to give them better things than play or pleasure: makes his promises good — gives exceeding great and precious things, and these for ever.

In the letter he admits that he had prayed much for the work of the day to be a success and then was happy to leave the rest to God: 'He did his own will: to him be all the glory.'[48]

Particularly in the last ten years of his life Romaine experienced a sweet communion with God and a solid reliance on his Word. This is not to say that he had not enjoyed such heavenly fellowship and faith before, far from it, but from the tone of his letters, as his final days drew near, the depth of his intimacy with the Redeemer he adored grew stronger still. It was as if the flower of the Saviour's love was in full bloom in his heart.

What a comfort — our day's work is done, we are walking as children in the light, and waiting to be sent for, whenever our Lord pleases. It need not be a violent death. It must be soon — in the course of nature. It may be in a moment. Come ever so soon, it will be a blessed time. When — and where — and how — all is settled by him — who says to you and to me, 'Fear not, I will be with you.'

William Romaine, 14 November 1794.[1]

16

'Waiting to be Sent for'

On 6 April 1791 Romaine wrote from Blackfriars to Thomas Coke of Shrewsbury, and in his usual manner imparted sound biblical advice in the spirit of humility:

> We are absolutely dependent on God, and the more we receive, the more we should look up to him for grace, that we may give him all the glory. This is our great lesson... When we have mercies we should not only thank the Giver, but the more, and better we thank him, we should thank him for thankfulness. This would keep our hearts truly humbled. And then we might have anything from God, because for giving us the grace, he would receive all the glory. A little of this is heaven...
>
> He who sitteth upon the throne is the God of all grace. And if he has given you ever so much, yet still he can give you more — not only fresh grace, but also greater degrees of it. He can increase the appetite — can make you open your mouth wider — and if you open it ever so wide, his divine bounty has said — I will fill it.

He then castigates himself for not receiving 'out of the fulness of Jesus so much as his exceeding great and exceeding precious promises encourage me to take and to make use of — by which means he loses the glory of his faithfulness, and I lose much of the blessedness of believing'. Finally, on the third page of his letter, he urges Coke to overflow with thankfulness for all the blessings he has enjoyed in so many areas of his life.[2]

Early in the same year (1791), Romaine, who had always been interested in missionary endeavours, tried to help his friend Thomas Haweis, who was in the process of sending two missionaries, Michael Waugh and John Price, to the South Seas. Haweis heard that Captain William Bligh was planning to embark for Tahiti to convey the bread-fruit plant to the British West Indian colonies. He immediately took steps to secure passages for his two missionaries aboard the *Providence* and to obtain leave for them from the government. In this he was assisted by Romaine, who evidently had some influence at the Admiralty, and by Ambrose Serle, a naval man himself and a prominent figure at the Admiralty, who had heard of Haweis's plans through his 'dear friend Mr Romaine'.[3]

Unfortunately, when Waugh and Price arrived in London, they began to lay down conditions which they wanted met before they would depart, one of which was to obtain Episcopal ordination. Haweis, who feared having to abort his 'cherished plan', did all he could to meet their demands. He consulted Romaine, who told him to approach Beilby Porteus, the Bishop of London. Haweis prepared a statement of the case and made out a copy of the Admiralty permit, both of which Romaine delivered to the bishop. He also persuaded Wilberforce to exercise his influence with the bishop. On 20 May 1791, Romaine wrote to Haweis with the news that

> ... the Bishop of London has refused to ordain them. But Mr Wilberforce will try him again. I have had a great deal of fatigue in attending on great men, but I repent not. When you come, there will be enough left for you to do, in order to equip them for such a long voyage: and to release me from every other concern about it, except prayer, which I am daily offering up for his blessing upon

the work, according to the full meaning of the prophecy in the 113th Psalm.[4]

Five days later Romaine wrote again, sharing further developments:

I find there is a private ship going to the South Seas, but not yet ready; a person concerned in her promised me a passage for missionaries which Mr Grant says will be ... preferable to a King's ship. On this account you need not hurry your friends, but leave them in Mr Spencer's hands, committing them to the care and teaching of our almighty head. You will see the Bishop's answer. He absolutely refuses me. Mr Wilberforce has engaged to talk with him on the subject.[5]

The bishop, however, simply referred the matter to John Moore, the Archbishop of Canterbury, who would not ordain them because they were not university men. Waugh and Price, on hearing the news, flatly refused to embark and so Haweis's missionary endeavours at this time came to a disappointing conclusion. Haweis was very appreciative of Romaine's efforts, saying in his biography of Romaine (1797): 'I have to acknowledge to his honour, the zealous help he afforded me about six years ago [in 1791], and his readiness to go to the Bishop of London, and be my advocate on the subject then in hand.'[6]

Inevitably, as Romaine grew older, he began to reminisce, often with a sense of distress at the service he had performed for his Master. Writing to a friend in 1792 he recollects: 'More than half a century ago, I was ordained to be a witness for Christ in this month of September. Looking backward, everything I can remember covers me with shame. Doing so little for such a Jesus — grudging to be laid out and spent for him — and, when he did vouchsafe to make use of me, so ready to take his glory to myself. I verily stand amazed at his infinite patience and kindness in all his dealings with me.'[7] In the middle of the next year, he said, 'I am an old preacher, and have seen enough of his glory to be ashamed of myself. I reprobate all my services; and, if I were to begin again, I would try to shoot higher.'[8] The only epitaph he wanted was: 'A sinner saved, a sinner saved.'[9]

Although the Bible was Romaine's 'supreme book', he avidly read the works of other men. Thomas Adam's writings were particularly prized by him. 'I owe more to this man (saving the honour of grace) than to all the world. May you read,' he says to Walter Taylor, 'as I did, to my first comfort, his lectures on the church catechism.'[10] He was much taken with Ambrose Serle's *The Christian Remembrancer*, his *vade-mecum* [go with me], as he called it. It was published in 1787 and went through numerous editions. Romaine thought it 'a most proper book for a journey — it is so well divided: chapters so short, and yet very experimental... I do not find that I can read it often enough.'[11] He sold many copies of it. 'It suits modern reading,' he said. 'If I had known the new edition was so forward, I would have proposed a new chapter, but it is too late. In my journeys through England last summer [1787], I disposed of great numbers — and had frequent opportunities of reading it myself.'[12] He advised James Ireland: 'Buy the *Christian Remembrancer* at my recommendation; you will thank me when we meet.'[13]

Serle was a Calvinistic writer who first became friendly with Romaine in 1764 and Romaine's letters to him in his *Works* (forty-seven in all) reveal the deep affection and sincere agreement in religious matters, which developed between them. His daughter Jane, who died in 1792 at the age of twelve, was Mrs Romaine's goddaughter. In June 1789, Romaine cheerfully complied with a request to write a recommendatory preface to Serle's *Christian Husbandry*, in the hope that the book would afford the reader 'seasonable and profitable meditations throughout the year'. He also says, 'If you are desirous of being thoroughly established in these two grand points of salvation, namely, the Godhead of Jesus Christ, and of the Holy Spirit, you will, I hope, find upon reading [Serle's former works] the Scripture doctrine of the Trinity, and will have reason to thank the author for writing, and me for recommending them.'[14] *The Gentleman's Magazine* (1812), reviewing Serle's writings, comments, 'Nowhere does the conviction of the vital importance of Calvinism as of the essence of the gospel appear more strongly than in Serle's books.'[15]

Back in 1771 Romaine had started the third part of his trilogy, *The Life, Walk and Triumph of Faith*, which was finally published early in 1795. After visiting the Taylor family in Southampton in 1787 he began to revise the work:

> This visit was greatly blessed [he told Taylor in November of that year], and produced one thing, which, as providence favours, I am now carrying into execution: it is my last testimony for Jesus. What he is — how he feels — what he has attained — who has been long an experienced believer — and in his own views is near death, and quite prepared to meet his God. I have kept it back for several years, that I might see and try whether anything new could be suggested on the subject from Scripture, or from my own life. But I am satisfied with what I had written, and I am now revising my papers. I beg you would help me with your prayers, that I may keep the ark steady, and hold forth nothing but what will tend to establish believers in their most holy faith.[16]

In the summer of 1792, he 'enjoyed some of the choicest blessings' in his meditations on the *Triumph of Faith*, although the writing part was still progressing slowly at the end of the year, partly because of 'so many [preaching] engagements'. 'I rather live the *Triumph of Faith* than write it,' he said.[17] His aim was to finish before he died. By the end of 1793 he was in earnest to complete the work and had started to transcribe it for the press. 'It has grown so voluminous,' he says, 'that I have resolved to throw aside all my papers, and write only just what I myself am at present, an old believer.' The treatise contained what he was 'still learning and living' and in his request for prayer he says,

'Pray that I may *live* it, and, in due time, *die* it.'[18] In October 1794, he sent it to the press and in November he writes to a friend: 'Favour me with your prayers for its success for the increase of true faith, and for its being the means of spreading the fame of our Jesus.'[19] And again: 'I am very busy printing my dying testimony for the truth of the gospel of Jesus, and for the power of it. If you live to see it, you will know somewhat more of his unspeakable grace and favour to W. Romaine.'[20]

When Romaine sent his friend William Cadogan a copy of *Triumph of Faith*, he wrote, 'Thank our divine teacher, the Holy Spirit, for leading me into the truth and for keeping me in it through such a long life, and for the most blessed prospect opened to me, when this life shall be ended.'[21] Thomas Wills was 'much refreshed' by Romaine's work. *The Gospel Magazine* for August 1901 comments that Romaine's 'pen and his life were alike sanctified and gifted by the Holy Spirit'. It calls his trilogy 'the gem of his writings' and 'precious compositions' that have 'for the past century maintained a high place in the esteem of the churches of God... There are a savour, sweetness, and power about these Christ-exalting pages such as win a spiritual mind, and meet with a joyful response from "the new man" in the believer.'[22]

During 1793 Romaine was involved in a controversy with Michael Nash, a collector of subscriptions for the *Societas Evangelica* (a society for the maintenance of itinerant preachers), and it seems a secretary of the Society for the Promotion of the French Protestant Bible. It all started in November 1792 when the committee of the French Bible Society nominated two or three of its members to call on Romaine to request him to preach on the Society's behalf. According to Nash, Romaine's 'known incivility seemed such a bar of access, that no one attempted to call on him for that purpose'. Nash then engaged one of Romaine's friends in conversation and told him that the Society wanted an eminent minister of the Church of England to espouse the Society's cause, upon which Romaine's friend, 'under a very strong conception' of success, pressed Nash to call on Romaine at about eight o'clock one morning. Nash continues his account:

> At this request I waited on him next morning at that hour. A servant opened the door; and on informing her master a gentleman wanted to speak with him, out he came from an adjacent room, and taking the street door in his hand, with no very pleasant countenance demanded my business; which he permitted me to open so far as to say, 'I have taken the liberty to wait upon you, Sir, in behalf of the French Bible Society;' and then sternly replied, 'I am not a friend to it — I am not a friend to it.' This abrupt answer, before I had properly explained my errand, induced me to depart a little chagrined: and on shutting the door, in a milder tone (as if conscience rebuked him) he added with emphasis, 'But I wish it may succeed with all my heart.'[23]

At the Society's next committee meeting Nash said, 'From the complexion of the latter part of his reply, he probably, upon mature reflection, might espouse the cause, and, if approved of, I would write to him.' So Nash drew up a letter, which received the Society's approbation, and on 4 January 1793 sent it to Romaine, who made no reply to it.

Two things in particular angered Nash. The first was a communication given to him that Romaine had said that he had 'not been applied to in behalf of the French Bible Society', which Nash regarded as blatantly untrue. And secondly, when he discovered that shortly afterwards Romaine had preached at Blackfriars, and made a collection for the French catholic refugees. In a letter to the Bishop of London, dated 10 May 1793, Romaine said he had 'subscribed to this labour of love for myself and friends 135-2-3' and had collected 'in my parish 25-5-6'.[24] In response, Nash wrote *Gideon's Cake of Barley*

Meal, a Letter to the Rev W. Romaine, on his Preaching for the Emigrant Popish Clergy, in which he accuses Romaine of 'voluntarily making a public collection for those implacable enemies of Christ, the Romish priests and Papists',[25] and of being 'foremost to encourage them, like locusts, to come and consume the substance of our poor'.[26] He regards Romaine's generosity towards foreigners as restricting his help and usefulness towards his own poor, and of showing support for the doctrines Papists follow.

One of the *Societas Evangelica* committee members, David Parker, 'of the King's Mews', denounced Nash and defended Romaine in *A Charitable Morsel of Unleavened Bread*, which was a reply to Nash's pamphlet. It was written so that others would not be prejudiced against Romaine. Parker, writing of Nash, says, 'You could not vent your spleen against any other person, it seems, than Mr Romaine: a man grown venerable by his years, his learning, and his long successful labours in the work of the ministry: whose character, when known, is as much out of the reach of slander from your pen, as yours is beneath contempt.'[27] Romaine had been accused of showing disrespect for Nash and of a 'bigoted attachment to forms and unchristian prejudices to the true cause of God', simply because he helped the needy Papists, who were French emigrants. How could you, asks Parker, 'censure and condemn him for such an act of kindness, for which all thinking and benevolent men must applaud him, as evincing the genuine influence of the gospel upon his own heart and those of his hearers?'[28]

Romaine had also been accused by Nash of a temper and a behaviour that were not according to the spirit of the gospel — 'as that natural surly moroseness in your carriage to strangers who approach you' will always keep the poor and needy from your door — and of 'carnal prejudices and churlishness'. In defence Parker gives a fine portrait of Romaine's character. He is

... one of the most laborious, faithful, exemplary ministers of Jesus Christ, which this age has produced. One who adorns in his life and conversation the gospel he preaches; abounding in every act of benevolence, and every work and labour of love, for the benefit of Christ's poor members. And not confining his benevolence to these alone, he extends it to others also, who appear to have any claim upon him. Hence arises your resentment against him...

I have had the honour of a pretty intimate acquaintance with him for more than thirty years; and I solemnly aver, that, during that long period, I do not recollect ever to have heard a morose, harsh, uncivil, or unkind expression drop from his lips; much less have I received from him any such behaviour as you charge him with. On the contrary, I have experienced, and hundreds more, who are ready to attest the same, the most affable, courteous, kind and gentlemanlike behaviour from him.[29]

'No man, nor minister of his day,' says Parker, 'lives a more abstemious, self-denied life than he does.'[30] And as far as the French Bible Society was concerned, Nash thought Romaine's comments to be 'paradoxical and mysterious', but it is clear that Romaine did approve of and support the Society, for he 'lent the Bible, by which the sheets that were printed off, were corrected; and for that very purpose'.[31] The *Evangelical Magazine* thought the defence of Romaine was unnecessary: 'The reply is written in a good style and a good spirit; but we are sorry that a gentleman who tells us that he has been honoured with Mr Romaine's friendship for thirty years, should think it worth his while to take any notice of such a contemptible performance.'[32]

In the same year, 1793, Nash published a second edition of *Gideon's Cake of Barley Meal*, which contained 'another letter sent to Mr Romaine prior to this, and sundry notes and remarks, wherein all the objections and replies of opponents that have come to the author's knowledge, are fully answered'.[33] And as Nash was not happy with Parker's reply, he retaliated with *An Answer to the 'Charitable Morsel of Unleavened Bread', Proving that Pamphlet to be a Beast with Seven Heads and Thirty Horns or Falsehoods*. The title betrays its contents. He also addressed a letter to the editors of the *Evangelical Magazine* (1793), which he called *The Barley Cake Defended from the Foxes*, a few extracts of which are quoted below. It must be pointed out that, true to character, Romaine did not enter the controversy, a 'wisdom and ingenuity' that even Nash seems to admire:

> Mr Romaine ... rises so superior to that littleness of soul which stimulates the illiberal to defame what they cannot with truth repel, that instead of depreciating the publication, he candidly allows every man at liberty to write his own sentiments; and only pleads the innocency of his motive in that unfortunate step, of *voluntarily* preaching, and publicly begging from house to house, for that great plague of all nations, and pest of all society, the Popish Priests. This admits the thing to be wrong.[34]

Nash claims that not one of Romaine's friends, with whom he has conversed, 'can produce an argument of any weight in his favour; but most acknowledge they disapprove of his conduct in espousing the priests'. He then continues his personal attack on Romaine's character:

> Some, indeed, have charged me with illiberality in touching so pointed his natural temper; but as almost the whole church of Christ have many years seen in him, with grief, that apparently unsubdued, which has been a stumbling-block to many sincere, though weak Christians, and given much occasion to the enemies of the Lord to triumph, it is incumbent upon every upright man and sincere friend to tell him seriously of it. I myself have heard his religion reproached on that very account...
>   I have seen it quite common among his own friends, when conversing about him to introduce some anecdotes

of his churlish moroseness to one or other, insomuch, that one of them said to me, 'You need not tell us of his sourness, we *all* know he is a crabbed temper.'...

I am aware of his plea, that he does it with a view to drive such from creature dependence, that they may seek God instead of man, I am certain he can find no scripture to justify that rudeness which he would not like to be treated with, nor submit to from another.[35]

Nash seems oblivious to the fact that in the same breath as he is charging Romaine with 'unchristianlike behaviour', he himself, in publicly condemning God's servant, has fallen into the same trap. To back up his accusations, and with apparent pleasure at producing a 'witness for the prosecution', he relates the following anecdote about a person he knew who was brought 'to a serious concern about eternal things':

She was deeply oppressed with the apprehension of having done the unpardonable sin ... and though she alternately sat under Mr Romaine, and the late Mr Hart, could get no solid peace; and therefore, in the grief and anxiety of spirit, with a trembling heart, she ventured to approach the austere Mr Romaine... It so happened, that he opened the door to her himself, when she politely apologized for giving him the trouble ... and he with an aspect and tone of voice apparently ferocious, replied, 'If you thought it a trouble, what did you come for?' Such a reception struck her speechless, and sent her heavy heart away bleeding with anguish... she never after attempted to tell her griefs to any minister; but was all her life (till very near the end) subjected to bondage through the fear of death.[36]

The only explanation that Nash can offer for Romaine's behaviour is: 'Perhaps, his own wounds have been so long healed, he forgets the smart of them; and having a steadfast

view of his own safety, is too unsolicitous to have those
Canaanites subdued which yet remain within him, and vex the
flock of Christ.' He then asks for Romaine's forgiveness if he
has injured him, and somewhat cheekily suggests that he should
read attentively his own book, *The Walk of Faith*.

Perhaps it is sufficient to note that Romaine, like his Master
before him, 'when he was reviled, did not revile in return; when
he suffered, he did not threaten, but committed himself to him
who judges righteously'; and that the *Societas Evangelica*, dis-
approving of Nash's attacks on so eminent a man, dismissed
him on 17 January 1794. Surely Romaine's passive response
and the Society's swift action against Nash reflect favourably on
the former and with disapprobation on the latter.

In the summer of 1793 Romaine's sister Dorothy Heslup
died, and on 26 July Romaine wrote to her grieving husband
at Horsley, Northumberland, where he was ministering to the
Independent congregation. 'I was very glad to see your testimony at last concerning my sister, and thank you for it. She
was the Lord's: she lived to him and on him, and she is with
him; where I hope you and I shall soon be with him, and like
him for evermore.' Exalt Christ, he said, 'with all your might, in
your pulpit and in your living... You will miss her more every
day. Your lesson is to pray him to fill up her absence with his
presence.'[37]

Generally speaking, Romaine suffered few health problems
but during the last ten years of his life there were times when the
infirmities of old age crept up on him and laid him low. In 1787,
he complained of being 'almost worn out and good for nothing.
My frame and my present feelings, the infirmities of mind and
body, keep me very close to my last lesson.' At this time he was
still preaching four or five times a week but it was too much for
him, and although his friends advised him to spare himself, love
constrained him to continue 'showing forth his praises before
men'. He was weary, and even writing letters was a burden. 'I
have dropped all my correspondents,' he says, 'and keep the little
spirits that remain for public preaching. Nobody knows what I feel

this morning, what uphill work it is, even to take up my pen.'[38]

In 1788, at the age of seventy-four, he was 'living in hopes' that it would not be long before he reached the promised land, and again complained that he had 'too much business for my age and growing infirmities'. In October 1791 he was 'very poorly', with his 'usual autumn complaint'; but his attitude was to say: 'I wish to live under an abiding sense of the certainty of death, and of preparation for it.' Two years before he died he wrote: 'Just on the verge of eternity. O it is a blessed prospect to be able to look forward with a hope full of glory and immortality: it makes age with its numerous infirmities, not only tolerable, but truly blessed. To live in the Lord, is heaven upon earth. To die in the Lord, is the heaven of heavens.'[39] In August 1794 he could praise God, that though 'my tabernacle be taking down, yet it is done with so much tender compassion, and so gently, that I am enabled to put old age among my blessings, and thank my God, that I have so few infirmities'.[40] Four months later his afflictions were 'very great', compounded no doubt by his wife's illness, which lasted about a month. Looking back over his life and the many years of good health he had enjoyed, he said with his usual discernment: 'I find inward health a great promoter of bodily health: and I would recommend my doctor, as the only giver of eternal health.'[41]

During the summer of 1794 he was as busy as ever visiting friends and family. In June he spent some time with his son in Reading before moving on to places such as Tiverton and Southampton, from where he wrote to James Ireland, whose hospitality he had enjoyed in Bristol. He intimated to his friend that the door of his life was soon to close: 'It is continually sounding in mine ears — "They sorrowed most of all, because they should see his face no more, &c." It is certain at my time of life, we cannot promise ourselves on any good ground a yearly visit to our friends. Our meetings must be before God — in the prayer of faith for them — which is the communion of saints — and praise to him for brotherly love with its heavenly fruits.'[42]

So in his eighty-first year he entered the field of battle for the last time. He was in good spirits, looking to his Saviour as his only hope and dependent on his all-sufficient grace. He was ready to die as he had lived, in complete submission to his Father's sovereign will, with the praises of Christ on his lips and the joy of salvation in his heart.

EPITAPH

In a Vault beneath, lies the mortal part of
The Rev. WILLIAM ROMAINE, A. M.
Thirty Years Rector of these united Parishes,
And Forty Six Years Lecturer of *St Dunstan's in the West...*
A Scholar of extensive learning, A Christian of eminent piety,
A Preacher of peculiar Gifts and Animation,
Consecrating all his Talents to the investigation of Sacred Truth.
During a Ministry of more than half a Century
He lived, conversed, and wrote, only to exalt the Saviour.
MIGHTY IN THE SCRIPTURES,
He ably defended with eloquence and zeal
*The equal Perfections of the TRIUNE JEHOVAH, exhibited in Man's
Redemption,*
The FATHER'S Everlasting Love,
The Atonement, Righteousness, & complete Salvation of the SON,
The regenerating influence of the ETERNAL SPIRIT...
And multitudes raised from guilt & ruin to the hope of endless felicity,
Became Seals to his Ministry, the Blessings & Ornaments of Society.
*Having manifested the purity of his principles in his life to the Age of
81,*
July 26, 1795, he departed in the Triumph of Faith,
AND ENTERED INTO GLORY.

The grateful Inhabitants of these Parishes, with other Witnesses of
these Facts, erected this Monument.[1]

17

'To Thee be Endless Praise!'

Romaine began his final year, 1795, with thanksgiving to God for keeping him in the truth through such a long life and 'for the most blessed prospect opened to me when this life shall be ended'.[2] Although he had never been 'laid by so much as this winter with a severe cough', he rejoiced that for fifty-nine years of preaching, God's goodness and mercy had followed him, and 'I give him full credit that he will not leave nor forsake me in this last stage of my journey.' His motto for that year was appropriately 'God with us'.[3] All his views of death were 'very comfortable and believing', and he was sure that God would make him a 'dying witness for Jesus and his love'.[4] For Romaine, heaven was to 'be with the Lord Christ, to see him face to face, to see him as he is, to behold the glory of God in the person of Christ Jesus... This is the highest enjoyment, to behold his glory.'[5]

Early in the year, Romaine reprinted *An Earnest Invitation*, originally published in 1757 and reprinted in 1779. Many copies were distributed to both clergy and laity of the Church of England, and once again it proved a useful stimulus to prayer. Sir Richard Hill received a number of copies along with a letter from Romaine: 'In some former years this treatise met with your approbation, and it pleased God to own it, and to bless it: at the desire of my friends I have reprinted it, in hopes it may, through the divine favour, bring his people again upon their knees. You know well, that prayer has dispersed blacker clouds than the present.'[6]

Before looking at the final days of Romaine's earthly pilgrimage, and God's faithfulness to him in his hour of need, we shall examine an incident that occurred about three weeks before his last illness. An article about Romaine appeared in the *Evangelical Magazine* for March 1796, about eight months after Romaine's death, which caused considerable disagreement among his friends. It was signed T. H. (Thomas Haweis), who owned it to be 'an anecdote of Mr Romaine more characteristic of the man than might be found in twenty lives of him'. Sometime in May 1795 Romaine was walking in London, followed closely by Gaskin of Islington and William Jones of Pluckley. These two men had formerly been his close friends, but, like many other old Hutchinsonian acquaintances, had long forsaken and shunned him. According to the article

> ... Dr Gaskin said, 'There goes Mr Romaine, just before us.'
>
> Mr Jones replied, 'He is an old acquaintance of mine,' and in his facetious manner, whipped by Mr Romaine, and turning round, stopped him full; just then Dr Gaskin was at his elbow.
>
> Mr Romaine looked at him. 'Do you know me, Mr Romaine?' said he.
>
> 'No,' said the venerable saint [Romaine], 'nor my Master neither;' and turning round on his heel, crossed the way, with contempt and indignation, leaving them confounded at this unexpected reception.[7]

William Goode, Romaine's curate and successor, was upset by the anecdote, so he immediately wrote from Blackfriars on 23 March 1796 to the editors of the *Evangelical Magazine* with a different version of events, which he received from an 'unquestionable authority, not long after they took place':

> The Rev Dr G. and the Rev Mr J. were walking together in Cheapside, when the sight of Mr Romaine at a distance gave rise to the following conversation.
>
> Mr J. 'There is Mr Romaine — do you know him?'
>
> Dr G. 'No, I have no personal acquaintance with him.'
>
> Mr J. 'Does he know you personally?'
>
> Dr G. 'I am not sure that he does; have you any knowledge of him?'
>
> Mr J. 'Yes. Some years ago we were very intimate, and he has been at my house some days together; I will speak to him.' As Mr Romaine came near, he was addressed by Mr J. in this manner: 'How do you do, Mr Romaine? I do not know whether you forget one William J. I do not forget you.'
>
> To which Mr Romaine replied, 'No, nor my Master neither, I hope.' Without waiting for a reply, he crossed the street, and passed on.[8]

In his letter, Goode interpreted Romaine's remark as a compliment to William Jones, as he had heard him speak of both men with great respect. He went on: 'No idea of disrespect need be attached to his immediately passing from them, for it was what Mr Romaine would frequently do to his most intimate friends, as he had almost as great an aversion to stop talking in the street as in the church, in the latter of which he was so remarkable and so worthy of imitation.'[9]

William Cadogan presents a third version, which he received from 'one present at the interview'. When Jones and Gaskin overtook Romaine in Cheapside, Jones cheerfully said to Romaine, 'Mr Romaine, I do not know whether you recollect one William Jones, but I do know that I do not forget you.' Romaine's reply was not distinctly heard by either man, except the words, 'No, nor my Master, I hope.' Without further ado Romaine crossed the street, leaving them 'not a little astonished at this unexpected reception'.[10] In support of Romaine's sudden departure, Cadogan says, 'He had a natural quickness, and sometimes roughness, in his manner, which were often mistaken, when not meant, for anger and rudeness. He was seldom in the street, but upon business; and being intent upon his engagement, and as frugal of his time as he was prodigal of his labour, he seldom saluted any man by the way, neither was it his custom to fall out by the way.'[11]

Thomas Haweis, the author of the original anecdote in the *Evangelical Magazine*, was not impressed by Goode's and Cadogan's arguments. He says that to claim Romaine 'meant compliment and not reproof is too absurd to be supported', and that, in view of his many rebukes from his high church friends 'for his serious mistakes and irregularities', it was 'perfectly natural and in character that he should speak and act as he did'. Apparently Gaskin had complained of Romaine's 'very great supposed rudeness'. Haweis then says that Charles Simeon had heard Gaskin 'repeat these very words and highly express his indignation at them'. He also claims to 'have proof from vouchers equally respectable that a tittle has not been misrepresented of Mr Romaine's words'.[12]

This is an unsavoury incident, not simply for Romaine's comments and their meaning, but for the disagreements it caused among his friends and acquaintances. There is no doubt, knowing Romaine's character, that he could have meant his remark in both the ascribed ways — as a compliment or as a rebuke. What is of more concern is the way his comments were 'reported abroad'. If Jones and Gaskin had followed the maxim 'love covers over a multitude of sins', then any supposed rudeness would have been quickly forgotten and presumably not revealed to the world by Haweis in the *Evangelical Magazine*. It also serves as a warning how a misunderstanding, by propagation, can be blown up out of all proportion and raise up supporters on both sides who are ready to take their stand against each other. The only consolation is that this wrangling did not take place while Romaine was alive — it would certainly have caused him unnecessary anxiety in the last days of his life.

The decline of Romaine's mortal life was gentle but rapid. He kept up his ministerial labours and summer excursions right up to the end, and his faith, so strong in health and life, was his support in death. His last Sunday preaching was Trinity Sunday, 31 May 1795. In the morning at Blackfriars he preached from 1 John 1:7, and in the evening at St Dunstan's his text was 2 Corinthians 13:14: 'The grace of the Lord Jesus Christ be with you all.' His last sermon at Blackfriars was on Tuesday morning from Psalm 103:13: 'Like as a father pitieth his children, so the Lord pitieth them that fear him.' His final sermon of all, an exposition of John 18 and sermon number four of that week, was preached the following Thursday evening, 4 June, at St Dunstan's. He mentioned to his curate, William Goode, that he must proceed as fast as he could to complete the gospel before the summer vacation stopped his lectures. After preaching he complained of languor.

The following day, Friday 5 June, before he had suffered any sickness, he called on a close friend and as soon as he was seated said abruptly, without any further introduction, 'Set thine house in order, for thou shalt die and not live.' His friend, surprised at the unexpected quotation of Scripture, inquired if it had any particular meaning. 'No,' replied Romaine, 'but the words are much impressed on my mind, and they are a proper admonition to us all.'[13]

That evening he went to his friend Whitridge's house at Balaam Hill, beyond Clapham, where he often resorted. He slept his usual time, and at six the following morning, 6 June, came down to breakfast. He presided over family devotions and among other petitions, prayed 'that God would fit them for, and support them under, the trials of that day, which might be many'. After breakfast he was ready to return to his house in Blackfriars to prepare for the coming Sabbath, when he suddenly felt ill. Initially he thought he would be able to continue with his usual work. The coach was ordered between eight and nine, and he and his friend set off together. On the way, as if knowing his earthly course was soon to end, he spoke with energy and deep

feeling on the subject of his own death, observing, 'O how animating is the view I now have of death, and the hope laid up for
me in heaven, full of glory and immortality!'[14]

He grew steadily worse through the next day and was unable to perform his Sabbath duties. His curate William Goode
stood up in his place and declared to the congregation their
pastor's inability to work, which excited from them sincere grief
and fervent prayers on his behalf. Romaine soon realised that
this sickness would end in death, which he prepared for with
'sweet serenity and firm reliance upon the truth and promises
of God'.

He stayed in London for three weeks under medical advice
and made use of the prescriptions ordered for him, although he
knew they would not save his life. 'You are taking much pains
to prop up this feeble body,' he said to his doctor. 'I thank you
for it, but it will not do now.'[15] He received great comfort from
his Hebrew Psalter, out of which he frequently read a verse or
two. He could not speak much due to his feebleness and saw
few people. On one occasion he was asked if he wanted to see
some of his friends, but he replied, 'I desire no better company
than I enjoy.'

His response to those who inquired about his health was: 'As
well as I expect to be this side of heaven.' Once he replied: 'As
well as I possibly can be whilst in this vile body, which plagues
and torments me.' To a friend who, noticing how low and weak
he appeared, asked if God's presence was with him, he said,
'It is indeed, for he is *my* God.' To another, who observed his
great frailty, he added, 'It is all mercy, all mercy.' Soon after the
beginning of his illness a friend on business called to see him
and expressed hope that he was better and happy in his views.
'Yes,' he replied, 'upon that point I have no doubt, for I have
much of the presence of Jesus with me.'[16]

To a minister, who was passing through London, and hearing of his illness called on him, he said, 'I do not repent of one
word that I have printed or preached on faith in Jesus: for I now
feel the blessed comforts of that precious doctrine.'[17] A friend

on a visit said to him, 'Heaviness may endure for a night, but joy comes in the morning.' He quickly answered, 'It has been a night *indeed*, but I have a blessed prospect in death, and a hope full of immortality.' On another occasion, he said, 'I have been in the deep waters, but have enjoyed much support, and wait to enter the courts of the Lord; for my soul is athirst for God, yes, even the living God.'[18] In this feeble state he sent a message to his curate, with whom he was unable to converse, desiring his prayers and urging all his friends and congregation not to forget him at the throne of grace. It was a request he sent to his curate on several occasions during his last days.

He did not receive much relief from the medicines he was prescribed, so after three weeks, on 26 June, he went to stay with a friend at Tottenham for a fortnight. For a while he gained strength and was able to walk in the garden. He returned to town where his curate visited him and thought him a little better. 'I have long lain at first in the arms of death, and, if recovering, it is very slowly. But this is but a poor dying life at best; however, I am in his hands, who will do the best for me.' He then added with force: '*I am sure of that*... I have lived to experience all I have spoken, and all I have written, and bless God for it.'[19] He commented to another friend, 'I have the peace of God in my conscience, and the love of God in my heart; and that you know is sound experience... I knew the doctrines I preached to be truths, but now I experience them to be blessings.'[20]

During his days of health he had often said, 'I desire to die with the language of the publican on my lips — "God, be merciful to me, a sinner."' Such were his sentiments when thanking a friend for visiting him: 'I thank you for coming to see a saved sinner.' At another time he stretched forth his arms and added, 'I shall soon be on Mount Zion that is above; there I shall dwell for ever, and there enjoy my everlasting rest.'[21]

The improvement in his health was only fleeting and soon it deteriorated to such an extent that he was advised to return to his friend at Balaam Hill, where he was first seized with illness. On 13 July he left the rectory house at Blackfriars and

was carried into the country. From this time his strength rapidly
declined. 'He had frequent spasms at his heart and shortness
of breath, attended with degrees of pain and convulsion; but
his faith and patience never failed him.'[22] He would often say,
'How good is God to me! What entertainments and comforts
does he give me! O what a prospect of glory and immortality
is before me! He is my God, through life, through death and to
eternity!'[23] A friend observing his patience under trial quoted
that Scripture 'My soul is even as a weaned child,' to which he
replied, 'Ah, but it is often cross whilst weaning.' 'True,' said his
wife, who was present, 'but when weaned it is quiet,' intimating
the state into which her husband's mind had been brought.

He continued to rise and sit up at this time, and to help
with the family devotions. In one of these gatherings he selected
for the morning lesson the chapter that records the sickness of
Hezekiah, and applying it to himself, said, 'Now I should have
nothing of this weakness and languor if I had no sin; but God
be thanked for hope in death, yea for life in death.'[24] On 23
July he sat at breakfast and with thankfulness said, 'It is now
near sixty years since God opened my mouth to publish the everlasting sufficiency and eternal glory of the salvation of Christ
Jesus; and it has now pleased him to shut my mouth, that my
heart might feel and experience what my mouth has so often
spoken.'[25]

The following day he was helped downstairs. When seated,
he said, 'O how good is God! With what a night he has favoured
me!' and then requested that prayer without ceasing be made
for him so that his faith and patience might not fail. His wife
came and enquired how he was feeling now he was up and
said, 'I hope, my dear, you now find God your support, and his
promises of life in Christ Jesus your comfort.' He responded,
'Yes, now that my heart and my flesh and my strength fail, *my*
God is the strength of my heart and my portion for ever.' He
then spoke to her with the most tender expressions of affection,
thanking her for her unwearied attention to him from the first

day of their union until now, adding, 'Come near, my love, that I may bless you. The Lord be with you, a covenant God for ever to save and bless you.' He then addressed his son with the same tenderness, and expressed his fervent hope and prayer that he was a son in the faith as well as a son in the flesh, and that he would continue to preach Christ after he had died.

The lady of the house, hearing him bless his wife, approached and said, 'Have you not a blessing for *me*, sir?' 'Yes,' he replied, 'I have. I pray God to bless you.' And so he said to everyone who came to him. On the same day a friend visited him and asked how he was feeling, 'My dear good friend, I am very weak and low.' 'But, sir, God is with you and will never leave you nor forsake you.' 'Yes,' he replied, with an air of triumph, 'he is my God for ever and ever, he will be my guide, even unto death.'[26]

On Saturday morning 25 July he was unable to go downstairs and so was placed on a couch, where he lay all day in great weakness of body, but strong in faith. At about three o'clock in the afternoon his beloved friend Whitridge returned from town and rushed upstairs to see him and to ask how he was. 'Very well, through mercy, and glad to see you.' He then took him by the hand and asked him if he was going back to town that afternoon. 'No, sir, I am come to be with you, and to pray God to bless you now with the comfort of his sweet salvation, and to bring you to the blessed possession and enjoyment of life everlasting.' To which he replied with earnestness, 'Amen, Amen, Amen!'[27]

At the close of the day he was thought to have said, 'Yea, though I walk through the valley and shadow of death, I will fear no evil, for thou art with me.' About an hour before he died Whitridge came to see him again. 'I hope, sir, you now find the salvation of Jesus inestimably precious to you.' He responded with a feeble voice, 'Yes, yes, yes, he is precious to my soul.' 'More precious than rubies?' inquired his friend. He recognised the Scripture and completed it, 'Yes, and all that can be desired is not comparable to him.' 'Now then,' said Whitridge, 'he is the chief of ten thousand.' 'Yes,' replied Romaine, 'he is a tree of life.'[28]

While he could still speak he lifted up his voice in prayer and praise, with an inexpressible joy flooding his soul. 'Many an happy hour,' one of his friends observes, 'have I spent with him, but none equal to the last; and respecting his own soul, I believe the last hour of his life was the happiest in all his life.'[29] Among his closing expressions were: 'Lord God Almighty, glory be to thee on high, for such peace upon earth, and good will unto men!'[30] The very last words he was heard distinctly to utter were: 'Holy, holy, holy, blessed and holy Jesus! To thee be endless praise!' Soon after, his breath failed and he could speak no more, but his lips continued to move. His hands were clasped and lifted up to God. Then, at about one o'clock in the morning of Sunday 26 July 1795, without a struggle or a groan, the battle was over and he slipped to his eternal rest and reward.

His relatives had intended to carry him to the tomb of his predecessors in private, but this was prevented by his many affectionate friends who wished to show their last respects to him by attending him to the grave:

> On Monday the third day of August 1795, the corpse was removed from Mr Whitridge's house at Balaam Hill in order to be interred in the rectory vault of Blackfriars Church. The funeral proceeded at about eleven o'clock in the forenoon, and was joined on Clapham Common by near fifty coaches, filled with the lamenting followers of their revered and beloved pastor. It was attended by many more on foot, who surrounded the hearse, or followed it weeping. By the time that the procession reached the Obelisk in St George's Fields, the multitude collected was very great indeed; but silence, solemnity and decorum universally prevailed. At the foot of Blackfriars bridge, the children of the charity school, together with the parish beadles, were waiting to attend.

The city marshals on horse back with their men, and with black silk scarfs and hatbands, rode before the hearse to the entrance of the church.[31]

The *Gentleman's Magazine* states that the large funeral procession passed over Blackfriars bridge in the following order: 'Six marshals; the children of Blackfriars school, the boys with crape round their hats, and the girls with black ribbons round their heads and across their stomachers; two city marshals on horseback; the two beadles of the parish; four men on horseback; the plume of feathers carried by two men; the hearse and six, two mourning coaches and four, and thirty-eight private carriages.'[32] The city marshals and their men had been called out by the Lord Mayor as a token of respect to Romaine's memory. The constables of the ward also attended to keep order and to prevent confusion.

Blackfriars was draped in black, as was St Dunstan's, and by the time the coffin arrived the pews were full of mourners. The funeral service was performed by William Goode to an affected congregation. A psalm was sung during the service and afterwards Romaine's body was placed in the vault of the church. Three more funeral sermons were preached the following Lord's day. Many congregations of the Calvinistic Methodists hung their pulpits in black as a token of respect. 'Sermons on the occasion were preached, probably in more places, than had ever before been known to lament together, over so afflictive an event to the Church of God.'[33] On 14 August 1795, Thomas Charles wrote to Miss Ashwell from Spafields, and summed up the sentiments of many when he said:

You have heard, doubtless, that the great *Romaine* is dead, and that Mr *Goode* has succeeded to his Church, to the universal satisfaction and joy of all lovers of the gospel. Mr R's death was triumphant; and his memory stands high in the minds of all of every party in the religious world. He long continued in the firmament of the

Church, a bright star, revolving in his appointed course with the Sun of righteousness full in view, continually receiving of his light and heat, and communicating them to others to the unspeakable benefit and comfort of their souls. May his mantle drop on his successor![34]

In the following weeks at least six funeral sermons were print-ed by his friends, William Bull, William Cadogan, Charles De Coetlogon, Thomas Wills and John Newton among them. Several of his particular friends united to erect a marble monu-ment to his memory in the church of St Ann's, Blackfriars, and on his memorial plaque in St Hilda's, Hartlepool, there is an autobiographical extract, which reads:

I was even as others are by nature a child of wrath and an heir of misery; I was going on in the broad way of destruction, careless and secure, and I am quite aston-ished to see the danger I was in; I tremble to behold the precipice over which I was ready to fall, when Jesus opened mine eyes and by the light of His Word and Spirit showed me my guilt and danger and put it into my heart to flee from the wrath to come. O what a merciful escape![35]

He left vast congregations at both St Dunstan's and Blackfriars, where his loss was greatly lamented. Soon, though, many who were partial to his ministry, drifted to other churches. In his will, which he had made in 1792, he bequeathed to his son William £200 'South Sea stock' and his 'library of books'. Everything else was left to his wife Mary, who was appointed sole executrix. It appears that his daughter had died some time before.

Skevington Wood rightly calls Romaine 'one of the ma-jor figures in the Evangelical section of the eighteenth centu-ry Awakening'.[36] His influence for good was deep and wide-spread and, in the words of his friend Thomas Haweis, he left the Church of God in a state 'abundantly more flourishing than he found it, and the Church of England especially profited by his labours'.[37] At his death the number of evangelical believers was 'amazingly increased. And the happy impulse given by his labours has left the most abundant tendency to accelerate the movement. Hundreds, many hundreds are labouring in the like cause, and with the like zeal ... with true purpose of heart, and signal blessings on their endeavours.'[38] Both Methodist connections were encouraged by him to stay within the Establishment and he did all in his power to raise up a body within the church that would rigorously and faithfully defend the Christian gospel.

With the message of man's sinfulness and the glory of Christ burning in his heart and resounding from his lips, and a life cast into the mould and form of God's Word, he earned the veneration, not only of his spiritual children, but of many who did not embrace the doctrines of God. In his death no one spoke against him, for the winds of persecution had ceased to blow; but the Word of life he loved and so earnestly preached lives on. He once prayed: 'Make [the Bible] my daily study. Render it my constant delight. Let my meditation of it be always sweet.' He went on:

> O thou holy and eternal Spirit, witness thus to thine own record — and let me experience it to be the power of God, as well as the truth of God. In this dependence upon thee in the use of it, let me be daily growing — until, by the will of God, I shall have served mine own generation; and then let it be the last act of my life, to seal the truth of thy testimony concerning Jesus. Let me find thy witness true in the hour of death, and beyond death all the promises made good to me, through Jesus Christ, in life everlasting. Amen and amen.[39]

The Lord, who had heard his cry, proved faithful to the end.

William Romaine was a steadfast, uncompromising, powerful witness for the whole counsel of God. His life was unsullied, and his great gifts and sound scholarship were richly sanctified and made meet for his Master's use.

The Gospel Magazine, August 1901.[1]

Few contemporary clergymen exercised a deeper or wider influence, or displayed a more perfect devotion to the cause they believed to be true, [than Romaine].

W. H. E. Lecky.

He was, in my humble opinion, a modern day patriarch: who, after having lived the life of faith, was translated, on the triumphant wings of faith, to the mansions of eternal rest and peace.

C. E. De Coetlogon.[2]

18

A Man for his Times

Many agree that Romaine was the right man in the right place at the right time. The strength of his character was ideally suited to persevere through years of opposition. His intrepid spirit enabled him to rebuke the wayward and to stand as an unbending pillar of truth in a godless London. An austere lifestyle added meaning and seriousness to the gospel message he preached, which was then ridiculed by many. He was not a man to be taken lightly or dismissed carelessly. He was an eighteenth-century John the Baptist, whose words were like fire in and out of the pulpit. He was a soldier, marching to war against the principalities and powers of this world, with the sword of the Spirit in his right hand and the shield of faith in his left, and always ready to submit to his Master's commands. He viewed the Christian life as a battle to be fought, not with idleness and self-indulgence, but with the weapons of prayer, integrity and diligence.

Romaine's character, criticized by those who have not taken into account his natural temperament and the ruggedness of the times, was naturally close and reserved, irritable to a certain degree and his short and quick answers were often interpreted as being rude. John Overton, who admits that all in all Romaine was 'the strongest man connected with the Evangelical branch of the revival', describes him as 'grave, severe, self-restrained, and, except to those who knew him intimately, somewhat repellent in manners'.[3] Hylson-Smith, following the traditional picture of Romaine, claims that he lacked 'warmth and pastoral sensitivity'.[4] Archibald Harrison calls him 'that good but dull man'. Elliot-Binns, while agreeing that he 'exercised a considerable influence on the movement and its adherents', comments that it would have been 'immeasurably greater but for certain defects of temperament'. He goes on:

> Romaine had an affectionate nature and a deep anxiety to promote the spiritual welfare of those under his care; but he was shy and reserved, severe in manner and difficult to approach, so that those who did not know him well might easily regard him as pedantic and morose. One gets the impression that he lived under considerable strain — the frequent opposition which he encountered may have helped this — which probably accounts for his occasional outbursts of irritability. Thus it came about that Romaine chiefly told on others through his preaching and writing rather than by personal dealings.[5]

While it is acceptable to describe Romaine as 'austere, a strict disciplinarian and one more calculated to inspire awe than love',[6] it is not accurate to portray him as deliberately provocative, uncaring or continually bad mannered. Yes, he could be rude and offensive in the things he said, but he was not hard-hearted, as many have suggested; rather he was a man of strength, unbending and resolute. It is certainly true that he did not fit into the mould of many modern preachers — all-smiling, back-slapping socialites — for he was more interested in saving souls than in flattering friends. He made his congregations tremble not laugh. He drove them from the mouth of hell, not with enticing words, but with the stick of God's wrath, before applying, with wisdom and sensitivity, the balm of Gilead. He lived as a man, whose sole purpose was to glorify God, and at no time did he compromise the truth in order to gain popularity. This must be kept in mind if we are to understand the man without misrepresentation.

It must be mentioned at this point that Romaine was a deeply humble man, as his letters demonstrate, and his teaching came from personal knowledge and experience. In a letter to his good friend Shrapnell (29 October 1772), he writes:

> You can never, never show forth all his praise, because an humble thankful heart is one of his gifts, and in your highest praises you return him nothing but his own. The humblest are the best at this work, and he is the great teacher of humility. He brings his scholars into self-abhorrence, that they may glorify him. When he has made you less than the least in your own eyes, then you will be glad Jesus should have all the honour of your salvation: and when he admits you into his presence and crowns you with glory, he will then make you perfectly humble, and perfectly willing to ascribe all your blessings to the rich, free, sovereign grace of God the Saviour.[7]

On another occasion he said: 'Depend upon it, man cannot be laid too low, nor Christ set too high. I would therefore, always aim, as good brother Grimshaw expresses it, to get the old gentleman down, and keep him down: and then Christ reigns like himself, when he is ALL and man is nothing!'[8] This was Romaine's constant desire, as he indicates in a further letter:

> Whatever it is which makes you pleased with yourself, is not true grace; and whatever makes you displeased with yourself, is not true grace, unless it brings you humbly to Christ, and makes you put more trust and confidence in him... I have learned [this] by long experience, though I know but little of [it], yet I am getting on in the school of Christ, and hope soon to be on the lowest form, for there

we learn most and safest... I would therefore wish you
to be the humblest man upon earth, not only that you
might know most, but also that you might love most.[9]

John Gadsby, in *Memoirs of the Principal Hymn Writers and
Compilers*, relates a story that points to Romaine's 'imperfect
humility':

In company with another minister, he was once staying
at the house of a friend, when it was desired that one of
them should engage in prayer, and it was thereupon arranged that R.'s friend should do so that evening and R.
the next. The Lord saw it good to shut the mouth of his
friend, so that he had to stop suddenly in the middle of
his prayer. Romaine seemed to feel no sympathy for his
friend, but was truly indignant and puffed up. The next
evening he was taught something of his own weakness;
for, though he eagerly read and as eagerly went on his
knees to pray, he became almost instantly so confused
that he had to rise, and was then glad of the sympathy
of his despised brother.[10]

There were other instances when he was too abrupt, displayed a
hasty temper and was unnecessarily sharp with others. Toplady
was told the following anecdote by Willett on 14 November
1769: 'A person called some time ago on Mr Romaine, and
complained of being grievously distressed and bowed down in
soul, without any ray of comfort from God. Mr Romaine's answer was: "Do you think, then, that no persons go to heaven
but those that have comforts?"'[11]

Sometimes his rebukes were too rough, especially if he suspected unfaithfulness, but he worked from the proverb: 'Open
rebuke is better than love carefully concealed.' He was a man
of piety and orthodoxy himself, and he expected others who
professed Christ to show the same earnestness in their daily
walk and loyalty to the fundamental doctrines of God. 'The

sharpness and severity with which he rebuked in a public shop, before several persons, not long before his death, the Rev Mr L[eicester], whom he charged with departure from the evangelical principles to the errors of the Swedenborgians, is well known.'[12] That was his nature. He zealously guarded the truth, and spared none whom he thought disgraced Christ by their actions or beliefs. 'Zeal for his great and only adorable master,' says Haweis in his defence, 'prompted him to these faithful offices of reproof; and if he erred, it was more in the manner of application, than in the justice of the cause which excited him to it.'[13]

Once, while Romaine and his wife were on their way to Augustus Toplady at Broad Hembury, they broke their journey at Tiverton, where Romaine went into a shop to get change for a guinea. He was followed by the Arminian Methodist and disciple of Wesley, Thomas Olivers, who was on a preaching tour in the area. Olivers immediately taunted Romaine about his trust in God's grace, observing, 'They say there's an act of grace coming out [from the king] for the release of imprisoned debtors; but I deny it to be an act of grace.' 'What, then,' said Romaine, 'would you call it?' Olivers replied, 'I would call it an Act of Insolvency, for nothing can be an act of grace but what is absolutely universal.' 'You are in error,' said Romaine, 'for if the king were to release only one debtor out of a hundred, it would certainly be an act of grace to that one.' 'I do not think so,' commented Olivers. Romaine, who had had enough of the fruitless conversation, simply retorted, 'Then enjoy your opinion,' and promptly left the shop.

When Romaine arrived at Broad Hembury, he related the incident to Toplady, who later wrote a letter 'to show the rudeness and impertinence of the illiterate and self-sufficient Arminian who wanted to draw into dispute a man of Mr Romaine's eminence, with whom he had never before exchanged even a single word'. Apparently, when Romaine next preached at Cullompton, some two weeks later, Olivers was in the congregation to listen to Romaine's free grace sermon from Lamentations

5:16. Olivers was 'prodigiously offended' by what he heard, and in the afternoon, when he preached at the Methodist meeting house, endeavoured to contradict 'all that Romaine had been advancing in the morning'.[14]

In many ways, Romaine was a 'rough diamond, but very pointed, and the more he was broken by years, the more he appeared to shine. There was indeed a light upon his countenance, and particularly when he preached, which appeared like the dawn, or the faint resemblance of glory.'[15] His abruptness came from an intense dislike of anything that pulled him away from the essential duties of a minister. If one met him in the street, for instance, and asked him how he was, his usual reply was: 'As well as I can be out of heaven,' before he hurried on. Once he made the same comment to a friend older than himself, and of a different communion, and added, 'There is but one central point in which we must all meet, Jesus Christ and him crucified.'[16] 'Christ crucified' was the subject always on his lips, the God-Man, whom, to use his own expression, he had 'taken for body and for soul, for time and for eternity, his present and his everlasting all'.[17] On another occasion, a friend stopped him on London Bridge and began a melancholy speech about the French successes. Romaine, who hated useless interruptions, rushed away, saying, 'I am in the ark.' Thus he redeemed his time, improving it to the best possible use, and by his quickness and activity, accomplished twice as much as other men in the same period.

Instead of entertaining 'the high and mighty', he preferred to study and pray over the sermon he was about to deliver to ordinary people:

Sir Harry Trelawny [the great Polperro landowner, who successively became a Methodist minister, an Anglican vicar and a Catholic priest!] earnestly requested Mr Neale, of St Paul's Churchyard, to introduce him to Romaine in his vestry. 'Well,' said Mr Neale, 'as you so much wish it, I certainly will, but mind, I do not promise

Sir Harry Trelawney
(sometimes spelled Trelawny).

The Trelawney estate near Polperro.

you he will not be angry with us both, as he never speaks to anybody there.' They met together before the service and Mr Neale ventured to say to Mr Romaine, 'Sir, I hope you will give me leave to bring in Sir Harry Trelawny, who is very desirous to speak to you.'

'O, Sir Harry Trelawny! I have heard of him, you may.' On Sir Harry's entering, Mr Romaine, looked at him kindly, and said in a solemn tone, 'Sir, you *stand upon ice* — now you must excuse me saying more, as it is contrary to my custom to admit persons here.[18]

On a similar occasion, to one who had taken up a great deal of his time by visiting him on a morning he regularly preached, he was compelled to say, 'Sir, I must now beg you would retire; as I really do not preach *by inspiration*,' meaning he needed time to prepare his sermon.[19]

There were lighter moments, too. One evening he was invited to a friend's house and after tea the lady of the house asked him to play cards, to which he made no objection:

The cards were brought out, and when all were ready to begin playing, Romaine said, 'Let us ask the blessing of God.'

'Ask the blessing of God!' said the lady in great surprise. 'I never heard of such a thing before a game of cards.'

Romaine then inquired, 'Ought we to engage in anything on which we cannot ask God's blessing?' This reproof put an end to the card playing.

On another occasion he was addressed by a lady, who expressed the great pleasure she had enjoyed under his preaching, and added that she could comply with his requirements, with the exception of one thing. 'And what is that?' asked Romaine.

'Cards, sir,' was the reply.

'You think you could not be happy without them?'

'No, sir, I know I could not.'

'Then, madam,' said he, 'cards are your god, and they must save you.'

It is recorded that this pointed remark led to serious reflections, and finally to the abandonment of card playing.[20]

One excuse for Romaine's hasty manner was the value he placed on time — there was little more precious to him and, in his view, not a moment should be wasted. He reasoned that the more time he spent counselling, the less time he had for reading, meditation and prayer; thus he strenuously avoided all unnecessary interruptions. He could not tolerate idle, godless chatter, but demanded honesty and plain speaking from all who visited him. 'It was not uncommon for him to tell those who came to him with cases of conscience and questions of spiritual concern, that he said all that he had to say in the pulpit.'[21] These people may have felt rebuffed at first, but when they attended his preaching at the next opportunity, they found that their difficulties had impressed him as much as themselves, and been the subject of prayer and careful consideration. His sermons in this regard were particularly useful, as they not only explained the text, but applied it to the case and condition of every hearer.

With the high value he placed on his daily walk with God and observing that most of his time was 'quite lost', he saw the necessity of 'husbanding it well, and of making the most of it'. This led him to settle and determine a fixed rule of living: 'Here is a new day, what lies before me to be done? What do I live for today? What am I now to propose to myself, as the end and aim of all my actions?' His conclusions were that only three things were to be done: 'First, I was to look to my conscience, that the peace of God might rule in it always and by all means. Secondly, I was to look to my heart, that it might be happy in the love of God; and thirdly, I was to watch over my tempers, my walk, and my conversation, that I might enjoy the peace and love of God.'[22]

In another letter his concern for living every moment with Christ-centred priorities is strikingly obvious: 'What a life is this! Hurry, hurry, hurry, from place to place, from this object to that; — weary with seeking, but never finding rest. Happy Christian, who is fixed to a point! Go where he will, ONE object is his ALL. The crucified Saviour is his happiness, his perfect, everlasting happiness; and this heaven he carries about with him.'[23] He keenly recognised the temptation to waste time that assails every minister, and of passing a day in non-essential duties and thereby accomplishing little or nothing for the kingdom of God.

Romaine's daily routine demonstrates how meticulous he was about the management of his time. During the last fifty years of his life he rose at five o'clock and breakfasted at six, with his Hebrew Psalter a constant companion. He always meditated on the Scriptures and often said how much his first repast was sanctified by the Word of God and prayer. His family devotions were at nine o'clock, and from ten o'clock he usually visited the sick and his friends. At one he had lunch, which consisted of some plain dish or cold meat, and a pudding. He drank little or no wine. After dinner he retired to his study, and sometimes went for a walk, which he deferred till after supper in the height of the summer. He supped at eight. Sometimes friends were admitted to his evening family devotions, which were deeply moving, and those privileged to be present enjoyed a most profitable time. If he returned their visit, he usually gave an exposition of Scripture at their domestic devotions. After devotions he again retired to his study before going to bed at ten o'clock.

From this strict timetable he rarely deviated, except occasionally when he was a guest in the house of a friend, then he had breakfast at seven and dinner at two. Once he was invited by a dignitary in the church to dine with him at five o'clock. As he wished to show respect to his intended host, instead of sending a written apology, he went to him personally, 'thanked him for the invitation, and excused himself by pleading his long habits of early hours, his great age and often infirmities'. In this way he avoided needless offence and maintained his routine.

It must not be thought from his strict timetable that he shunned conversation or friendships, for his character in private life was 'remarkably amiable'. 'In company he was polite, affable and instructive, without affectation; and in domestic life, where the tempers of most men are tried and discovered, he had none superior to him as a master, a father and a husband.'[24] Cadogan, in his funeral sermon for Romaine, comments:

> As a friend and companion he was among the best that I ever knew — plain but polished in his manners; and as cheerful in his behaviour, as he was happy in his soul. As a scholar he could converse on any subject and accommodate himself to any undertaking... [He was] a most entertaining and edifying companion in the house, in the field, and in the garden. He could speak of most natural things with a peculiar favour, because he could point out the spiritual things to which they are related: all, therefore, that received him into their houses were the better for his visits.[25]

De Coetlogon notes that his 'powers of conversation were considerable: easy, unaffected and always pious'.[26] William Goode, who had a close communion with him for nearly ten years, 'with the most uninterrupted cordiality and good understanding', and who 'loved him as a father and served him as a friend', says this about him:

> As a man he was a firm, faithful, and instructive friend, a lively and edifying companion. He possessed a natural cheerfulness of disposition, and firmness of mind, which, sanctified by grace, shone forth in the holy joy, and confidence of faith.
>
> He had a quickness of apprehension, and a readiness of determination. In his conversation, as

well as in his writings, he was short, and sententious;
which was often misunderstood for want of temper and
irritation. But in his *domestic* character he shone forth
the ornament of his profession, and an evidence of
the power of grace: the kindest of husbands, the most
affectionate of fathers, and the best of masters. Of this
we have the most convincing proof, since all who were
about him loved him, and those who were the nearest to
him loved him the most.[27]

At times he could be quite playful. Once he met the great Welsh
preacher Daniel Rowland in a bookshop, probably in Bristol.
He had already ordered 100 copies of Rowland's sermons,
eight of which had appeared in English in 1774, and it is said
that he considered the Welsh preacher 'the greatest minister in
the whole world'. On seeing him, Romaine exclaimed somewhat humorously, 'What, do you, the most eminent divine,
come here to buy books? I thought you had the Spirit of God to
study his word and compose your sermons!' Rowland replied
mischievously, 'I find that Romaine lately published some to be
read, and how are they to be got, unless purchased from booksellers, where they are to be sold?'[28]

In one of his letters, Romaine said, 'It is a great prize to
meet with a real friend, and a greater still to meet with an approved one. A friend of Christ's making is better still, because
he makes everlasting friends.'[29] Among his friends was the
warm-hearted James Ireland, a wealthy sugar refiner, who lived
at Brislington, a suburb of Bristol. He has been called the 'John
Thornton of the West' because of his patronizing services to the
evangelical cause. It was through his instrumentality that the
Bristol Clerical Society was formed, which enabled young men
to secure a place in the universities. Romaine often visited him
at Brislington and many of his letters make affectionate mention
of his family. Romaine had great respect for 'perhaps the most
learned of all the evangelicals', Thomas Clarke, the 'walking
synopsis', as he called him. 'He gives you the opinion of every

Daniel Rowland.

William Kinsbury.

commentator, and then gives his own, which is worth all the rest put together.'[30] William Kinsbury, pastor of the Independent Church in Southampton, 'whose meeting he constantly attended ... and whose ministry he so highly esteemed', was also a close friend — many of Romaine's letters to Walter Taylor include greetings to Kinsbury — along with many who have been mentioned earlier.

It is worth mentioning that Romaine's church provision was very poor, especially when compared to the money he could have made, with his abilities and learning, in a different vocation. Before he went to Blackfriars it amounted to only £18 per annum, which was wholly inadequate to support himself and his family. Thankfully, his necessities were met by kind friends. But in spite of his poverty he was always ready and willing to give to others. On 21 February 1789 he wrote to a fellow minister and enclosed a £10 gift: 'Accept a small token of great love. I choose to send it in my life time, rather than by legacy. I have only to desire, that you would *mention it to nobody*, except God, — and to myself, when you see me... Then I will give my reasons for your not taking notice of it, and I am sure, they will satisfy you.'[31] Four years after Romaine's death the recipient sent a copy of this letter to the *Gospel Magazine*, along with a warm testimonial to Romaine's friendship. Thomas Hervey, a poor clergyman, having only a small chapelry at Underbarrow near Kendal, was also occasionally sent money by Romaine.

Romaine's wants were astonishingly few, and those who sat at his table were amazed at the lack of self-indulgence he displayed — an abstemiousness that lasted to his dying day. It may well have been this temperance, coupled with his singular regularity, which kept him in such good health. Occasionally he was attacked by a fever, which affected him for a while, but he persevered in his labours and pursued his normal duties. When he died, because of his frugality, he was able to leave a liberal provision for his surviving relatives.

Romaine had a deep concern and pity for sinners, but a

William Dodd at Tyburn,
27 June 1777, his place of
execution. He is accompanied
by Joseph Harris.

genuine abhorrence of sin, a combination that is seen in his relationship with a friend, William Dodd (1729-1777), who at one time leaned towards Hutchinsonianism and distinguished himself as a popular preacher, his sermons on behalf of charities being particularly successful. Through similar interests the two men had become acquainted. Sadly, Dodd turned away from Christian principles and, through living carelessly and beyond his means, fell heavily into debt. Ashamed of his former friends, he told Romaine that he would be glad to see him at his house, but hoped that he would not acknowledge him if they met in public. Thus their intimacy ceased until Dodd was imprisoned for forgery.

Once, Romaine, on his way from Newgate Prison, met one of Dodd's faithful friends at the bottom of the Old Bailey. Their conversation soon turned to the unhappy backslider. Romaine expressed sorrow at Dodd's imprisonment and disappointment that his former friend was visited by ungodly companions. Dodd's friend was surprised and hurt that Romaine had received such an untrue report, particularly as Dodd always spoke highly of Romaine. He assured Romaine that he had been misinformed and that all who visited him were those whose minds were duly and deeply impressed like his own. Not only that but the horror of his circumstances precluded all levity and impertinence from the prisoner. Romaine was pleased to hear the truth and promised to do all he could to set the record straight. He then left Dodd's friend at the door of St Dunstan's, where he was to preach the evening lecture.

Romaine visited Dodd on several other occasions. A gentleman one day met him at the prison, and wanting to know Romaine's thoughts on the matter, took care to leave Newgate at the same time. As they were walking out together, he asked Romaine, 'if he, who knew so much of the human heart, thought poor Dodd a real sincere penitent. Mr Romaine answered, "I hope he may be a real penitent, but there is a great difference between saying and feeling, *God, be merciful to me, a sinner*."'[32] After further visits Romaine became more certain of Dodd's repentance, for three days before Dodd's execution he wrote to Mrs Medhurst and said, 'I have seen poor D[odd]: he is a very great penitent. The Lord has brought him through the fire, a miracle of mercy. Before this reach you, it is likely he will be adoring the love of a triune God.'[33] Dodd had preached to his fellow-prisoners in Newgate chapel on 6 June 1777, a sermon that had been written by Samuel Johnson, before he was hanged at Tyburn Tree on 27 June. Johnson afterwards described Dodd as a 'man whom we have seen exulting in popularity, and sunk in shame... He was at first what he endeavoured to make others; but the world broke down his resolution, and he in time ceased to exemplify his own instructions.' He concludes by saying that in prison Dodd showed 'regret and self-abhorrence' over his 'deviations from rectitude'.[34]

There is another anecdote that shows Romaine's hatred of sin, and his compassion for the sinner.

He was walking in the street with a gentleman, when he overheard a poor thoughtless man solemnly calling upon Jehovah to damn him for ever to the bottomless pit. Mr Romaine stopped, took half-a-crown out of his pocket, and said, 'My friend, I will give you this if you will repeat that oath again.'

The man started and said, 'What, Sir, do you think I will damn my soul for half-a-crown?'

Mr Romaine mildly replied, 'As you did it just now for nothing, I could not suppose that you would refuse to do it for a reward.'

The poor creature, struck, as Mr Romaine meant he should be, replied, 'God bless and reward you, Sir, wherever you are. I believe you have saved my soul. I hope I shall never swear again as long as I live.'[35]

At another time, he heard a man call on God to damn his soul for Christ's sake. He went up to the man and put a hand on his shoulder and said, 'My friend, God has done many things for Christ's sake, and he may do that too.' The man was taken aback as the reproof pierced his heart, and it was the means of turning him to God.[36]

In the early days of his ministry, especially when influenced by Hutchinsonianism, he kept aloof from Methodists, with whom he was in all essential points of doctrine one in heart and sentiment. These zealous men had awakened great attention in London, and in the churches where they preached huge congregations gathered. But on account of 'irregularity' the churches were soon shut against them and they were driven into the fields or forced to erect their own chapels. Romaine, for his part, 'seldom, if ever, frequented their places of worship, and studiously avoided forming any connections, which should expose him to the charge of Methodism'. He would not employ lay preachers or countenance their methods; thus he stood alone for a considerable time in the Church of England and, in the opinion of Haweis, there was no one else who 'distinguished himself with like labour, zeal and fidelity'.[37]

During this early period he also tended to express his attachment to the Establishment in a bitter spirit, thereby offending some of his dissenting brethren with his severe remarks — men whom he later acknowledged as the 'excellent of the earth'. But he knew his faults and was always willing to own up to wrongdoing. As he matured he became more liberal in spirit and less hasty in speech, as the following instance demonstrates. Thomas Towle, an eminent dissenting minister, had often with pleasure attended Romaine's lectures at St Dunstan's. On one occasion he heard what he regarded as an unjust censure cast on the dissenters by Romaine. So he determined to challenge his brother on the matter:

> He was accordingly introduced, and with Christian apologies for the freedom he was taking, began to state the cause of his visit and the subject.
>
> 'Sir,' said Romaine very rudely, rising to show him the door, 'I don't want to have anything to say to you.'
>
> 'If you will hear me, sir,' said Mr T., 'I am ready to acquaint you with my name and that I am a protestant dissenting minister.'
>
> 'Sir,' said he, cutting him short, 'I desire neither to know your name nor your profession,' and most ungraciously led him to the door and shut it after him.
>
> Some time after to the great surprise of Mr T., Mr Romaine waited upon him. 'Sir,' said Mr R., 'I am come to take shame for my behaviour to you the other day, so unlike a Christian I acknowledge, and unbecoming my profession, for which I can make no apology, but beg your pardon; for though I have neither changed my sentiments, nor seen reason to alter my preference for the Church of England, I am conscious, I am bound to allow every other brother the same right of judging for himself, which I exercise, and therefore, without renouncing

our respective principles of church order, or being different towards them, I hope we shall hereafter exercise mutual candour and charity to each other, and I cannot but profess my high respect and esteem for my gospel brethren of whatever denomination.'[38]

Towle accepted Romaine's apology. The two men shook hands and their difference respecting church government never again became a matter of dispute; instead, they had a constant friendly relationship until Towle died. When Towle was asked about the above incident, he closed by saying, 'I have not the smallest suspicion, but that, as long as I live, I shall remember him with veneration, as an eminently consistent and respectable character.'[39]

On a different occasion he had offended a dissenting minister in Bristol by his apparent dislike of those outside the Church of England. In 1793, two years before he died, he surprised 'Mr T.' with a visit and, after apologizing for his intrusion, addressed him in the following manner: 'Sir, I have been very high church in the former years of my life, but the Lord has brought me down; and now I can rejoice in, and wish well too, the ministers of my master, of whatever denomination.'[40] Age and experience mellowed his judgement, and his mind ceased to put undue importance on non-essential matters, a change of attitude that William Goode noted in his funeral address:

In his earlier years he had resisted the offer of much temporal advantage, and endured much opposition in [the Church of England], rather than depart from its communion; well convinced that he was in the line of duty, and God, who had placed him there, would provide him his work, and supply his necessities. His firmness has sometimes been interpreted into bigotry, as I conceive, through inattention and misunderstanding. If such a temper might arise in the fervency of youth, maturer wisdom had meliorated his disposition; at least, I

> must profess, that the many years I have been with him
> (though many opportunities offered) I have never once
> heard him express anything but the most cordial love to
> all, 'who loved our Lord Jesus Christ in sincerity': this
> was his only rest — denominating all things else but the
> scaffolding of the building, that must be taken down be-
> fore the whole shall appear in its glory. And I am in pos-
> session of a letter that discovers the most unbounded
> liberality and candour of his mind.[41]

Another dissenting minister, who lived in the country and
whose work had been blessed, served a poor congregation,
and therefore was unable to support himself and his family. He
approached Romaine and made his situation known. Romaine
received him kindly, encouraged him to continue in the ministry, and promised to do everything he could to supply his need.
He made the case known to several of his friends, who gladly
contributed. Each year he collected the subscriptions and trans-
ferred them to the worthy minister in the country. In this way
Romaine demonstrated that he was willing to uphold any minister, whether of the Established Church or not, who preached the
gospel of Christ. Similarly, he raised no less than £300 a year for
the benefit and comfort of the poor in his own parish.

A further example of his catholicism of spirit is occasioned
by one of his visits to Southampton, the city that refused him
every Church of England pulpit. He stayed for some time at
Portswood Green and preached frequently in Walter Taylor's
laundry to as many as could squeeze into that room. On the
Lord's Day and on lecture evenings, he attended with his host
the ministry of William Kinsbury, and during his visits never
once entered the doors of the Established Church. He did not
want to support by his presence the place where the gospel was
not preached. In a letter dated 5 January 1790, he states: 'It is
to me matter of great thankfulness that the Lord has such able
witnesses to succeed us. I do not forget brother Kinsbury, nor
Mrs, nor the family, nor the CHURCH; our national sins begin

to find us out. I pray for Mr K's witness against infidelity, and its offspring profaneness, and their natural effects, WAR.'[42] Some years later John Newton visited Portswood Green and preached to Taylor's congregation, who then met in a place of worship that opened out of the old laundry, and where three hundred persons could gather to hear the gospel.

The above examples demonstrate that in his later days Romaine was more liberally minded towards those ministers who did not belong to the Church of England, although he himself was always 'firmly attached to the articles of its faith, to the forms of its devotion, and to its ecclesiastical authority'.[43] The *Gospel Magazine* for October 1796 reports that he was 'accessible, affable and conversable' towards non-conformists in the latter part of his life.[44] 'The excellent of the earth,' says Haweis, 'without respect to their denomination, he honoured, attended, countenanced. It was not in his view a matter of first importance, whether men assembled at church or at meeting, provided they gathered to the true Shiloh, and without that, it was no matter where they assembled.'[45]

The service he offered the Church of England was not weakened by his catholicism, but rather strengthened as he reached a wider audience. Many of the younger workers looked up to him with the 'highest reverence and affection', and consulted him about the pressures they endured. He always exhorted them to remain faithful to the church and, where possible, to submit to the unreasonable demands of their superiors, rather than be driven from their curacies. It is well known that his counsel kept many serving the church who otherwise would have left due to the 'insolence, ill-usage and oppression' they encountered. Sadly, many church rulers were ready to expel any curate whom they suspected of 'Methodism', a term they used to describe an enthusiastic Christian.

It is obvious that Romaine was by no means perfect. Overton and Relton, in an attempt to explain his rough, unsociable nature, suggest that 'his foreign extraction may have been a hindrance to his understanding English ways', as if all Englishmen

are refined in manners and genial in society. Yet in the same
breath they describe him as 'absolutely without reproach ... his
earnestness and piety, his orthodoxy and loyalty to the Church
unquestioned'.[46] Goode says this of him:

> As a Christian — I have frequently admired the cheer-
> fulness, the consistency, and fervour of his piety. He
> evidently lived much with God; inflexibly abstracted
> from the world; much in the enjoyment of his redeem-
> er's presence, and in the realizing views of eternity in
> its most glorious and animating light. His devotion was
> pure and sincere, glowing lively from a heart filled with
> the love of Christ... His whole conduct was in unison
> with his profession.[47]

In case we are accused of only quoting the remarks of his
friends, we offer the testimony of a group of gentlemen who
were among his fiercest opponents:

> It appears that Mr Romaine was indefatigably active
> during a ministry of near sixty years, in discharging the
> duties of his profession, and in promoting charitable de-
> signs. Whatever peculiar theological notions he might
> entertain, his piety appears to have been most fervent
> and sincere; his charity ever watchful for opportunities of
> doing good; his literary attainments respectable, and his
> knowledge at all times wholly devoted to the advance-
> ment of religion.[48]

Ryle's closing portraiture of Romaine gives an excellent overall
picture of 'a great man, and a mighty instrument in God's hand
for good':

> [Romaine] stood in a most prominent position in London
> for forty-five years, testifying the gospel of the grace of
> God, and never flinching for a day. He stood alone, with

almost no backers, supporters or fellow-labourers... He stood there witnessing to truths which were most unpopular, and brought down on him opposition, persecution and scorn. He stood in a most public post, continually watched, observed, and noticed by unfriendly eyes, ready to detect faults in a moment if he committed them. Yet ... he maintained a blameless character, firmly upheld his first principles to the last, and died at length, like a good soldier at his post, full of days and honour. The man of whom these things can be said must have been no common man... In [eighteenth-century] England ... there were not four spiritual champions greater and more honourable than William Romaine.[49]

'Prepare yourself and arise, and speak to them all that I command you. Do not be dismayed before their faces, lest I dismay you before them. For behold, I have made you this day a fortified city and an iron pillar, and bronze walls against the whole land ... They will fight against you, but they shall not prevail against you. For I am with you,' says the LORD, 'to deliver you.'

Jeremiah 1:17-19.

The labours of Mr Romaine, and of those men of God who united with him in 'holding forth the word of life', were truly astonishing. They were not suffered to labour in vain, or spend their strength for nought, when called to go forth in the name of his Divine Master. His word directs — 'In the morning sow thy seed, and in the evening withhold not thine hand; for thou knowest not whether shall prosper either this or that.'

Aaron Seymour.[1]

19

'An Iron Pillar and a Bronze Wall'

Marcus Loane is right when he refers to Romaine as 'that iron pillar of the truth'. The church historian Philip Schaff says something similar when he comments that Romaine 'stood forth as the main pillar of evangelization, which was reviving in the Church of England after the reaction against Puritanism consequent upon the Restoration a hundred years before'. J. B. Owen makes the bold claim that as a writer and preacher none ever 'attained a greater popularity; and, what is infinitely more important, none were ever more signally blessed with proofs of usefulness in his ministry'.[2]

There is no question that Romaine was an extraordinarily popular and powerful preacher; for through the course of fifty years, as he fearlessly proclaimed Jesus Christ and him crucified, with peculiar emphasis and effect, many were converted from a life of degradation and sin to a saving knowledge of the Redeemer; the attention of his regular hearers increased in fervour, and their love and reverence for the Word deepened to a remarkable degree. There was nothing spectacular in what he said or did, but there was an uncommon power invested in the words he uttered that caused many unenlightened clergymen to react against him. So much so that at one meeting of clergymen a resolution was passed that 'Romaine's preaching was calculated to do harm.'[3]

In appearance, he was a little 'above the middle stature' with a commanding presence in the pulpit. His dress was plain but always neat. His countenance was 'prepossessing, and, when discoursing on the excellencies of Jesus Christ, illuminated with a majestic and pleasing smile',[4] made all the more attractive by a full set of teeth. His voice was weak but harmonious, which, towards the end of his life, became lower in tone and volume; but it was still distinct and audible, and he always possessed free and easy elocution and clear articulation. His powers of intellect and memory were considerable, and neither were impaired as the years went by. The writer in the *Evangelical Magazine* (1795) says:

> His body was certainly the residence of a capacious and exalted mind. His understanding was strong and manly, his perception quick and penetrating, and his literary acquirements such as entitled him to superior respect among the wise and intelligent. By partial admirers he was made the standard of critical knowledge; but for our own parts we have been free to confess that some of his criticisms never appeared to us to merit a rank among his chief excellencies. However, he made all these point to the Lord Jesus Christ, the great object of his supreme confidence and affection. Had his conscience been pliant and accommodating, he certainly possessed those natural and acquired talents, calculated to accelerate his early preferment in the church; but in his adherence to truth he was firm and inflexible.[5]

Apart from the wrinkles on his face in later life, his body bore no signs of weakness. He walked quickly and vigorously — 'with the erectness and celerity of youth' — right up to the end of his life, and the last time Thomas Haweis saw him ascend the pulpit stairs, though very steep, he climbed them with the same agility as ever. He never wore glasses in the pulpit and his eyesight was always good, as the following anecdote illustrates. One morning, when Haweis was preaching at Blackfriars, he was struck as he glanced into Romaine's Hebrew Bible that his eyes had not grown dim with age, for the writing was so small that Haweis, a younger man, 'could scarce read it with spectacles'. In fact, so wonderfully were his physical and mental faculties preserved, that De Coetlogon exclaims that a more 'accurate, animated or impressive sermon was scarce delivered by any person, in the vigour of his days and powers, than was uttered by him ... at the advanced age of *eighty*'![6]

In the pulpit he did not use his intellect to impress his hearers with wise and persuasive words, but sought to unveil the sinfulness of man and the unmerited grace of God in Christ Jesus. 'He remembered nothing but his Master's work and glory, and studied nothing but how best to impress his excellency and salvation on the minds of men.'[7] All that he said was based on the 'mighty influence of that faith which the Holy Ghost inspires, and the unutterable pleasure that results from an uniform dependence on the infinite merits of Jesus Christ'.[8] He proclaimed with great fervour all the leading doctrines of the gospel, and he never grew tired of going over the same ground again. 'No man of distinguished abilities ever preserved so great a sameness of subjects, or supported so great a variety in *discussing* those subjects. As these enter into the hopes and fears, the joys and sorrows, the trials and triumphs, the wants and supplies; in short, into the life and death of Christians, they were to his hearers ever new and ever sweet.'[9] De Coetlogon underlines the 'sameness' of the doctrines he preached:

The peculiar talent, with which this eminent minister was favoured of God, appears to have been, not that of harrowing up the souls of his hearers, and driving them into the regions of horror and despair; terrifying their distracted imaginations, or afflicting their wounded consciences; but of illustrating the preciousness of Christ; enforcing the duty of faith; and administering the balm of Gilead to the troubled spirit. His principal subjects were indeed the two former, in order to the latter: for, however he might be led occasionally to digress from them, he seemed always to return to them with renewed ardour.

Upon this ground, some have thought fit to start an objection to the usefulness of his ministry, from its perpetual sameness. But, might we not start a similar objection to the sun itself from its perfect uniformity?... And, notwithstanding the general ideas and plan of all the discourses of this valuable preacher were the same, who, that had a taste for devotion or doctrine, did not admire that assemblage of truth, beauty and utility; that divine simplicity and heavenly unction, with which they were ever enriched.[10]

Thomas Robinson of St Mary's, Leicester, agreed that Romaine's subject changed little, but he always spoke 'as though it were quite new; as though he had just found and dug it out of the mine. "Have you changed your subject yet, Mr Romaine?" "No, brother, my subject is still the same — waiting faith."'[11] This 'sameness' is illustrated again and again in his sermon notes. For example, his notes for 23 January 1785 are taken from Psalm 56:3-4:

When in fear the Psalmist fled to God and he was to him an Almighty refuge. If you put your trust in him, you will find a safe place to trust to in time of need and God will protect and keep you till you arrive safe in heaven. Whatever you meet with in the world trust in Christ — whatever distresses your poor heart look up to him. There is no growth but by faith... The Bible is to be read with prayer... The more you try the word of God the more you will approve it... The holy Psalmist was in such a situation he had nobody to fly to but God — is it not a wise thing to be provided with an antidote against death and sin? There is a remedy for fear nowhere but in the

> arms of faith... A true Christian is always at prayer in the constant dependence upon his word.[12]

Romaine never compromised the truth, either by accommodation, or by hiding or disguising the less attractive parts to make them inoffensive, but preached the whole counsel of God as he understood it. 'He was too full of the election of grace, the divine righteousness and complete redemption, which is in the Son of God, to bend these truths to the temper of half-hearted professors, or to accommodate Calvinistic doctrines to Arminian gospellers.'[13] He preached the same truth of Christ dying on the cross for sinners to the rich and poor, to the wise and foolish, to the fashionable and vulgar, and urged all to embrace the freedom and fulness of the gospel.

In the preface to his *Discourses upon Solomon's Song*, he stated: 'The great subject of all my preaching ... is Christ Jesus the Lord, inviting and calling careless sinners from the error of their ways, and pressing them to come to Christ for the pardon of their sins, for strength to subdue sin, and for grace to do good works, pleasant and acceptable unto God.'[14] In the *Life of Faith*, he wrote: 'The corruption of our nature by the fall, and our recovery through Jesus Christ, are the two leading truths in the Christian religion.'[15] George T. Fox mentions four doctrines on which Romaine majored: the new birth — the 'absolute necessity of a man's being born again'; the imputed righteousness of Christ; a present salvation, which he 'clearly and earnestly enforced, when he had all the world against him'; and the existence of two natures in the regenerate man.[16]

His writings, which helped to spread evangelical truth in the Church of England throughout the eighteenth and into the nineteenth century, and his preaching always centred on the essential truths and explained them in the fullest and strongest manner.

He professed to teach no holiness, but what arose from
faith in the truth. He admitted nothing good as the produce of unrenewed man, nor acceded to the high opinion
of themselves, entertained by those, who suppose they
have ability to think or do anything pleasing to God. He
allowed no sanctification but that of the Spirit, through
the sprinkling of the blood of Jesus Christ. Though no
man more pressed upon the conscience to walk closely
with God as dear children, none stated more distinctly
the divine principles from which this must originate, the
sovereign, free and everlasting love of God, the Saviour
to his elect.[17]

He felt it his responsibility to enforce all the fundamental doctrines as well as duties of the Christian faith, for he conceived
that 'belief of divine truth was [just] as essential to the Christian
character as the sanctification of the spirit and the obedience of
the life. It appeared to him, that to deny is to give up the cause
of revelation at once, that the *principles* of Christianity are as
important in their nature and place as its *precepts*; and that both
must stand or fall together.'[18]

In the words of his biographer, William Cadogan,

He fainted not in the discharge of [his ministry], nor had
recourse to the hidden things of dishonesty to recommend it: but used great plainness of speech, that by
manifestation of the truth he might commend himself to
every man's conscience in the sight of God. He spoke
freely of the manners of the great, and endeavoured
to bring them to an acquaintance with their own heart,
as the seat and source of all iniquity, and with Jesus
Christ, as the great purifier of the heart through faith in
his blood.[19]

William Goode goes to the heart of Romaine's preaching when
he comments that the 'very name of Jesus seemed to kindle

at once the ardour of divine love: his soul was raptured at the sound; everything else yielded to the irresistible energy'.[20] He possessed, says Goode, 'the most exalted views of the Saviour of guilty men, and therefore he "preached Christ" — his sole subject — his all in all; knowing at the same time he could "warn every man" of his sin and danger, could "teach every man" in the way of peace, truth and righteousness, without deviating from this one subject, which he did with that peculiar wisdom with which God had favoured him'.[21]

T. Sharp in *Select Pulpit Sentences of W. Romaine* provides a good summary of his message: 'Jesus was his darling theme; Jesus, in the glory of his adorable person; Jesus, in the efficacy of his blood and righteousness; and Jesus, in the fulness of his great and all gracious salvation. Nor, indeed, was this holy man ever in his element, but when making mention of the name and righteousness of his divine Master, a subject which was literally, to him, ever full and ever new.'[22] Thomas Wills, who knew Romaine for more than twenty years, preached a funeral sermon for Romaine 'as a fresh testimony of triumphant faith in the immediate view of death, and a token of respect to the memory of one of the greatest ministers of the gospel in the present day'.[23] Wills concurs with Sharp when he sums up all of Romaine's sermons by saying,

> Christ is all, in all... I am bound to say, to the best of my knowledge, no one in all London, either in the Establishment or out of it, did or could preach Jesus more constantly, sweetly and successfully, than this aged father in Christ... All his preaching was nothing but Jesus ... he seemed to have a peculiar dispensation. And what an honour did his master put upon him, to keep him so steady to that one point, without varying, for near half a century.[24]

Romaine's style of preaching was simple and plain — he used short sentences and purely evangelical thoughts. He did not use flowery language or express especially profound ideas, nor did he rise very high in feeling or imagination, yet he commanded attention and focused on Christ in a straightforward and earnest manner. He spoke from his own experience, as one who felt what he delivered, with 'such energy and unction, such dignity of elevation, such earnestness of persuasion, such sweetness of love'.[25] He regarded preaching as a 'heart work' and so appealed more to the heart than the head. His expositions displayed a deep understanding of the Bible, which was his constant companion and on which he fed deeply, and, in all that he said, he seemed to possess more than he expressed.

> As a *reader* he was the best we ever remember to have heard. As a *preacher* he had the happy talent of saying much in a little. His text was generally explained in a few minutes, and the remainder of the time appropriated to the application and improvement of his discourse. His style was neither mean nor flowery, and was well adapted to the generality of a pious and Christian auditory. Few examples have occurred, of similar standing, diligence and liveliness of address, to the end of his labours.[26]

Goode was so impressed with his preaching that he was ready to resign his own commission, so inferior were his talents. In his portrayal of Romaine the preacher, who in London preached forty-six courses of lectures, and went through the whole Bible by way of exposition once and many parts twice, he comments:

> His voice possessed an admirable sweetness; his countenance a liveliness of expression; his eyes sparkled with delight, and every feature expressed the sensibility of his heart while engaged in his delightful work; his very countenance was a sermon. Yet all was

natural and unaffected... His energy, his pathos, his lively action, arose from the fervour of his spirit in love to Christ...

Early in life he was a *Boanerges*, and there is a peculiar fire, energy, and alarming tendency, in his early compositions: but this had given way to a milder manner, and more delightful subjects in general. Yet still, when such subjects occurred, he touched them with uncommon force and effect, so as to astonish and alarm the soul... His favourite subjects were the glory of Christ, and the great privileges of the gospel...

There was also a peculiar style in his preaching, which to us seemed most calculated to enlighten the understanding, to warm the affections, to animate the desires, and to sanctify the heart in the love of God. Zealous for the glory of Christ, and jealous in his spirit of everything that might detract therefrom, he could not bear without sensible indignation anything of a contrary tendency.[27]

His sermons, which were the fruit of diligent, prayerful and painstaking study of the Scriptures, were not as long or delivered with as much energy as many of his brethren, which may account, at least in part, for his remarkable and sustained health. Due to his extensive labours and in order to fulfil all his engagements, he stopped writing out his sermons, but he spoke with such 'clearness, precision and facility, that to any person who had not looked up to him, [his sermon] could not be distinguished from writing, except that it gave him a happier freedom of address, and afforded him occasion to seize and introduce circumstances, that arising on the spot, and from the objects before him, were peculiarly striking and impressive'.[28] Of his written sermons, Ryle remarks: 'For simplicity, pith, point, and forcibleness — for short, true, vigorous sentences — they will bear a favourable comparison with almost any evangelical sermons of' the eighteenth century.[29]

There is a good description of one of Romaine's sermons in the *Evangelical Magazine* (January 1800). The anonymous writer, from whose diary the extract is taken, heard Romaine, then seventy-nine years old, preach his annual sermon at Blackfriars on New Year's Day 1794 from Romans 15:13, 'The God of hope':

> The sermon was short and good, but without much order or method. The people were very attentive, and to all appearance much affected and comforted. I observed that he did not attempt to *prove* anything, but took all his doctrines for granted. Like the venerable prophets of old he came with 'Thus saith the Lord.' And without endeavouring to convince his hearers that what he advanced was the true and proper sense of the passages he quoted, as though the grand truths of the Gospel were doubtful, he pointed out the suitableness of his doctrine to the people of God, and the utility of believing it upon the testimony of God alone, who not only authorized but commanded their assent and reliance. He adduced several portions of Scripture, in which the word *'hope'* was contained, and paraphrased them with great earnestness and judgment. This is an easy way of preaching — perhaps the best.[30]

His contemporary De Coetlogon says this about Romaine, the preacher:

> As a *preacher*, though in the perpetual custom of delivering sermons without any notes, he was neither inaccurate, wild, visionary, rhapsodical, nor enthusiastic; but, in his *method*, exact: in his *language*, correct: in his *arguments*, pointed and concise: in his *manner*, serious, earnest and affectionate: and in his *style*, possessed, in an unusual degree, of the very enviable gift of express-

ing himself with the most intelligible simplicity, without a shade of vulgarity. So that, while the meanest of his hearers might clearly understand, those, who had been favoured with a more liberal education, could not but admire that peculiar excellence, that happy talent.[31]

Many of Romaine's well-known contemporaries testified to the strength of his doctrine and the power of his preaching. John Wesley, in describing the preaching of John Berridge, said that he spoke 'with all the propriety of Mr Romaine'. Henry Venn rejoiced in his 'gracious ministry'. Samuel Walker of Truro, writing to his friend Thomas Adam on 7 June 1758, reports that the aide-de-camp to the Bishop of Cork was 'so shaken by a sermon of Romaine's, as to become a bold professor'.[32] James Hervey, after hearing Romaine preach, wrote in a letter to a friend about 'the strong meat he received from Romaine's words concerning Christ's vicarious suffering in the form of dying for sinners and being obedient on their behalf'. He goes on: 'Romaine ... shows how our justification is based on the complete sufficiency of Christ's sacrifice in matters of our punishment and guilt.' These words and Romaine's emphasis on the illumination and influence of the Holy Spirit 'were highly comforting to Hervey'.[33] Howel Harris, the great Welsh preacher, wrote in his diary for 13 April 1769: 'Heard Mr Romaine at St Dunstan's. Excellent sermon.'[34]

In 1761, John Newton wrote to an old correspondent and urged him to attend Romaine's ministry with the words: 'I wish you dare hear him often.'[35] On one occasion, shortly before his conversion, William Huntington started to discuss religion with a friend who emphatically told him that Whitefield, Romaine and all the good London preachers taught that only the elect would be saved. Huntington vehemently opposed this doctrine, but his friend had 'learnt so many passages of Scripture from hearing Whitefield and Romaine that he was soundly defeated in the debate'.[36]

William Cadogan says that those who heard him preach

often remarked, 'It was as though he had been in heaven, and
came back to earth to tell us what is doing there.'[37] In *Lives of
Eminent Christians*, John Frost tells us that Romaine's 'fame as
a preacher was at one time so great, that booksellers offered
him, but without effect, large sums for permission to place his
name in the title pages of religious compilations'. One unscrupulous publisher named Pasham bought a house on Finchley
Common for the purpose of printing a beautiful edition of the
Bible with annotations by Romaine, so arranged that they could
be cut off — 'an artifice to evade the patent enjoyed by the
king's printer'.[38]

The evangelical periodicals of the eighteenth century contain numerous obituaries of ordinary people who were either
converted or strengthened in their faith under Romaine's
preaching. In 1757, John Wesley, when visiting Hartlepool,
found that Romaine had been the 'instrument of awakening
several; but, for want of help, they soon slept again'.[39] A couple
who were truly awakened by Romaine's preaching were Mr and
Mrs William Smyth of Dublin. In June 1776, Mrs Smyth, who
loved the theatre, travelled to London with her brother-in-law
to watch the famous actor Garrick perform for the last time.
During her stay she was the guest of the Duchess of Leeds.

> Hearing of the immense crowds that attended
> [Romaine's] ministry, and the astonishing effects pro-
> duced by his preaching, Mrs Smyth expressed a strong
> desire to hear a man so singular and so renowned.
> The fashionable circle by whom she was surrounded
> were unanimous in their reprobation of the man and the
> doctrines he promulgated. In vain it was urged that he
> was a Methodist — an enthusiast — one whom it was
> improper for her to hear — and that to procure admit-
> tance to a place so crowded was utterly impracticable.
> Mrs Smyth had been gratified in seeing Mr Garrick, and
> in mingling with the immense crowd that witnessed his
> last acting. The more Mr Romaine was reprobated, and

the greater the difficulty of obtaining admission to the church, the more urgent was Mrs Smyth to hear him: nothing could deter her, and go she would, in defiance of every remonstrance.

Mr Romaine preached from that remarkable passage in the 90th Psalm — 'Who knoweth the power of thine anger? Even according to thy fear, so is thy wrath.' There the Lord met Mrs Smyth with the blessings of his grace; and she was led to a happy acquaintance with the great deep of corruption in a heart deceitful above all things and desperately wicked.

Mr Smyth's state of mind was little short of derangement. With the utmost anxiety he hastened to London: Mrs Smyth explained the change that had taken place in her principles and feelings, and the abandonment of all her former notions of religion. Mr Smyth was overwhelmed with surprise but agreed to accompany her to hear Mr Romaine, and judge for himself; and he too was constrained, as a poor sinner, to take refuge at the foot of the cross! From that time the happy change commenced, for which hundreds have since had reason to bless God.[40]

In 1786, the Smyths built Bethesda Chapel at their own expense and it became a centre of evangelical witness in Dublin. Through William Smyth's influence, his brother Edward joined the Methodists and for a number of years assisted Wesley and Lady Huntingdon.

John Russell, who became a famous portrait painter, also profited from Romaine's ministry. He was converted at Lock Chapel under Madan's preaching on the same day as Romaine's probation sermon at Blackfriars. He afterwards heard Romaine on many occasions. On one of these occasions, he took his friend Miss Hannah Faden, who was soundly converted. Romaine then had the privilege of marrying them on 5 February 1770. An interesting excerpt from Russell's diary for 1768 shows that it was not always easy lecturing at St Dunstan's: 'I was, with the whole church, much disturbed by a man's bawling out and insulting Mr Romaine ... as he was preaching, and making a ridicule of what he said and praising him ironically.'[41]

William Talbot of Kineton was one of Romaine's converts. Samuel Walker, writing to Thomas Adam on 25 July 1759, put it this way: 'By what I can gather, he [Talbot] began with the law; then the Moravians came in his way, and a year or two ago, he was settled by Romaine.'[42] John Clayton, after he was awakened under the preaching of Romaine, trained for the ministry at Lady Huntingdon's college at Trevecca. He later became a Congregational minister and exercised considerable influence on that denomination. In 1783 he was invited by Newton to join the Eclectic Society. Thomas English was another Romaine convert. After sitting under his preaching for four years, he too trained at Trevecca and was ordained in 1775.

The Bishop of Derry heard Romaine at Lady Huntingdon's chapel while he was living in Bath for the benefit of his health, and was greatly blessed. Daniel Wilson, who became the Bishop of Calcutta, traced his early religious impressions to the time when, as a boy, he attended Blackfriars first with his parents and then with his uncle. On one occasion, Wilson was very impressed when Henry Venn was ushered into the pew next to his own to hear Romaine. John Ford, the physician, not only regularly heard Romaine's Tuesday morning lectures at Blackfriars and his Thursday evening lectures at St Dunstan's, but went privately to him for instruction in Hebrew. He later joined the Countess of Huntingdon's connection. William Wilberforce, so influential in the abolition of the slave trade, heard Romaine preach in 1785.

Sir Richard Hill was confirmed in his faith by hearing Romaine, and Cornelius Winter 'heard with delight and to profit Messrs Romaine, Jones, Madan, Venn — each of them had a message from God for me'.[43] The preaching and writings of Romaine impressed Thomas Kelly, son of Judge Kelly and the author of over 700 hymns, with 'the awfulness of eternity, and a few remarks from John Walker completed his determination to devote himself to spiritual things'.[44] Richard Jones, the son of a farmer living in the parish of Llangollen, ran away to London, where he attended the ministry of Whitefield and Romaine, 'and before long was led captive by the power that went with their ministrations'.[45] Charles Glover on removing to London in 1775 became a new man under the ministry of Romaine. Later in life he built a chapel on his premises in Spring Hill, Birmingham, to provide the poor of the neighbourhood with a religious service on Sabbath evenings.

Paul Avril went to hear Romaine for many years and has left a valuable record of some of the sermons he heard and the blessings he received under them — blessings that were common under Romaine's preaching. After being convicted of sin Avril 'fell into deep legality in which his mind was fixed on his own self'. This in turn led him to despair as he could find nothing to recommend him to God. He started to believe that he had committed the unforgivable sin, but soon, thanks to Toplady and Romaine's preaching, he could say, 'But out of this snare the Lord delivered me.' He was also helped out of his despondency by Romaine's tract *A Dialogue Between a Believer and an Awakened Soul*, which 'proved very seasonable to me', and by a sermon Romaine preached at the Lock Chapel on 27 December 1775 from Isaiah 19:20, in which he declared, 'Jesus calls, bids, invites, yea, commands thee to come, poor doubting soul, and declares he will not cast out any poor sinner who is enabled to come.' Avril comments: 'O how did my heart burn within me while Christ, by the mouth of his minister, talked with me and opened to me the Scriptures... This is a sermon much to be remembered by me.' After his deliverance, he wrote: 'Of all the ministers I heard, I was particularly attached to Mr Romaine and Mr Toplady, and omitted not an opportunity, if possible, of hearing them. I missed not once if I could help it.'[46]

Avril found Romaine's *Walk of Faith* a 'great help' and his *Life of Faith* was useful to him in his spiritual pilgrimage. On Whit Sunday 1777 he heard Romaine preach from 1 Corinthians

2:11-12: 'This sermon was unspeakably blessed to my soul. He prayed much that the weak in faith might be built up and strengthened, that the mourners in Zion might be comforted; the answer of which fervent prayers of this good man I experienced at the Lord's table after sermon, and was much refreshed and strengthened.'[47] On 7 November 1779 he heard Romaine in the morning when a verse he quoted

> ... darted into my mind with wonderful power. I immediately felt uncommon joy and peace flowing into my heart. A blessed, unspeakable calm ensued. It is impossible to express by words what I then felt. I praised the Lord with great freedom, liberty, and enlargement when at home on my knees... I evidently felt my sins forgiven and blotted out... This Lord's day was a day of the Lord's power in my soul. I was made willing to receive Christ. I found sweet rest, joy, and peace in believing. The promises were sealed on my heart. I felt the pardon of my sin, though I had experienced the pardoning love of God in a very evident manner, and in a lesser degree on many other occasions.[48]

On Sunday evening, 10 December 1780, Avril went to St Dunstan's 'rather uncomfortable, dark, dull, and dead in my frame, expecting no particular or extraordinary blessing from the preaching; but the Lord met me in his sanctuary'. He received a 'precious and sweet visit from the Lord' under the sermon and beheld 'unspeakable glory in the text and the quotations from Scripture'. When he arrived home they were 'wonderfully opened and applied to my soul, sweeping away my doubts, chasing the dullness, deadness, and darkness from my mind, and causing me to rejoice and glory in the Lord... Mr Romaine, in his concluding prayer, begged much that a great blessing might attend what he had been delivering. I believe his prayers were answered towards me then, and when I was returned home also.'[49] And so Avril's record in *The Gospel Standard* for 1865 goes on with account after account of Romaine's sermons and their wonderful effects.

During Romaine's summer holidays, when many of his parishioners moved out of London and St Dunstan's was shut against him, Romaine travelled far and wide preaching the gospel. While his mother was alive he spent the summers in the north of England, and afterwards in the west, where many churches were ready to receive him. Everywhere he journeyed friends welcomed him and opened their homes for their neighbours to come and 'hear a sermon from Romaine'. He was always willing to preach in these domestic congregations, and, as he put it, to say a word for his Master in every place. Southampton, Bradford and Bristol were frequently visited by him, and from his letters, a sweet savour of Christ attended his ministrations. In one of his letters, written on 31 October 1783 to that 'excellent man' Walter Taylor, he opens by saying, 'I sit down to tell you of great mercies which have followed us all our journey, and brought us home in peace. Southampton mercies not the least — Heckfield, Reading, Blackfriars.'[50]

When he found the church doors shut against him, in places such as Southampton, his friends invited him to preach for them on the Lord's Day, and often in the week too, and he never declined. Much good was done by these occasional labours. It was on one of these journeys that an incident occurred that demonstrates his determination to preach Christ come what may. He was visiting Bootle in Cumberland, where he had been invited to preach by the churchwarden W. Parks and where his preaching 'caused considerable sensation and was instrumental in the awakening of many'.[51] He read prayers in the desk and then started to climb into the pulpit to deliver his sermon, but could not open the old pulpit door. He pulled hard at it but it would not budge. He immediately suspected that the blacksmith of the parish, an inveterate enemy to the gospel, had played a trick on him, so he asked the clerk to sing a long psalm, while he ran to find a pair of pincers and a hammer to break open the pulpit door. He quickly returned and, with as little noise as possible, achieved his objective. He then preached powerfully to all present.

During the sermon a sudden storm of thunder and lightning crashed and flashed overhead and the congregation was terrified. Making the most of the opportunity, he spoke powerfully on the terrible majesty of Jehovah and on what a dreadful thing it is to fall into the hands of the living God. In order to close the pulpit against him in future, his sermon was misrepresented by his enemies, who claimed he had taken it upon himself to deal out wrath and damnation to a vulnerable congregation, before stating, 'If the lightning were to be fatal, he and Mr Parks would be safe.'[52] These summer excursions occurred almost every year until his death. He maintained his annual trips to Durham until 1791, and as late as 1789 he preached in Plymouth at the Church of King Charles the Martyr. After the long vacation he returned to London in full vigour and health, apparently refreshed by serving his master. Once he had 'to preach twelve times in fourteen days — and rather not well, till preaching comes, and then I get better. No Master like mine. His service is perfect freedom.'[53]

His services at Blackfriars and St Dunstan's were hardly ever less than four or five times a week, and often he preached elsewhere when others demanded his labours — a workload he maintained right into his seventies. He never courted assistance, although, when visited by his brethren, he often invited them to preach for him. Once when Thomas Haweis arrived unexpectedly at Blackfriars, Romaine, already robed ready for the service, insisted that Haweis preached, and quickly took off his robe and put it on his visitor. 'Every man of us,' remarks Haweis, 'esteemed it a favour done to us, and a token of marked respect, rather than as a relief sought for himself.'[54]

He tried hard to conduct the services with strict reverence and good order, and expected a high standard of behaviour from all who came to worship. He complained against those who were in the habit of turning up late, acting as if they came to church only to hear the sermon while ignoring the other parts of worship, but even he was not able to eradicate completely this habit. He also reproved those who started to talk in the church or churchyard, in the vestry or boardroom, immediately after the service. He not only spoke against such conversations, but frequently interrupted them when he came out of the church 'by tapping the shoulders of those who were engaged in them; and once, if not oftener, by knocking their heads together, when he found them particularly close, and whispering in their ears that they had forgotten the parable of the sower'.[55]

He himself carefully avoided the same faults. He was always in church sometime before the service, and as soon as it was over, he retired to his own house, without ever speaking a word, except to his curate, clerk or parish officers, and that only in the vestry when necessary. It is said that a woman once greeted him as he came down the pulpit stairs by telling him he had been 'greater that night than ever'. He answered her with the words of John Bunyan, that the 'devil had told him so before he left the pulpit'.

He had a deep love and respect for the Church of England, and as his strict observance of her rules became generally known, some pulpits that were closed to Whitefield, Wesley and other leaders of the evangelical movement were open to him. He took full advantage of this freedom and many of his holidays were spent in the service of the Establishment. The *Evangelical Magazine* (1795) says that his attachment to the church was 'regular and steady', and that he 'preached in a greater number of her pulpits than any clergyman for a century past'.[56] In all these pulpits he declared the gospel of Jesus Christ without making any concessions to his opponents. He was faithful to the high calling he had received, unwavering in his stand for the truth, resolute and strong amidst persecution — like an iron pillar and a bronze wall that stood against the enemy, until eventually the power of his message and the godliness of his life won them over. At Blackfriars, his election to the living was violently opposed,

> yet the purity of his doctrine and propriety of his conduct conciliated the esteem of those who had taken the most decided part against him; and after his death, the whole parish petitioned the Chancellor to appoint Goode his successor. He was extensively and justly celebrated as a minister raised up for exalted services in the church of God, yet no man ever spoke or wrote in terms more expressive of conscious nothingness in himself.[57]

Perhaps the most appropriate way to sum up his ministry is to pick out three of the annual mottoes he chose for his church: in 1785 he chose 'go forward', in 1788 he decided on 'looking unto Jesus', and in 1789 it was 'the Lord reigneth'. On 7 January 1785, he wrote to a friend about the first of these mottoes:

> Our motto this year was 'Go forward.' All in a wrong way till set right. He who sets us in the right way has provided everything needful to keep us going, pressing on, till he bring us to the end of our journey; to which he encourages us by promises, by examples, by setting before us the shortness of the journey, and what awaits us at the end of it... Going forward, till we finish our course with joy. I am in the last stage; and, for the prospect of safety and happiness through life and death, blessed, most blessed be the name of my Jesus.[58]

Bibliography

Primary Sources

Cadogan, William, *Works of William Romaine: Life and Letters (vol. 7)*. London, T. Chapman, 1796.

Davis, Donald G., *The Evangelical Revival in Eighteenth Century England as Reflected in the Life and Work of William Romaine (1714-1795)*. Edinburgh Ph.D. thesis (unpublished), December 1949.

Evangelical Magazine, November 1795. London, T. Chapman, 1795.

Haweis, Thomas, *The Life of William Romaine*. London, T. Chapman, 1797.

Select Letters of William Romaine. Glasgow, William Collins, 1830.

Whole Works of William Romaine. London, B. Blake, 1837.

Other Works by Romaine Consulted

A Full Christ for Empty Sinners. Halifax, Milner and Sowerby, 1852.

A Modest Apology for the Citizens and Merchants of London, who Petitioned the House of Commons against Naturalizing the Jews. London, W. Webb, 1753.

An Answer to a Pamphlet Entitled 'Considerations on the Bill to Permit Person Professing the Jewish Religion to be Naturalized'. London, H. Cooke, 1753.

The Christian Sabbath (a sermon on Exodus 31:12-14). Cheltenham, 1845.

The Life, Walk and Triumph of Faith. Cambridge & London, James Clarke & Co. Ltd, 1970.

The Life, Walk and Triumph of Faith. London & New York, G. Routledge & Co., 1856.

The Necessity of Receiving Christ in our Hearts (a sermon on Luke 2:7). London, 1758.

Libraries Consulted (with material, mostly unpublished)

Bridwell Library, Dallas
British Library, London
Beinecke Rare Book and Manuscript Library, New Haven
Bodleian Library, Oxford
Drew University Methodist Library, Madison
Evangelical Library, London
Evangelical Library of Wales, Bridgend
John Rylands University Library, Manchester
Lambeth Palace Library, London
National Library of Wales, Aberystwyth
New College Library, Edinburgh
State Library of New South Wales, Sydney

Periodicals

Arminian Magazine, vol.3, 1780.

Banner of Truth Magazine, September 1961.

Baptist Magazine, vol.16, 1824.

Christian's Magazine, 1790.

Christian Observer, 1803, 1841.

Evangelical Magazine, November 1793, 1794, November 1799, January 1800, December 1800, September 1802, June 1803, December 1806, November 1807, December

1807, August 1808, November 1808, December 1808, August 1814, January 1815, August 1901.

Evangelical Quarterly, January 2000, Tyson, John R., *Lady Huntingdon and the Church of England*.

Evangelical Register, August 1835.

Gentleman's Magazine, November 1748, March 1752, 1762, January 1766, April 1766, August 1795, 1812.

Gospel Magazine, February 1771, June 1771, January 1774, February 1774, February 1780, October 1796, August 1799, March 1840, August 1901, September 1901, January 1970.

Gospel Standard Magazine, April-September 1865.

Free Church of England Magazine & Harbinger of the Countess of Huntingdon's Connexion, June 1866, September 1866, February 1868.

History of the Works of the Learned, vol.6, August 1739.

London Gazetteer, February 1752, March 1752.

Monthly Review, May 1755, June 1755, September 1758, August 1762, September 1764.

Notes and Queries, July-December 1897.

Peace and Truth, April-June 1937.

Pamphlets, Sermons and Printed Letters

Adams, William, *A Test of True and False Doctrines*. London, B. White & T. Cadell, 1770.

An Apology for the Parishioners of St Dunstan's in the West. C. Sympson, 1759.

Brown-Lawson, A., *William Romaine (1714-1795): Distinctive Evangelical*.

Evangelical Library Essay, 1987.

Cadogan, William, *The Continuance and Constancy of the Friendship of God, as a Covenant God with his People*. London, 1795.

Clark, George, *A Defence of the Unity of God*. London, 1789.

Coles, Elisha, *A Practical Discourse of God's Sovereignty*. Bath, W. Gye, 1776.

De Coetlogon, C. E., *The Life of the Just Exemplified in the Character of the Late W. Romaine*. London, Messrs Rivington, etc., 1795.

Description of the Monument Erected to the Memory of W. Romaine. London, 1795.

Dodwell, William, *A Dissertation on Jephthah's Vow*. London, 1745.

Douglas, John, *An Apology for the Clergy*. London, S. Bladon, 1755.

Douglas, John, *The Destruction of the French Foretold by Ezekiel*. London, M. Cooper, 1755.

Elliot, Richard, *The Scripture Testimony of Christ*. London, 1775.

Felton, William, *A Letter to Mr Romaine, Containing Remarks on his Discourses upon the Law and the Gospel*. London, 1761.

Fox, G. T., *The Life and Doctrine of Romaine: A Sermon*. London, Seeley, Jackson & Halliday, 1876.

Goode, William, *Faith Triumphant in Death*. London, 1795.

Hill, Richard, *A Letter to Dr Adams of Shrewsbury*. London, E. & C. Dilly, 1770.

Mason, William, *Methodism Displayed and Enthusiasm Detected*. London, 1756.

Mason, William, *The Christian Communicant*. London, Chas. J. Thynne, n.d.

Murray, James, *Sermons to Asses*. London, 1768.

Mortimer, Thomas, *Die, and be Damned*. London, Hooper & A. Morley, 1758.

Nash, Michael, *An Answer to the 'Charitable Morsel of Unleaven Bread', Addressed to the Author*. London, 1793.

Nash, Michael, *Gideon's Cake of Barley Meal*. London, 1793.

Nash, Michael, *The Barley Cake Defended from the Foxes*. London, 1793.

Newbon, Joseph, *The History of the Parish of St Ann, Blackfriars*. London, Judd & Co., 1876.

Parker, David, *A Charitable Morsel of Unleavened Bread*. London, J. Mathews, 1793.

[Philo-Patriae], *Considerations on the Bill to Permit Persons Professing the Jewish Religion to be Naturalized by Parliament*. London, R. Baldwin, 1753.

Samuel, D. N., *A Winnowing Ministry: Romaine, Huntington and Experimental Preaching*. Totton, Berith Publications, 1999.

Some Remarks on the Progress of Learning since the Reformation, Especially with Regard to the Hebrew. London, M. Cooper, 1746.

Suter, Andrew Burn, *The Worthies of St Dunstan's*. London 1856.

The First of a Series of Letters to the Author of Pietas Oxoniensis. London, B. White & T. Cadell, 1770.

Thomas, Ivor, *St Andrew-by-the-Wardrobe with St Ann Blackfriars: A Short Guide*. London, 1966.

Wilcox, Thomas, *A Choice Drop of Honey from the Rock of Christ*. London, 1823.

The Gospel Tract Society, Tract no.7, London, 1824.

Wills, Thomas, *The Dying Believer*. London, 1795.

Secondary Printed Sources

Abbey, Charles J. & Overton, John H., *The English Church in the Eighteenth Century*. London, Longmans, Green & Co., 1902.

Allen, John, *The Spiritual Magazine*. London, A. Kidwell & S. Lee, 1810.

Aveling, Thomas W., *Memorials of the Clayton Family*. London, Jackson, Walford & Hodder, 1867.

412 'An Iron Pillar'

Balleine, G. R., *A History of the Evangelical Party in the Church of England*. London, Longmans, Green & Co., 1909.

Bebbington, D. W., *Evangelicalism in Modern Britain*. London, Routledge, 1995 reprint.

Berridge, John, *The Works of John Berridge*. London, Ebenezer Palmer, 1864.

Beynon, Tom, *Howell Harris, Reformer and Soldier 1714-1773*. Caernarvon, The Calvinistic Methodist Bookroom, 1958.

Bickersteth, Robert (editor), *A Memoir of John Newton*. London, Seeley, Jackson & Halliday, 1865.

Blackwell Dictionary of Evangelical Biography 1730-1860. Oxford, Blackwell Publishers Ltd, 1995.

Boswell, James, *The Life of Samuel Johnson* (2 vols). London & Toronto, J. M. Dent, 1928.

Bready, J. Wesley, *England Before and After Wesley*. London, Hodder & Stoughton Ltd, 1939.

Broome, Edward W., *Rowland Hill: Preacher and Wit*. London, Cassell, Petter, Galpin & Co., n.d.

Bull, Josiah, *But Now I See: The Life of John Newton*. Edinburgh, Banner of Truth Trust, 1998 reprint.

Bull, Josiah, *John Newton of Olney and St Mary Woolnoth*. London, The Religious Tract Society, n.d.

Bull, Josiah (editor), *Letters by John Newton*. London, The Religious Tract Society, n.d.

Bumpus, T. Francis, *Ancient London Churches*. London, T. Werner Laurie Ltd, n.d.

Burder, Henry Forster, *Memoir of George Burder*. London, F. Westley & A. H. Davis, 1833.

Cadogan, William, *Discourses of the Honourable and Reverend W. B. Cadogan*. London, F. & C. Rivington, 1798.

Carpenter, S. C., *Eighteenth Century Church and People*. London, John Murray, 1959.

Carter, C. Sydney, *The English Church in the Eighteenth Century*. London, Longmans, Green & Co., 1910.

Cecil, J., *Remains of Richard Cecil*. London, Knight & Son, 1854.

Cecil, Richard, *Life of William Bromley Cadogan*. London, The Religious Tract Society, n.d.

Collingwood, C. S., *Memoirs of Bernard Gilpin*. London, Simpkin, Marshall & Co., 1884.

Cook, Faith, *Selina Countess of Huntingdon*. Edinburgh, Banner of Truth Trust, 2001.

Cook, Faith, *William Grimshaw of Haworth*. Edinburgh, Banner of Truth Trust, 1997.

Cragg, George C., *Grimshaw of Haworth*. London, The Canterbury Press, 1947.

Cragg, G. R., *The Church in the Age of Reason (1648-1789)*. Harmondsworth, Penguin Books, 1960.

Cunningham, George Godfrey (editor), *Lives of Eminent and Illustrious Englishmen* (vol.6). Glasgow, A. Fullarton & Co., 1836.

Dale, R. W., *The Evangelical Revival and Other Sermons*. London, Hodder and Stoughton, 1880.

Dallimore, Arnold, *George Whitefield* (2 vols). Edinburgh, Banner of Truth Trust, 1989.

Dargan, Edwin Charles, *A History of Preaching* (vol.2). Grand Rapids, Baker Book House, 1970 reprint.

Davies, Horton, *Worship and Theology in England: From Watts and Wesley to Maurice 1690-1850*. London, Oxford University Press, 1961.

Davies, G. C. B., *The Early Cornish Evangelicals 1735-60*. London, SPCK, 1951.

Davies, Rupert. George, A. Raymond & Rupp, Gordon (general editors), *A History of the Methodist Church in Great Britain* (4 vols). London, Epworth Press, 1965 & 1978.

Dictionary of National Biography (22 vols). London, Oxford University Press, 1960.

Dorney, Henry, *Contemplations*. Bath, 1773.

Douglas, J. D. (general editor), *Dictionary of the Christian Church*. Grand Rapids, The Zondervan Corporation, 1978.

Edwards, Brian H., *Through Many Dangers*. Darlington, Evangelical Press, 2001 reprint.

Ella, George M., *Augustus Montague Toplady: A Debtor to Mercy Alone*. Go Publications, 2000.

Ella, George M., *William Huntington: Pastor of Providence*. Darlington, Evangelical Press, 1994.

Ella, George M., *James Hervey, Preacher of Righteousness*. Eggleston, Go Publications, 1997.

Ella, George M., *Mountain Movers*. Eggleston, Go Publications, 1999.

Ella, George M., *William Cowper: Poet of Paradise*. Darlington, Evangelical Press, 1993.

Elliot-Binns, L. E., *The Early Evangelicals: A Religious and Social Study*. Greenwich, The Seabury Press, 1955.

Elliot-Binns, L. E., *The Evangelical Movement in the English Church*. London, Methuen & Co. Ltd, 1928.

Evans, Eifion, *Daniel Rowland*. Edinburgh, Banner of Truth Trust, 1985.

Fisher, George Park, *History of the Christian Church*. London, Hodder & Stoughton, 1892.

Frost, John, *Lives of Eminent Christians of Various Denominations*. Philadelphia, 1852.

Gadsby, John, *Memoirs of the Principal Hymn Writers and Compilers of the 17th, 18th & 19th Centuries*. London, John Gadsby, 1882.

George, M. Dorothy, *London Life in the Eighteenth Century*. London, The London School of Economics and Political Science, 1951 reprint.

Gillies, John, *Historical Collections Relating to Remarkable Periods of the Success of the Gospel*. Edinburgh, Banner of Truth Trust, 1981 reprint.

Goode, William, *A Memoir of the Late W. Goode*. London, R. B. Seeley & W. Burnside, 1828.

Green, John, *The Church of England Vindicated from the Rigid Notions of Calvinism*. London, B. White & T. Cadell, 1770.

Green, V. H. H., *John Wesley*. London, Thomas Nelson Ltd, 1964.

Haweis, Thomas, *An Impartial and Succinct History of the Rise, Declension and Revival of the Church of Christ* (3 vols). London, 1800.

Heitzenrater, Richard P., *Wesley and the People Called Methodists*. Nashville, Abingdon Press, 1995.

Hennell, Michael, *John Venn and the Clapham Sect*. London, Lutterworth Press, 1958.

Hervey, James, *A Collection of the Letters of the Late James Hervey*. London, 1763.

Hervey, James, *Letters from James Hervey to Lady Frances Shirley*. London, John, Francis & Charles Rivington, 1782.

Hervey, James, *Letters of James Hervey*. Edinburgh, John Grieg, 1845.

Hervey, James, *The Select Works of James Hervey*. London, R. Thurston, 1828.

Hervey, James, *The Works of James Hervey* (7 vols). London, F. & C. Rivington, 1797.

Hill, Richard, *A Review of all the Doctrines Taught by John Wesley*. London, E. & C. Dilly, 1772.

Hindmarsh, D. Bruce, *John Newton and the English Evangelical Tradition*. Cambridge, William B. Eerdmans, 2001.

Hole, Charles, *A Manual of English Church History*. London, Longmans, Green & Co., 1910.

Hughes, Hugh J., *Life of Howell Harris*. Stoke-on-Trent, Tentmaker, 1996 reprint.

Hylson-Smith, Kenneth, *Evangelicals in the Church of England 1734-1984*. Edinburgh, T&T Clark, 1989.

Jackson, Thomas, *The Life of Charles Wesley* (2 vols). London, John Mason, 1841.

Jay, William, *Memoirs of the Life and Character of C. Winter*. London, 1812.

Jenkins, David Erwyd, *The Life of Thomas Charles of Bala* (3 vols). Denbigh, Llewelyn Jenkins, 1908.

Jones, Thomas, *The Works of Thomas Jones*. London, 1763.

Knight, Helen C., *Lady Huntingdon & her Friends*. Grand Rapids, Baker Book House, 1979.

Knox, Vicesimus, *Considerations on the Nature and Efficacy of the Lord's Supper*. London, 1799.

Lewis, Donald M. (editor), *The Blackwell Dictionary of Evangelical Biography 1730-1860* (2 vols). Blackwell Reference.

Loane, Marcus L., *Cambridge and the Evangelical Succession*. London, Lutterworth Press, 1952.

Loane, Marcus L., *Oxford and the Evangelical Succession*. London, Lutterwoth Press, 1950.

London Encyclopaedia (editors: Ben Weinreb & Christopher Hibbert). London, Papermac, 1993.

Martin, Bernard, *John Newton*. London, William Heinemann, 1950.

Martin, Roger H., *Evangelicals United: Ecumenical Stirrings in Pre-Victorian Britain, 1795-1830*. London, The Scarecrow Press, 1983.

Mason, William, *A Spiritual Treasury for the Children of God*. London, The Religious Tract Society, 1765.

Middleton, Erasmus, *Biographia Evangelica* (4 vols). London, J. W. Pasham, 1780.

Millar, John Hepburn, *The Mid-Eighteenth Century*. Edinburgh, William Blackwood & Sons, 1902.

New, Alfred H., *The Coronet and the Cross*. London, Partridge & Co., 1858.

Newton, John, *The Christian Correspondent*. Hull, 1790.

Nichols, John, *Illustrations of the Literary History of the Eighteenth Century* (8 vols). London, Nichols, Son & Bentley, 1817-1858.

Nuttall, Geoffrey F., *Howel Harris 1714-1773: The Last Enthusiast*. Cardiff, University of Wales Press, 1965.

Overton, John Henry, *The Church in England*. London, Gardiner, Darton & Co., 1897.

Overton, John Henry, *The Evangelical Revival in the Eighteenth*

Century. London, Longmans, Green & Co., 1900.

Overton, John Henry, *The True Churchmen Ascertained*. London, Mawman & Rivington, 1801.

Overton, John H. & Relton, Frederic, *A History of the English Church 1714-1800*. London, Macmillan & Co., 1906.

Palmer, Ebenezer, *Palmer's Select Pocket Divinity* (vol.1). Halifax, Milner & Sowerby, 1852.

Pattison, Mark, *Essays* (2 vols). Oxford, Clarendon Press, 1889.

Pattison, T. Harwood, *The History of Christian Preaching*. Philadelphia, American Baptist Publication Society, 1903.

Philip, Robert, *The Life and Times of George Whitefield*. London, George Virtue, 1842.

Pibworth, Nigel R., *The Gospel Pedlar: The Story of John Berridge*. Welwyn, Evangelical Press, 1987.

Pratt, Josiah, *Memoir of Josiah Pratt*. London, 1849.

Reynolds, John Stewart, *The Evangelicals at Oxford, 1735-1871*. Oxford, Basil Blackwell, 1953.

Roberts, Gomer M. (editor), *Selected Trevecka Letters (1747-1794)*. Caernarfon, 1962.

Roberts, Richard Owen, *Whitefield in Print*. Wheaton, Richard Owen Roberts, 1988.

Roth, Cecil, *A History of the Jews in England*. Oxford, Clarendon Press, 1941.

Rupp, Ernest Gordon, *Religion in England 1688-1791*. Oxford, Clarendon Press, 1986.

Ryle, J. C., *Christian Leaders of the Eighteenth Century*. Edinburgh, Banner of Truth Trust, 1978 reprint.

Sandeman, Robert [Palaemon], *Letters on Theron & Aspasio* (2 vols). Edinburgh, Sands, Donaldson, Murray & Cochrane, 1759.

Schlenther, Boyd Stanley, *Queen of the Methodists, the Countess of Huntingdon and the Eighteenth Century Crisis of Faith and Society*. Durham, Durham Academic Press, 1997.

Scott, Thomas, *The Life of Thomas Scott*. London, 1822.

Serle, Ambrose, *Christian Husbandry*. London, J. Mathews, 1789.

Seymour, A. C. H., *The Life and Times of Selina Countess of Huntingdon* (2 vols). Stoke-on-Trent, Tentmaker, 2000 reprint.

Sharp, Cuthbert, *History of Hartlepool*. Hartlepool, Hartlepool Borough Council, 1978.

Sharp, T., *Select Pulpit Sentences of W. Romaine*. Woolwich, 1831.

Sidney, Edwin, *The Life and Ministry of Samuel Walker*. London, R. B. Seeley & W. Burnside, 1838.

Sidney, Edwin, *The Life of Rowland Hill*. London, 1861.

Sidney, Edwin, *The Life of Sir Richard Hill*. London, R. B. Seeley & W. Burnside, 1839.

Simon, John S., *John Wesley the Master Builder*. London, Epworth Press, 1927.

Simon, John S., *The Revival of Religion in England in the Eighteenth Century*. London, Charles H. Kelly, n.d.

Steer, Roger, *Church on Fire: The Story of Anglican Evangelicals*. London, Hodder & Stoughton, 1998.

Stephen, Leslie, *History of English Thought in the Eighteenth Century* (2 vols). London, Smith, Elder & Co., 1876.

Telford, John, *A Sect that Moved the World*. London, Charles H. Kelly, n.d.

Thompson, W., *The History & Antiquities of the Collegiate Church of St Saviour, Southwark*. London, Elliot Stock, 1904.

Tidball, Derek J., *Who are the Evangelicals?* Marshall Pickering, 1994.

Toplady, Augustus Montague, *The Works of Augustus Toplady*. London, J. Chidley, 1837.

Tyerman, Luke, *The Life and Times of John Wesley* (3 vols). London, Hodder & Stoughton, 1890.

Tyerman, Luke, *Wesley's Designated Successor: The Life, Letters and Literary Labours of John William Fletcher*. London, Hodder & Stoughton, 1882.

Vaughan, Edward Thomas, *Some Account of Thomas Robinson*. London, Sherwood, Neely & Jones, 1816.

Venn, John, *The Life and Letters of Henry Venn*. Edinburgh, Banner of Truth Trust, 1993 reprint.

Walsh, John. Haydon, Colin & Taylor, Stephen (editors), *The Church of England c.1689-c.1833 from Toleration to Tractarianism*. Cambridge, Cambridge University Press, 1993.

Watson, John Selby, *The Life of William Warburton*. London, Longman, Green & Roberts, 1863.

Watts, Isaac, *The Works of Isaac Watts* (6 vols). London, J. Barfield, 1810.

Watts, Michael R., *The Dissenters*. Oxford, Clarendon Press, 1999 reprint.

Webber, F. R., *A History of Preaching in Britain and America (part 1)*. Milwaukee, Northwestern Publishing House, 1952.

Wesley, Charles, *The Journal of Charles Wesley* (2 vols). London, Wesleyan Methodist Bookroom, 1849.

Wesley, John, *The Journal of John Wesley* (8 vols). London, Epworth Press, 1938.

Wesley, John, *The Letters of John Wesley* (8 vols). London, Epworth Press, 1931.

Wesley, John, *The Works of John Wesley* (14 vols). London, Wesleyan Conference Office, 1872.

Wesley, John, *Wesley's Standard Sermons* (2 vols). London, Epworth Press, 1931.

Whitefield, George, *The Works of George Whitefield* (6 vols). London, Edward & Charles Dilley, 1771-1772.

Williams, John, *Memoirs of the Life & Ministry of Robert Hawker*. London, Ebenezer Palmer, 1831.

Williams, William, *Welsh Calvinistic Methodism*. Bridgend,

Bryntirion Press, 1998 reprint.

Williamson, George C., *John Russell*. London, George Bell & Sons, 1894.

Wood, A. Skevington, *The Inextinguishable Blaze*. Exeter, The Paternoster Press, 1967.

Wood, A. Skevington, *Thomas Haweis 1734-1820*. London, SPCK, 1957.

Wright, Thomas, *The Life of Augustus M. Toplady*. London, Farncombe & Son, 1911.

Zabriskie, Alexander Clinton, *The Rise and Main Characteristics of the Anglican Evangelical Movement in England and America*. Philadelphia, Church Historical Society, 1943.

Notes

Abbreviations

(D) Donald G. Davis, *The Evangelical Revival in Eighteenth Century England as Reflected in the Life and Work of William Romaine (1714-1795)* (Edinburgh Ph.D. thesis, December 1949).

(EM) *Evangelical Magazine*, November 1795 (London, T. Chapman, 1795).

(H) Thomas Haweis, *The Life of William Romaine* (London, T. Chapman, 1797).

(L) *Select Letters of William Romaine* (Glasgow, William Collins, 1830).

(W) William Cadogan, *Works of William Romaine: Life and Letters (vol.7)* (London, T. Chapman, 1796).

(WWWR) *Whole Works of William Romaine* (London, B. Blake, 1837).

Preface

1. H, p.3.
2. Ibid., p.12.
3. Ibid., p.5.
4. L, pp.161-162.
5. Ibid., p.173.
6. Ibid., p.183.
7. J. C. Ryle, *Christian Leaders of the Eighteenth Century* (Edinburgh, Banner of Truth Trust, 1978 reprint), p.154.
8. L, p.85.

Chapter 1 — Early Years

1. H, p.11.
2. Josiah Bull, *But Now I See: The Life of John Newton* (Edinburgh, Banner of Truth Trust, 1998 reprint), p.328.
3. H, p.3.
4. Ryle, *Christian Leaders of the Eighteenth Century*, p.iv.
5. Actually, Romaine travelled to various parts of the country a good deal.
6. Ryle, *Christian Leaders of the Eighteenth Century*, p.150.
7. D, p.12.
8. John Wesley, *The Works of John Wesley* (London, Wesleyan Conference Office, 1872), vol.2, p.415.
9. L, p.199.
10. G. T. Fox, *The Life and Doctrine of Romaine: A Sermon* (London, Seeley, Jackson & Halliday, 1876), p.6.
11. Ibid., p.23.
12. Romaine's family was not among the French Protestants who took refuge in England after the revocation of the Edict of Nantes in 1685.
13. W, p.11.
14. Ibid.
15. Ibid., p.129.
16. L, p.168.
17. WWWR, pp.674-675.
18. L, p.154.
19. Ibid., p.183.
20. Ibid., p.197.
21. Ibid., p.201.
22. *Dictionary of National Biography* (London, Oxford University Press, 1960), vol.7, p.1258.
23. Erasmus Middleton, *Biographia Evangelica* (London, J. W. Pasham, 1780), vol.2, p.204.
24. C. S. Collingwood, *Memoirs of Bernard Gilpin* (London, Simpkin, Marshall & Co., 1884), p.180.
25. W, p.13.

26. William Goode, *Faith Triumphant in Death* (London, 1795), p.24.
27. H, p.18.
28. *Gospel Magazine*, August 1901, p.543n.
29. *Dictionary of National Biography*, vol.10, p.342.
30. John C. English, *Church History: Studies in Christianity & Culture*, vol.68, September 1999.
31. John H. Overton & Frederic Relton, *A History of the English Church 1714-1800* (London, Macmillan & Co., 1906), p.204.
32. John Wesley, *The Journal of John Wesley* (London, Epworth Press, 1938), vol.6, p.6.
33. H, p.19.
34. *Evangelical Magazine*, June 1803, p.261.
35. Ibid., December 1806, p.533.
36. WWWR, p.931.
37. H, pp.66-67.

Chapter 2 — A Man of Learning

1. Overton & Relton, *A History of the English Church 1714-1800*, p.151.
2. Goode, *Faith Triumphant in Death*, pp.30-31.
3. L, p.34.
4. *Theatrical Review*, 1763, p.74.
5. Alfred H. New, *The Coronet and the Cross* (London, Partridge & Co., 1858), p.105.
6. Leslie Stephen, *History of English Thought in the Eighteenth Century* (London, Smith, Elder & Co., 1876), vol.1, pp.345-346.
7. *Internet Encyclopedia of Philosophy*, William Warburton 1698-1779.
8. *Dictionary of National Biography*, vol.20, p.766.
9. John Hepburn Millar, *The Mid-Eighteenth Century* (Edinburgh, William Blackwood & Sons, 1902), p.120.
10. *History of the Works of the Learned*, vol.6, August 1739, pp.88, 90.

11. Ibid., p.91.
12. WWWR, p.747.
13. Ibid., pp.747-748.
14. Ibid., p.762.
15. Ibid., p.761.
16. H, p.22.
17. W, p.19.
18. *History of the Works of the Learned*, vol.6, August 1739, p.92.
19. John Nichols, *Illustrations of the Literary History of the Eighteenth Century* (London, Nichols, Son & Bentley, 1817-1858), vol.2, pp.104-105.
20. Ibid., p.52.
21. WWWR, p.762.
22. EM, p.439.
23. Arnold Dallimore, *George Whitefield* (Edinburgh, Banner of Truth Trust, 1989), vol.2, p.421. Referring to his learning, Bentley said that Warburton had a 'monstrous appetite but bad digestion'.
24. John Selby Watson, *The Life of William Warburton* (London, Longman, Green & Roberts, 1863), p.178.
25. H, p.23.
26. W, pp.16-17.
27. WWWR, p.782.
28. W, p.17.
29. Ryle, *Christian Leaders of the Eighteenth Century*, p.154.
30. WWWR, pp.909, 915.
31. William Dodwell, *A Dissertation on Jephthah's Vow* (London, 1745), pp.i-ii.
32. *Some Remarks on the Progress of Learning since the Reformation, Especially with Regard to the Hebrew* (London, M. Cooper, 1746), p.19.
33. Ibid., pp.9-10.
34. Even Romaine's 'erratic' printer Jacob Ilive possessed a great love for the Hebrew language.
35. W, p.21.

36. *Some Remarks on the Progress of Learning since the Reformation*, p.11.
37. H, pp.44-45.

Chapter 3 — A New Heart

1. Rupert Davies & Gordon Rupp (general editors), *A History of the Methodist Church in Great Britain* (London, Epworth Press, 1965), vol.1, p.289.
2. William Romaine, *The Life, Walk and Triumph of Faith* (Cambridge & London, James Clarke & Co. Ltd, 1970), p.362.
3. M. Dorothy George, *London Life in the Eighteenth Century* (London, The London School of Economics and Political Science, 1951 reprint), p.27.
4. Ibid., p.42.
5. Ibid., p.286.
6. L. E. Elliot-Binns, *The Early Evangelicals: A Religious and Social Study* (Greenwich, The Seabury Press, 1955), pp.235-236.
7. H, pp.23-24.
8. EM, p.439.
9. W, p.26.
10. H, pp.25-26.
11. *Gentleman's Magazine*, November 1748, p.525.
12. Ben Weinreb & Christopher Hibbert (editors), *The London Encyclopaedia* (London, Papermac, 1993), p.718.
13. Ibid., p.728.
14. H, pp.26-27.
15. L, pp.380-381.
16. Ibid., p.81.
17. Ibid., pp.81-82.
18. Ibid., p.82.
19. Romaine, *The Life, Walk and Triumph of Faith*, p.393.
20. L, pp.87-93.
21. Ibid., pp.93-95.

Chapter 4 — Evangelicals in London

1. John Venn, *The Life and Letters of Henry Venn* (Edinburgh, Banner of Truth Trust, 1993 reprint), pp.361-362.
2. John Walsh, Colin Haydon & Stephen Taylor (editors), *The Church of England c.1689-c.1833 from Toleration to Tractarianism* (Cambridge, Cambridge University Press, 1993), p.43.
3. Mark Pattison, *Essays* (Oxford, Clarendon Press, 1889), vol.2, p.42.
4. Edwin Sidney, *The Life of Rowland Hill* (London, 1861), pp.514-515.
5. Ibid., p.516.
6. Overton & Relton, *A History of the English Church 1714-1800*, p.236.
7. D. Bruce Hindmarsh, *John Newton and the English Evangelical Tradition* (Cambridge, William B. Eerdmans, 2001), p.291.
8. Elliot-Binns, *The Early Evangelicals*, p.241.
9. Ibid., p.246.
10. Hindmarsh, *John Newton*, p.294.
11. Luke Tyerman, *The Life and Times of John Wesley* (London, Hodder & Stoughton, 1890), vol.1, p.548.
12. Thomas Jones, *The Works of Thomas Jones* (London, 1763), p.viii.
13. WWWR, pp.817-828.
14. Venn, *The Life and Letters of Henry Venn*, p.91.
15. *Monthly Review*, August 1762, p.260.
16. Edwin Sidney, *The Life of Sir Richard Hill* (London, R. B. Seeley & W. Burnside, 1839), p.520.
17. Jones, *The Works of Thomas Jones*, p.iii.
18. New, *The Coronet and the Cross*, p.163.
19. Tyerman, *The Life and Times of John Wesley*, vol.2, p.325.
20. G. R. Balleine, *A History of the Evangelical Party in the Church of England* (London, Longmans, Green & Co., 1909), p.55.
21. Bull, *But Now I See*, p.113.

22. W. Thompson, *The History and Antiquities of the Collegiate Church of St Saviour, Southwark* (London, Elliot Stock, 1904), p.26.

23. Venn, *The Life and Letters of Henry Venn*, p.24.

24. Marcus L. Loane, *Cambridge and the Evangelical Succession* (London, Lutterworth Press, 1952), p.127.

25. Venn, *The Life and Letters of Henry Venn*, p.25.

26. A. C. H. Seymour, *The Life and Times of Selina Countess of Huntingdon* (Stoke-on-Trent, Tentmaker, 2000 reprint), vol.1, p.297.

27. Ibid.

28. Overton & Relton, *A History of the English Church 1714-1800*, pp.197-198.

29. Venn, *The Life and Letters of Henry Venn*, p.152.

30. George M. Ella, *William Cowper: Poet of Paradise* (Darlington, Evangelical Press, 1993), p.509.

31. John Telford, *A Sect that Moved the World* (London, Charles H. Kelly, n.d.), p.68.

32. Tyerman, *The Life and Times of John Wesley*, vol.2, p.336.

33. Wesley, *The Journal of John Wesley*, vol.6, p.391.

34. Michael Hennell, *John Venn and the Clapham Sect* (London, Lutterworth Press, 1958), p.80.

35. Ibid., pp.104-105n.

36. Charles J. Abbey & John H. Overton, *The English Church in the Eighteenth Century* (London, Longmans, Green & Co., 1902), p.388.

37. Overton & Relton, *A History of the English Church 1714-1800*, p.237.

38. *Dictionary of National Biography*, vol.3, p.1308.

39. A. Skevington Wood, *Thomas Haweis 1734-1820* (London, SPCK, 1957), p.85.

40. Seymour, *The Life and Times of Selina*, vol.1, pp.230-231.

41. D, p.264.

42. Wood, *Thomas Haweis*, pp.91, 97.

43. Elliot-Binns, *The Early Evangelicals*, p.243.

44. *Dictionary of National Biography*, vol.4, p.670.
45. Overton & Relton, *A History of the English Church 1714-1800*, p.191.
46. Abbey & Overton, *The English Church in the Eighteenth Century*, p.386.
47. *Dictionary of National Biography*, vol.17, p.1012.
48. Hennell, *John Venn and the Clapham Sect*, pp.202-203.
49. Abbey & Overton, *The English Church in the Eighteenth Century*, p.387.
50. *Dictionary of National Biography*, vol.17, p.1012.
51. Robert Bickersteth (editor), *A Memoir of John Newton* (London, Seeley, Jackson & Halliday, 1865), p.134.
52. *Dictionary of National Biography*, vol.14, p.397.
53. Hindmarsh, *John Newton*, p.327.
54. Ibid., p.249.
55. Kenneth Hylson-Smith, *Evangelicals in the Church of England 1734-1984* (Edinburgh, T&T Clark, 1989), p.39.
56. A. Skevington Wood, *The Inextinguishable Blaze* (Exeter, The Paternoster Press, 1967), p.208.
57. Ibid., p.209.
58. Balleine, *A History of the Evangelical Party in the Church of England*, p.62.
59. Bull, *But Now I See*, p.262.
60. Ibid., p.263.
61. Alexander Clinton Zabriskie, *The Rise and Main Characteristics of the Anglican Evangelical Movement in England and America* (Philadelphia, Church Historical Society, 1943).

Chapter 5 — St Dunstan's, St George's and Gresham College

1. H, pp.53-54.
2. *London Encyclopaedia*, p.725.
3. Elliot-Binns, *The Early Evangelicals*, p.164.
4. *Dictionary of National Biography*, vol.19, p.558.
5. H, p.55.

6. EM, p.446.
7. Helen C. Knight, *Lady Huntington & her Friends* (Grand Rapids, Baker Book House, 1979), p.64.
8. D. N. Samuel, *A Winnowing Ministry: Romaine, Huntington and Experimental Preaching* (Totton, Berith Publications, 1999), p.2.
9. Seymour, *The Life and Times of Selina*, vol.1, p.186.
10. Thomas Jackson, *The Life of Charles Wesley* (London, John Mason, 1841), vol.1, p.549.
11. Tyerman, *The Life and Times of John Wesley*, vol.2, pp.71-72.
12. *London Encyclopaedia*, pp.728-729.
13. Ryle, *Christian Leaders of the Eighteenth Century*, p.157.
14. H, p.47.
15. EM, p.445n.
16. Ryle, *Christian Leaders of the Eighteenth Century*, p.160.
17. *Evangelical Magazine*, November 1799, p.443.
18. H, p.49.
19. Seymour, *The Life and Times of Selina*, vol.1, p.189.
20. *London Encyclopaedia*, p.224.
21. George M. Ella, *James Hervey, Preacher of Righteousness* (Eggleston, Go Publications, 1997), pp.85-86.
22. Ibid., p.135.
23. James Hervey, *Letters from James Hervey to Lady Frances Shirley* (London, John, Francis & Charles Rivington, 1782), p.50.
24. WWWR, pp.810, 811, 812.
25. *Dictionary of National Biography*, vol.8, pp.593-594.
26. Bodleian Library, *The London Gazetteer*, 15 February 1752, MS Rawlinson fol.4, 315.
27. Ibid., 6 March 1752, MS Rawlinson fol.4, 315.
28. Davis argues unconvincingly that Romaine was not the author of the lecture. See D, p.63.
29. W, p.34.
30. *Gentleman's Magazine*, March 1752, p.99.
31. Ibid., p.100.

32. Ibid., p.101.
33. EM, pp.446-447.
34. British Library, MS 6194, f.294. English translation by H.
    D. Glover.

Chapter 6 — A Widening Ministry
1. Ryle, *Christian Leaders of the Eighteenth Century*,
   pp.157-158.
2. John Allen, *The Spiritual Magazine* (London, A. Kidwell & S.
   Lee, 1810), p.viii.
3. *Dictionary of National Biography*, vol.1, p.308.
4. Cecil Roth, *A History of the Jews in England* (Oxford,
   Clarendon Press, 1941), p.214.
5. D, p.67.
6. *Dictionary of National Biography*, vol.19, p.1209.
7. D, p.67.
8. William Romaine, *A Modest Apology for the Citizens and
   Merchants of London, who Petitioned the House of Commons
   against Naturalizing the Jews* (London, W. Webb, 1753),
   p.iv.
9. Ibid., pp.vi-vii.
10. Ibid., p.ix.
11. Ibid., pp.xi-xii.
12. George Whitefield, *The Works of George Whitefield* (London,
    Edward & Charles Dilley, 1771-1772), vol.3, p.15.
13. William Romaine, *An Answer to a Pamphlet Entitled:
    Considerations on the Bill to Permit Persons Professing the
    Jewish Religion to be Naturalized* (London, H. Cooke, 1753),
    p.i.
14. Quoted in D, p.72.
15. W, pp.35-36.
16. Tyerman, *The Life and Times of John Wesley*, vol.2, p.
    203.
17. Augustus Montague Toplady, *The Works of Augustus Toplady*
    (London, J. Chidley, 1837), p.505.
18. EM, p.446.

19. WWWR, pp.924, 927, 929.
20. *Christian Observer*, 1803, p.345.
21. WWWR, p.372.
22. Ibid., pp.372-373.
23. Ibid., p.378.
24. James Hervey, *The Works of James Hervey* (London, F. & C. Rivington, 1797), vol.7, p.35.
25. *Monthly Review*, May 1755, p.399.
26. Ibid.
27. WWWR, p.933.
28. Ibid., p.930.
29. Ibid., p.828.
30. George Clark, *A Defence of the Unity of God* (London, 1789), pp.5-6.
31. WWWR, p.829.
32. Ibid., p.837.
33. Ibid., p.833.
34. Whitefield, *The Works of George Whitefield*, vol.3, p.122.
35. W, p.30.
36. EM, p.445.
37. Ryle, *Christian Leaders of the Eighteenth Century*, pp.159-160.
38. W, p.30n.
39. John Douglas, *The Destruction of the French Foretold by Ezekiel* (London, M. Cooper, 1755), p.16.
40. Ibid., p.21.
41. *Monthly Review*, June 1755, p.479.
42. Faith Cook, *Selina Countess of Huntingdon* (Edinburgh, Banner of Truth Trust, 2001), p.158.
43. WWWR, p.871.
44. Ibid., p.872.
45. Ibid., p.877.
46. Ibid., p.878.
47. Ibid., pp.883-884, 885.
48. W, pp.32-33.
49. Ryle, *Christian Leaders of the Eighteenth Century*, p.159.

Chapter 7 — Prayer, Preaching and more Persecution

1. WWWR, p.802.
2. Ibid., p.889.
3. C. Sydney Carter, *The English Church in the Eighteenth Century* (London, Longmans, Green & Co., 1910), p.91.
4. *London Encyclopaedia*, p.774.
5. W, p.45.
6. Ibid., pp.46-47.
7. Ibid., p.54.
8. Edward Thomas Vaughan, *Some Account of Thomas Robinson* (London, Sherwood, Neely & Jones, 1816), p.249.
9. W, pp.55-67.
10. Ibid., p.53.
11. WWWR, p.803.
12. Ibid., p.865.
13. Ibid., p.870.
14. Ryle, *Christian Leaders of the Eighteenth Century*, p.178.
15. EM, p.449.
16. Josiah Bull, *John Newton of Olney and St Mary Woolnoth* (London, The Religious Tract Society, n.d.), p.100.
17. James Hervey, *Letters of James Hervey* (Edinburgh, John Grieg, 1845), pp.433-434.
18. Ella, *James Hervey*, p.245.
19. WWWR, p.889.
20. Ibid., p.896.
21. Ibid., pp.796-797.
22. Wood, *Thomas Haweis*, p.51.
23. Edwin Sidney, *The Life and Ministry of Samuel Walker* (London, R. B. Seeley & W. Burnside, 1838), p.329.
24. *Free Church of England Magazine and Harbinger of the Countess of Huntingdon's Connexion*, June 1866, p.149.
25. WWWR, p.785.
26. Fox, *The Life and Doctrine of Romaine*, p.12.
27. *Evangelical Magazine*, September 1802, p.338.
28. Wood, *Thomas Haweis*, p.51.
29. H, pp.76-78.

30. Ibid., pp.13-14.
31. Ibid., p.76.
32. Ibid., pp.65-66.
33. Josiah Bull (editor), *Letters by John Newton* (London, The Religious Tract Society, n.d.), pp.202-203.
34. Quoted in D, p.98.
35. Charles Wesley, *The Journal of Charles Wesley* (London, Wesleyan Methodist Bookroom, 1849), vol.2, p.217.
36. Robert Sandeman, *Letters on Theron & Aspasio* (Edinburgh, Sands, Donaldson, Murray & Cochrane, 1759), vol.2, p.481.
37. WWWR, p.954.
38. L, p.192.
39. John Rylands University Library, *Folio of Letters Chiefly to the Wesleys*, I, p.183.
40. William Romaine, *The Necessity of Receiving Christ in our Hearts* (London, 1758), p.28.
41. *Free Church of England Magazine and Harbinger of the Countess of Huntingdon's Connexion*, September 1866, p.233.
42. Thomas Mortimer, *Die, and be Damned* (London, Hooper & A. Morley, 1758), p.iv.
43. WWWR, p.667.

Chapter 8 — Romaine and the Other Leaders of the Revival

1. New, *The Coronet and the Cross*, p.96.
2. Seymour, *The Life and Times of Selina*, vol.1, p.352.
3. *Free Church of England Magazine and Harbinger of the Countess of Huntingdon's Connexion*, September 1866, p.257.
4. Jackson, *The Life of Charles Wesley*, vol.2, p.163.
5. Sidney, *The Life and Ministry of Samuel Walker*, pp.488-489.
6. See author's work on Samuel Walker.
7. Sidney, *The Life and Ministry of Samuel Walker*, p.497.

8. G. C. B. Davies, *The Early Cornish Evangelicals 1735-60* (London, SPCK, 1951), p.178.
9. *An Apology for the Parishioners of St Dunstan's in the West* (C. Sympson, 1759), p.8.
10. Ibid., pp.9-11.
11. Balleine, *A History of the Evangelical Party in the Church of England*, pp.52-53.
12. EM, p.446.
13. Balleine, *A History of the Evangelical Party in the Church of England*, p.54.
14. WWWR, p.438.
15. Ibid., p.441.
16. *Monthly Review*, September 1758, p.317.
17. Cook, *Selina*, p.182.
18. Seymour, *The Life and Times of Selina*, vol.1, p.475.
19. Ibid., pp.475-476.
20. *Free Church of England Magazine and Harbinger of the Countess of Huntingdon's Connexion*, September 1866, p.257.
21. Seymour, *The Life and Times of Selina*, vol.1, p.561.
22. John Wesley, *The Letters of John Wesley* (London, Epworth Press, 1931), vol.5, pp.82-83.
23. Whitefield, *The Works of George Whitefield*, vol.3, p.238.
24. Wesley, *The Letters of John Wesley*, vol.4, p.58.
25. *Arminian Magazine*, vol.3, 1780, p.612.
26. Nigel R. Pibworth, *The Gospel Pedlar: The Story of John Berridge* (Welwyn, Evangelical Press, 1987), pp.56-57.
27. Seymour, *The Life and Times of Selina*, vol.1, p.477n.
28. Ibid., p.477.
29. WWWR, pp.710-711.
30. John Gadsby, *Memoirs of the Principal Hymn Writers and Compilers of the 17th, 18th & 19th Centuries* (London, John Gadsby, 1882), p.116.
31. *Evangelical Magazine*, January 1815, pp.10-11.
32. Ibid., p.11.

33. Hindmarsh, *John Newton*, p.105.
34. Seymour, *The Life and Times of Selina*, vol.1, p.353.
35. *Evangelical Magazine*, August 1814, p.308n.
36. L, pp.101-102.
37. Faith Cook, *William Grimshaw of Haworth* (Edinburgh, Banner of Truth Trust, 1997), pp.282-283.
38. Seymour, *The Life and Times of Selina*, vol.1, p.354.
39. W, p.44n.
40. Cook, *William Grimshaw*, p.255.
41. Middleton, *Biographia Evangelica*, vol.4, p.413.
42. Ibid., p.407.
43. L, pp.172, 173.
44. WWWR, pp.35, 36.
45. Ibid., pp.38, 39.
46. William Felton, *A Letter to Mr Romaine, Containing Remarks on his Discourses upon the Law and the Gospel* (London, 1761), pp.3-4.
47. Gadsby, *Memoirs of the Principal Hymn Writers*, p.116.
48. Quoted in D, p.138.
49. Wesley, *The Works of John Wesley*, vol.3, p.70.
50. John Rylands University Library, MAM PLP 91.18.3.
51. Ibid.
52. H, pp.141, 142.

Chapter 9 — Stalwart for the Truth

1. *Gospel Magazine*, January 1970, p.43.
2. New, *The Coronet and the Cross*, p.154.
3. Gomer M. Roberts (editor), *Selected Trevecka Letters (1747-1794)* (Caernarfon, 1962), pp.91-92.
4. Tyerman, *The Life and Times of John Wesley*, vol.2, p.448.
5. Seymour, *The Life and Times of Selina*, vol.1, p.409.
6. Tom Beynon, *Howell Harris, Reformer and Soldier 1714-1773* (Caernarvon, The Calvinistic Methodist Bookroom, 1958), p.153.
7. Seymour, *The Life and Times of Selina*, vol.1, p.411.

8. Ibid., p.413.
9. *Free Church of England Magazine and Harbinger of the Countess of Huntingdon's Connexion*, February 1868, pp.42-43.
10. Seymour, *The Life and Times of Selina*, vol.1, p.419.
11. Ibid., p.420.
12. Tyerman, *The Life and Times of John Wesley*, vol.2, pp.464-465.
13. Seymour, *The Life and Times of Selina*, vol.2, p.424.
14. Gadsby, *Memoirs of the Principal Hymn Writers*, p.116.
15. L, p.45.
16. *Dictionary of National Biography*, vol.17, p.1110.
17. Seymour, *The Life and Times of Selina*, vol.1, p.455.
18. L, p.175.
19. Seymour, *The Life and Times of Selina*, vol.1, p.416.
20. L, p.39.
21. Ibid., p.48.
22. Thomas Wright, *The Life of Augustus M. Toplady* (London, Farncombe & Son, 1911), pp.36-37.
23. Ibid., p.46.
24. Quoted in D, p.161.
25. H, p.80.
26. L, pp.168-169.
27. Lambeth Palace Library, *Fulham Papers*, Osbaldeston vol.1, ff.79-80.
28. EM, p.449.
29. L, p.37.
30. Ibid., p.168.
31. Ibid., p.50.
32. W, p.387.
33. WWWR, p.151.
34. Ibid.
35. *Monthly Review*, September 1764, p.225.
36. Elliot-Binns, *The Early Evangelicals*, p.168.
37. Wesley, *The Journal of John Wesley*, vol.5, pp.105-106.
38. Wesley, *The Letters of John Wesley*, vol.5, p.266.

39. Romaine, *The Life, Walk and Triumph of Faith*, p.xviii.
40. T. Francis Bumpus, *Ancient London Churches* (London, T. Werner Laurie Ltd, n.d.), p.288.
41. *Baptist Magazine*, vol.16, 1824, p.484.
42. William Romaine, *The Life, Walk and Triumph of Faith* (London & New York, G. Routledge & Co., 1856), pp.xi, xii.
43. Sidney, *The Life of Rowland Hill*, p.22.

Chapter 10 — Elected to Blackfriars
1. L, p.176.
2. WWWR, p.671.
3. L, p.56.
4. National Library of Wales, Calvinistic Methodist Archive, Trefeca 2838c.
5. L, p.161.
6. *London Encyclopaedia*, pp.710-711.
7. Ibid., p.70.
8. W, p.69.
9. Seymour, *The Life and Times of Selina*, vol.1, p.433.
10. Ryle, *Christian Leaders of the Eighteenth Century*, p.166.
11. H, p.149.
12. L, pp.159-160.
13. WWWR, p.944.
14. Seymour, *The Life and Times of Selina*, vol.1, p.437.
15. L, p.60.
16. Ibid., p.170.
17. Seymour, *The Life and Times of Selina*, vol.1, p.434.
18. Sidney, *The Life of Sir Richard Hill*, p.87.
19. H, p.86.
20. John Newton, *The Christian Correspondent* (Hull, 1790), p.56.
21. Seymour, *The Life and Times of Selina*, vol.1, p.436.
22. L, pp.174-175.
23. H, pp.89-90.
24. *Evangelical Magazine*, November 1807, pp.492-493.
25. Ibid., p.493.

26. Seymour, *The Life and Times of Selina*, vol.1, p.406.
27. Michael R. Watts, *The Dissenters* (Oxford, Clarendon Press, 1999 reprint), pp.453-454.
28. *Evangelical Magazine*, December 1807, p.537.
29. William Mason, *A Spiritual Treasury for the Children of God* (London, The Religious Tract Society, 1765).
30. William Mason, *The Christian Communicant* (London, Chas. J. Thynne, n.d.), p.vii.
31. *Evangelical Magazine*, 1794, pp.5-6.
32. WWWR, p.705.
33. Ibid., pp.705-706.
34. Ibid., p.706.
35. Robert Philip, *The Life and Times of George Whitefield* (London, George Virtue, 1842), pp.513-514.
36. H, pp.93-95.
37. State Library of New South Wales, *Thomas Haweis Papers*, vol.5: ZML A3024, pp.193-195.
38. Ibid., p.195.
39. *Evangelical Register*, August 1835, p.271.
40. Seymour, *The Life and Times of Selina*, vol.1, p.560.
41. Cook, *Selina*, p.225.
42. WWWR, pp.707-708.
43. L, pp.163, 164.
44. Ibid., pp.69-70.
45. Ibid., p.72.
46. WWWR, p.711.
47. *Gentleman's Magazine*, January 1766, p.45.
48. L, pp.176-177.
49. EM, pp.448-449.
50. Bumpus, *Ancient London Churches*, pp.287-288.
51. Seymour, *The Life and Times of Selina*, vol.1, p.435.
52. Ibid.
53. EM, p.448.
54. L, p.79.
55. D, p.188.

Chapter 11 — 'A Single Eye to his Glory'

1. Ryle, *Christian Leaders of the Eighteenth Century*, p.168.
2. Ibid.
3. W, p.78.
4. *Gentleman's Magazine*, April 1766, p.197.
5. W, p.84.
6. Thomas Wills, *The Dying Believer* (London, 1795), pp.24-25.
7. W, pp.82-83.
8. Michael Nash, *An Answer to the 'Charitable Morsel of Unleavened Bread', Addressed to the Author* (London, 1793), pp.12-13.
9. H, p.155.
10. WWWR, pp.681-682.
11. Venn, *The Life and Letters of Henry Venn*, p.121.
12. L, p.84.
13. Seymour, *The Life and Times of Selina*, vol.1, pp.455-456.
14. Ibid., p.563.
15. WWWR, p.682.
16. Wesley, *The Letters of John Wesley*, vol.5, p.107.
17. Ibid., p.108.
18. Middleton, *Biographia Evangelica*, vol.4, p.408.
19. WWWR, p.682.
20. W, pp.73-74.
21. Ibid., pp.74-75.
22. Bodleian Library, MS Montagu d.15, ff.254-6.
23. L, pp.101-102, 103.
24. James Murray, *Sermons to Asses* (London, 1768), p.i.
25. Ibid., p.iv.
26. Seymour, *The Life and Times of Selina*, vol.1, p.390.
27. Cook, *Selina*, p.338.
28. L, p.106.
29. George, *London Life in the Eighteenth Century*, p.57.
30. Ibid., p.339.
31. L, pp.106-107.
32. Sidney, *The Life of Sir Richard Hill*, pp.156-157.

33. L, pp.200-201.
34. Ibid., pp.99-100.
35. Ibid., p.186.
36. Seymour, *The Life and Times of Selina*, vol.1, p.461.
37. L, p.112.
38. William Adams, *A Test of True and False Doctrines* (London, B. White & T. Cadell, 1770), p.5.
39. Ibid., pp.6-7.
40. Sidney, *The Life of Sir Richard Hill*, p.159.
41. John Green, *The Church of England Vindicated from the Rigid Notions of Calvinism* (London, B. White & T. Cadell, 1770), pp.123-124.
42. Wright, *The Life of Augustus M. Toplady*, p.146.
43. Seymour, *The Life and Times of Selina*, vol.1, p.420.
44. WWWR, p.731.
45. Ibid., p.733.
46. Ibid., p.734.
47. L, pp.127-128.
48. Tyerman, *The Life and Times of John Wesley*, vol.3, p.77.
49. John Wesley, *Wesley's Standard Sermons* (London, Epworth Press, 1931), vol.2, p.342.
50. Richard P. Heitzenrater, *Wesley and the People Called Methodists* (Nashville, Abingdon Press, 1995), p.242.
51. *Gospel Magazine*, February 1771, p.41.
52. Ibid., p.44.
53. Wesley, *The Letters of John Wesley*, vol.5, pp.223, 225.
54. *Gospel Magazine*, June 1771, p.271.
55. Richard Hill, *A Review of all the Doctrines Taught by John Wesley* (London, E. & C. Dilly, 1772), p.83.
56. Wesley, *The Works of John Wesley*, vol.4, pp.471-472.

Chapter 12 — An Eighteenth-Century Puritan

1. Abbey & Overton, *The English Church in the Eighteenth Century*, p.373.
2. H, pp.157-159.
3. WWWR, p.734.

4. L., p.180.

5. Ibid., pp.187-188.

6. Romaine, *The Life, Walk and Triumph of Faith*, p.89.

7. WWWR, p.733.

8. Ibid.

9. L, pp.128, 129-130.

10. H, p.179.

11. George M. Ella, *William Huntington: Pastor of Providence* (Darlington, Evangelical Press, 1994), p.119.

12. George M. Ella, *Mountain Movers* (Eggleston, Go Publications, 1999), p.258.

13. Ella, *William Cowper*, p.56.

14. Fox, *The Life and Doctrine of Romaine*, pp.5-6.

15. Abbey & Overton, *The English Church in the Eighteenth Century*, p.374.

16. *Gospel Magazine*, January 1970, pp.41-42.

17. Wesley, *The Letters of John Wesley*, vol.6, pp.60-61.

18. L, p.192.

19. Abbey & Overton, *The English Church in the Eighteenth Century*, p.374.

20. L, pp.195-196.

21. W, p.381.

22. L, pp.142-143.

23. Ibid., p.v.

24. Seymour, *The Life and Times of Selina*, vol.2, p.36.

25. Ibid., pp.305-306n.

26. L, p.129.

27. Ibid., pp.189-190.

28. Ibid., p.190.

29. W, p.164.

30. L, p.190.

31. Ibid., pp.135, 136.

32. Thomas W. Aveling, *Memorials of the Clayton Family* (London, Jackson, Walford & Hodder, 1867), pp.11-12.

33. Ibid., p.13.

34. H, p.98.

35. Ibid.
36. L, p.197.
37. Henry Dorney, *Contemplations*, (Bath, 1773), pp.iv-vi.
38. Seymour, *The Life and Times of Selina*, vol.2.
39. Toplady, *The Works of Augustus Toplady*, p.848.
40. *Christian Observer*, 1841, p.720.
41. John Rylands University Library, MAM PLP 91.18.4.
42. *Evangelical Magazine*, August 1808, p.324.
43. WWWR, p.963.
44. Ibid., p.964.
45. Ibid., p.972.
46. Ibid., p.985.
47. Ibid., p.990.
48. Ibid., p.994.
49. Ella, *William Cowper*, p.193.
50. Isaac Watts, *The Works of Isaac Watts* (London, J. Barfield, 1810), vol.4, p.376.
51. Ibid., p.377.
52. Balleine, *A History of the Evangelical Party in the Church of England*, p.137.
53. WWWR, p.997.
54. Ibid., p.998.
55. Hindmarsh, *John Newton*, p.264.
56. Seymour, *The Life and Times of Selina*, vol.2, p.52.
57. WWWR, p.989.
58. Ibid., p.997.
59. H, p.180.

Chapter 13 — A Man After God's own Heart

1. WWWR, p.623.
2. Elisha Coles, *A Practical Discourse of God's Sovereignty* (Bath, W. Gye, 1776), pp.iii-v.
3. W, pp.148-149.
4. Ibid., p.149.
5. Ibid., pp.149-150.
6. Bull, *But Now I See*, p.224.

7. David Erwyd Jenkins, *The Life of Thomas Charles of Bala* (Denbigh, Llewelyn Jenkins, 1908), vol.1, pp.50-51.
8. Bodleian Library, Vet.A5 e.6335.
9. H, p.171.
10. Cook, *Selina*, p.377.
11. H, p.171.
12. Ibid., pp.172-173.
13. L, p.145.
14. Ibid., p.146.
15. W, p.128.
16. WWWR, p.621.
17. L, pp.243-244.
18. *Gospel Magazine*, February 1780, p.76.
19. Ibid., p.78.
20. Ibid., p.80.
21. W, p.155.
22. Ibid., p.159.
23. Jackson, *The Life of Charles Wesley*, vol.2, pp.323-324.
24. W, p.121.
25. Ibid., pp.173-174.
26. Ibid., p.181.
27. Ibid., p.243.
28. Ibid., p.174.
29. Ibid., p.178.
30. L, pp.383-384.

Chapter 14 — The Trials of 'An Old Man'
1. W, pp.240-241.
2. Bodleian Library, MS Autograph c.24, ff.343-4.
3. L, p.151.
4. W, pp.88-89.
5. L, p.293.
6. Ibid., pp.293-294.
7. Ibid., p.245.
8. Ibid., p.292.
9. W, p.304.

10. Ibid., p.234.
11. L, p.211.
12. Ibid., p.155.
13. H, pp.101-102.
14. L, p.152.
15. W, p.397.
16. L, p.246.
17. W, pp.132, 133.
18. Ibid., p.141.
19. Ibid., p.172.
20. Ibid., p.129.
21. Ibid., p.131.
22. Ibid., pp.130-131.
23. Ibid., p.184.
24. John Rylands University Library, MAM PLP 91.18.5.
25. *Gospel Magazine*, August 1901, pp.544-545.
26. Ibid., p.544.
27. W, pp.97-101.

Chapter 15 — 'Looking to Jesus'

1. L, p.206.
2. Ibid., pp.203, 204.
3. Ibid., pp.248-249.
4. W, pp.251-252.
5. Ibid., p.199.
6. William Goode, *A Memoir of the Late W. Goode* (London, R. B. Seeley & W. Burnside, 1828), p.26.
7. Ibid., p.27.
8. WWWR, p.631.
9. New College Library, CM/R25.
10. W, pp.252-253.
11. L, p.203.
12. W, pp.204-205.
13. Ibid., p.209.
14. L, pp.224-225.
15. H, pp.102-103.

16. W, p.220.
17. Ibid., pp.291-292.
18. Ibid., p.215.
19. Ibid., pp.214-215.
20. H, p.104.
21. W, p.221.
22. L, p.237.
23. Ibid., p.238.
24. W, p.285.
25. WWWR, p.649.
26. W, p.298.
27. Ibid., pp.200-201.
28. L, p.237.
29. Ibid., p.238.
30. Ibid., p.240.
31. WWWR, p.649.
32. Ibid., p.650.
33. W, p.295.
34. L, p.221.
35. W, p.136.
36. Ibid., pp.287-288.
37. Ibid., p.294.
38. John Williams, *Memoirs of the Life & Ministry of Robert Hawker* (London, Ebenezer Palmer, 1831), p.24.
39. Ibid., p.25.
40. W, p.200.
41. Ibid., p.205.
42. Ibid., p.187.
43. Ibid., p.356.
44. Ibid., p.262.
45. L, pp.231-232.
46. Ibid., p.233.
47. W, p.381.
48. WWWR, p.665.

Chapter 16 — 'Waiting to be Sent for'

1. W, p.302
2. John Rylands University Library, MAM PLP 91.18.7.
3. Wood, *Thomas Haweis*, pp.177-178.
4. State Library of New South Wales, *Thomas Haweis Papers*, vol.5, ZML A3024, pp.192-199.
5. Ibid.
6. H, p.203.
7. WWWR, p.661.
8. L, p.202.
9. WWWR, p.661.
10. Ibid., p.629.
11. W, p.272.
12. Ibid., p.205.
13. Ibid., p.259.
14. Ambrose Serle, *Christian Husbandry* (London, J. Mathews, 1789), pp.iii-iv.
15. *Gentleman's Magazine*, vol.2, 1812, p.193.
16. WWWR, p.632.
17. W, pp.224-225.
18. WWWR, p.662.
19. Beinecke Rare Book and Manuscript Library, *Letter of Romaine's* (22 November 1794).
20. W, p.303.
21. William Cadogan, *The Continuance and Constancy of the Friendship of God, as a Covenant God with his People* (London, 1795), p.172.
22. *Gospel Magazine*, August 1901, p.542.
23. Michael Nash, *Gideon's Cake of Barley Meal* (London, 1793), pp.89-90.
24. Lambeth Palace Library, *Fulham Papers*, Porteus 35, ff.96-97.
25. Nash, *Gideon's Cake of Barley Meal*, p.2.
26. Ibid., p.25.
27. David Parker, *A Charitable Morsel of Unleavened Bread* (London, J. Mathews, 1793), p.4.

28. Ibid., p.9.
29. Ibid., pp.11-12.
30. Ibid., p.15.
31. Ibid., p.33.
32. *Evangelical Magazine*, November 1793, p.218.
33. *Dictionary of National Biography*, vol.14, p.99.
34. Michael Nash, *The Barley Cake Defended from the Foxes* (London, 1793), p.7.
35. Ibid., pp.10-11.
36. Ibid., pp.11-12.
37. L, pp.201-202.
38. W, pp.202, 203.
39. Ibid., p.286.
40. Ibid., p.299.
41. Ibid., p.280.
42. Ibid., p.301.

Chapter 17 — 'To Thee be Endless Praise!'
1. H, p.207.
2. W, p.134.
3. WWWR, pp.650-651.
4. L, p.241.
5. Ibid., p.331.
6. W, p.144.
7. Ibid., p.38n.
8. Ibid., p.39n.
9. Ibid., pp.39-40n.
10. Ibid., pp.39-41.
11. Ibid., p.41.
12. H, p.70.
13. EM, p.450.
14. H, p.186.
15. W, p.105.
16. Ibid., p.106.
17. H, p.188.
18. W, p.106.

19. Ibid.
20. Ibid., pp.106-107.
21. H, p.190.
22. W, p.107.
23. H, pp.186-187.
24. Ibid., p.191.
25. W, pp.107-108.
26. H, p.193.
27. Ibid., p.194.
28. Ibid.
29. T. Sharp, *Pulpit Sentences of W. Romaine* (Woolwich, 1831), p.127.
30. Ibid.
31. W, pp.109-110.
32. *Gentleman's Magazine*, August 1795, p.701.
33. H, p.205.
34. Jenkins, *The Life of Thomas Charles of Bala*, vol.2, pp.156-157.
35. Wood, *The Inextinguishable Blaze*, p.142.
36. Ibid., p.141.
37. H, p.196.
38. Ibid., pp.202-203.
39. L, p.384.

Chapter 18 — A Man for his Times

1. *Gospel Magazine*, August 1901, p.600.
2. C. E. De Coetlogon, *The Life of the Just Exemplified in the Character of the Late W. Romaine* (London, Messrs Rivington, etc., 1795), p.27.
3. Abbey & Overton, *The English Church in the Eighteenth Century*, pp.372-373.
4. Hylson-Smith, *Evangelicals in the Church of England 1734-1984*, p.28.
5. Elliot-Binns, *The Early Evangelicals*, pp.167-168.
6. Overton & Relton, *A History of the English Church 1714-1800*, p.175.

7. H, pp.97-98.
8. Hindmarsh, *John Newton*, p.140.
9. W, pp.388-389.
10. Gadsby, *Memoirs of the Principal Hymn Writers*, p.115.
11. Toplady, *The Works of Augustus Toplady*, p.506.
12. H, p.211.
13. Ibid., p.138.
14. Wright, *The Life of Augustus M. Toplady*, pp.145-147.
15. W, p.101.
16. Ibid.
17. Ibid., pp.101-102.
18. Sidney, *The Life of Rowland Hill*, p.515.
19. De Coetlogon, *The Life of the Just Exemplified in the Character of the Late W. Romaine*, p.23.
20. Ryle, *Christian Leaders of the Eighteenth Century*, pp.170-171.
21. W, p.87.
22. Ibid., pp.361-362.
23. L, p.68.
24. W, p.88.
25. William Cadogan, *Discourses of the Honourable and Reverend W. B. Cadogan* (London, F. & C. Rivington, 1798), pp.178-179.
26. De Coetlogon, *The Life of the Just Exemplified in the Character of the Late W. Romaine*, p.21.
27. Goode, *Faith Triumphant in Death*, p.30.
28. Eifion Evans, *Daniel Rowland* (Edinburgh, Banner of Truth Trust, 1985), p.358.
29. W, p.151.
30. Balleine, *A History of the Evangelical Party in the Church of England*, p.121.
31. *Gospel Magazine*, August 1799, p.304.
32. W, p.95.
33. WWWR, p.742.
34. James Boswell, *The Life of Samuel Johnson* (London & Toronto, J. M. Dent, 1928), vol.2, pp.110-111.

35. W, p.96.
36. Gadsby, *Memoirs of the Principal Hymn Writers*, pp. 115-116.
37. H, p.46.
38. Ibid., pp.129-130.
39. W, p.93.
40. H, p.132.
41. Goode, *Faith Triumphant in Death*, pp.32-33.
42. H, p.133.
43. De Coetlogon, *The Life of the Just Exemplified in the Character of the Late W. Romaine*, p.22.
44. *Gospel Magazine*, October 1796, p.408.
45. H, pp.104-105.
46. Overton & Relton, *A History of the English Church 1714-1800*, p.153.
47. Goode, *Faith Triumphant in Death*, pp.31-32.
48. John Henry Overton, *The True Churchmen Ascertained* (London, Mawman & Rivington, 1801), p.328.
49. Ryle, *Christian Leaders of the Eighteenth Century*, p.179.

Chapter 19 — 'An Iron Pillar and a Bronze Wall'
1. Seymour, *The Life and Times of Selina*, vol.1, p.470.
2. Ella, *Mountain Movers*, p.255.
3. Gadsby, *Memoirs of the Principal Hymn Writers*, p.116.
4. EM, p.453.
5. Ibid., pp.453-454.
6. De Coetlogon, *The Life of the Just Exemplified in the Character of the Late W. Romaine*, p.26.
7. Goode, *Faith Triumphant in Death*, p.31.
8. EM, p.454.
9. Ibid.
10. De Coetlogon, *The Life of the Just Exemplified in the Character of the Late W. Romaine*, pp.25-26.
11. Vaughan, *Some Account of Thomas Robinson*, pp.248-249.
12. Lambeth Palace Library, MS 3169, *Sermon Notes* (27).

13. H, pp.143-144.
14. WWWR, p.438.
15. Ibid., p.153.
16. Fox, *The Life and Doctrine of Romaine*, pp.7, 11, 15, 17.
17. H, p.145.
18. De Coetlogon, *The Life of the Just Exemplified in the Character of the Late W. Romaine*, p.23.
19. W, p.33.
20. Goode, *Faith Triumphant in Death*, p.12.
21. Ibid.
22. Sharp, *Select Pulpit Sentences of W. Romaine*, p.5.
23. Wills, *The Dying Believer*, p.i.
24. Ibid., pp.2-3.
25. Goode, *Faith Triumphant in Death*, p.11.
26. EM, p.454.
27. Goode, *Faith Triumphant in Death*, pp.33-35.
28. H, pp.160-161.
29. Ryle, *Christian Leaders of the Eighteenth Century*, p.178.
30. *Evangelical Magazine*, January 1800, p.18.
31. De Coetlogon, *The Life of the Just Exemplified in the Character of the Late W. Romaine*, p.22.
32. Sidney, *The Life and Ministry of Samuel Walker*, p.436.
33. Ella, *James Hervey*, p.135.
34. Beynon, *Howell Harris*, p.222.
35. Bull, *But Now I See*, p.112.
36. Ella, *William Huntington*, p.52.
37. Cadogan, *Discourses of the Honourable and Reverend W. B. Cadogan*, p.183.
38. John Frost, *Lives of Eminent Christians of Various Denominations* (Philadelphia, 1852), p.479.
39. Tyerman, *The Life and Times of John Wesley*, vol.2, p.277.
40. Seymour, *The Life and Times of Selina*, vol.2, pp.201-202.
41. George C. Williamson, *John Russell* (London, George Bell & Sons, 1894), p.21.
42. Sidney, *The Life and Ministry of Samuel Walker*, p.479.

43. William Jay, *Memoirs of the Life and Character of C. Winter* (London, 1812), p.44.
44. Jenkins, *The Life of Thomas Charles of Bala*, vol.3, p.175.
45. Ibid., vol.1, p.407.
46. *Gospel Standard*, April 1865, pp.101, 106.
47. Ibid., May 1865, p.149.
48. Ibid., pp.151-152.
49. Ibid., p.152.
50. H, p.100.
51. Seymour, *The Life and Times of Selina*, vol.2, p.526.
52. Henry Forster Burder, *Memoir of George Burder* (London, F. Westley & A. H. Davis, 1833), p.83.
53. L, p.252.
54. H, p.107.
55. W, p.80.
56. EM, p.455.
57. Ibid.
58. W, p.191.

Index